PENGUIN BOOKS

THE GLORY BARONS

DOUGLAS HUNTER is a writer, editor and graphic designer. He is the author of *Open Ice: The Time Horton Story; A Breed Apart: An Illustrated History of Goaltending; War Games: Conn Smythe and Hockey's Fighting Men; Champions: An Illustrated History of Hockey's Greatest Dynasties* and *Scotty Bowman: A Life in Hockey*. He is also the author of four books on yachting and boat design. He lives on Georgian Bay's Severn Sound with his wife, Debbie, and their three children.

THE GLORY BARONS

THE SAGA OF THE EDMONTON OILERS

DOUGLAS HUNTER

Penguin Books

PENGUIN BOOKS

Published by the Penguin Group

Penguin Books Canada Ltd, 10 Alcorn Avenue, Toronto, Ontario, Canada M4V 3B2

Penguin Books Ltd, 27 Wrights Lane, London W8 5TZ, England

Penguin Putnam Inc., 375 Hudson Street, New York, New York 10014, U.S.A.

Penguin Books Australia Ltd, Ringwood, Victoria, Australia

Penguin Books (NZ) Ltd, cnr Rosedale and Airborne Roads, Albany,
Auckland 1310, New Zealand

Penguin Books Ltd, Registered Offices: Harmondsworth, Middlesex, England

First published in Viking by Penguin Books Canada Limited, 1999
Published in Penguin Books, 2000

1 3 5 7 9 10 8 6 4 2

Manufactured in Canada

CANADIAN CATALOGUING IN PUBLICATION DATA

Hunter, Douglas, 1959–
The glory barons : The saga of the Edmonton Oilers

ISBN 0-14-028126-6

1. Edmonton Oilers (Hockey team) — History   I. Title.

GV848.E35H85 2000   769.962'64'09712334   C00-931628-0

Visit Penguin Canada's website at www.penguin.ca

THE GLORY
BARONS

THE SAGA OF THE EDMONTON OILERS

In tribute to Bob Carse,
who was there before everyone.

PROLOGUE

O N FRIDAY, OCTOBER 24, 1997, the Edmonton Oilers were in the middle of a three-game home stand, preparing for a match that night against the Pittsburgh Penguins at Northlands Coliseum. Bob Turner was in the back of a limousine with his wife, headed to Edmonton International Airport to catch a flight. He unfolded a copy of that day's *Edmonton Journal*. He began to read. He began to fight a rising tide of disbelief.

For more than four years, the Oilers and Northlands had been front and centre in Turner's life. In 1994, the fifty-year-old senior partner in the local law firm Milner Fenerty had represented the city of Edmonton and its non-profit corporation, Economic Development Edmonton, in the difficult negotiations with Oilers owner Peter Pocklington—the self-made salesman-entrepreneur, bon vivant and slayer of socialism—over the terms of Pocklington's lease at the city-owned Northlands. The city had listened to Pocklington's insistence that major concessions were required in the Northlands lease, not only to make the Oilers profitable, but also to keep the team in Edmonton. The result had been a deal some decried as a giveaway to Pocklington, as it had granted him the right to run the arena virtually for his own profit for ten years. But three years into the new deal, the long-term presence of the Oilers that the city thought it had secured was plunged into doubt. Pocklington's business empire had been under seige from its principal creditor, the provincial bank known as Alberta Treasury Branches (ATB) since 1989, and Pocklington could no longer ward off pressure from ATB to cash in assets to address a mountain of non-performing loans. Since June 5, 1997, the Oilers, at the urging of ATB, had been for sale, and Turner had been party to efforts to drum up a friendly local buyer.

There was much speculation in the press about how secure a grip the city had gained on the franchise in return for the major concessions made to Pocklington in the 1994 agreement. No one knew the facts of the matter better than Turner, who continued to represent both the city and EDE in matters of the man known as Peter Puck and his troubled NHL franchise. Turner had helped draft the 1994 deal; he knew the team couldn't leave Edmonton without the city's permission. And he knew the city wouldn't give its permission without first checking with him.

Thus it came as a considerable surprise to Turner when he encountered the banner headline "SOLD!" in the *Edmonton Journal* on his ride to the airport. The Oilers, it seemed, were being purchased by Leslie Alexander, owner of the Houston Rockets of the National Basketball Association, and might or might not be heading to Houston. Turner could scarcely believe the news. Had he been away from the planet for the last few weeks? he asked his wife. That a conclusive deal could have been made between Alexander and Pocklington without Turner knowing about it was extraordinary.

Scenarios were being excitedly debated in the newspaper. Pocklington had met with Alexander in Denver earlier in the week to finalize an agreement by which Pocklington would retain a minority position in the team and Alexander would retire Pocklington's ATB debts. The team would continue to operate in Edmonton for three years. If it was profitable at that time, Alexander would sell the team to local investors and be rewarded, it was believed, with an expansion franchise for Houston. If, however, the team was losing money—and by Pocklington's accounting, even with the lease deal of 1994, the team was still losing several million dollars a season—Alexander would pack it off to Houston.

This all made for fascinating reading, but Turner could not help but see a gaping flaw. Where, in all of this, was some recognition of the Location Agreement, which Pocklington had signed in 1994? In return for essentially being given Northlands to run as his own facility, Pocklington had pledged to keep the Oilers in Edmonton until 2004. Further, Pocklington had apparently put together the Alexander deal without involving two important shareholders in Oilers Hockey Inc., the company that owned the team—namely the city, through EDE, and Northlands Park, the non-profit entity that owned the grounds on which city-owned Northlands Coliseum was located. EDE and Northlands Park had secured what was called a "golden" share in the team, as well as what amounted to a lien, through the 1994 negotiations. These gave them stringent controls on any sale that would break the Location Agreement.

Turner was amazed. But then, he was dealing with Peter Puck, who since arriving in Edmonton in 1971 had incited amazement with almost every move he made. There was a period in the early eighties when some astounding new development in his public or private life hove into view with alarming regularity, giving his existence a tabloid-television veneer. A hostage taking in which he was accidentally shot by police. An unsuccessful sexual harassment suit by his psychic. Hair-raising jet-boat racing escapades. Confessions of a near-death experience. High-stakes backgammon games with his fellow dealmeister, Nelson Skalbania, in which Monet canvases changed hands with a roll of the dice. And just for good measure, a quixotic run at the leadership of the federal Progressive Conservative party as he dreamed of becoming the country's prime minister. Selling the Oilers to a Houston millionaire was just the latest, albeit the most egregious, in a long series of jaw-dropping manoeuvres by the man so many Edmontonians unfortunately had grown to hate as his eroding financial circumstances began to impact on their beloved Oilers. It was no use for his friends to try to remind people of all the charitable things he had done for Edmonton, many of them unpublicized, when the times were good—his support of local theatre, of health care facilities, of the education of underprivileged youth, the mere fact that he took the sad-sack Oilers of the WHA into the NHL and gave the city a team that won five Stanley Cups. Once Pocklington began to bail, Edmontonians began to to get wet.

At first, his efforts to stay afloat consisted of ridding himself of the team's star players, above all Wayne Gretzky. Then he tried to take the team to Hamilton or Minneapolis–St. Paul in 1993 to get a better building lease. Finally he had no choice but to sell the team entirely, and he had found a Texan who could well end up taking the team south of the border. As Turner's limo rolled on toward the airport, as the mayor, Bill Smith, and the head of EDE, Rick LeLacheur—both of whom had just returned from a provincial trade mission to Asia— scrambled to bring themselves up to speed on Pocklington's loop-the-loop, it was clear that the city had just hit serious turbulence in its efforts to find a local buyer for the team whose decline had broken so many hearts.

PETER POCKLINGTON owed his fellow Albertans an awful lot of money through non-performing loans his various enterprises had received from Alberta Treasury Branches. How much he owed the ATB was confidential, but it was believed this arch-conservative champion of hands-off government had been receiving ATB loans for his Oilers since the early 1980s, and that the team's indebtedness stood at over $100 million, possibly as high as $120 million. Loans incurred through other business ventures were likely pressing Pocklington's total indebtedness to about $155 million, giving him a substantial share of the ATB's $700 million in non-performing loans. (Much of the rest, defaulted on by the West Edmonton Mall, was an unexploded bomb awaiting detection beneath the provincial government.) By the early 1990s, Pocklington's freewheeling entrepreneurial style was seriously cramped by the fact that the ATB was standing at his side, carefully watching over the assets he had pledged in order to get cash from the government bank.

The ATB had its own considerable problems. Critics charged that the ATB, established in 1938 by Alberta's Social Credit government (which was deeply suspicious of the international banking system) as a public lender for farmers, small businesses and individuals, had metamorphosed in the 1980s into a candy store from which the Progressive Conservative government could dispense goodies. Pocklington had received loans and loan guarantees in 1987 to extricate himself from the mess of a nasty strike at his Gainers meat packing plant in Edmonton, as he staged one of the most publicized showdowns between capital and organized labour in modern Canadian history. That money had been supplied by the PC government of Don Getty through the ATB, rather than directly from government coffers, to keep the deal clear of public scrutiny. Pocklington would subsequently allege—and Getty would hotly deny—that the loan was essentially made to get him to make the strike go away. The strike did go away, but then so did Gainers. The government was compelled to step in and take over the company in 1989, when Pocklington defaulted on loan payments. The government sold the operation to Burns Foods at a considerable loss; the Burns/Gainers facility was then bought by Maple Leaf Foods in October 1996, but in 1998 the whole operation was about to shut down for good as another strike hit the plant and Maple Leaf opted to consolidate its hog processing operations at one giant plant in Manitoba.

While the forces conspiring against the Oilers remaining in Edmonton were complex, the Gainers loan default was fundamental to Pocklington's decision to sell the team. Under the master agreement Pocklington had signed in the government bailout of Gainers in September 1987, Pocklington could be held personally liable for the company's debts. After selling off Gainers, the government was still short $38 million, plus interest, on the Gainers loans, and it wanted it back from Pocklington. Suits and countersuits flew, with Pocklington claiming he was shortchanged $20 million when the province took Gainers away from him and failed to receive what he thought was its full value as the business was sold to cover the loans and loan guarantees. The government in turn sued Pocklington, alleging he had improperly moved assets from the security he had pledged for the loans.

Before the Gainers fiasco, many public dollars already had been spent cleaning up a major Pocklington financial spill. When his Edmonton-based Fidelity Trust, the largest trust company in the province, collapsed in 1984, the bailout of customers by the Canadian Deposit Insurance Corporation nicked Canadian taxpayers for $359 million. Pocklington went on to compile a lengthy history of brinkmanship with the people of Edmonton. His habit of hiring, or promising to hire, replacement workers in his disputes with the unionized employees of Gainers presaged his showdowns with the city and its hockey fans in the 1990s.

After missing the playoffs for the first time in 1992/93 (and missing out on the postseason revenues), Pocklington had declared himself sufficiently unhappy with the team's lease at Northlands that he was prepared to move the Oilers to Hamilton, Ontario. Like Edmonton, Hamilton had built a municipal arena, Copps Coliseum, in hopes of attracting an NHL franchise. But whereas Northlands, built in 1974, got its NHL team when the Oilers of the WHA moved into the NHL in 1979, Hamilton's effort proved fruitless, as the city was passed over in the 1991 expansion (and again in 1997). Hamilton was in the delicate position of not wishing to appear to court an NHL team in another Canadian city, whose municipal leaders were trying to hang on to it, but Hamilton was only too happy to accommodate Pocklington if he did decide the Oilers would have to leave Edmonton. A move to Hamilton did not transpire, but at the start of the 1993/94 season, Pocklington was preparing to move the team to

Minnesota; the state had just lost the North Stars to Dallas. Northlands Coliseum had to secure a court injunction to enforce its lease and keep the Oilers in place.

In the wake of the showdown over the planned relocation to Minnesota came the new deal for Pocklington at Northlands in 1994. The negotiations occurred at a critical point in NHL history, for the Winnipeg Jets were in the throes of a torturous struggle over the team's future between taxpayers, fans, team ownership, local business and two levels of government. In 1991, the municipal and provincial governments had agreed to underwrite any losses the Jets franchise incurred, in exchange for 36 percent of the team's equity. The ownership group, led by Barry Shenkarow, in return pledged that, should it decide to bail out, it would sell its 64 percent stake for $32 million by 1996 to an approved local buyer. Failing the appearance of a satisfactory local buyer, the Shenkarow group could sell the team to whomever the league would approve, which would almost certainly mean the Jets heading south of the border.

At the root of the Jets' woes was an antiquated municipal arena, built in 1955 for $2 million, which the city proposed replacing for $65 million. In Edmonton, the arena issue wasn't nearly as dire. Although Northlands had needed some sprucing up in 1994 (in particular the installation of luxury corporate boxes) to pull in more revenue, it wasn't in the same league as the aging Winnipeg Arena, which had sustained all the updating it could.

Civic leaders and citizens of Edmonton shared with their Winnipeg counterparts an enthusiasm for public support of professional sports. The Edmonton Eskimos, one of the strongest and most celebrated franchises in the Canadian Football League, was publicly owned, and many of the key figures in the battle to keep the Oilers in Edmonton were connected with the Eskimos operation. There was a strong (although not unanimous) sentiment in Edmonton that the city's international reputation and general prosperity depended on sporting events.

This feeling was partly due to a natural rivalry with Calgary to the south. The Flames and the Oilers had regularly waged war in the NHL playoffs in the 1980s, with the Flames finally earning a Stanley Cup of their own in 1988/89. In the CFL, the Eskimos and the Calgary Stampeders were natural West Division rivals. There was more than a little jealousy to be tasted in the air in Edmonton when Calgary did such a splendid job of hosting the 1988 Winter Olympics, and Edmonton began to covet its own edition of the Olympic Games.

The sentiments of two men in particular were fundamental to the success of any effort to keep the Oilers franchise alive and in Edmonton. One was the city's lawyer, Bob Turner; the other was Rick LeLacheur. A forty-eight-year-old civic dynamo from the Edmonton suburb of St. Albert, LeLacheur had been hired as the first president of Economic Development Edmonton when Turner spearheaded its creation in 1993. A non-profit corporation wholly owned by the city, EDE was designed to boost tourism and encourage economic growth and diversification. Virtually from the beginning of his term as the head of EDE, LeLacheur viewed the Oilers as a key component of the local economy.

By 1994, people like Turner and LeLacheur were striving to preserve a franchise that bore little resemblance to the team responsible for the profusion of championship banners in the Northlands rafters. The magical eighties, in which the dynamic young Oilers won their string of Stanley Cups, were long gone and unlikely ever to be recaptured. The trade of Wayne Gretzky in August 1988 was the watershed in the team's history—and arguably in the history of the modern NHL—but it had been preceded by the trade of star defenceman Paul Coffey to Pittsburgh in November 1987. A wholesale dismantling of the core of the Oilers championship lineup was postponed until after the 1990/91 season. Jari Kurri (who had chosen to play in Italy in 1990/91 rather than report to the Oilers), Mark Messier, Grant Fuhr, Glenn Anderson and Steve Smith were all dealt away; Adam Graves, who had joined the club for the 1989/90 Stanley Cup drive, was lost to free agency; and Charlie Huddy went to Minnesota on May 30, 1991, in the expansion draft.[1] Early in the 1991/92 season, Jeff Beukeboom was sent to the New York Rangers, where Messier and Graves had landed. Kevin Lowe, Esa Tikkanen, Glenn Anderson and Craig MacTavish then joined them, making for seven Cup-winning Oilers in the New York lineup when the Rangers won the 1993/94 Stanley Cup. The Rangers acquired the nickname of "Oilers East" (Gretzky was added in 1996/97) and for Edmonton fans, the success enjoyed by the Rangers in 1993/94 served to remind them of what might have been in Northlands, had the championship lineup of the eighties not been broken up by an owner who had come to demand virtually complete control of their municipal arena.

The question of just how viable the Oilers were, based in Edmonton, was clouded by Pocklington's financial straits. To be sure, Pocklington's public struggles had masked the factors underlying the Oilers' plight. The league's economics had changed tremendously since the team had escaped from the sinking World Hockey Association to join the NHL in 1979.

Foremost, the Canadian dollar's purchasing power had seriously eroded. When the WHA began playing in October 1972 (with the Edmonton team making its debut as the Alberta Oilers), the Canadian dollar was actually worth two cents more than the American greenback, making it possible for Canadian WHA teams like the Oilers to engage in a salary war with NHL clubs, most of which were in the United States. In 1977, right after Pocklington took over the near-bankrupt Oilers franchise from Nelson Skalbania, the Canadian dollar lost ten cents in value; by 1979, when the Oilers joined the NHL, the U.S. dollar was worth $1.17 Canadian. When the Oilers won their first Stanley Cup, in May 1984, the American currency was up to $1.29, and it kept climbing, reaching $1.40 in January 1986.

The Oilers were then in the midst of one of the greatest regular-season performances in league and franchise history. By today's measure of the game's operating costs, the low purchasing power of the Canadian currency should have crippled the Oilers in mid-dynasty. Instead, they were able to win three more Stanley Cups, their survival abetted by a weak players' union run by an autocratic, owner-friendly head, Alan Eagleson. Without an active free-agency market, player salaries could be held in check, and as the U.S. dollar retreated to $1.13 by the fall of 1991, the true circumstances of a franchise like the Oilers, however successful in the 1980s, were obscured. Eagleson's highy publicized fall from grace in January 1992 precipitated a more militant union, determined to make up the ground lost in the complacent eighties. The players struck before the 1991/92 playoffs; a so-called lockout by the owners reduced the 1994/95 season to forty-eight games. Along the way, free agency was liberalized, salaries began to climb, and the Canadian dollar wilted in the heat of the American economy. By the time the 1992/93 season was over, the U.S. dollar was approaching $1.30; at the end of 1993/94, it was at $1.38.

For Canadian teams, who had to pay almost all their player salaries and travel costs in U.S. currency, the deteriorating exchange rate placed an almost absurd surcharge on their operating costs. At the league's semi-annual meeting in December 1995, the Calgary Flames' part-owner, Harley Hotchkiss, took advantage of his new post as chairman of the league's board of governors to press through approval of the Canadian Supplementary Currency Assistance Plan, which provided some relief to the small-market Canadian teams.[2] But with the U.S. dollar headed for $1.50, Hotchkiss appeared to be fighting a losing battle: not only with a sinking dollar, but with a league whose economic structure was becoming irreversibly hostile to a city like Edmonton. Pocklington was losing his grip on the Oilers, but so were the fans. The City of Champions, as it liked to call itself, was a breath away from being sent to the minors.

PART ONE

Chapter One

N THE END, the city of Edmonton lost its team, with the sad realization that the professional game was becoming an American one, economically more suited to places like Denver and Los Angeles and San Francisco, where the arenas had higher revenue potential. It didn't matter how many championships the team had produced, how fierce the rivalry had been with Calgary, how dedicated the local population was to hockey. The decision to cease operations was driven, it was said, purely by dollars. The owner was simply losing too much money.

The abrupt disappearance of the Edmonton Flyers from the Western Hockey League in June 1963 sounded all the familiar notes in the almost timeless struggle by small-market Canadian hockey teams to resist the ferocious undertow of the American sporting business. Edmonton seemed to be locked in a thirty-five-year cycle of professional hockey boom and bust. The Eskimos of the old Western Hockey League had been lost in 1926, when the league closed shop and sold its player contracts en masse to NHL teams. Just over thirty-five seasons later, the Flyers, who had been around since 1945/46, played their last seventy games in 1962/63 before being abruptly disbanded. And in 1998, thirty-five years after the Flyers were lost, the Oilers were facing imminent extinction. Though separated by decades, the crises faced by the Eskimos, Flyers and Oilers were remarkably similar. They demonstrated that, beneath the veneer of modern issues such as cable television market revenues and municipal tax burdens, the essential pressures on teams off the beaten track of the American economy had not changed.

Foreshadowing the plight of the Oilers in the 1990s, the Eskimos died in 1926 because they and their league could no longer compete for the best players with a growing NHL. The WHL's forerunner, the Pacific Coast Hockey Association, had launched a salary war with the NHL's forerunner, the National Hockey Association, back in 1911, and beginning in 1915 the respective champions of the two leagues had met in a final series to determine the winner of the Stanley Cup. In 1921, another professional loop, the Western Canada Hockey League, arose, with a twenty-four-game schedule featuring the Edmonton Eskimos, Regina Capitals, Calgary Tigers and Saskatoon Crescents. Two years later, in 1923, the NHL, PCHA and WCHL entered into a cooperative agreement, and the PCHA and WCHL began playing an interlocking schedule. Although the professional western game was still strong enough to produce the Stanley Cup champions of 1924/25, the Victoria Cougars, the league enterprise overall could no longer compete with the NHL for the best players as the eastern league began expanding. Boston and a second Montreal club, the Maroons, joined the NHL in 1924/25; in 1925/26 came the New York Americans and Pittsburgh Hornets. After playing a final season as the Western Hockey League in 1925/26, the NHL's only significant rival folded, providing the player contracts that for 1926/27 helped fill the rosters of three more new NHL teams: the Detroit Cougars, Chicago Blackhawks and New York Rangers. The Blackhawks got their start by buying the lineup of the Portland Rosebuds, the Detroit franchise by swallowing the lineup (and the name) of the Victoria Cougars. The Edmonton Eskimos scattered. Goaltender Bill Tobin landed in Chicago and ended up becoming the Blackhawks' general manager. Boston acquired Eddie Shore, one of the greatest defencemen in the history of the game. As the

Eskimos departed, the city was left in the barrens of professional hockey.

But for a brief return to the minor pro game in the short-lived Western Canada and Northwest leagues in the mid-Depression era, Edmonton waited until after the Second World War for another shot at the professional hockey ranks. By then, the line between the Canadian amateur Senior game and outright professional hockey was a subtle one. Many players on Senior teams were under contract to NHL or affiliated minor professional clubs. In 1945/46, the Edmonton Flyers, Calgary Stampeders, Saskatoon Elks and Regina Caps formed the Western Canada Senior Hockey League, and in 1947/48 the Flyers won the first national championship of any significance for Edmonton when they captured the national Senior trophy, the Allan Cup.

Professional hockey in the meantime moved into the American Midwest and west coast, setting in motion a dynamic that would influence the the game's history to the present day and Edmonton's at times precarious role in it. Immediately after the war, two new leagues brought sixteen new teams into the ranks of outright professional hockey. The Pacific Coast Hockey League stitched together the key sites along the continent's western shore: in British Columbia, Vancouver and New Westminster; in Washington, Seattle (and later Tacoma); in Oregon, Portland; in California, Oakland, Hollywood, San Diego, Los Angeles, Fresno and San Francisco. In the American Midwest, the United States Hockey League brought a paying game to Kansas City, Omaha, St. Paul, Minneapolis, Tulsa, Fort Worth, Dallas and Houston.

The postwar experiment of professional hockey in the United States from the Mississippi west had a quick setback. The USHL folded after 1950/51, and that same season California was erased from the professional map as the Pacific Coast league was reduced to six teams in the northwest: Victoria, Vancouver, New Westminster, Seattle, Portland and Tacoma. While California stayed out of the minor pro game, the International Hockey League, a six-team loop centred on

Detroit, rapidly expanded to reestablish the game in the Midwest. While some teams became affiliated with NHL clubs, many were independently owned and operated, and in the 1990s this league would prove to be a thorn in the NHL's side in some markets.

Back in Canada, the professional nature of much of the country's Senior hockey activity became above board as individual teams and, in some cases, entire provincial leagues (as in Quebec in 1952/53) were transformed by the NHL into fully professional enterprises. It was an important initial step in the eventual decline of Canada's grip on its own game. When Senior teams entered the outright professional domain, their fate was left to the whims of their sponsoring NHL clubs. They could be shut down entirely if sponsorship was cut off. And while the team itself might not be physically moved, by transferring all the players under contract to another location, the NHL club could effectively relocate the operation. As time passed, these relocations were almost all pointed southward, into the United States. Senior hockey leagues continued in Canada despite many teams being converted to professional status and entered in new leagues, but by the 1960s the Senior game was in serious decline. Once the teams that had turned professional vanished, there was almost nothing left of a once-vibrant network of community teams.

In 1951/52, the Edmonton Flyers, Calgary Stampeders, Vancouver Canucks, New Westminster Royals and Saskatoon Quakers left the Senior game to join the PCHL, and in 1952/53, the PCHL and the Western Canada Senior League merged to create the Western Hockey League. The Detroit Red Wings, who had lost the Omaha Knights as a sponsored team when the USHL folded, took a gamble on the new venture and became the lone NHL club to sponsor a WHL team in the 1950s. The Flyers, owned by the Edmonton Exhibition Board, forerunner of Northlands Park, were leased to the Red Wings for $1 a season.

Bud Poile was hired as the Flyers' player-coach for its first WHL season.[1] Poile played the better part of two seasons in Edmonton before moving behind the bench exclusively. He won the WHL championship with the Flyers on his first try, in 1952/53, and again in 1954/55. The team lineup enjoyed a parade of players who were on their way either out of or into the NHL, with a few hirelings oscillating between the majors and minors. Among them were Dutch Reibel, Larry Wilson, Al Arbour, Bronco Horvath, Gord Hannigan and Larry Hillman. For three seasons the team enjoyed the superb goaltending of Glenn Hall, who was from Humboldt, Saskatchewan, but became so attached to Edmonton that he retired to a farm in nearby Spruce Grove after his celebrated NHL career. The Flyers of the 1950s also featured a number of home-grown forwards who had notable NHL careers, all of whom had played for the local Junior team, the Oil Kings. Johnny Bucyk was an Edmonton native, Vic Stasiuk was from Lethbridge, and Norm Ullman hailed from Provost.

There was reasonable prosperity in Edmonton in the Flyers' glory days, with the discovery of Alberta's oil reserves in 1947 having fuelled a new natural resources industry. By 1961 there were about 250,000 people in the provincial capital, and in addition to the oil and gas industry and the surrounding farming economy, Edmonton was thriving as a gateway to northern Canada. The Flyers of the 1950s and early 1960s were the city's first taste of a celebrated professional hockey team, but the team's existence depended entirely on the sponsoring support of the NHL's Detroit Red Wings, far to the east. Edmonton did not have the independent resources to thrive in even the minor pro game, and as the WHL developed ambitions to become a pro league that could challenge the NHL, the city was destined to become a casualty of the brewing rivalry.

In 1958, Poile predicted that the WHL could well form a West Division in the NHL. Certainly there was something absurd about the NHL calling itself "National" when it comprised only six teams in the northeast. In the same year that Poile voiced the hope that the WHL could serve as a one-step expansion for the NHL, baseball's Brooklyn Dodgers moved to Los Angeles, and won the World Series the following year. If major-league baseball could figure out how to operate on both coasts, surely the NHL could, too, and Los Angeles in particular was eager to move into the NHL.

The NHL, however, rebuffed all overtures for expansion, as it had since the end of the Second World War. Ostensibly, the reason was concern for the quality of the game—if more teams were added, surely the skill level would be diluted. A more likely explanation was sheer hegemony. NHL franchise owners didn't want to increase their own numbers; they wanted to control as much of the professional and amateur game as they could and maintain an artificial exclusivity. Territorial agreements with minor pro leagues like the American Hockey League saw the NHL give up the possibility of intruding on markets like Philadelphia and Cleveland in return for the other leagues remaining minor pro in character, their teams supported by sponsorship agreements. These agreements saw the NHL parent clubs supply the cream of the minor pro talent. The NHL teams and their sponsored minor clubs also controlled the rights to the main resource of new players: the Canadian amateur system.

The importance of these arrangements to the NHL's profitability becomes clear when seen from the perspective of labour and wages. By limiting the number of starting positions in the six-team NHL to about one hundred jobs in total, the league had the upper hand in setting player salaries. It was basic supply and demand. When the number of qualified players exceeded the number of starting jobs, labour costs were naturally suppressed. The vast majority of players were issued two-way contracts—that is, contracts that specified salary levels based on the league to which the NHL assigned them. The NHL naturally paid the most, with an assignment to a second tier league like the AHL or WHL paying less, and duties with a Canadian Senior league less again. Players without a starting spot on the main NHL team had no choice but to settle for significantly less money—as little as half their NHL rate—in a minor pro assignment. Consequently, the network of minor pro affiliates the NHL teams oversaw served not only as a development system, but as a low-cost overflow for surplus talent. It was a place the NHL owners could park players cheaply, which was preferable to allowing them to earn a major-league wage with a new franchise. The affiliate system also served as a disciplinary tool. Problematic players—particularly those chafing for more money—could be banished to the minors and suffer the financial consequences. It was an effective brake on labour unrest.

Expanding the league would greatly increase the number of player positions at the elite wage level. There is an important distinction to be made between elite wages and elite ability. Some so-called minor-league clubs had very strong lineups. The Cleveland Barons of the AHL of the late 1940s and early 1950s held their own against top NHL clubs in exhibition matches, and were probably good enough to qualify for the playoffs in the NHL, had they been permitted to join the league. Team owner Jim Hendy was led down the garden path by the NHL board of governors as he tried in vain to meet their conditions for bringing the Barons into the NHL. If season ticket sales weren't the problem, then it was Hendy's net worth. In the 1950s, there was enough talent in the AHL alone to have provided for at least two more NHL clubs, which would have done no worse than the struggling Blackhawks and Rangers.

If the NHL didn't want the Barons of the AHL, it certainly didn't want the entire WHL. If the NHL agreed to add the WHL as a western division, the NHL would have twice as many starting jobs overnight, and that would place upward pressure on salaries. There would also be twice as many owners, which would make it more difficult to operate a cartel with minimal dissent. The NHL could keep a lid on labour costs so long as the players could be herded by the small circle of owners. The league twice had close calls with embryonic players 'union drives, in 1947 and 1957. On both occasions, the owners were able to divide and conquer the would-be unionists. With twice as many players in the league, many of them just released from the confines of the minors, it would not be so easy to keep at bay an effort to organize.

In short, the economic pressures that would so inform the history of the Edmonton Oilers predated the debut of the World Hockey Association in 1972. They were in plain sight as the NHL turned the corner into the 1960s and confronted a rising threat from the WHL. The Edmonton Flyers were doomed to be caught in the crossfire.

In 1961/62, the Flyers won another WHL championship, just as there was a major front-office shakeup in Detroit. Jack Adams was practically the only general manager the Red Wings had ever had, having been preceded in the job by Art Duncan in the team's inaugural NHL season, 1926/27. In 1962, the irascible Adams was put out to pasture by owner Bruce Norris, his job being handed over to former star Sid Abel, who had coached the Wings since taking over from Jimmy Skinner in 1957/58. Adams had been the only person to both coach and manage the Red Wings, and he had given up the coaching duties in 1947. Bud Poile expected Abel to similarly give up the coaching job—to him. Having served in the Red Wings' minor-league trenches for a decade, having just earned his third WHL title, Poile felt he'd earned a shot at the bench job in Detroit. But Abel decided to keep the coaching position for himself. Poile quit, accepting a four-year contract as general manager of the WHL's San Francisco Seals.

The WHL had beaten the NHL to the coast. Tired of waiting for the NHL to move west of Chicago, both San Francisco and Los Angeles had secured WHL teams for 1961/62, forming a southern division with Portland and Spokane. The new operations in the major California centres fuelled the WHL's ambition. It wasn't based on their lineups, for their teams were mostly composed of career minor-leaguers and former NHLers entering their twilight years. It was based on the fact that their league had established a footprint in territory the NHL seemed foolishly determined to ignore. If a few additional cities could be added, a major U.S. television contract could be negotiated, and the resulting revenues would take care of the problem of finding first-class players. They wouldn't need to worry about trying to steal players under contract to NHL clubs. They would just have to get them right out of the Junior hockey ranks, securing their services before the NHL did.

The NHL's persistent dominance of the pro hockey system in its archaic configuration as a small railway league based in the northeastern United States and Canada required time to stand still. The quaint NHL loop denied the fact that California had risen up through westward migration and the industrial and agricultural wealth fuelled by the Second World War; that television broadcasting had expanded to become the dominant force in professional sports; that jet aircraft had changed continental travel patterns so that lengthy road trips were possible. The league tried to defy the shifting economic patterns, clinging to its aging arenas in urban centres with nineteenth-century industrial roots.

Poile's departure for San Francisco, the new frontier of the game, was an auspicious turn of events for Edmonton. Without Poile, the Flyers were orphaned in the Red Wings system. One season after winning the WHL title, the Flyers' wins dropped from thirty-nine to twenty-four as they missed the playoffs altogether, even though they had twelve of seventeen players from the championship season. Poile's Seals, meanwhile, won the first of two consecutive WHL titles. Among the players in the lamentable 1962/63 Flyers roster was a career minor-leaguer named Doug Messier, who had a two-year-old son named Mark.

At the WHL's annual meeting in June 1963, Sid Abel brought the hammer down on the Flyers. Ten minutes before the meeting was to start, Abel confronted Flyers general manager Al Anderson, and informed him that the Red Wings were withdrawing all player support for the team. Without the Red Wings' money and contracted players, there was a franchise, but no actual team. Anderson had no choice but to suspend operations for the 1963/64 season while the Edmonton Exhibition Board weighed its options. Though stung by the loss of the Flyers, fans could find enough to cheer for in the Oil Kings, who were in the midst of an unprecedented seven consecutive appearances in the Memorial Cup finals. Edmonton passed on getting the Flyers going again. Without an Edmonton team in the WHL, the Calgary Stampeders, whose performance had also slipped in 1962/63, were without a traditional rival and gate draw. Calgary, too, dropped out of the WHL. The Winnipeg Warriors had already been lost in 1961.

As would prove to be the case in the NHL in the 1990s, arena facilities were a major factor in the inability of Canadian cities to hold on to franchises, and in the ability of American cities to attract them. The Vancouver Canucks, the only Canadian team left in the WHL, were stuck in a rink with a capacity of 5,000. Edmonton Gardens, which had been home ice to the Flyers, had a capacity of 5,200. The five American WHL franchises had facilities that could handle much larger crowds. The Spokane Comets had moved to Denver; renamed the Invaders, they were playing in a 10,000-seat rink. Portland, Los Angeles and San Francisco could accommodate 11,000 fans, while a new rink in Seattle had a capacity close to 14,000. So long as teams in larger arenas could actually attract sufficient fans, the profitability consequences were indisputable. More fans bought more tickets and brought in more money. Teams playing in newer, larger American arenas were going to be more viable than ones in antique Canadian ones.

Sid Abel blamed the decision to break off the long and productive relationship with the Flyers on money—specifically the loss of $110,000 in 1962/63. "Detroit lost a lot of money in Edmonton last season, and the team finished third [in the North Division]," he explained at the WHL meeting. "The year before they won the regular season race and the playoff championship and the Wings still lost money. Under those circumstances I think it's a good idea to get out."

Coincidentally, Detroit was getting out of the WHL just as the NHL was getting into the American Midwest. Jack Adams had been paid off with a fresh assignment: overseeing the creation of a fully NHL-sponsored development loop, the Central Professional Hockey

League. As Detroit pulled the plug on Edmonton in the WHL, the sponsoring NHL clubs withdrew their support for the four-team Eastern Professional Hockey League, which had grown out of Canadian Senior teams in Ontario and Quebec that had been turned professional. The CPHL was meant to take over the EPHL's development role, with rosters limited mostly to players under the age of twenty-three. Each NHL club would sponsor one of the CPHL teams. For the debut 1963/64 season, Detroit took the Cincinnati Wings, Boston the Minneapolis Bruins, New York the St. Paul Rangers, Montreal the Omaha Knights, Chicago the St. Louis Braves. They were joined the next season by the Tulsa Oilers, sponsored by the Toronto Maple Leafs.

In the space of just three seasons, the minor pro hockey landscape had been almost entirely Americanized. As recently as 1961/62, the EPHL had featured six Canadian teams, in Ottawa-Hull, Kingston, Kitchener, Sudbury, North Bay and Sault Ste. Marie. In 1963/64, the only Canadian teams left in the minor pro game, other than the WHL's Vancouver Canucks, were the Quebec Aces (another former Senior team) in the American Hockey League and the Windsor Bulldogs and Chatham Maroons, one-season wonders of the IHL. The replacement in the WHL of the Denver Invaders by the Victoria Cougars (owned by the Maple Leafs) in 1964/65 was a brief and illusory resurgence.

After dropping out of the WHL for the 1963/64 season, Edmonton had no choice but to drop out for good. No credible plan presented itself for returning the Flyers to the WHL. The game, and its money, had gone south. The WHL's ambitions of challenging the NHL for tier 1 bragging rights was leading it to explore the possibility of establishing franchises in places like St. Louis, Buffalo, Pittsburgh and Baltimore. Quebec City was also considered, but not Edmonton or Calgary. The key to getting an American network contract was having an American league. Edmonton, one of Canada's northernmost metropolises, was about 300 miles north of the Montana border, which itself was far removed from any urban centre American media buyers considered desirable.

The NHL still refused to consider expansion, not even putting the subject on the agenda for its annual meeting in June 1964. But the Western Hockey League expansion feelers, combined with lectures on "national" programming from American TV networks, finally forced the NHL to act. Without teams in the major California markets, there was no chance of getting a network contract. The NHL had also failed to see that rival networks would be willing to support rival leagues. NBC was not going to walk away from professional football, just because CBS had a two-year, $35 million contract with the National Football League. Instead, NBC signed up with the NFL's rival, the American Football League. Maybe the AFL didn't play as sophisticated a game, but it made for good TV, and that made it worthwhile for NBC executives to spend $35 million for a five-year deal. The lesson was clear: a second-class product could attract first-class money. What was to stop the WHL from doing what the AFL had done?

In March 1965, the NHL cut off the WHL threat at the pass by deciding to move forward with expansion. Taking in the WHL as a six-team west division could have given the NHL three more Canadian teams, in Vancouver, Edmonton and Calgary. Added to the existing teams in Montreal and Toronto, this would have made the NHL almost half Canadian in ownership. Instead, by selecting six new teams one franchise at a time, in February 1966 the NHL was able to stay clear of Western Canada altogether. It cherry-picked the prime WHL locations in Los Angeles and San Francisco, elevated two locations in the CPHL, Minneapolis and St. Louis, and backfilled in the east with Philadelphia and Pittsburgh, both of which were AHL territories.

The WHL's ambitions of becoming a rival major league had been tamed. By the time the NHL announced its six expansion sites, all the WHL clubs had NHL sponsors. In 1967/68 the WHL retreated into a five-team enterprise in Portland, San Diego, Phoenix, Seattle and Vancouver. The league folded in 1974, but the dream of a league that would challenge the NHL for fans and players did not die. On the contrary, Phoenix and San Diego joined the new rebellion, which had been under way since 1972. It was officially called the World Hockey Association, but it might be better characterized as Billy's Revenge. A western Canadian hockey promoter had teamed up with a pair of Californians who knew nothing about the sport but saw an opportunity to create a new major league. In the process that promoter, Billy Hunter, brought the paying game back to the Canadian prairies, and back to Edmonton. The team was called the Oilers, but they were affectionately known to some simply as Billy's Boys. The boys, who had been scattered hither and yon by the contrary winds of professional hockey, were back in town.

CHAPTER TWO

AVING OUTMANOEUVRED the Western Hockey League with the 1967 expansion that doubled its size, the NHL enjoyed a brief period of hegemony before encountering the first serious challenge to its dominance of the professional game since the 1920s and the old WHL. In the early 1970s, a pair of Californians, lawyer Gary L. Davidson and promoter Dennis A. Murphy, who had never actually seen a hockey game, were inspired by the success of another upstart operation, the American Basketball Association. The ABA hit the courts in 1967/68, just as the NHL doubled its size.

At the time, the National Basketball Association was a ten-team league (the NHL had twelve), and there was pent-up demand among investors and cities for franchises the NBA was declining to provide. The situation with the NHL was no different. The NHL's expansion into Buffalo and Vancouver in 1970 merely cleaned up loose ends, granting franchises to locations that had expected to be chosen in the original 1967 expansion. Basketball and hockey shared a similar season and the same building, an arena that could seat about 16,000. Davidson and Murphy put together the World Hockey Association concept in April 1971, after the ABA had made it through its fourth season, and incorporated the league in Delaware on June 10 of that year.

Following the ABA, the WHA attempted to bring some novelty to its product to distinguish it from the dominant league. The ABA used a three-point shot and a red, white and blue ball; the WHA introduced regular-season overtime and a red and blue puck. On November 1, 1971, in a press conference at the Americana Hotel in New York City, the WHA announced its initial loop for the 1972/73 season: ten teams would play in Edmonton, Calgary, New York, Winnipeg, Chicago, St. Paul, Miami, Dayton, Los Angeles and San Francisco. Three weeks later, two more franchises were announced: one for New England and one for Ontario. The New England franchise was placed in Boston as the Whalers; the Ontario franchise chose Ottawa and became the Nationals.

There was much shuffling of franchises before the first puck was dropped. Miami moved to Philadelphia to become the Blazers; San Francisco went to Quebec to become the Nordiques; the Dayton Aeros relocated to Houston (and kept their name); and the Calgary Broncos were turned into the Cleveland Crusaders. As hockey neophytes, Davidson and Murphy were given little chance of success. (At the press conference announcing the New York Raiders franchise, Davidson stumbled badly when he introduced the team's coach, veteran NHLer Camille Henry, as "Henry Camille.") But the league held a player draft in Anaheim on February 12, 1972, and began making headlines when it was able to sign a number of NHL stars whose rights they had parcelled out among themselves. Bobby Hull's signing of a ten-year, $2.75 million contract with the Winnipeg Jets had the greatest impact on the league's credibility, but there were many other star signings. The defending Stanley Cup champions, the Boston Bruins, lost Derek Sanderson, Gerry Cheevers and Ted Green; the Philadelphia Flyers lost goaltender Bernie Parent to the Miami Screaming Eagles, which then landed in the Flyers' backyard as the Philadelphia Blazers. But the league had its greatest success in attracting NHL journeymen and minor-leaguers, who could double their salaries joining the new enterprise. Not every franchise was a success, and relocations occurred at a frenetic pace in the first few seasons. But the WHA, contrary to its detractors' predictions, did not go away, and even began to expand, riding a wave of new arena construction around North America.

Working behind the scenes with WHA architects Davidson and Murphy was Billy Hunter, an indefatigable prairie hockey promoter born in Saskatoon in 1920. Hunter had played for the Notre Dame College Hounds, a Junior team in Wilcox, Saskatchewan; a team-mate was Garth Boesch, a defenceman who starred with the Maple Leafs in the 1940s, and the college also produced the Leafs' Nick and Don Metz. After serving in the RCAF during the war, Hunter went into the sporting goods business in North Battleford, revived the North Battleford Beavers Senior team, and in 1946 took over the Regina Caps Senior team with a partner. Hunter's chequered career was launched. (Running hockey teams was in his blood: his father, Jack, had managed the Saskatoon Quakers of the old WHL in the 1920s.) A long association with prairie hockey brought Billy to Edmonton, where he owned, managed and sometimes coached the Edmonton Oil Kings, the city's Major Junior A team, as well as owning its 5,200-seat arena, the Gardens. Marked by flaming red hair and a promoter's gift for hyperbole, Hunter came to run one of the most celebrated teams in Canadian Junior hockey history.

The Ontario league was the powerhouse of tier I Canadian Junior hockey in the 1960s, but the national Junior championship, the Memorial Cup, required a showdown between east and west. Though consistently thin on future NHL talent, the Oil Kings reached every Memorial Cup final from 1960 to 1966, a streak unprecedented and never repeated. Playing a hard-hitting western game, the Oil Kings overcame the odds to win twice in seven tries, in 1962/63 and 1965/66.

For his WHA team—also initially called the Oil Kings—Hunter had envisioned a lucrative Alberta rivalry with a Calgary-based team, the Broncos, but when the Broncos' owner was unable to make a $100,000 franchise payment in April 1972, the franchise was transferred to Cleveland. Left alone in the province, Hunter switched the name of his club before the start of the first WHA season to the Alberta Oilers.

Where other WHA teams attempted to secure fan bases by luring marquee talents from the NHL, Hunter adopted a less expensive strategy: key in on Alberta-born players, or players who had played their Junior hockey in the province, to give fans familiar faces. Many former Oil Kings (and some former WHL Flyers) were the targets of his drafting and signing efforts. Because so many players who had starred for Hunter as Oil Kings were lassoed by him for the WHA Oilers, the team became known as "Billy's Boys."

Hunter secured Dennis Kassian from his 1960/61 Oil Kings, who lost to the St. Michael's College Majors in that year's Memorial Cup finals. He also got Edmonton native Eddie Joyal, who was with the Oil Kings in 1958/59 and 1959/60 before joining the Edmonton Flyers for two seasons. As a Detroit property, Joyal then lasted three seasons with the Red Wings before becoming one of five Detroit players in a seven-player swap with Toronto in May 1965, which mainly saw Marcel Pronovost become a Maple Leaf and Andy Bathgate become a Red Wing. Chosen by the Los Angeles Kings in the 1967 expansion draft, Joyal managed a steady career at centre with the Kings until he was thrown into another seven-player swap, this time with Philadelphia, two weeks before the first WHA draft. Joyal signed with Hunter and finished his playing career in Edmonton, after four seasons as an Oiler, in 1975/76.

Defenceman Bob Wall was a Detroit property who played for the Hamilton Red Wings when they defeated the Oil Kings in the 1961/62 Memorial Cup finals. He then joined the Edmonton Flyers for seven games in their last season, 1962/63. Wall appeared sporadically on defence for Detroit from 1964/65 to 1966/67, before being selected by Los Angeles in the 1967 expansion draft. He had been traded from Los Angeles to St. Louis and back to Detroit when Hunter chose him in the WHA draft. Wall was with the Oilers for two seasons before being traded to San Diego.

Val Fonteyne was an old hand on left wing when Hunter selected him in the draft. Though he had never played for Hunter in Edmonton, he was born in nearby Wetaskiwin and like many local players had been a Detroit property. Fonteyne played with the Red Wings, the Rangers and the Red Wings again from 1959/60 to 1966/67, before being chosen by Pittsburgh in the 1967 expansion draft. He was a Penguins regular when Hunter drafted him, and he spent his last two professional seasons with the Oilers.

Another veteran that Hunter secured was right winger Bill Hicke, a Montreal Canadien in the late 1950s and early 1960s who was with the Rangers when taken by Oakland in the 1967 expansion draft. Hicke's career was ebbing when Hunter selected him—he spent most of 1971/72 in the Central and American leagues. He finished his career with Edmonton in 1972/73.

Among Hunter's more youthful signings was left winger Brian Carlin, a twenty-two-year-old Calgarian who had played three seasons of Junior hockey with the Calgary Centennials and another with the Medicine Hat Tigers before being drafted 86th overall by Los Angeles in 1970. His first professional season, 1971/72, had been spent mostly with L.A.'s American league affiliate, the Springfield Kings, and he accepted Hunter's offer to play with the Oilers. He lasted little more than one season.

The Oilers scored a rare victory against the NHL in the battle for new talent in signing Ken Baird. The former Flin Flon Bomber defenceman, who had 211 penalty minutes in his final Junior season in 1970/71, had been Oakland's first pick (15th overall) in the 1971 amateur draft. Oakland assigned him to Oklahoma City in the Central league for most of 1971/72, where he amassed 196 penalty minutes in fifty-nine games. Drafted by Hunter, Baird came to Edmonton to play four full seasons with the Oilers, then sporadically with Edmonton, Calgary and Winnipeg until 1977/78, before playing in Germany for two years.

Hunter made a special effort to secure players who had been part of his 1965/66 Memorial Cup-winning team. Defenceman Al Hamilton, born in Flin Flon, Manitoba, had played on the Oil Kings from 1963/64 to 1965/66. As a Rangers property, he broke into the New York lineup fulltime in 1969/70, only to be taken by the Buffalo Sabres in the 1970 expansion draft. After being drafted by Hunter, Hamilton signed with the new WHA team and became a franchise player, lasting until 1979/80, the Oilers' first NHL season.

Centre Jim Harrison, born in Bonnyville, Alberta, had been a Boston property playing for the Estevan Bruins when Hunter added him to the Oil Kings lineup for the 1965/66 Memorial Cup finals. He broke into the Boston lineup in 1968/69, then was traded to Toronto for Wayne Carleton in December 1969. Harrison was taken by Calgary in the inaugural WHA draft, but when the Calgary franchise was transferred to Cleveland, Hunter was able to buy his rights (along with those of goaltenders Ken Brown and Jack Norris, both former Estevan players) in May 1972. Harrison, with eighty-six points, and Hamilton, with sixty-one, were Hunter's top two points producers in the Oilers' first WHA season.

Other players selected from the 1965/66 Oil Kings were right winger Ron Anderson and defencemen Doug Barrie and Bob Falkenberg, all of whom signed with Hunter. He missed out on the team's goaltender, Don McLeod, who was drafted by Houston but found his way to the Oilers, long after Hunter had ceased to be involved, in 1977/78. Hunter also drafted Garnet Bailey, an overlooked talent acquired by Boston in the 1966 amateur draft after he helped the Oil Kings defeat the Bruins' heavily favoured farm team, the Oshawa Generals, in the Memorial Cup finals. But Bailey declined to come over to the WHA and the Oilers, sticking with the NHL and winning a Stanley Cup with Boston in 1971/72. He finally reached the Oilers as a free agent signing for 1978/79, his final major professional season.

Another local-hero draft pick was Glen Sather, a former Oil Kings captain who had played on the 1962/63 Memorial Cup-winning team. Though Hunter was unable to sign him, Sather would figure enormously in the team's history. Born in High River, Alberta, in 1943, Sather was a tenacious checking left winger who belonged to the Detroit Red Wings. The Red Wings assigned him to their Central Professional Hockey League team in Memphis for 1964/65, where he produced forty-eight points and ninety-eight penalty minutes but made no long-term impression. The Boston Bruins picked him up in the CPHL inter-league draft in June 1965 and moved him to their own CPHL affiliate, the Oklahoma City Blazers. There, he fell under the direction of player-coach Harry Sinden.

As a player, Sinden had won a world championship for Canada in 1958 with the Whitby Dunlops of the Ontario Senior League, one of the last Canadian amateur teams to win a world title. (British Columbia's Trail Smoke Eaters were the final Canadian amateur team to accomplish the feat, in 1961.) Sinden's future was as a coach, not as a player, and for four seasons he made his mark as a player-coach in the minor pro game. With the Kingston Frontenacs of the Eastern Professional Hockey League, Sinden won a regular-season title in 1962/63 (though was unable to win the league championship), then moved to the new Central Professional Hockey League to serve as player-coach of Boston's affiliate, the Minneapolis Bruins. For 1965/66, Boston moved its affiliate to Oklahoma City, and there Sinden won his first league title, the Adams Cup.

The Bruins at the time were in a long and dispiriting slump, not having made the playoffs since 1958/59. Lynn Patrick, who had been the team's general manager since 1954/55, was replaced in the summer of 1965 by Hap Emms, while former team captain Milt Schmidt continued to coach. Schmidt was poised to move up into the general manager's job, which would create a vacancy down at the bench. By winning the Adams Cup with the Blazers in the spring of 1966, Sinden, at thirty-three, was deemed fit to become for 1966/67 the Bruins coach—the youngest coach in the NHL at the time.

His Blazers had been filled with future NHLers, some of whom would participate in the Bruins' rapid ascent as Stanley Cup contenders. Sinden had already played with and coached Ted Green, Don Awrey and Ed Westfall. On the 1965/66 Blazers he had goaltender Gerry Cheevers as well as Derek Sanderson, Don Marcotte and Dallas Smith, all of whom would win the Stanley Cup with Boston. He also had goaltender Doug Favell, who would play with Philadelphia and Toronto, and Terry Crisp and Joe Watson, who would win Stanley Cups with Philadelphia.

And then there was Sather. "I was impressed with Glen's understanding of the game even as a young man," Sinden recalls. Sather became a long-standing close friend of Sinden's, though not a player who figured in Sinden's future as a Stanley Cup-winning coach. Sather, who set an Oklahoma City franchise record with 147 penalty minutes in 1966/67, excelled through sheer competitive determination. As the Bruins assembled a powerful and talented team, there was increasingly less room for his services. After Sinden called him up from Oklahoma City for five games in 1966/67, Sather played two full seasons in Boston. However, in thirteen playoff games in 1967/68 and 1968/69, he didn't record a single point. His only statistical contribution was eighteen penalty minutes incurred in ten playoff games in 1968/69.

The Bruins were on the brink of success. In the 1968/69 semi-finals, they came up short against the defending Stanley Cup champions, the Montreal Canadiens, losing in six games. Three games, including the series-clincher, went into overtime, and the more experienced Canadiens won all of them. Sinden made almost no changes to this lineup for 1969/70, save on left wing. Don Marcotte, Sather's Oklahoma City team-mate, got a starting job. So did Garnet Bailey, the former Edmonton Oil King. Left unprotected at the June 1969 intra-league draft, Sather was selected by the Pittsburgh Penguins.

So began for Sather an NHL career that repeatedly brought him within sight, but never within touch, of the Stanley Cup. Dropped by the impending champions, the Bruins, in the summer of 1969, he was acquired by an expansion team that had yet to make the playoffs.

With former Detroit and Toronto defensive star Red Kelly coaching, the Penguins were able to reach the 1969/70 playoffs with a losing record, but were eliminated by the St. Louis Blues, who were on their way to a third consecutive appearance in the finals under coach Scotty Bowman. Bowman lost (for the third consecutive time) to the representative of the NHL's Eastern Division, Sinden's Bruins.

On January 26, 1971, Sather got a break: the Penguins traded him to a Stanley Cup contender, swapping him for Syl Apps Jr. of the New York Rangers. In 1971/72, Sather reached the finals as the Rangers met up with the Bruins.

It was not the best year to tackle Boston in the finals. The Bruins had run away with the 1970/71 season, scoring 108 goals more than any other team. But with an unheralded rookie, Ken Dryden, in goal, the Canadiens upset the Bruins in the quarter-finals. The Bruins were determined not to repeat the humiliation the following year. Sinden had left the Bruins after the 1969/70 Cup win in a salary dispute, going into the residential construction business, and would return as general manager for 1972/73. With Tom Johnson coaching, the Bruins knocked off the Maple Leafs in five in the opening round of the 1971/72 playoffs and swept the Blues in four, outscoring St. Louis 28-8. Sather and the Rangers kept the finals close, but not close enough. Four games were decided by one goal, but the Bruins won in six.

At the beginning of the 1973/74 season, the Rangers traded Sather to St. Louis. He had his best NHL season, with forty-four points in sixty-nine Blues games, which made him marketable the following summer. On May 27, 1974, the Montreal Canadiens sent Rick Wilson to the Blues, who had missed the playoffs. The defenceman from Saskatchewan had completed his first of three seasons at the University of North Dakota when the Canadiens chose him 66th overall in the 1970 draft. Called up from the Nova Scotia Voyageurs of the AHL in 1973/74, Wilson played in twenty-one regular-season games, but in none of Montreal's playoff appearances as the Canadiens were downed by the Rangers in the opening round. In return for Wilson and Montreal's fifth-round pick in that summer's draft, St. Louis gave Montreal their fourth-round pick in the same draft and the ubiquitous "future consideration." On June 14, 1974, St. Louis and Montreal agreed on the future consideration: Glen Sather.

It was Sather's last shot at a Stanley Cup. Unfortunately, as in Boston in 1968/69, his stint with the Canadiens came one year too soon. Montreal had been rocked in 1973/74 by a sub-par performance and dissent between players and coach Scotty Bowman. Having already lost Marc Tardif, Réjean Houle and J.C. Tremblay to the WHA, further defections followed, as Frank Mahovlich signed with the Toronto Toros. Goalie Ken Dryden returned after spending a year articling to complete his law degree (although his decision to sit out 1973/74 was inspired by dissatisfaction over his contract), but the Canadiens were not quite ready to return to league dominance. (Also, unfortunately for Sather, the team was already stocked with excellent young left wingers: Steve Shutt, Murray Wilson, Yvon Lambert and Bob Gainey.) In the 1974/75 semi-finals, the Canadiens lost to the Buffalo Sabres in six games. Sather was sent to the Minnesota North Stars that July for cash and Minnesota's third-round pick in the 1977 draft. In the season that followed Sather's trade, Montreal began its run of four consecutive Stanley Cup victories.

Sather's own NHL run was all but over. He turned thirty-two at the beginning of the 1975/76 season, the property of a struggling franchise that would win only twenty games. Sather contributed nine goals and ten assists, and turned to the WHA to extend his playing career. The team that hired him, the Edmonton Oilers, had never dealt away his rights. For the end of a playing career, it was at least a homecoming.

IN THE FOUR-AND-A-HALF years that passed between Sather's drafting by Billy Hunter and his belated appearance in the team roster in the fall of 1976, the Oilers franchise had been through a steady march of changes. By the measure of a league in which franchises folded tents and moved to new territories with the regularity of desert nomads, the Oilers could be called a success, but by the measure of professional hockey in general, the Oilers were tenacious survivors.

The first seasons were ad hoc efforts. When the Calgary Broncos were turned into the Cleveland Crusaders before the first season, Hunter abandoned his plan to call the team the Edmonton Oil Kings. He switched it to the Alberta Oilers, intending to split home games between Calgary and Edmonton. (Like other league novelties, this concept was borrowed from the regional franchise model employed by the American Basketball Association. The Carolina Cougars, for example, played in Greensboro, Raleigh and Charlotte—a foreshadowing of the NHL's Carolina Hurricanes playing their initial home games in Greensboro while a new arena was built in Raleigh.) The regional franchise concept was abandoned before the start of the first season, however. While still named the Alberta Oilers, the team played home games exclusively at Hunter's cramped Edmonton Gardens, averaging about 3,800 fans per game. Hunter fired his coach, Ray Kinasewich, halfway through the season and took over the bench himself. The team finished tied for fourth in the six-team Western Division with a 38-37-3 record, forcing a one-game playoff with the Minnesota Fighting Saints. The Oilers lost 4-2, and were left without playoff revenues.

With the team firmly established in Edmonton, Hunter changed its name to the Edmonton Oilers for 1973/74. It again played to a 38-37-3 record, finishing third in the west. Minnesota eliminated Edmonton in five games, but the team could look forward to a vast improvement in their humble surroundings. The City of Edmonton had decided to build a major-league arena, and the Oilers would move into it for 1974/75.

The propensity of North American cities for building civic arenas in the hope of attracting a major-league hockey or basketball franchise would became captured by the phrase, "If you build it, they will come." The phrase itself didn't exist until Alberta novelist W.P.

Kinsella bestowed it upon a disembodied voice in *Shoeless Joe*, published in 1982. The words compelled Kinsella's protagonist to build a baseball diamond in the middle of a cornfield, to conjure the spirits of the scandal-tinged 1919 Chicago White Sox. When the novel was turned into a popular 1989 feature film, *Field of Dreams*, starring Kevin Costner, the phrase entered the general lexicon. The civic construction boom those words came to describe and even encourage was already under way a full decade before *Shoeless Joe* was written.

One of the most notable early successes in the publicly financed arena boom was Nassau Veterans Memorial Coliseum in Long Island, New York. The new facility, built by the affluent suburban county, had no major-league hockey tenant when designed in 1970, but the arrival of the WHA quickly took care of that. The New York Raiders franchise was considering the Coliseum for its home, but the NHL hustled in a team ahead of it, granting the Islanders franchise to a syndicate led by Roy Boe, who owned the Nets of the ABA. The Islanders began playing in 1972/73, and soon new public arenas were under construction in Indianapolis, Denver and Cleveland, as well as in Edmonton.

In Edmonton, the Coliseum was the showpiece of the exhibition grounds known as Northlands Park. The city-owned Northlands Coliseum was modelled on the Pacific Coliseum in Vancouver, home of the Canucks of the NHL (and, beginning in 1973/74, the Blazers of the WHA). Relatively lavish for its time, it was designed not to give the WHA's Oilers a fancier home rink but to attract an NHL franchise to the city. When construction began in 1973, there was no guarantee that the WHA, let alone Billy Hunter's humble Oilers, would survive more than a season or two. But as the WHA and the Oilers hung in, the city, by default, came to bank on the Oilers' potential to cross over into the NHL as its means of bringing truly big-league hockey to Northlands.

After the Oilers relocated to Northlands, Billy Hunter sold the team to a local investor, Dr. Charles Allard, whose enthusiasm was short-lived. Dr. Allard enjoyed neither the public spotlight of ownership nor the losses associated with the team, and he quickly sold the Oilers for $300,000 to Nelson Skalbania, a hyperkinetic real estate flip artist from British Columbia, with whom he had done multimillion-dollar property deals through the Allard family's North West Trust Company. Skalbania's friend, auto sales magnate Jim Pattison, already owned the Vancouver Blazers; together they would buy AAA baseball's Vancouver Canadians in 1980.

The secret to Skalbania's financial success was rapid-fire property deals. Hanging tough through a steady flow of red ink from a second-rate sports franchise like the Oilers was not Skalbania's style, nor was the team as attractive an investment as he first thought. In the fall of 1976, he quickly decided to take on a partner, an emerging Edmonton capitalist named Peter Pocklington, with whom he'd done about $200 million in real estate deals.

PETER POCKLINGTON arrived in Edmonton from southern Ontario in August 1971, catching the first curl of the wave of prosperity that swept across Alberta in the ensuing decade.

He showed up in time for a watershed provincial election, held on August 30. While long the voters' party of choice federally, the Progressive Conservatives had been in the doldrums provincially until they launched a revitalization in the 1960s. The rural, Bible-thumping conservatism of Ernest Manning's Social Credit party then ruled the province. After Calgary lawyer Peter Lougheed won the provincial PC leadership in 1965, the party began to march ahead. While Joe Clark, running in Calgary South, failed to win a seat in the 1967 election, Lougheed was elected in Calgary West, as was former Edmonton Eskimos quarterback Don Getty in Edmonton. They didn't win power, but the Lougheed-led party had a toehold. Social Credit faded badly in the wake of Manning's retirement in 1968. Six years after assuming party leadership, Lougheed became premier.

Lougheed came to power with a majority government in the

August 1971 election, just before the western Canadian economy ignited. Oil and gas had been part of Alberta's economic landscape since vast reserves were discovered in 1947, but the OPEC crisis of 1973 made the province truly wealthy. Oil was considered almost inflation-proof; the price was below US$3.00 per barrel from 1959 to 1967, and was $3.56 when Lougheed won power. It was still that price two years later. Then, in the fall of 1973, the Middle East War sent oil's price skyrocketing. Jumping to $4.31 as tensions rose in August 1973, it leapt to $10.11 in January 1974 and kept climbing, with the Iranian hostage crisis of 1979 helping press it beyond $20.

The oil-price run-up should have been financially devastating to Pocklington, who acquired an Edmonton car dealership when he arrived in town two years earlier. But being in the business of retailing gas-eating machines at a time of runaway fuel prices proved not to be a problem. The local economy was in overdrive, and people were buying cars, no matter how much it cost to top up their tanks. And Pocklington, only thirty years old, was already diversifying into the other attractive commodity of the 1970s, real estate. Even before arriving in Edmonton, he had begun to invest money in American property, and would prove to be a prescient investor in Phoenix, Arizona, a future sunbelt mecca, where he accumulated up to five hundred acres of land by buying on the down cycle.

The tales of Pocklington's rise from humble beginnings in London, Ontario, as the son of an insurance executive have been coloured with hyperbole worthy of Billy Hunter. What is undisputable is that he proved to be an outstanding deal-maker at a young age.[1] Cars gave him his start—by his own account one of his earliest deals was selling the family Oldsmobile without first telling his dad, although the $800 profit he turned helped mitigate the consequences. A visit to his grandfather's farm in Carberry, Manitoba, at fifteen led him to the realization that a junker not ravaged by road salt on the Prairies could be had for $150, shipped back east to Ontario (taking advantage of cheap haul-back rates) for $25, and sold for $500. Details of his early exploits vary, but to Peter Gzowski (in *The Game of Our Lives*) Pocklington offered that he went broke at twenty-one selling finance companies contracts to car sales and personally guaranteeing the loans, not counting on the fact that the buyers might default. At some point he became a management trainee at Eaton's in Toronto, a serious miscalculation, then abandoned the department store trade to return to London and sell Fords. Fired by a dealer after asking for a raise, at twenty-three (or twenty-four; accounts vary) Pocklington became the youngest Ford dealer in Canada when he bought a small operation in nearby Tilbury, followed by another in Chatham.

Edmonton was next. He had asked Ford Canada for a larger dealership, and had been directed there to look at one for sale. "The deal took about half an hour," he would recall. "It just felt right." He had the foresight to move it to the suburbs, as Westown Ford. As the oil boom hit, Edmonton sprawled spectacularly. Despite its cowboy persona, Alberta, like its ten-gallon cousin Texas, became increasingly urban. Calgary's population grew from 279,000 to 470,000 between 1961 and 1976, Edmonton's from 259,000 to 554,000. Edmonton was the country's sixth-largest city in 1976; it had become bigger than Quebec City, and almost as big as Winnipeg. By 1991, Edmonton had surpassed 800,000, with Calgary at 750,000; both had become bigger than Winnipeg, and were exceeded in size only by Montreal, Toronto, Ottawa and Vancouver. Alberta's population had become 80 percent urban, with only about 57,000 of its 2,000,000 citizens living on the farm. Big Sky country had become essentially as urbanized as Ontario.

Pocklington would pride himself on gut-instinct deal-making decisions, on not getting lost in details, on not losing the long-term view through short-term greed. While Nelson Skalbania, his new-found business associate out West, often looked for quick profits with rapid rollovers of properties, Pocklington began to build a diversified empire. The cash flow from the auto business helped fuel his real estate deals, and with real estate profits he branched into agribusiness, natural resources and financial services.

The inclination of self-assured entrepreneurs to venture into the risky but ego-gratifying world of professional sports franchises saw to it that Pocklington ended up buying some, and then all, of the Edmonton Oilers.

The Oilers were on the brink of collapse after 1975/76, having finished fourth in the five-team Canadian division with twenty-seven wins in eighty-one games. Skalbania, the new owner gripped by serious second thoughts about a near-worthless asset with about $1.6 million in debt, convinced Pocklington to relieve him of half the team's equity. Pocklington and Skalbania split up the team at the very press conference that Skalbania called to announce he had just bought it from Dr. Charles Allard. Pocklington was dining with his wife, Eva, at the Steak Loft in Edmonton in October 1976, when he saw Skalbania come in with a crowd of reporters in tow. The two men bartered their way to a new ownership arrangement. Pocklington gave Skalbania a vintage Rolls Royce Phaeton used in the film *The Great Gatsby*, a painting by Maurice Utrillo (Skalbania and Pocklington both had considerable fine art collections), and a diamond ring worth about $150,000 that happened to be on Eva's finger. Pocklington put the value of the swap at $700,000. In acquiring half the team, he also agreed to take on half the $1.6 million in debt, putting him $100,000 in the hole. He now had half a hockey team that was in danger of never being worth anything if they didn't figure out how to get into the NHL.

Chapter Three

THE WHA REACHED its apex in 1974/75, the season the Oilers moved into Northlands Coliseum. In a quest for greater credibility, the league's All Stars, who had been blackballed from Team Canada in 1972, played their own series against the Soviet national team before the season began. While they lost four, won two and tied one, the event proved that the WHA was no bush league. A total of fourteen teams led to the creation of three separate divisions, with Edmonton sharing the new Canadian Division with the Quebec Nordiques, Toronto Toros, Winnipeg Jets and Vancouver Blazers. Although the Oilers finished last in the five-team division and missed the playoffs (albeit with a respectable thirty-six wins in seventy-eight starts), the league in which they played was never stronger.

But at the end of the 1974/75 season, the league's fortunes began to flag. The Chicago Cougars and Baltimore Blades (a midseason relocation of the Michigan Stags) folded. The Vancouver Blazers became the Calgary Cowboys. A new franchise, the Denver Spurs, was awarded to St. Louis businessman Ivan Mullenix for 1975/76. Playing in the city's new McNichols Arena, the Spurs (which displaced the CHL team of the same name) attracted only minor pro crowds of about 3,000, and made a midseason move to Ottawa. Ottawa had already lost the Nationals to Toronto, where they had begun playing as the Toros in 1973/74. The relocated Spurs, dubbed the Civics, made a brief showing at the Ottawa Civic Centre before folding on January 17, 1976. Five weeks later, the Minnesota Fighting Saints vanished, with twenty-one games left to play in the season.

The Cleveland Crusaders were also in trouble, and for 1976/77 were relocated to Minnesota in an attempt to revive the Fighting Saints. Toronto was abandoned as the Toros were moved to Birmingham, Alabama, to become the Bulls. The Canadian Division was scrapped for 1976/77, with the league's twelve surviving teams aligned in Eastern and Western divisions.

It was in this shrinking league that Glen Sather became an Edmonton Oiler for his last tour as a professional player. Now owned by Nelson Skalbania and Peter Pocklington, the Oilers had proprietors with the wherewithal to stave off imminent collapse—a reasonable probability for a team that had won only twenty-seven games in 1975/76 and had rapidly drained the enthusiasm for solo ownership of both Dr. Charles Allard and Skalbania. With eighteen games left in 1976/77, the Oilers, though slightly improved, had only twenty-five wins and were destined again to finish behind Calgary in the race for the final playoff spot in their division. Skalbania's enthusiasm for the team was all but spent; his new co-investor, Pocklington, was poised to acquire the team outright.

As their season fizzled, the Oilers produced one of the oldest management ruses in professional sport. When a team is doing badly, management can always find an untested coach to be the fall guy. When the season is over and the playoffs have been missed yet again, the hapless coach can be fired, buying management some time with the owners.

That, at least, was how the scenario presented by the Edmonton Oilers in 1976/77 was widely interpreted, no more so than by Glen Sather, the subject of the coaching change. Trailing Calgary for the final playoff spot, Sather, the team captain, was abruptly made player-coach by coach and general manager Bep Guidolin. (Guidolin had been coach of the Oshawa Generals when the Edmonton Oil Kings upset them in the Memorial Cup finals of 1965/66.) "I was a scapegoat, because Guidolin never expected us to make the playoffs," Sather would say. As he later quipped, "I entertained my first thoughts about becoming a coach the day Guidolin told me I was either going to coach or sit in the crowd."

Sather rose magnificently to the occasion. As player-coaches went, he'd had an excellent role model, his old friend Harry Sinden, in Oklahoma City. The rag-tag Oilers responded to the change and went on a tear, winning nine, losing seven and tying two, just as the Cowboys were embarking on a disastrous road trip. Edmonton eased past Calgary with three points to spare, securing the final playoff spot in the Western Division.

The Oilers' playoff run was over quickly as they lost in five games to the Houston Aeros in the division semi-finals, but Sather had made an important impression on Peter Pocklington. The team's co-owner intervened directly in the Oilers' operations and hired Sather as the new coach. Meanwhile, he continued to search for a general manager to replace Guidolin, whose buck-passing scheme had backfired.

Pocklington's intervention had its own immediate consequences, however. Gord Robson, the operations manager appointed by Skalbania, tendered his resignation, objecting not to Sather as a coach but to the way in which Pocklington had taken matters into his own hands. Robson argued it would be harder to hire a new general manager, now that Pocklington had picked the coach first. Skalbania declined to rally to Robson's cause. With Sather as his new hand-picked coach, Pocklington soon had a new general manager as well—the WHA's former vice-president of operations, Larry Gordon. The Oilers also acquired a new outright owner, as Pocklington bought out Skalbania's share for $500,000, with a promise to pay him another $500,000 if the team was accepted into the NHL.

The Oilers' 1976/77 playoff drive, however much a boon to Glen Sather's career, proved a setback for the WHA, for it helped kill off

Edmonton's short-lived provincial rival, the Calgary Cowboys. Jim
Pattison had attracted reasonable crowds of 10,000 with his Vancouver
Blazers, but could not win the battle for fan affection and market
prevalence against the NHL's Canucks. Pattison had relocated the team
to Calgary for 1975/76, but his Cowboys were forced to play in an
ancient minor pro building, the Corral, and were slow to build fan
support. Missing the playoffs in 1976/77 sealed their fate. Pattison
announced that if the Cowboys didn't sell at least 4,400 season tickets
by May 31, the team was through. With one month to go, only 1,100 had
been purchased. The Cowboys became one more casualty in a league
that had been in retreat for the past two seasons. The reincarnation of
the Minnesota Fighting Saints had already closed shop, forty-two
games into the 1976/77 season. With the loss of the San Diego Mariners
and Phoenix Roadrunners, in addition to Pattison's Cowboys, the WHA
began 1977/78 with eight teams, all in one division.

Though scaled back considerably from 1974/75, the WHA still had
fight left in it, and with Howard Baldwin, owner of the New England
Whalers, serving as league president, efforts to strike a merger deal
with the NHL increased. A merger between the NHL and the WHA could
not be entertained in strict legal terms, because it would reopen the
free-agency clause in the NHL's 1976 collective bargaining agreement.
This was the first such agreement negotiated between the league and
the NHL Players' Association, which was formally certified as a union
in Canada that year. A possible bonanza of free agency for players in a
newly merged superleague would have been too much for the NHL's
owners to tolerate. Furthermore, a merger between the two leagues as
they existed would have created a surfeit of troubled franchises.

The NHL's expansion efforts alone since 1967 had produced an
excess of failed and failing teams. Three of the six original expansion
clubs of 1967 were on the ropes as the merger talks became more serious. St. Louis was on the verge of bankruptcy when acquired by
Ralston Purina in the summer of 1977. In 1978, two other 1967 expansion teams, Minnesota and California (which had moved to

Cleveland in 1976/77) merged and continued playing in Minnesota. Kansas City, an ill-advised expansion site in 1974, rapidly got into trouble and in 1976/77 was relocated to Denver, to play as the Colorado Rockies. The Rockies were quickly at loggerheads with Denver City Council over the amenities at McNichols Arena, and began making plans for a relocation to the Meadowlands facility in New Jersey, which would finally come to pass in 1982. The 1972 franchise additions, the Atlanta Flames and New York Islanders, also had viability problems. The Flames were proving unprofitable, and while the Islanders were becoming Stanley Cup contenders in the late 1970s, their majority owner was having financial difficulties. The NHL had planned to expand to twenty-five teams by 1979, but was having trouble keeping eighteen teams afloat. Some of the opposition within the NHL to a merger with the WHA was founded on the reasonable position that the league could not consider taking on additional teams while it had so many troubled operations in its existing ranks.

By 1977/78, the WHA's stronger franchises were holding on in the hope of a reconciliation with the league's rival. There was some inspiration to be found in the end of the battle between the National Basketball Association and the American Basketball Association. In an attempt to avoid a free-agency nightmare like that predicted for the NHL, it was decided not to merge the leagues. Rather, an expansion was held for the 1976/77 season, with four ABA teams joining the NBA: the Denver Nuggets, San Antonio Spurs, Indiana Pacers and New York Nets. The Nets happened to be owned by Roy Boe, the New York Islanders' majority shareholder, and Boe's participation in the rivalries between both the NHL and the WHA, and the NBA and the ABA, was illuminating. Boe favoured an end to the NHL–WHA feud, given that he had been able to bring his ABA Nets into the NBA. More importantly, Boe's position on the NHL–WHA merger issue was supported by the Islanders' local rivals, Madison Square Garden, which owned not only the New York Rangers of the NHL but the New York Knicks of the NBA. The rivalry between the Rangers and Islanders, jacked up by the

Islanders' victory over the Rangers in the 1974/75 opening playoff round, had been prefaced by a solid exhibition-game rivalry between the Nets and Nicks before the 1976 NBA expansion was concocted.

While MSG consistently supported the NHL–WHA truce initiative, Boe's ability to continue arguing for an end to hostilities faded. Losses generated by the Nets, coupled with the debt burden created by the $10 million expansion fee the NHL had commanded for the Islanders in 1972, were pushing Boe's sports empire under. In 1978, Islanders general manager Bill Torrey teamed up with minority owner John Pickett to put together a new ownership group and steer the club out of receivership. The Islanders' position on the inter-league dispute did not change. Pickett was among the NHL owners to favour a negotiated end to the war against the WHA.

Most of the NHL owners, in fact, were in favour of ending hostilities in 1978, but any deal required the approval of three-quarters of the board of governors. For the league even to come within a vote or two of approving a quasi-merger required a major shift in opinion within the ownership ranks. Initially the NHL's power bloc of Bill Wirtz in Chicago and Bruce Norris in Detroit, who firmly supported long-standing league president Clarence Campbell, would not hear of anything short of the WHA's unconditional surrender. Campbell was utterly intransigent. The lessons of the American Football League, which was launched in 1959 and survived to force a merger with the NFL in 1970, or of the ABA, which had hung in against the incumbent NBA, were lost on him. Campbell was an Edmonton lawyer who had returned from serving on the prosecution team of the Nuremberg war crimes trials to assume the league presidency in 1946. Campbell had seen various threats to the NHL's monopoly on tier I professional hockey in North America come and go, and was adamant that the WHA would go away of its own accord. He had already cut off the Western Hockey League's ambitions to become a national league with an all-important national U.S. television deal, by launching the NHL's first postwar expansion in 1967/68.[1]

An early advocate of a quick, negotiated settlement with the WHA was Ed Snider, majority owner of the Philadelphia Flyers. Snider was one of seven NHL franchise owners to face a WHA team in his territory when the WHA made its debut in 1972/73.[2] The WHA's threat to the NHL was measured less in territorial invasions than in the player salary escalation it had ignited. The new standards in compensation forced Snider to sign his captain, Bobby Clarke, to a five-year, $500,000 contract at the start of the 1972/73 season. Down the road in New York, the Rangers were spending a small fortune to keep intact a first-rate roster that had lost the 1971/72 Stanley Cup finals to Boston. Snider, in concert with the New York Rangers' chief executive, Bill Jennings, had tried to bring a civilized end to the WHA before it had completed its first season. Working with several other NHL franchises, Snider and Jennings hammered out a plan wherein WHA franchises would pay a total of $40 million to join the NHL. This clandestine initiative blew up in Snider's face when Wirtz, Norris and Campbell caught wind of it. Battle lines were drawn, both between the NHL and WHA and within the NHL itself over its policy toward the new league.[3]

Contrary to Clarence Campbell's assurances, the WHA was not going away in any great hurry. It had even begun to make a dent in the fortunes of one of the league's great franchises, the Montreal Canadiens. In January 1972, the Molson family had sold the Canadiens to the Bronfmans, and the new owners had almost immediately been forced to confront the consequences with the WHA's debut of the expansion of the professional hockey labour market. Star defenceman J.C. Tremblay defected to the Quebec Nordiques for their first season, and after Montreal's 1972/73 Stanley Cup win Marc Tardif and Réjean Houle jumped to the WHA and subsequently joined Tremblay on the Nordiques. Frank Mahovlich left the team to sign with the Toronto Toros after the 1973/74 season, and that summer, the Canadiens saw their first draft pick, Cam Connor, opt for a career in the WHA.

Snider narrowly lost his bid to succeed Norris as chairman of the league's board of governors (the ruling body, with one representative from each club) in June 1974, Wirtz edging him by one vote. Wirtz then stripped Snider of his duties on the board's finance committee and blocked his participation in all of the league's standing committees.

The NHL was dangerously adrift, its expansion program blemished by ongoing viability problems among its six teams from 1967/68 and the debacle of Kansas City. The aging Campbell needed to be replaced, and while the Wirtz–Norris bloc carried the day in finding his successor, by finessing the selection in June 1977 of lawyer John Ziegler from Norris's Red Wings organization, they at least engineered the arrival of a new paid hand who believed it was time to put an amicable end to the WHA. The war subsided to the point where trades and sales of player contracts were actually being conducted between NHL and WHA teams.

Ziegler's assets in tackling the WHA dilemma included good personal relations with both Howard Baldwin, president of the WHA, and Alan Eagleson, head of the NHL Players' Association. Eagleson's goodwill was crucial, because the autocratic head of the NHLPA was unusually tight with ownership ranks for a union president and could be counted on to bring the union membership along. Fundamentally, a merger between the NHL and WHA was bad for players, as it would reduce employment opportunities and remove the upward pressure on player salaries that the bidding war between the two leagues had produced. Peter Pocklington and Glen Sather, who both knew Eagleson, offered Eagleson a $1 million bonus if he could arrange a merger of the leagues. In the end, no incentive was necessary (or paid). The end of the WHA would come without any special effort from Eagleson beyond delivering his union's blanket approval.

Eager to wind up the WHA before the start of his first season as NHL president, John Ziegler came close to his goal in the summer of 1977, one year after the NBA had negotiated an end to the war with the ABA. Terms for a basketball-inspired NHL expansion had been negotiated; it would take in the Edmonton Oilers, Winnipeg Jets, Quebec Nordiques, Cincinnati Stingers, New England Whalers and Houston Aeros. To meet the 75 percent majority requirement, fourteen of eighteen governors were required to approve the move. In a secret ballot, it failed by one vote. The two leagues had no choice but to embark on another contrary season.

Nelson Skalbania had gone to New York in the summer of 1976, as soon as he acquired the Oilers from Allard, to hold talks with the NHL about merging the leagues. The failure to strike a merger deal in 1977 had been a factor in his decision to sell his half of the Oilers to Pocklington. But Skalbania wasn't out of the picture entirely. In real estate, he was the king of leverage—the art of realizing large gains through a small investment. But leverage is also a tool of power and influence. Owning something everyone else wants or needs is a sure-fire way to get otherwise intransigent opponents to see things your way. Businesspeople recognize this as the acquisition of a strategic asset. The underworld knows it as kidnapping. In Skalbania's case, his hostage was an entirely willing one, who set his own ransom price. Skalbania's return to the professional hockey scene in 1978, with its audacious, broad-daylight abduction, would help lever the two leagues into becoming a sporting monopoly.

OVERALL, THERE was too much hockey, and there were too few fans in North America. In 1977/78 the Central Hockey League lost the Phoenix Roadrunners (crossovers from the WHA) in December, the American Hockey League lost the Hampton Hulls in February, and fans in Syracuse, Maine, Binghampton, Philadelphia, Erie, Mohawk Valley and Johnston lost the entire North American Hockey League before the season even began. In 1978/79, the Pacific Hockey League—where the phoenix-like Phoenix Roadrunners had been resurrected—followed the NAHL into oblivion. The 1977/78 WHA season was the last one for the Houston Aeros. Once one of the strongest

WHA teams on the ice, featuring Gordie Howe and his sons Mark and Marty, the Aeros had lost all three Howes to the Whalers as free agents in the summer of 1977. After producing the league's third-best regular-season record in 1977/78, the Aeros closed down, with a half-dozen players relocating to the Jets, who were suffering from the loss of free-agent stars Anders Hedberg and Ulf Nilsson to the New York Rangers.

In the summer of 1978, the WHA and NHL were back at the bargaining table. Lawyer Michael Cardozo had been hired to represent four of the WHA franchises: the Oilers, owned by Peter Pocklington; the Jets, represented by controlling shareholder Michael Gobuty; the Nordiques, owned by Carling O'Keefe Breweries; and the New England Whalers, owned by a group that included the Aetna Insurance Company. The gist of the proposal brought forward by Cardozo was that at the NHL's discretion, four (or five, if Cincinnati was included) WHA clubs would be admitted to the NHL, just as the NBA had admitted four ABA clubs in 1976. Each WHA club admitted to the NHL would pay $4 million. The NHL would use a portion of this money to buy several of its own weak franchises, which would be "moved" to the locations of the teams being admitted from the WHA. The rest of the money would be held in escrow, for the WHA clubs to use as a cleanup fund to buy out the remaining WHA clubs and make any necessary payments to the WHA Players' Association. The new NHL clubs would get to keep all their players, and the players left over from the other WHA teams and the NHL teams being purchased and relocated would form a pool, from which they would be distributed in a draft by the teams in the expanded NHL.[4]

The proposal didn't fly, for a number of reasons. First, the payment to owners of NHL teams that would be collapsed, about $2 million, was far too low, considering the league had been charging five times that amount for new franchises a few years earlier. Allowing the WHA clubs to keep all their players was another non-starter, because all NHL clubs had lists of players they'd drafted and had been unable to sign when the players opted for the WHA, or whose rights they still held after the players jumped to the rival league. Rights to players in the WHA were also regularly included in NHL trades. To waive their claim on them now would have left the trade books horribly unbalanced.

A particular sore spot was the wont of WHA teams to employ "underage" players, thereby securing new talents before they came up at the NHL annual amateur draft. Both the NHL and the WHA had a draft age limit of twenty that respected Canadian Junior hockey's maximum-age eligibility. However, some WHA clubs had been flouting the regulation in the face of anti-trust rulings in the United States (which forbade collusive limitations on employment according to age) by signing teenagers as free agents before their Canadian Junior eligibility had expired. This was the case of the WHA copying another page from the old ABA operations manual. The ABA had strengthened its game by beating the NBA to new talent, and signing players before they completed their college careers. The WHA team most notorious for accumulating teenagers who had not played out their Junior eligibility was the Birmingham Bulls, owned by Toronto's John F. Bassett. Birmingham had so many underage players that they were known as the "Baby Bulls."

One Baby Bull was a particular source of vexation for the NHL. Ken Linseman had played three seasons of Junior hockey as a Kingston Canadien when he decided to sign with the Bulls in 1977, rather than wait to turn pro in his NHL eligibility year, 1978. Linseman was a top prospect, having scored 114 goals in 128 games in his last two seasons in Kingston, and another year in the Junior ranks would have meant sacrificing hundreds of thousands of dollars in earnings. Linseman sued the NHL, claiming the league interfered with his right to earn a living by practising age discrimination. Drafted by Philadelphia in 1978, he reported to the Flyers for the NHL career he wanted, which eventually took him to Edmonton. The American courts ruled that the minimum draft age of both the NHL and WHA was in violation of anti-trust regulations, and the NHL would have to lower the minimum draft age accordingly.

In the meantime, a considerable gap existed between the age of rookies in the WHA and those in the NHL. The predilection of the WHA for gathering teenage talent meant it had many future stars on team rosters. Increasingly less able to compete with the NHL on raw salaries, the WHA had found an edge by scooping players before they turned twenty. And the most celebrated prospect awaiting capture by the WHA in the summer of 1978 was a seventeen-year-old phenomenon named Wayne Gretzky.

By then, the dynamics of acquiring underage players had shifted significantly. Initially, signing teenagers was a way for WHA clubs to get to talent without having to outbid the NHL for it, since the NHL was not going to ante up until a player became draft-eligible. But as the merger talks with the NHL stalled, the young stars emerged as strategic assets. If signed to long-term contracts, they became well-fed and well-treated hostages. If the NHL was serious about being the premier league with the premier talent, it was going to have to make room for the WHA teams pleading to get in. Just as Joe Namath had given the New York Jets and the AFL legitimacy in the league's final seasons, and Julius Irving had boosted the reputation of the ABA, Wayne Gretzky in particular could do the same for the WHA.

Gretzky had been pegged as the next big thing to come out of Canada on hockey skates since he was ten years old, when he recorded 378 goals and 120 assists playing Atom in Brantford, Ontario. In an age of specialists—snipers, playmakers, checkers, penalty killers— Gretzky was far more than a capable generalist. He excelled in all aspects of the game except body checking and fighting, which was all to his credit for purists who decried the rise of goonery and the dumbing down of the Canadian game. For all the press he attracted, scouts were not convinced he was a shoo-in to rule, or even survive in, the brawny NHL. A marginal six-footer when fully grown, he was a lean 170 pounds who relied on agility, not raw speed, to minimize physical punishment. What Gretzky looked like was far less important than what he saw. Harry Sinden, the old friend of the man who came to coach Gretzky, Glen Sather, would pay him the highest compliment. "Gretzky sees a picture out there that no-one else sees. It's difficult to describe it because I've never seen the game he's looking at."

Gretzky had the potential not only to excel at the game the NHL played, but also to change it. And as much as he defied the sport's conventions, he also defied its hierarchies and regulations as he progressed through its successive tiers. In 1975 his parents attempted to have him play, at fourteen, and as an out-of-towner, with the celebrated midget-level Young Nats of Toronto's notoriously competitive Metropolitan league. Their plan met with pronounced resistance. To meet the league's residency requirement, a player *and his family* had to live within the league's geographic limits. Rather than move the whole family to greater Toronto, the Gretzkys made their son a legal ward of the family with whom he boarded. This legal ruse did not satisfy opposing teams in the MTHL, and when the Ontario Minor Hockey Association declared illegal his transfer from his hometown Brantford league to the MTHL, the mess went to court, where the Gretzky family lost.

Gretzky then joined the Junior B Nats, which weren't subject to any residency restrictions. After two seasons as a Nat, he was drafted third overall in Canada by the Sault Ste. Marie Greyhounds of the OHA Major Junior A. There, he tried to secure the number 9 worn by Gordie Howe, his childhood hero. (In 1972, Howe attended a Brantford hockey banquet at which Gretzky hauled in the bulk of the silverware. Gretzky's father, Walter, snapped a much-reproduced photograph of Howe playfully pressing a stick against the young Wayne's neck.) The Howe number wasn't available. Gretkzy tried 19, and a few weeks later settled on 99. In his first game with the Greyhounds, he produced a hat trick, and in 1977/78, his only season in Major Junior hockey (he had played three games with the Peterborough Petes in 1976/77), he tallied a record 182 points in sixty-four games, with another twenty-six points in thirteen playoff games.

By then Gretzky was a client of agent Gus Badali, a former Junior B player and coach who had been auditing confections for Famous Players Theatres while negotiating contracts for many of the teen-age hockey players being lured to the WHA. Badali broke into the agent business by delivering Mark and Marty Howe of the Toronto Marlboros, along with their father Gordie, to the Houston Aeros in 1973/74. He first saw Gretzky play as a Nat in Junior B, and in coming to know Walter he took on the client that allowed him to leave Famous Players behind.

Star quality had been an important component since the WHA's inception. Not every player on a team roster had to be NHL quality— as long as there were enough of them to give the new game marquee appeal. Signings like Gerry Cheevers, Ted Green and Derek Sanderson from the Stanley Cup champion Bruins of 1971/72 were major coups for the infant league (even though only Ted Green stuck it out for the rest of his career). The most celebrated signing was Bobby Hull, awarded his multimillion-dollar contract by the Winnipeg Jets. Hull had already played fifteen NHL seasons on left wing with Chicago when he switched leagues, and peaked in the WHA in 1974/75, when he scored a record seventy-seven goals in seventy-eight games on a line with Swedish imports Anders Hedberg and Ulf Nilsson. By 1978/79, his career was all but over as he appeared in only four Jets games. The New England Whalers had signed away Gordie Howe and his sons from Houston in 1977, but after turning forty in March 1978 the elder Howe's long-term potential as a fan attraction was extremely limited.

Hull's decline at the time of the Linseman suit and the WHA's fla-grant enthusiasm for so-called underage players should have pro-vided a noteworthy flashback to the Golden Jet's own beginnings. Like other stars of his era, Hull was only eighteen when his parent club, the Blackhawks, introduced him to the NHL full time in 1957/58.

Gretzky was about four months away from his eighteenth birthday when he made his professional debut in the fall of 1978.

John F. Bassett wanted Gretzky as a Baby Bull in Birmingham, but couldn't afford him. At a WHA meeting at the Hotel Toronto that summer he steered Nelson Skalbania, the new owner of the Indianapolis Racers, toward Badali and Gretzky. The Racers were a team on death's door after finishing last in 1977/78. The franchise was in such precarious shape that it wasn't included in the group of WHA clubs that had pitched the NHL in the summer of 1978 on crossing over to the established league. Skalbania had picked up the team for one dollar, in exchange for guaranteeing its debts.

At the same WHA meeting at which Skalbania was tipped off to Gretzky's availability by Bassett, the new Racers owner bumped into Gus Badali in the lobby of the Hotel Toronto. Handed $1,000 in plane fare by Skalbania, Badali loaded himself, Gretzky and his parents onto a flight to Vancouver, where Skalbania feted them in his 17,000-square-foot mansion. A fitness freak with little real knowledge of hockey, Skalbania sized up his potential acquisition in a footrace. "I had never seen Gretzky play, but I had heard all the reports and went from there," Skalbania told Peter C. Newman in *The Acquisitors*. "We went on a six-mile run, and when he beat me, that was it." The contract was drawn on a piece of paper on Skalbania's lawn while he and Gretzky were still perspiring from the run. Gretzky signed not with the Racers, but with Skalbania personally, in the form of a personal services contract. Reports on its details varied. He signed Gretzky either to a four-year deal which, with signing bonus, amounted to $1.125 million,[5] or a seven-year deal worth $1.75 million.

Gretzky's signing was an inspired move by Nelson Skalbania, who leapt at the opportunity that holding the young man's contract presented. Having bailed out of owning the Oilers, he had recognized that in the present state of the hockey business, owning a showpiece player the NHL wanted was far more important than owning a struggling WHA team that it probably didn't. The player was the lever to get the NHL to accept an otherwise unappealing team into its ranks. And once in, it could always be moved somewhere more profitable.

In truth Gretzky, not the Racers, was the franchise Skalbania owned. All Skalbania had to do now was to keep the Racers afloat long enough to become part of the renewed merger negotiations with the NHL.

Whatever the specifics of Gretzky's contract with Skalbania, its life was measured in days, not years. The arrival of Gretzky in Indianapolis helped Skalbania push season tickets, but he was only able to increase them from 2,500 to 2,700. The team's financial circumstances quickly deteriorated; operating debts ballooned to $2 million. After only eight games with the Racers, in which he scored three goals and assisted on three others, Gretzky was both too expensive and too valuable for Skalbania to keep on the payroll. Skalbania needed to cash in his asset, and he went to Michael Gobuty, a real-estate investor he knew who had a controlling share of the Winnipeg Jets.

Skalbania couldn't reach a deal with Gobuty, who apparently had received advice that Gretzky was overrated and was too slight to cut it in the NHL. He then turned to his former partner in the Oilers, Peter Pocklington, and offered him the precocious seventeen-year-old.

Gretzky had played his fourth professional game against the Edmonton Oilers on October 20, giving Glen Sather his first glimpse of the player who would provide the foundation for his future NHL dynasty. As he told *Toronto Star* writer, Milt Dunnell, in 1984, "I thought Wayne must be a stick boy or some kid who hung around with the team. Then, the game started and he went around one of our veterans like he was a lamp post." Gretzky scored twice in the second period in a span of thirty-nine seconds. When Skalbania came to Pocklington to offer him Gretzky, Sather urged the Oilers' owner to sign Gretzky and anyone else Skalbania was offering. That November, Pocklington struck a deal for three Indianapolis players: Gretzky, left winger Pete Driscoll and goaltender Ed Mio.

Gretzky was overwhelmingly the most important component of

the deal, for reasons beyond raw skill. Driscoll and Mio were slender assets simply because whoever employed them in the WHA might have them only for the remainder of the season, should an NHL absorption of the stronger WHA teams go through. Gretzky was the only one of the three on whom no NHL team had a rights claim, being too young ever to have been drafted by an NHL team. His team-mates (who were twenty-four) had both been selected in the 1974 NHL and WHA amateur drafts. Both were chosen by Vancouver of the WHA, while Driscoll was chosen by Toronto of the NHL and Mio by Chicago of the NHL. Both went into the WHA, and compiled résumés typical of players in an upstart league struggling for stability. In 1975 Driscoll and the rest of the team hit the road again to become the Calgary Cowboys. Two seasons later, the Cowboys were out of business, and Driscoll was signed as a free agent by the Quebec Nordiques for 1977/78. After twenty-one games, the Nordiques sold him to Indianapolis, and now he was being sold to Edmonton.

Mio was about to begin his third of four seasons at Colorado College when selected by the Blackhawks in the 1974 NHL draft. Though the U.S. college game was considered a long-shot development system, the Blackhawks had done well by Tony Esposito, another Canadian who had played goal for an American college, and whom they'd picked up from Montreal in the 1969 intra-league draft. Like other WHA players, Mio lived a double professional life. While he plied his trade in the WHA as a property of Calgary, Birmingham and then Indianapolis, he was also enjoying a phantom NHL career as his playing rights swapped hands. In May 1978, the Blackhawks sent his rights, along with future considerations (Pierre Pilote), to Minnesota in a deal for Doug Hicks (a future Oiler) and Minnesota's third-round pick in the 1980 draft. It was precisely because of such deals that NHL owners refused to consider the proposal Pocklington and three fellow WHA owners tabled in June 1978 for joining the NHL. Having just surrendered Hicks and a future draft pick to get the rights to Mio, the North Stars were not going to agree to allow any WHA club that came into the NHL to keep him on its roster. While Driscoll was largely a forgotten man in the Leafs organization, Mio was a priority to the North Stars. If the WHA was dissolved in the near future, the North Stars would consider him rightfully theirs. Sather's grip on Mio, who became such a close friend of Gretzky that he served as the best man at Gretzky's wedding in 1988, might be temporary.

Gretzky's status as an underage player and the NHL's ongoing problem with the Linseman draft age suit imposed an implicit time-line on the negotiations to bring the WHA's more viable franchises into the NHL. For the sake of whoever employed Gretzky in the WHA, a deal had to be done before he became draft-eligible in the NHL. At the latest, that would come when Gretzky reached age twenty in 1980, but was likely to come in the summer of 1979 as the NHL lowered its draft age. The NHL had experimented with a younger draft age before, permitting teams to select one eighteen-year-old in either the first or second round in 1974. There was no reason the NHL couldn't try another limited draft of eighteen-year-olds in 1979, which would ensure that some established NHL club had a claim on Gretzky before the next season. Pocklington first needed Gretzky to ensure the value and viability of his franchise, but then he needed a deal that would get the Oilers into the NHL, with Gretzky intact as an Oiler.

Deals involving Pocklington or Skalbania—never mind *between* them—tend toward the Byzantine. Pocklington is believed to have paid $850,000 to Skalbania for the contracts of the three Racers, although not much was in actual cash. According to Peter Gzowski (writing in *The Game of Our Lives*), Pocklington paid Skalbania $300,000 up front, along with a $250,000 note that was to be applied against the $500,000 Pocklington had promised to pay his former Oilers partner if and when Edmonton made it into the NHL. As the Racers continued to cost Skalbania dearly in the ensuing months, Pocklington redeemed the note for $100,000—in effect, Skalbania agreed to take $100,000 now and waive his right to a potential $250,000 later. Thus, Pocklington's cash outlay in acquiring Gretzky (and two other players[6]) amounted to $400,000, not the $850,000 sometimes reported.

Skalbania's Indianapolis Racers lasted until December 15, 1978, less than halfway through his first season as owner. Skalbania folded the team as his attention was gripped by the biggest deal of his life, a property acquisition from Genstar valued at $100 million. Skalbania had to raise a lot of cash in a short period of time, and couldn't afford to keep losing money with the Racers while doing so. The gambler had bet—for now—on real estate, not professional hockey.

After the Racers died, Pocklington and Sather acquired another Skalbania property, signing defenceman John Hughes as a free agent in January 1979. A former Toronto Marlboro who had been chosen 41st overall by Vancouver in the 1974 NHL amateur draft, Hughes had instead reported to Cincinnati, which selected him in the WHA draft that year. He spent a season on loan from Cincinnati to Phoenix, then two seasons in Cincinnati proper. A trade to Houston made him an Aero in the team's last season, 1977/78, after which Skalbania bought his contract from Houston. Like Minnesota with Ed Mio, Vancouver was not prepared to relinquish its NHL rights to Hughes.

As Hughes arrived in Edmonton from Indianapolis in the wake of Gretzky, Mio and Driscoll, Peter Pocklington planned the second Gretzky contractual celebration in the city in less than a year. After concluding the negotiations for his contract with Gretzky at his Vancouver home the previous summer, Skalbania had decided to hold a press conference in Edmonton while they were all en route to Indianapolis. It gave him a chance to crow about the big one that had just gotten away from the NHL. Now it was Pocklington's turn, and he outdid Skalbania in both pomp and contractual terms. Pocklington helped Gretzky celebrate his eighteenth birthday on January 26 by announcing his new contract at centre ice of Northlands Coliseum, before a crowd gathered to watch the Oilers play the Cincinnati Stingers. Gus Badali had been convinced to bind his client to Pocklington for twenty-one years under a personal services contract that would pay Gretzky between $4 million and $5 million, although the final haul depended on any raises that resulted from its renegotiation schedule. Its most important aspect was that Gretzky was Pocklington's—and not the Oilers'—personal employee until 1999. "The contract is for personal service," Pocklington reminded the press. "There's no way anyone's going to touch him when we join the NHL." Skalbania's strategy of holding the game's premier new talent agreeably hostage in the midst of the WHA's merger talks with the NHL had been adopted by Pocklington. Gretzky's decision to bind himself to Pocklington for what would have amounted to his entire professional career gave Pocklington more personal leverage than the WHA could hope for in getting a merger deal done.

Watching the birthday cake in the shape of Gretzky's trademark "99" get served up at centre ice was a Cincinnati Stingers lineup that included a player who had celebrated his own eighteenth birthday eight days earlier, and who had begun the 1978/79 season as Gretzky's replacement in Indianapolis. Mark Messier was the son of Doug Messier, the former Edmonton Flyer, now a school teacher and Junior hockey coach in St. Albert, south of Edmonton. Mark had played tier II Junior hockey with the Mets of Spruce Grove, just west of the city, in 1976/77, and had picked up some fill-in assignments on his dad's St. Albert Saints. His one glimpse of Major Junior hockey came in a seven-game playoff stint with the Portland Winter Hawks in the spring of 1978. (Messier had grown up in Portland while his father played for the Buckaroos of the WHL after the Edmonton Flyers folded.) Messier distinguished himself with four goals and an assist in seven games as the Hawks lost in seven to the defending Memorial Cup champions, the New Westminster Bruins, who went on to capture their second consecutive Canadian title. From there, the seventeen-year-old graduated directly into the professional ranks when he was signed to a ten-game tryout with Indianapolis after they lost Gretzky to Edmonton. He got to play in five. When the Racers folded, he was signed as a free agent by Cincinnati. Aside from his seven games in a losing playoff cause in western Canadian Junior hockey, Messier was a complete unknown, and his tour of duty in the WHA in 1978/79 did little to raise his general profile. In five games with Indianapolis, he had no goals or assists. With Cincinnati, he scored just once. Gretzky and Messier, two underage players sharing the Northlands ice, occupied opposite ends of the professional spectrum. Gretzky was on his way to scoring forty-six goals and sixty-four assists in his first professional season, third best in the WHA. Messier, with eleven points in the entire season, appeared to exemplify the rank and file of marginal talents who had been dragooned into filling out the rosters of WHA clubs in the league's last gasp.

WHILE PETER POCKLINGTON was celebrating signing Gretzky to his twenty-one-year contract, an expansion scheme to bring four WHA teams into the NHL was being finalized for submission to the NHL board of governors at a special meeting in Key Largo, Florida, on March 7–8. Pocklington and his fellow owners in Winnipeg, Quebec and Hartford had agreed to a fairly stiff set of admission terms. "We're getting raped," said Jets general manager John Ferguson, "but it's the only answer for hockey." Peter Pocklington also conceded the agreement was lopsided. "It's going to be very expensive for us, but there is no alternative. We can end the silly hassling between the leagues and put all our efforts into building one league."

Each incoming WHA team would pay a US$6 million expansion fee—not $4 million, as the WHA teams had proposed the previous summer. They would also have to make indemnification payments to the two WHA franchises, in Birmingham and Cincinnati, that were not being admitted. Cincinnati was to receive $3.5 million, Birmingham $2.85 million, bringing the individual indemnification bill for each of the four expansion clubs to exactly $1,587,500. Each club would be required to have $1.5 million in available working capital for its 1979/80 operations, and insurance for the next two seasons in the form of bank notes worth $1.5 million. The four teams also posted a $50 million bond to protect the NHL against any liabilities or legal action that might arise, and agreed to bear all costs of paying off the contracts of any players or officials left unemployed by the pseudo-merger. The existing NHL teams would be allowed to reclaim players whose rights they held. The WHA teams would only be allowed to protect two goaltenders and two skaters from this reclamation draft, in addition to the forty-five WHA players to whom no NHL team held rights.

Two WHA players were given special consideration in the agreement. Gordie Howe would not have to be included on any protected list and would not be available in any draft. And Wayne Gretzky was deemed untouchable.

Unquestionably, Gretzky would have gone first overall in the amateur draft that summer (in which WHA players who were nineteen by the end of the 1979/80 season were eligible for selection), had some special accommodation not been made to ensure he remained out of bounds. Pocklington had the exclusive rights to his personal services, yet the Oilers might not have had the right to use him as an NHL player once another team secured his playing rights at the draft. Making sure the expansion process allowed Gretzky to remain in Edmonton was fundamental to clinching a deal between the NHL and the four WHA teams. The NHL agreed to allow Pocklington to include Gretzky in his list of protected players and thus exempt him from the draft.

The expansion plan, as with the proposal unsuccessfully tabled in 1977, would need 75 percent of the board's approval. With the merger of the Cleveland Barons and Minnesota North Stars having reduced the NHL by one team, this meant thirteen of seventeen votes were required.

Since Pocklington and his three fellow WHA owners had made the June 1978 proposal, a significant complication had arisen in the politics of the merger/expansion. Three months after the failed vote, in September 1978, the Bronfman family empire announced it was selling the Montreal Canadiens to Molson Breweries. Under a contract with the NHL known as the Trans-Border Agreement, Molson held the exclusive national broadcast rights in Canada to the games of the Canucks, Maple Leafs and Canadiens, as well as the Canadian broadcast rights for all fourteen American-based NHL teams. The national broadcast rights for the three existing Canadian NHL teams—which formed the backbone of Molson's co-production with CBC television of "Hockey Night in Canada"—were a major stumbling block in the expansion effort. Three of the four WHA teams being proposed for membership in the NHL were Canadian. If they were to join, Molson would have to pony up for their national rights as well, potentially doubling the fees required to stage "Hockey Night in Canada"—or, conversely, requiring the negotiated national rights fee to be distributed between six teams, not three. Purchasing the Canadiens in September 1978 had given the brewery a seat on the league's board of governors and a crucial vote to wield against an expansion of the NHL in Canada. Ironically, for nationalists who lamented the domination of the Canadian game by American interests, the most formidable opponent to an expanded NHL presence north of the border came from within.

None of the established Canadian NHL teams were keen to have the Oilers, Jets and Nordiques in the league. More teams would just slice up the national broadcast revenues into twice as many pieces, with no guarantee that the monies would correspondingly double. And Vancouver didn't like the idea of an unbalanced schedule requiring Canucks fans to sit through more games against a divisional rival like the Oilers than against an eastern powerhouse and traditional fan favourite like the Canadiens—a concern shared by the Los Angeles Kings.

John Ziegler tried to avert a "no" vote from at least Montreal by ruling before the Key Largo meeting that Molson would have its exclusive national broadcast rights guaranteed for five more years. In other words, the brewery wouldn't have to pay the Oilers, Nordiques or Jets anything for the national broadcasts of their games as Ziegler stripped them of their rights for their first five seasons in the NHL. (These teams would still be able to sell their local, i.e., cable, rights.) Ziegler's generosity flopped. Montreal voted against the expansion, as did Vancouver, Toronto and Los Angeles. A fifth "no" vote by the Boston Bruins—who didn't want the Hartford Whalers in their backyard, and also objected to taking on more teams when several existing NHL franchises were on the rocks both financially and in fan support—sank the expansion by one vote.

Both leagues were bearing down on another spring of playoff hockey when the Key Largo vote failed. The pro-expansion forces within the NHL regrouped to find one team among the five dissenters that might be swung to the "yes" side. Frank Griffiths, owner of the Canucks, was targeted. By guaranteeing that the league would employ a balanced schedule for at least two seasons, Griffiths agreed to switch his vote. The board was reconvened in Chicago later that month, and the "yes" side got a pleasant surprise when Montreal also decided to change its vote. When word spread that the Canadiens had opposed adding three more Canadian franchises to the NHL, a boycott of Molson products had erupted in the Canadian WHA cities. The Canadiens' owners decided that selling beer was more important than perpetuating a hockey broadcasting monopoly, and made the vote fourteen for, three (Toronto, Los Angeles and Boston) against.

The Bruins were so angered by the expansion approval that they considered suing the league. Harold Ballard, majority owner of the Leafs, persisted in voicing his opposition. "There are maybe eight or nine players in their whole league who will be any good in our league. Meanwhile, we add four new teams to the seventeen in our league, which already has enough problems and enough lousy teams. Here we are in Chicago, where they draw only nine thousand for the New York Rangers. How many will they draw for the Edmonton Oilers? Who the hell are the Edmonton Oilers?"

As it happened, the Oilers, led by Gretzky, were on their way to the WHA playoff finals, the last to be held for the Avco Cup before the league was wound down. Come October, the Oilers would be playing in the NHL. Precisely who those Oilers would be was another matter.

Chapter Four

I F THE NHL HAD learned anything from the debacle of the 1967 expansion draft, it was not in evidence twelve years later, on June 13, 1979, when the expansion draft was held for the four WHA clubs being admitted to the NHL ranks. The league had been roundly criticized for the unfair advantage given in 1967 to the "Original Six" teams, who were allowed to protect eleven skaters and two goaltenders while avoiding a universal amateur draft until 1969. But compared to 1979, the 1967 process for stocking the rosters of the six new NHL clubs was an act of generosity on the part of the established clubs. Many NHL teams had been battered by the WHA's poaching of talent, and resentment over the rival league's escalation of player salaries ran deep. The 1979 expansion was payback time. Edmonton, Winnipeg, Quebec and Hartford came into the NHL under the worst terms of any expansion.

The admission of the four teams involved four phases of player selection. First, the WHA had to be formally wound down with a dispersal draft to redistribute the rights to players held by Birmingham and Cincinnati among the four expansion teams. When this was done, the NHL would then hold a reclamation draft, in which the existing seventeen league teams would claw back any players on the four expansion club rosters whose NHL rights they held. These rights applied to players who had jumped from the NHL to the WHA after their contracts with an NHL team had expired (and whose rights may subsequently have been traded to another NHL team), and to prospects who had been selected in an NHL amateur draft but had opted to sign with a WHA team instead. There were some restrictions on the reclamation process. Anyone reclaimed would have to remain on the club's roster for two years, and was ineligible to be traded or demoted to the minors. If the reclaiming club could not fit the player into its roster, the expansion club could retain him for $100.

Most NHL clubs held rights to between four and six WHA players. Chicago had more than average, with nine, while Montreal stood head and shoulders above all other teams, with twenty-one. The Canadiens' huge claim on WHA players gave the defending Stanley Cup champions considerable influence on how players would actually be selected in the coming drafts.

Once the reclamation draft was over, the league would move on to the third phase, the expansion draft. The former WHA clubs would begin the process by making their four "priority selections"—two skaters and up to two goaltenders—which were in addition to any players whose rights they had retained when the reclamation draft was over. The existing NHL clubs would each submit their protected list of fifteen skaters and two goaltenders, with their remaining con-tracted players (and players whose rights they held) made available. Because no NHL player who had just completed his first year under contract was draft eligible, the established clubs had an easier time sheltering players with the protected list. No NHL team could lose more than four skaters and one goaltender. For each player lost, a club would receive $125,000 from the $24 million pool of expansion fees. As well, there were about seventy NHL players whose contracts would expire by June 1, making them free agents. Clubs took the risk of not protecting them, hoping no expansion club would bother choosing a free agent given the league's onerous compensation system. Because any team that lost a free agent was entitled to compensation from the signing team in the form of cash, draft picks, a player of equal value, or some combination thereof, free agency was almost non-existent among premier players in the NHL of the late 1970s. If the free agents passed untouched through the expansion process, the clubs holding their rights could then sign them to new deals before the start of the next season.

The final phase of the NHL's absorption of the four WHA clubs was the most contentious one: the annual amateur draft, usually held at the same time as the annual general meeting in June. A basic draft plan had been agreed to in the expansion agreement, but squabbling over details of its format caused the league to delay the draft until August 9. The draft pool had been muddied by the status of the WHA's underage signings, who also happened to be among the most lucrative players on the WHA team rosters. The NHL's draft-eligibility age since 1974 had been twenty (the age the player would turn in the following year). Because of Ken Linseman's anti-trust suit and extensive lobbying by player agents, the league had come under considerable pressure to reduce the draft age to eighteen.

But the league also had to weigh the concerns of the Canadian Junior system, which had become alarmed by the damage inflicted on its team lineups by the underage-free-agent phenomenon that had seen talents like Wayne Gretzky head for the WHA before their Junior playing eligibility had expired. The Canadian Major Junior Hockey League, as the NHL's traditional source of new talent, had looked to the NHL for firmer support. But even with the elmination of the WHA, the draft age would have to move downward to avert damaging antitrust rulings and a full-blown revolt by player agents with teenage clients.

A compromise was reached between a professional league that was interested in securing younger talent and a Canadian development system that didn't want to see its Junior teams robbed of players in their prime. The eligibility age for the 1979 draft was dropped to nineteen, with certain conditions. Only nineteen-year-olds who had been professionals in the WHA were eligible, and if they weren't added to the selecting team's roster for the 1979/80 season, they had to be offered back to the Junior club they had been with prior to jumping to the WHA. Should the Junior club decline to take the player back, the NHL club could then send him to the minors. In 1980, the NHL would begin conducting an unrestricted draft of eighteen-year-olds. In light of the fact that so many players in the draft pool were no longer amateurs, the league changed the name of the amateur draft to the "entry draft."

A timetable was established for the summer's flurry of player selections. After the WHA held its dispersal draft and the NHL clubs reclaimed their players, the four expansion clubs would submit their lists of priority selections on June 7. The NHL trade deadline was set for June 9, with teams required to submit their protected list for the expansion draft on June 10. The annual meeting was scheduled from June 11 to 13, and at 9 a.m. sharp on June 13, the expansion draft would begin. Two months later, the entry draft would be held.

The league's expansion program had a potentially fatal flaw: it did not have the NHL Players' Association's approval for the expansion, and wouldn't get it until a special meeting in Nassau, set for June 5 and 6. This would be followed by a meeting between the NHLPA and agents in Toronto on June 7 and 8 to debate the eligibility rules for the entry draft. While the NHL had avoided ushering in wide-open free agency by structuring the merger with the WHA as an expansion, the plan still required the approval of the NHLPA, which was three years into its first five-year collective bargaining agreement (CBA) with the league. By leaving the meeting with the NHLPA until June 5–6, mere days before the expansion process and annual general meeting, the NHL had delivered the union a golden opportunity to wrest major concessions from the league. The NHLPA could refuse to endorse the CBA, go on strike and throw the whole NHL–WHA marriage into chaos.

The union had sound reasons for playing hardball. Many players and agents were unhappy with the so-called free-agency provisions of the first CBA. The compensation system was too discouraging for teams to regularly sign free agents. As a result, players had little or no mobility. The union was considering pressing for a change in the compensation system, which would allow a signing team to reward the player's former team simply with future draft picks, rather than having to hand over cash or a player of comparable worth. But although NHLPA head Alan Eagleson had made noises in the spring, while the NHL was voting on the expansion plan, that the association might strike, there was no real hope of this happening. Eagleson was close to league president John Ziegler and to many owners, and as an international hockey czar in charge of the Canada Cup tournament, his life would be much simpler if the WHA went away. The Canada Cup was the property of the NHLPA, making the tournament his personal domain. Getting rid of the WHA would ensure that the top professionals in North America were playing in one league and were represented by one union—Eagleson's union. The Canada Cup would be that much easier for him to package for sponsors and advertisers.[1] Another Canada Cup was set for 1981, and its marketing value would be diminished if young stars in the WHA like Gretzky weren't able to play because of a failed merger.

If the league had any real concerns about the NHLPA not agreeing to a renewed CBA, it would never have risked scheduling the necessary meeting so close to its annual general meeting and the expansion timetable. And sure enough, in Nassau, the association caved in under Eagleson's guidance, voting thirty to one to allow the expansion to go ahead. The membership bought into the notion that professional hockey was in mortal peril, and that it was time for the players to set aside their own agenda for the greater good of the sport.

"We couldn't be greedy," NHLPA president Bobby Clarke explained after the vote. "We still have too many clubs in financial trouble. What good does it do now if we try to rob the owners, but then three teams go under next year? We lose jobs, we lose more money, we lose, period. We had to do what was right for the game, not what was right for us."

As it happened, no teams went under as the league stabilized at twenty-one clubs. Meanwhile, an entire rival league, which had almost singlehandedly forced player salaries (including Clarke's) upward, had been eradicated, and with the collapse of Cincinnati and Birmingham[2] there were two fewer major-league clubs offering employment. Furious, Montreal agent Norm Caplan charged Eagleson with orchestrating a "sellout." The position of Caplan and other agents—that their teenage professionals from the WHA should be declared free agents, and not be tossed into the entry draft pool— was also ignored by the Players' Association at the Toronto meetings that followed the Nassau capitulation. It was an enormous blunder by the union. Fifteen years would pass before any significant reform came to the free-agency provisions of the CBA.

The "good for the game" argument would hound the players through the next decade, as they often tried scrupulously to do the right thing and not to appear selfish or arrogant to the fans, especially when it came to turning out for international tournaments like the Canada Cup. The Oilers, led by Wayne Gretzky, would eventually feature prominently in these campaigns. While providing splendid entertainment and a boost to national pride when Canada won in 1984 and 1987, they would also be duped into making pension plan contributions through the tournament that they were not actually required to provide.[3]

Mike Gartner was one of those prize teenage prospects delivered to WHA teams by agent Gus Badali, then denied free agency and, with the NHLPA's approval, declared eligible for the entry draft in August 1979. The right winger had signed with the WHA's Cincinnati Stingers as an underage free agent in May 1978, after a ninety-point season with the Niagara Falls Flyers of the OHA Major Junior A. Initially offered a contract with Birmingham, he signed for slightly more money with Cincinnati.[4] Turning nineteen that October, he played his first professional hockey season as a Cincinnati Stinger alongside Mark Messier, with fifty-two points in seventy-eight games. Gartner would play nineteen seasons in the NHL and participate in two Canada Cup campaigns, in 1984 and 1987. In 1982 he became the NHLPA player rep for the Washington Capitals, and rose steadily through the union ranks to become the NHLPA head in 1993 after Alan Eagleson's ouster, serving until his retirement from play in 1998. Gartner then joined the NHLPA head office as director of business relations.

Looking back on the terms of the WHA's quasi-merger with the NHL, Gartner can only speak with wonder. "It's remarkable that you had a company, the NHL, having endemic problems competing because their competitor was taking all the quality assets [the players] away from them. So this company says, we're going to allow our competitor to merge with us. And not only are we not going to have to pay anything, they're going to have to pay us to come on board. So we're going to eliminate our competition, take all their employees, and they're also going to pay us to do it."

Gartner says the elimination of the WHA under the terms agreed to by all parties marked the dawn of "the golden years of the eighties for NHL owners. They had the collective bargaining agreement totally in their favour, with no rights for the players. I remember Ed Snider [owner of the Philadelphia Flyers] coming into a meeting one time during a CBA negotiation in the mid-eighties. He put his feet up on the table and said, 'So, what do you guys want to talk about?' He knew the CBA was the greatest thing in the world. And it was. For the owners.

"Players now can differentiate between what's just good for the game and what's just good for the owners," Gartner observes. "I don't think players in general were able to do that as much in the past. What owners have felt was fair was not always fair. Using the guise of 'What's good for the game,' they've gotten a lot. Players now will do what's good for the game, and they'll do what's good for the players."

WHEN THE WHA dispersal draft began, the Oilers' strategy was being directed by general manager Larry Gordon and coach Glen Sather, who were also respectively president and vice-president of hockey operations for the team. Sather, however, had tremendous corporate momentum. At the end of the 1978/79 season, Harry Sinden had fired Don Cherry as coach of the Boston Bruins and was in search of a replacement. "I offered the job to Glen, kind of half-jokingly. I could see he and Peter had a pretty good relationship." Having become impressed with Sather in his suicide-mission coaching debut in the spring of 1977, Pocklington had him pegged as a fast-track executive. Sather was already established in business himself, having run a hockey camp in Banff for ten years before becoming the Oilers' coach, and had made solid real estate investments around the resort town. There was little doubt that, as the Oilers entered the NHL, they were Sather's team, and that he would eventually succeed Larry Gordon.

The WHA dispersal draft began with a large swath of quality players declared off-limits, as the prime underage prospects were set aside for distribution in the entry draft in August. While twenty-eight players would be divvied up among the four teams joining the NHL, the pickings were slim. The dispersal draft participants were resigned to redistributing marginal talents, free agents they had no guarantee of actually being able to sign, and aging players at the end of their careers. They also had to pick players who would promptly be stolen away by NHL clubs in the reclamation draft. The Oilers ignored the Birmingham Bulls lineup entirely in choosing nine players from the Cincinnati list, but didn't find a starter. The Oilers' best selection was Mike Liut, a Canadian goaltender who spent four years in the American collegiate game at Bowling Green and was drafted by both the New England Whalers of the WHA and the St. Louis Blues of the NHL in 1976. After Liut's WHA rights were dealt by the Whalers to Cincinnati, he joined the Stingers for the 1977/78 and 1978/79 seasons. Liut would be one of the leading goaltenders of the NHL in the early 1980s, but he wasn't to play for Glen Sather. Following his selection by the Oilers in the dispersal draft, Liut was grabbed by the Blues in the reclamation draft.

The only dispersal selections who made it into the Oilers organization were defencemen Byron Baltimore and Bryan "Bugsy" Watson. Baltimore managed two games as an Oiler in 1979/80, and spent two seasons in the Central league. Bryan Watson, a journeyman defenceman who had played in Pittsburgh with Sather in 1969/70 and 1970/71, had made an eleventh-hour jump to the WHA from the NHL after being released by the Washington Capitals on March 2, 1979. Watson played twenty-one games with Cincinnati to round out the last WHA regular season, as well as three playoff games. Selected by his old friend in the dispersal draft, Watson retired from playing and signed on as an assistant coach with the Oilers. It may have been one of Sather's most fortuitous selections that June, for Watson had been able to watch Mark Messier in action with Cincinnati firsthand.

Reg Thomas, a Cincinnati left winger who had been chosen 29th overall by Chicago in the 1973 draft and had spent his professional career in the WHA, proved to be a practical selection. The Oilers flipped him later that summer to Toronto, for the Leafs' sixth-round pick in 1981. (The Leafs then dealt Thomas to Quebec in December.) As thin a return as this might have seemed, good scouting would allow the Oilers to use this pick to acquire a starting defenceman, Steve Smith, who joined the lineup full time in 1985/86.

Sather's new fellow NHL executives gave him a rough welcome to the league as the reclamation draft gutted the Oilers. Twelve players from the 1978/79 lineup that had taken the Oilers to the WHA finals, most of them young and promising, were lost. Sather was left without a starting goaltender. Unable to keep Liut from the WHA dispersal draft, he also lost Ed Mio and Dave Dryden. Mio was reclaimed by Minnesota, who had acquired his NHL rights from Chicago (the team that had drafted him in 1974) in a May 1978 trade. Dryden was snatched back by the Buffalo Sabres, the team he had left to join the WHA experiment in 1974. The only netminder the Oilers had was

Hannu Kampurri, a free agent signing from Helsinki who had made two appearances in 1978/79.

Having been cleaned out of starting goaltenders, Sather also had his defence corps decimated, as four solid blueliners decamped. He lost his highest scoring defenceman, Paul Shmyr, a regular WHA All Star, when Minnesota reclaimed him. Dave "the Bammer" Langevin came to the Oilers in 1976/77 straight out of the American college ranks, where he had played four seasons in his native state for the University of Minnesota-Duluth. Both the Oilers and the New York Islanders had claimed him in their respective league drafts in 1974. The Islanders, having just lost in the 1978/79 Stanley Cup semi-finals to the Rangers, took the three-season Oiler veteran back as they began rebuilding a team that would produce the first of their four consecutive Cup wins the following spring. The third starting defenceman lost was John Hughes, who had been acquired in January 1979 as a free agent after the Indianapolis Racers folded. He had been drafted by Vancouver in 1974, and the Canucks now laid claim to him. The fourth was Risto Siltanen, a twenty-year-old Finn who had played in two World Junior Championships (and made the tournament All Star team on both occasions) before the Oilers picked him up as a free agent for twenty games in 1978/79. After he made the World Junior All Star team alongside Gretzky in 1978 (and also played for Finland at the World Championships), the St. Louis Blues dedicated their 13th pick (173rd) overall to securing his NHL rights at the draft that summer. Siltanen was now reclaimed by the Blues.

Sather lost a fifth defenceman to retirement, as Jim Neilson, with whom he'd played in New York, came to the end of the major-league road. Neilson, about to turn thirty-nine, had spent sixteen seasons in the NHL before Sather signed him as a free agent in the summer of 1978. He played thirty-five games with the Oilers.

There was more decimation at centre, as Sather lost four pivots from his forward lines: Dennis Sobchuk, Stan Weir, Steve Carlson and Doug Berry. The loss of three wingers rounded out the damage done.

Right winger Jim Mayer vanished, reclaimed by the New York Rangers, who had made him a draft afterthought at 239th overall in 1974. Mayer had played only two games for Edmonton; the greater losses were left wingers Dave Semenko and Dave Hunter. Semenko, an enforcer who had racked up 265 penalty minutes with the Brandon Wheat Kings in 1976/77, was a top draft pick of both Houston in the WHA and Minnesota in the NHL in 1977. Semenko, however, joined the Oilers for 1977/78 after seven games with the Wheat Kings. In 142 games with the Oilers in 1977/78 and 1978/79, Semenko produced thirty-six points and 298 penalty minutes. Minnesota had used its second pick in the 1977 draft to take Semenko 25th overall. He joined Ed Mio and Paul Shmyr in being reclaimed by the North Stars from the Oilers roster.

Edmonton had no claim to Dave Hunter; he had been signed as an underage free agent in June 1978, as the tough twenty-year-old who had played for Canada at the World Junior tournament in 1977 left behind his Junior days with the Sudbury Wolves. In addition to his thirty-two points and 134 penalty minutes in the regular season, Hunter had amassed forty-two minutes and five points in thirteen playoff games in the spring of 1979. But Hunter belonged to Montreal, who had made him their second choice, 17th overall, in the 1978 draft.

Also lost in the reclamation draft was Bengt Gustafsson, a twenty-one-year-old right winger from Sweden whom the Oilers had signed as a free agent in March 1979 and had used in two playoff games that spring. Gustafsson had been chosen 55th overall in the 1978 draft by Washington, and the Capitals reclaimed him, employing him profitably for nine seasons.

Retirements by veterans exacerbated the Oilers' losses. Bill Goldsworthy was another Sather crony who had found his way to the Oilers. He had played with Sather as a Bruins prospect in Oklahoma City, with the Bruins proper in 1965/66 and 1966/67, and in Minnesota in 1975/76. At thirty-five, his playing careeer was over. The

1978/79 campaign also closed out the major-league career of one more Sather crony, Garnet "Ace" Bailey. Bailey, one of the last of "Billy's Boys" on the Oilers, had played Junior hockey for Billy Hunter's Edmonton Oil Kings before entering the Bruins system with Sather. After being selected by Hunter in the inaugural WHA draft in 1972, Bailey was finally signed on by Sather for 1978/79, and he played thirty-eight games. He would play eight more games before retiring, in Wichita and in Houston, the Oilers' affiliates in the Central league.

Some hasty repairs were made to the lineup following the reclamation draft through the "priority selection" granted the former WHA teams. The Oilers were the only expansion team to fill both their priority selection spots for goaltenders, retrieving Dryden and Mio. Gretzky took one of the skaters' spots; the remaining spot, which the Oilers initially were expected to use for Gustafsson, was devoted instead to Ron Chipperfield.

Sather had been able to retain the rights to seven players in the course of the reclamation draft. In addition to his priority selections, he could count on still having the Oilers' five leading points-producers from 1978/79. As well as Gretzky, he had right wingers Blair MacDonald and Bill Flett, and centres Brett Callighen and Ron Chipperfield. MacDonald's seventy-one points were bested only by the 104 generated by Gretzky. MacDonald was an Oilers original, drafted in 1972, although he didn't join the team until 1973, after his Junior career with the Cornwall Royals was over. After a mid-decade detour to Indianapolis, he returned to Edmonton in September 1977 in a seven-player deal.

The bona fide original, however, was Al Hamilton, Sather's former team-mate on the Oil Kings. About to turn thirty-three, Hamilton's career was nearing its end. He had been a defensive mainstay for the entire history of the team in the WHA. Though protected by Sather after producing forty-four points in 1978/79, Hamilton would only play another thirty-one games with the Oilers before retiring.

Brett Callighen, the team's third-best scorer, was a professional-hockey wild card. Never seen in Junior action, never drafted by an NHL team, Callighen went from playing for Centennial College in Ontario collegiate play to a minor pro career, mainly in the International League with Kalamazoo in 1974/75 and 1975/76. New England signed him as a free agent in October 1976, and traded him to Edmonton in February 1977. In the efforts to extricate Edmonton from the problem of a previous deal, in which Dave Dryden had refused to report to New England after his trade there, Callighen ended up being sent to New England once more (as a "future considerations" trade) and back again (with Dryden) in the summer of 1977.

Team captain Ron Chipperfield was a high-scoring Brandon Wheat King when drafted by Vancouver of the WHA and California of the NHL in 1974. Chipperfield opted for the upstart league that fall, and moved with the team to Calgary in 1975/76. When the Cowboys folded after 1976/77, the Oilers signed him as a free agent. California had traded Chipperfield's NHL rights to Philadelphia in December 1974, and Sather made sure he stayed in Edmonton by protecting him in the expansion draft.

Bill "Cowboy" Flett was a rare player who managed to be part of a deal between clubs in the NHL and WHA, when the Atlanta Flames sold him to Edmonton in December 1976.[5] A Toronto property in the 1960s, Flett had participated in the Philadelphia Flyers' 1973/74 Stanley Cup win after a seven-player deal sprung him from Los Angeles in 1972. Born east of Edmonton in Vermilion, Alberta, the rangy, bearded right winger was returning to home turf with the Oilers. However, Flett's career was at an end; he would play just twenty games in 1979/80.

One of the few able defencemen Sather had left was Joe Micheletti, a native Minnesotan who spent four seasons playing for the University of Minnesota before joining the Calgary Cowboys in 1976/77. He came to Edmonton via Winnipeg after Calgary folded, and his forty-seven points tied him with Paul Shmyr, now lost, for top defensive points production on the team in 1978/79. Not surprisingly, Sather protected him.

Pete Driscoll, the third player acquired from Indianapolis along with Gretzky and Mio, was also protected, although he, like Flett, did not have a long-term future with the team. The left winger would play sixty games over the next two seasons as Sather broke in new talent.

At least Driscoll could play, which was more than could be said for many of the players being offered by the established NHL teams in the expansion draft on June 13, 1979. The day before the draft, Sather publicly pronounced his dissatisfaction with the dog's breakfast of talents he was required to use to fill out a roster. "At one time, there were 761 names up for grabs," he commented. "After poring over the names, only fifty-three excited us a little. Too many of the players have huge, out-of-sight contracts, problems with their present coach or GM, a drinking problem, or are already retired, like Bobby Orr. And that doesn't include the guys who aren't very good, period."

Having made the WHA clubs pay dearly to get into the league they had so vexed for much of the last decade, having stripped them of so much talent through the reclamation draft, the NHL's existing franchises were now offering the expansion clubs a ratty, often improbable selection of cast-off properties from which to create some semblance of a roster. There was an almost farcical quality to the expansion draft at times, as teams picked players they had no real hope of using or any desire to actually sign, for no other reason than they were supposed to pick people.

Teams fell back on old league habits, trying to cut pre-draft deals that ensured the expansion clubs got something in return for promising to leave certain unprotected players alone. With the draft a closed-door exercise, it was not always possible to know who promised what to whom. The Oilers made a straight deal with Montreal in the hours leading up to the draft to give up their second-round pick in 1980 in exchange for Montreal's Dave Lumley and Dan Newman. Lumley, a Torontonian who had played at the University of New

Hampshire, had been selected 199th overall by the Canadiens in 1974, and had managed a three-game glimpse of the NHL with Montreal in 1978/79. Lumley would be on hand for two Oilers Cup wins. Newman, another former collegian who had been picked up by Montreal on waivers from the New York Rangers in October 1978, would see ten games with the Oilers before being dealt away.

Edmonton resolved to look beyond the expansion draft, toward the entry draft in August. A key goal in the expansion draft was to focus on free agents who, if they chose to sign with another club, would entitle the Oilers to compensation. As Larry Gordon would explain, "We've saved ourselves from $350,000 to $500,000 by drafting free agents. And if they don't sign with us, we get compensation from the clubs they do sign with. We've now got some money to play with . . . some money to sign some Juniors in the [entry] draft." In hindsight, though, it's hard to see if any money ultimately flowed Edmonton's way.

The expansion and reclamation drafts clearly had more activity going on behind the scenes than in the actual proceedings. "Glen had so many cards in play," Dave Dryden recalls, "I don't know how he kept track of them all." Improbable oversights in the reclamation draft hinted at deals that never made it into the formal registry of league trades. The haggling was plainly ferocious. By all rights, the Oilers should have lost both Ron Chipperfield, to Philadelphia, and Blair MacDonald, to Los Angeles, in the reclamation draft, but didn't.

The expansion draft was as much improvised as executed. While the league originally had decreed that existing teams would be allowed to protect only fifteen skaters, deal-making between these teams and the expansion clubs quickly jacked the number up to nineteen. And the Canadiens, with a Stanley Cup-winning lineup to protect (and so many reclamation opportunities giving them extra bargaining leverage), were able to engineer an opening to the expansion draft that entirely served their agenda.

Established clubs had the option of receiving, for every player lost, an extra spot on the protected list rather than the $125,000 compensation. Montreal arranged to sacrifice three lesser players in the opening picks of the draft to make more room on the protected list. As Winnipeg took Peter Marsh first, Edmonton took Cam Connor second and Hartford took Alan Hanglseben third, Montreal filled in the protected spots it acquired with Bill Nyrop, Gilles Lupien and Rod Langway. Exactly what each club received in return for going along with the Montreal scheme is impossible to say, but in Edmonton's case, it can be noted that the Oilers exited the expansion draft with Dave Hunter back in the roster, even though he wasn't actually selected in the draft.[6] The Oilers emerged from the reclamation and expansion drafts with another prize unattributable to any formally recorded deal: from Minnesota North Stars general manager Lou Nanne (a friend and former roommate of Sather's from his stint with Minnesota in 1975/76), the Oilers acquired Minnesota's third and fourth round picks in the upcoming entry draft.

Cam Connor, acquired by Edmonton with the second pick in the expansion draft, had been one of the NHL's notable draft losses in the earlier wars with the WHA. Montreal had used its first pick, fifth overall, in 1974 to choose the hard-hitting right winger from the Flin Flon Bombers, but Connor had opted to sign with the WHA's Phoenix Roadrunners. Montreal was finally able to sign him for 1978/79, but on a talent-rich team Connor played only twenty-three games and was deemed expendable in the 1979 draft. The Oilers were able to sign Connor, but would trade him before their first NHL season was over.

Sather was forced to make some long-shot choices in the expansion draft. No club could lose more than five players, and Sather accounted for two far-fetched selections that were struck off the Pittsburgh Penguins' roll call. Tom Edur was a capable defenceman who left Junior hockey after one season with the Toronto Marlboros to sign with Cleveland of the WHA as an underage free agent in August 1973. Harry Sinden drafted him for the Bruins in 1974, 54th overall, but Edur remained in the WHA with the Crusaders. Sinden finally sold his rights to Colorado, and Edur signed with the Rockies for 1976/77. Twenty games into 1977/78, Edur was dealt to Pittsburgh for Dennis Owchar. Edur produced fifty-five points that season, but as a Jehovah's Witness he announced his retirement in protest against hockey violence. Sather was unable to coax him into an Oilers uniform. Wayne Bianchin was a once-prized left winger, who was Pittsburgh's second choice (23rd overall) in the 1973 draft. After one season with the Penguins, he spent most of 1974/75 and 1975/76 in the minors. He'd secured a starting job in 1976/77 with the Penguins, but spinal surgery had cut short his 1978/79 season at forty games and there was some question of whether he could even play again in the NHL. Sather would get eleven games out of him in 1979/80 before he went to play in Italy.

Another gamble was Inge Hammarstrom, who had helped pave the way for European talent in the NHL when in 1973 he joined the Toronto Maple Leafs with Borje Salming as a free agent signing. Hammarstrom was traded to St. Louis in November 1977, and after completing the 1978/79 season with the Blues he had gone home to Sweden, firm about not returning to the NHL. He was true to his word, playing three more seasons of professional hockey in Sweden, declining to try the NHL again with Edmonton—or with any other NHL team, which would have entitled the Oilers to compensation.

Fortunately for the Oilers, who had lost so many quality defencemen in the reclamation draft, there were good pickings among the league's defencemen. As it turned out, of sixteen "new" players Sather bothered to select in the expansion draft (leaving the retrieved Hunter aside), all four who made the Oilers' roster for the team's first NHL season were defencemen. And two had been among the highest-drafted blueliners in recent years.

The Islanders may have stolen away Dave Langevin, but the Oilers could take some solace in plucking Pat Price from the Islanders' defence corps. Price had been an All Star with the Saskatoon Blades in Canadian Western Junior hockey when he answered the 1974 WHA draft by reporting to the Vancouver Blazers. The Islanders drafted him 11th overall with their first pick in 1975, and Price came over to the NHL. Price was an early reclamation project of Sather's, for the once-vaunted prospect had become a walking argument against prospects leaving the Junior ranks for a pro career too soon. Signed by Vancouver at eighteen, he immediately crashed a Ferrari, and his reputation had remained troubling. Price saw his selection by Sather as a welcome second chance. His twenty-five penalty minutes in seven playoff games in 1978/79 showed he had a physical game in reserve, and with Edmonton and later Pittsburgh, Price would play a much tougher game while contributing more than thirty points a season.

Colin Campbell had been another high draft pick on defence, going 27th overall as the Pittsburgh Penguins' third selection in 1973. Like Price, he played initially with Vancouver in the WHA, in 1973/74, then joined the NHL's Penguins in 1974/75. While he would last only one season in Edmonton, heading to Vancouver after being let go on waivers in October 1980, his brush with the Oilers was a distant presage of his experiences on the coaching staff of the New York Rangers in the 1990s. As the Rangers' associate coach, "Collie" would oversee a host of former Edmonton stars who arrived for New York's 1993/94 Stanley Cup victory. Promoted to coach in 1995, he would acquire Gretzky as well in 1996/97. A player Sather cut from the team after its first season in the NHL would end up inheriting a bevy of Stanley Cup champions that Sather's boss, Peter Pocklington, could no longer afford.

Sather achieved one of the few coups of the expansion draft by taking defenceman Lee Fogolin from the Buffalo Sabres. The Sabres were in a state of front-office mayhem as the draft approached. Scotty Bowman had been fielding offers of a new job after coaching Montreal to a fourth consecutive Stanley Cup that May, and the Sabres were in a race with the Toronto Maple Leafs to sign him. The Sabres won, by offering him a high-paying package that included the roles of coach, general manager and director of player personnel.

The deal wasn't announced until June 11, the day after the Sabres staff had to submit their protected list for the expansion draft. Bowman could not have been pleased to discover that left off it was Fogolin, who had been Buffalo's first pick (11th overall) in the 1974 draft. The highly capable Fogolin would be named the Oilers' captain in 1981 and would win two Stanley Cups with the team.

Chicago provided Edmonton a fourth defenceman through the expansion draft, as Doug Hicks began a stint in Edmonton that lasted almost three seasons. But as things stood, when the expansion draft ended, the only players Sather had who would bring the Oilers the Cup in 1983/84 were Fogolin, Hunter and Gretzky. Sather had tremendous work ahead of him over the summer to begin to lay the foundations of a champion team.

In the time at hand between the expansion draft on June 13 and the entry draft on August 9, Sather went to work getting back players he'd lost through reclamation and couldn't recover via priority selection or backroom deal-making. First, Stan Weir quickly boomeranged when the Leafs let him go on waivers on July 4. To get Risto Siltanen back from St. Louis, Sather had to surrender one of his few serviceable defencemen, Joe Micheletti, but he got the Blues to throw in minor pro forward Tom Roulston. Getting Dave Semenko back from Minnesota was potentially far pricier. Sather's friend Lou Nanne had his eye on a favourite son of Minnesota, collegiate star Neil Broten, and he needed Edmonton's second-round entry-draft pick to have some hope of securing him. Sather gave Nanne his second- and third-round selections in return for Semenko.

The 1979 entry draft was one of the most intriguing, and most patently unfair, drafts the NHL had ever held. The normal draft process was for teams to choose in each round in the reverse order of their finish in the previous regular season. It was also the policy of the league to allow expansion clubs to pick first, before the established clubs began their reverse-order selections. Not this time, though. Despite having structured the arrival of the four WHA clubs as an expansion and not a merger (and with the expansion fees to go with it), and despite having stripped these teams of so many asset players, the established NHL clubs could not resist placing these latest expansion teams in the worst possible position in the divvying of new talent. The expansion agreement struck in March dictated that for the 1979 draft the existing clubs would follow the standard reverse-of-finish pecking order for the first seventeen selections in each round. The last four selections in each round were then left to the former WHA clubs, who would choose in their own reverse order. No former WHA club would pick higher than 18th, and because the Edmonton Oilers finished first overall in the last WHA regular season, they were relegated to the last pick in every round. Most of the prizes in the draft pool were the teenage free-agent signings from the WHA that the NHLPA had agreed to have dumped into the entry draft rather than be granted free agency. Because the former WHA teams had been assigned such poor draft positions, most of these top prospects would be gone before they had a chance to choose one.

Four Birmingham Bulls in the 1979 draft pool were sure to go higher than 18th. Defenceman Rob Ramage was agreed to be the best prospect in the entire pool, and was sure to be picked first overall, by Colorado. Rick Vaive and Craig Hartsburg were top-ten certainties, and Michel Dion could go in the first round. Bulls goaltender Pat Riggin, Gaston Gingras and Keith Crowder were also available, but could wait until the second round. Over on the Cincinnati Stingers, Mike Gartner would be taken in the first few picks, and while Mark Messier was draft eligible, he was too unknown a quantity to predict when he would be selected.

Aside from the inclusion of the teenage WHA players, the 1979 draft was a major departure from the previous year in permitting about half as many selections. The 1978 draft had been the second largest ever held by the NHL; with 234 selections, it had been exceeded only by the 247 of the 1974 draft, in which the league had allowed limited selection of players as young as eighteen in the heat of its battle with the WHA. For this first entry draft, the maximum number of players permitted for selection was 126, chosen over six rounds. It was the last NHL draft held in private. A telephone conference call was used to link the participating team offices with the league office in Montreal.

As the draft began, the Oilers' selection schedule was far from promising. They had the last pick in the first round, at 21st, then nothing in the second round, due to the Semenko deal. The third- and fourth-round picks acquired from Minnesota let them back in at 48th and 69th (having relinquished their third-round pick at 63rd to Minnesota.) Then came the Oilers' remaining picks at the ends of the fourth (84th), fifth (105th) and sixth rounds (126th—dead last).

Where the 1978 amateur draft had prioritized offensive talent, the 1979 entry draft was tilted toward blue-line skill. Led by ex–"Baby Bull" Rob Ramage, defencemen dominated the selection process, accounting for picks one (Ramage), six (Craig Hartsburg), seven (Keith Brown), eight (Ray Bourque), eleven (Mike Ramsey), twelve (Paul Reinhart), fifteen (Brad McCrimmon) and sixteen (Jay Wells). The teenage WHA prospects also figured strongly. In addition to Ramage and Hartsburg, Mike Gartner went fourth, Rick Vaive fifth and Michel Goulet 20th.

Of the four WHA teams, Hartford and Winnipeg stumbled in their first-round picks, making weak selections of right wingers Ray Allison and Jimmy Mann. Quebec did well with Goulet, and then it was Edmonton's turn.

The persuasion for Sather to pick Kevin Lowe, captain of the Quebec Remparts, as the ninth and last defenceman (and last player) chosen in the opening round, came from Oilers' chief scout Barry Fraser. The talent spotter, a former Ontario Hydro worker in northern Ontario, had gotten into the business bird-dogging for the Kitchener Rangers of Ontario's Major Junior A as a hobby, then turned it into a profession in the WHA, first with the Cleveland Crusaders for four years, followed by the Houston Aeros for two.

When the Aeros folded following the 1977/78 season, Fraser came to the Oilers. While Sather was ultimately calling the shots at the 1979 entry draft, Edmonton's selection performance helped establish Fraser's reputation as superb judge of talent.

Lowe had been a second-team All Star in the past two seasons in Quebec Major Junior A, and had completed his final campaign with eighty-six points in sixty-eight regular-season games, though he hadn't reached a Memorial Cup finals or represented Canada at a World Junior Championship. And while defenceman Mike Ramsey, a standout on the American team at the world Juniors, had been taken by Buffalo 11th overall, his highly regarded team-mates, right winger Dave Christian and centre Neal Broten, were still available when Edmonton came to make its first pick. So were all the stars of the bronze-medal Swedish team: the tournament's top goaltender, Pelle Lindbergh, defenceman Thomas Jonsson, centre Thomas Steen and left winger Mats Naslund.[7] But Fraser had tagged a player who had ability and poise, and a mind for the game that would impress Sather immediately, just as Sather's had once impressed Harry Sinden. With Lowe, however, Sather had a player who was capable of playing at an elite level, whereas in Sather, Sinden had a player who was destined to excel in management.

The Oilers sat out the second round while an uneven draft effort unfolded. Having been passed on by Edmonton, Jonsson, Naslund and Lindbergh were all spoken for in the round (Steen would linger until the 103rd pick, by Winnipeg), which ended strongly with picks by Winnipeg, Quebec and Minnesota (using the pick acquired from Edmonton as part of the Semenko deal). The two overlooked American Juniors, Dave Christian and Neal Broten, went to Winnipeg and Minnesota, while Quebec scored with centre Dale Hunter. All three would play more than 1,000 games in the NHL.

When the draft resumed in the third round, Montreal held the opening two picks. The Canadiens picked up a defensive journeyman in Craig Levie of the Edmonton Oil Kings, then made an impressive selection in centre Guy Carbonneau. There followed a series of blunders by Detroit and Vancouver. The Red Wings, selecting 45th and 46th, threw away their selections on right winger Jody Gage, who lasted sixty-eight games in the NHL, and defenceman Boris Fistric, who never made the league at all. Vancouver followed with goaltender Ken Ellacott, who made a dozen NHL appearances. Next up was Edmonton, who used the 48th pick to choose a player who had never played a regular-season Major Junior A game, and who had scored once in his previous season in the WHA. The Edmonton Oilers chose Mark Messier.

Messier's low profile skimmed below the radars of other scouting efforts. There was simply no track record to pique interest. Among the WHA's underage free-agency signings for 1978/79 who were the stars of the 1979 NHL entry draft, Messier rated no mention. The free spirit with the bulldog work ethic, the prototypical western Canadian power forward, came into the professional game in his own way and on his own terms. He had raw talent that had to be witnessed to make a man like Sather believe he was a more important choice than any number of quality players still available. For while Messier proved to be one of the most inspired draft picks ever made in the NHL, he was not plucked out of the deepest reaches of the talent pool. The 1979 draft still had many quality players, a number of whom would have long NHL careers, going for the asking when the Oilers fingered Messier. In the third round alone, Atlanta took right winger Tim Hunter at 54th; Boston, right winger Keith Crowder (the last Baby Bull) at 57th; Montreal, goaltender Rick Wamsley at 58th; and the New York Islanders, goaltender Rollie Melanson at 59th. Messier was less a talent overlooked by other teams than one the Oilers hit on by overlooking more obvious choices.

Messier was a gutsy call, a well-founded hunch. A rink-rat as a kid, Mark had skated in practices at age six with the Portland Buckaroos of the WHL when his father was with the team. He had been in action for almost the entire 1978/79 WHA season, giving

Sather a chance to scout him in person. And he had played on the Cincinnati Stingers with the Oilers' new assistant coach, Bugsy Watson. Back in March, Sather had tipped his hand to his enthusiasm for the prospect. "If he's available in the draft of kids this summer, I'll take him in a minute," Sather had promised. "He's good in the corners and big and strong. Surprisingly so. I remember him knocking 215-pound Dave Langevin over once. This is a boy who jumped all the way from tier II [Junior hockey] to the pros in one season and didn't look terribly out of place. I think he'd make a hell of a choice for us."

Six picks into the fourth round, at 69th, Barry Fraser was pulling another plum out of a pie which by then was supposed to be little more than crumbs. This time he was arguing the case for another low-profile prospect, collegiate player Glenn Anderson.

The son of a B.C. commercial fisherman, the Vancouver-born right winger was two months away from his nineteenth birthday, and had just completed a year with the University of Denver's hockey program, producing fifty-five points in forty games. Despite inroads made by collegiate players in the NHL draft, sentiments still ran against the system, which it was felt had too many practices and too few games. Before the entry draft, Fraser spent a week at the Canadian Olympic team training camp in Calgary, watching Anderson work out with Don Spring, Paul Pageau, Jim Nill, Paul MacLean, Kevin Primeau and Kevin Maxwell. All except Nill and MacLean (who had been chosen by St. Louis, 89th and 109th overall, in 1978) would be available in the upcoming draft, and Fraser was convinced Anderson was the best of the bunch.[8] At six feet one inch, Anderson had not only size, but tremendous speed also. In a red-line to red-line dash, Fraser timed him at a blistering 6.3 seconds. Anderson had scoring and playmaking ability, but his mobility was mesmerizing. He could go around an opponent as easily as over him. Opponents who tried to stop him by getting in his way would find themselves knocked on their backsides or left spinning in a spray of ice chips. Sather listened to Fraser, and took Anderson.

The three remaining Oilers picks were forgettable. Given the exalted reputation the Oilers would gain for fingering major talents in Europe at subsequent drafts, it's worth noting that in choosing Maxwell Kostovich at 84th (a left winger from the Portland Winter Hawks who never made the NHL), they passed on two quality Swedish players: defenceman Thomas Eriksson, taken by Philadelphia at 98th, and the curiously discounted Thomas Steen.[9] (The Oilers also chose Portland centre Mike Toal 105th, who played three NHL games. Chicago then scored at 112th with defenceman Doug Crossman, who played 914 NHL games, and down at 120th Boston unearthed forward Mike Krushelnyski, whom Sather would acquire in 1984 and use on three Stanley Cup-winning teams before losing him to Los Angeles in the Gretzky trade.)

The efforts at the draft of Edmonton's fellow WHA refugee clubs varied. Hartford clearly stumbled. Its best pick proved to be right winger Ray Neufeld, down at 81st, who lasted 595 games in the NHL. Winnipeg and Quebec both did solid jobs. Five of Winnipeg's six picks made the NHL (albeit for only twelve games in the case of the fourth pick, Pat Daley), and came away with three selections who had long, productive careers: Dave Christian (1,009 games on right wing), Thomas Steen (950 games at centre) and Tim Watters (741 games on defence). Quebec probably did the most consistent drafting job of all four expansion clubs. Five of six selections were keepers. Left winger Michel Goulet played 1,089 NHL games; centre Dale Hunter 1,345 games; defenceman Lee Norwood played 503 games; left winger Anton Stastny (an Iron-Curtain gamble who first had to be spirited out of Czechoslovakia) 650 games; and defenceman Pierre Lacroix 274 games. Measured on the basis of games played (as tallied at the end of the 1997/98 season), the Nordiques were the winners in the draft derby among the former WHA teams. They found more NHLers than anyone else, who combined for the most games: 3,861, compared with Edmonton's 3,730, Winnipeg's 3,005 and Hartford's 1,133.

But in choosing Lowe, Messier and Anderson, the Oilers had

accomplished a draft-day miracle. Sather and his staff had selected three players outside the top twenty who would each play more than 1,000 games in the NHL and (as of 1997/98) produce 3,142 points and share in six Stanley Cup victories—five for Edmonton, one for New York. With Gretzky already in hand, Sather had four of the most potent talents of the 1980s before his team even held its first NHL training camp. And far from being proven a case of beginner's luck, Sather's Oilers would turn in performances at the next two entry drafts almost as dazzling as the one that gained so little initial attention in 1979.

CHAPTER FIVE

LIKE ALL GREAT sporting dynasties, the Edmonton Oilers of the 1980s were a product of place and time—of where they played, both geographically and in the game's history. And that history included the evolution of both the game's strategy and its economic environment. Yet the Oilers developed a unique capacity to inspire "what ifs" and "if onlys"—an often contradictory sense that circumstances both favoured and punished the team.

As financial pressures forced Peter Pocklington to deal away the team's stars in the early 1990s, Glen Sather would give voice to the idea that the Oilers were doomed because the championship lineup had come together in Edmonton, and not some eastern seaboard megalopolis. "Can you imagine what that team might have done in a market like Toronto or Montreal or New York that could have afforded to keep it together?" he wondered in 1993. By then, seven of his former Cup winners were in New York, preparing to win the Rangers their first Stanley Cup since 1939/40. Oilers coach Ron Low, the team's goaltender in the dynasty's formative years, would pick up Sather's if-only-elsewhere theme, wondering aloud how many more goals the high-scoring Oilers could have amassed in the 1980s if they had been based in the east, and not been so drained by their lengthy road trips.

The Edmonton Oilers in retrospect—a retrospect informed

largely by the modern economics of the game—have come to be seen as a championship team that happened in entirely the wrong place, wrong both for its own good and for the good of the league overall. Yet the championship Oilers would never have existed without Edmonton. They could not have happened in New York or Toronto or Montreal. Ultimately, these were places that only the mature team could have moved to, not where it could could have come from.

WHEN THE OILERS joined the NHL, the league was in the latter stages of accepting that the old way of playing the game was not the only way, that there was room in the NHL for Europeans and anyone who played a European style of passing game. Even so, the game had not yet been transformed. As anyone who has watched international hockey can attest, fancy passing does not necessarily mean wide open offence. Rigorous puck control and forechecking on the larger international ice surface can produce dull games with few scoring chances. The game Wayne Gretzky and the Oilers helped create in the NHL was something entirely different. It was fast, clever, creative, and above all it was committed to scoring as many goals as possible.

As the 1980s began, the NHL was already allowing more goals per game on average than it had since the Second World War, about 1.5 goals per team more than in the mid-1950s. There was no philosophical basis for this scoring ascent; it was almost entirely due to diluted talent. The NHL's haphazard expansion efforts of the 1970s, as it tried to shut the WHA out of potential markets, had thinned the ranks of quality players and created up to half a dozen particularly poor teams that the better clubs could score against without mercy. As the NHL's average per-team scoring climbed toward the four-goal mark in the late 1970s, there was no real change in coaching strategy to account for it.[1]

Considered in isolation, goals against are meaningless. What matters at the end of the day (or, more precisely, at the end of the game) is that a team scores more goals than it allows. There's no merit in a team limiting opponents to, on average, 2.5 goals per game when its offence can only produce 2.0 in return. A championship NHL team, regardless of its era, generally must produce an average scoring surplus of one goal per game, and the very best, like the Montreal Canadiens of the 1970s, have achieved a two-goal surplus. By this measure, a team that wins games by an average 5-3 score is as capable as one that wins 4-2. But until the Gretzky-era Oilers came along, having an offence consistently potent enough to achieve a five-goal average was almost unheard of. Scoring that many goals almost certainly meant taking defensive risks, and in the late 1970s accepting mediocre goals-against numbers was anathema to the game's prevailing philosophy.

The modern blueprint for a championship team had defensive thrift as its foundation. Preventing goals was the priority. The history of dynastic NHL clubs—in particular the Detroit Red Wings of the 1950s and the Montreal Canadiens of the 1950s, 1960s and 1970s—showed that if a team had outstanding goaltending and a strong defence corps, it could limit opponents to about two goals per game. The forward lines were a mix of checking specialists, two-way generalists, playmakers and the occasional exceptionally gifted sniper. With a strong power play, such a team could produce about four goals a game, giving it a comfortable two-goal scoring margin. The Stanley Cup winners of the 1950s were model outfits—physically tough as well, to withstand a determined checking game. Their scoring stars were men like Gordie Howe in Detroit and Maurice Richard in Montreal, who could give as good as they took. The idea of employing enforcers did not arise until the mid-1960s, when Montreal's John Ferguson became an on-ice policeman for a team with smaller, fleet-footed stars like Yvon Cournoyer, whom he protected against the tenacious checking styles of teams such as Toronto and Detroit.

The Montreal team went through repeated successful overhauls, extending its championship run right through the 1970s, and its blueprint proved especially influential. As the Canadiens recorded a new string of Cup victories in the early 1970s, their model was being adapted by a new team, the New York Islanders.

Established as an expansion franchise in 1972, the Islanders were built from the defence up in the Canadiens tradition. The team's general manager, Bill Torrey, had grown up in Montreal near the Forum, and as a young man would sneak into the building to watch the team practise under coach Dick Irvin. The Islanders' chief scout, Jim Devellano, came to the team from the St. Louis Blues, where the coach and general manager was Scotty Bowman, a product of the Canadiens Junior development system. Bowman had gone into coaching in the mid-1950s under Sam Pollock, who became the Canadiens' general manager in 1964. Bowman had built the 1967 expansion franchise in St. Louis using the Montreal blueprint, emphasizing strong goaltending (securing Glenn Hall and then Jacques Plante, an Oiler in 1974/75) and a tough defence. It got the Blues to three consecutive Stanley Cup finals, after which, in 1971, Bowman returned to the Montreal fold to coach the Canadiens. One of the defencemen Bowman had selected for the Blues in the 1967 expansion draft was Al Arbour, a reliable stay-at-homer who had been in and out of the minors since the early 1950s with the Red Wings and the Maple Leafs. Bowman had given Arbour the Blues to coach in 1970/71, and for the Islanders' second season, 1973/74, Devellano persuaded general manager Torrey to hire Arbour. With Torrey, Devellano (who became assistant GM) and Arbour, the Islanders were hard-wired to build and maintain a Canadiens facsimile. When the Canadiens' string of championships ended after Bowman left to become coach and general manager of the Buffalo Sabres in 1979, the Islanders stepped in to form the next dynasty, winning four consecutive Stanley Cups.

In their best years (1978/79 and 1980/81), the Islanders were among the highest-scoring teams while vying for the lead in fewest goals allowed. Torrey had made goaltender Billy Smith his first selection in the 1972 expansion draft; paired with Glenn "Chico" Resch, acquired from the Canadiens within days of the first draft, Smith became the anchor of one of the best netminding duos of the 1970s. After Resch was traded to Colorado in March 1981, Rollie Melanson became Smith's capable partner. The defence was anchored by Denis Potvin, drafted first overall in 1973 and heir apparent to Bobby Orr and Brad Park as the game's preeminent offensive defenceman. In 1980/81, Potvin broke Orr's single-season playoff points record (with twenty-five to Orr's twenty-four, set in 1971/72). The Islanders' attack was built around two gifted players: centre Bryan Trottier, who was one of the game's better defensive forwards as well as one of its most accomplished playmakers and scorers, and right winger Mike Bossy, a pure sniper who from his Calder-winning debut in 1977/78 until 1985/86 scored at least fifty goals in every season. At their peak in 1980/81, the Islanders churned through the playoff record book. In addition to Potvin's defensive points record,[2] Bossy scored a record nine power-play goals that spring. In one playoff game against Edmonton, Potvin set or matched three defensive playoff records for a single-game performance: most points (five), most goals (three), and most power-play goals (three). It was the discipline of this machine, more defensively rigorous than even the Canadiens, that the Oilers would have to overcome to present an alternative blueprint for winning.

The ideal ingredients to create success in Edmonton and to force a change in the NHL game were all in place when Wayne Gretzky entered the league with the Oilers. The team had the right ownership, the right management, and what would prove to be the right location for a young team developing a new style of game. It also had the right lineup, which is to say that it had virtually no lineup at all. The bench was empty, save for a few key seats, the most important one being occupied by Gretzky.

For all the disparaging remarks Peter Pocklington would invite over the ensuing years, he was a good owner for the Oilers as they entered the NHL. He had money, and he did not have some dangerously deluded notion of himself as a hockey sage. He would play a minimal role in the day-to-day affairs of the team, leaving its management almost entirely to Glen Sather. Before acquiring Gretzky, the most important personnel decision he made was promoting his coach to general manager and then to team president as well. It was Sather who convinced Pocklington to buy Gretzky's contract from Skalbania; it was Sather who, hobbled by the onerous terms under which Pocklington agreed to bring the Oilers into the NHL, made a contender from them. Above all, it was Sather who saw the possibilities of Gretzky, not simply as an individual star and gate attraction, but as the departure point for creating a team and a whole new game plan to go with it.

Necessity, in the case of the Oilers, was the mother of opportunity. Because the Oilers came into the league as a quasi-expansion franchise, with so few quality players, Sather had no choice but to build a team. And with the teenage Gretzky as his main asset, he had a once-in-a-lifetime chance to create something truly new: not just another team that adhered to the Canadiens-inspired blueprint of tenacious control, but a team that dared to play in a flat-out offensive press.

Like his close friend and former coach Harry Sinden, Sather had the rare experience of being given a team to build that had at its core the most talented player of his generation. In Sinden's case, it had been Bobby Orr. The superlative defenceman came straight out of Canadian Junior hockey to join the Bruins lineup at eighteen in 1966/67, just as Sinden was being promoted from his Central league coaching job with the Oklahoma City Blazers to run the Boston bench. The Bruins missed the playoffs for the eighth consecutive season that year, but Sinden had the fundamental ingredients of a championship club before the start of the next season. After a disappointing playoff performance in the spring of 1967, the Chicago Blackhawks made one of the worst trades in league history, sending Phil Esposito, Ken Hodge and Fred Stanfield to the Bruins. When acquired from Chicago, Esposito predicted to Sinden that they would win the Cup in three years. The Bruins were right on schedule when they swept the St. Louis Blues in 1969/70.

Although the two teams were wildly different in many aspects, Sinden's Bruins were the closest the NHL came to creating a team like the Oilers before Sather actually did the job. And Sather, of course, had played for these Bruins, on the eve of their success, in 1968/69. While Boston was a far more physical team—no one would ever think of calling Sather's Edmonton outfit the Big, Bad Oilers—the two clubs bore a basic similarity in their commitment to offensive production. In 1970/71, the Bruins scored a record 399 regular-season goals—108 more than the next best effort, by Montreal. Esposito obliterated the offensive records with seventy-six goals in seventy-eight games, as he, Orr, Johnny Bucyk and Ken Hodge all gathered more than 100 points and locked up the top four positions in the scoring race. These Bruins also foreshadowed the Oilers in their exceptional goaltending pairing of Gerry Cheevers and Eddie Johnston, who, like Grant Fuhr and Andy Moog in Edmonton, were not going to win awards for goals-against stats but whose first-class skills kept the opposing team to about three goals a game (in Boston's case) while the offence produced five or six.

Sinden says the comparison of the Bruins he coached and the 1980s Oilers is a fair one, but the most important component to him was the resident superstar. Like Gretzky (and later Messier), Orr raised the level of the game of everyone around him by his example, his commitment, his inspiration. "We had guys in Boston who had never come close to achieving what they did when Orr came, and it wasn't just because Orr was passing them the puck. Gordie Howe was like that too. Detroit in the 1950s was a good team with one good line. The superb play of Howe brought everybody up."

Boston's dominance of the game, however, was brief. After winning a second Cup in 1971/72, the team was debilitated by defections to the new WHA and by the rise of an even more physical club, the Philadelphia Flyers. Ultimately in the 1970s, the traditional Canadiens style of "score four, allow two" prevailed, as Montreal won Cups in 1970/71, and 1972/73 and four in a row from 1975/76 to 1978/79, after which the Islanders took over.

While the Bruins provided a foreshadowing of an offensive-minded NHL championship club, Glen Sather's main inspiration for the team he fashioned came from the Winnipeg Jets of the WHA. Overall, the WHA played a higher-scoring game than the NHL (partly because regular-season overtime was used). The difference in raw statistics between the leagues owed much to the WHA's embrace of the European game, long before most NHL clubs were prepared to admit there was room for the European style in their game plan, never mind European players. Prejudices were deep-seated in the NHL. It was felt Europeans couldn't adapt to the smaller North American ice surface, and that they weren't physically tough enough to play in the corners or in the slot. For Europeans to make an impact in North America, team management would have to be convinced it had any need for them. The Canadian Junior system was the overwhelming choice for new talent, and only late in the 1970s did the American college system (featuring Canadians alongside Americans on playing scholarships) begin to make significant inroads at the NHL draft. Scouting within the NHL was inconsistent from team to team, and in 1976 the league introduced the Central Scouting Bureau to produce reports of prospects that could be accessed by all clubs. The number of NHL scouts that might attend a major international tournament like the European Junior Championship could be counted on the fingers of one hand. They already knew the best Canadian Juniors—who cared about the Finns and Swedes? As for Russians and Czechs, the Iron Curtain kept them far out of reach.

Over in the WHA, though, the need to find talent in the salary war with the NHL pressed the league in two directions. While some clubs signed Canadian Juniors before they became draft eligible in the NHL, others looked to Europe.

The Jets were successful because they didn't make the mistake of trying to shoehorn overseas talent into the prevailing playing style. The Jets embraced the European game wholeheartedly, allowing the imported stars to play the way they knew best. They were the first North American professional team to use European techniques such as criss-cross attacks by forwards and neutral zone regrouping. Fred Shero claimed his intensive study of the Russian game inspired the short-pass offence of the Philadelphia Flyers, but the game played by Shero's Broad Street Bullies was a pale reflection of the swirling, inventive choreography demonstrated by the Jets. Shero could talk the Russian game, but with the talent limits of the Flyers, he was wont to practise a dump and chase—and hit—style.

In 1975/76, the Jets won fifty-two of eighty-one games and the WHA championship, while their fellow Canadian Division members, the Oilers, were floundering with twenty-seven wins. The Jets featured nine overseas players;[3] when they won the WHA title again in 1977/78, they had eight Europeans.[4] In 1977/78 they led the league in goals for (381, or 4.76 per game) and were second by one goal to the New England Whalers in fewest goals allowed (270, or 3.38 per game).

The Jets won a third WHA championship, the last one contested, defeating Sather's favoured Oilers in the spring of 1979. The Jets were no longer the European powerhouse of the North American professional game, having lost Ulf Nilsson and Anders Hedberg (who together had contributed 100 of the Jets' 381 goals in 1977/78) to the New York Rangers. But the kind of game the Jets had been able to play in the unique hothouse environment of the WHA was inspiring to Sather, who had never played any game like it personally, but was enchanted by its excitement and grace. When the 1979 absorption of four WHA teams by the NHL provided a unique opportunity for his club to make a fresh start, and build a team like none before it, Sather rose to the challenge.

Why Sather? Foremost, because he had a mind for the game's architecture that rivalled Gretzky's on-ice vision. Sather was typical of many great coaches and managers (like Harry Sinden) in that his playing career was far less spectacular than the one that followed in management. Sinden never rose above the minor pro ranks, becoming a player-coach in the CHL before taking the Bruins coaching job. Sather at least plugged away in a grinder's role in the NHL and WHA before being frog-marched behind the Edmonton bench by Bep Guidolin. Pocklington recognized as much ability in Sather as Sather did in Gretzky, and that cascading trust permitted a team-building program totally dedicated to bringing a Jets-like game to the NHL.

Sather would do it foremost with Gretzky, who came along when the NHL was open to the possibilities of his talent, but certainly not unanimously impressed with his teenaged skills. Even in his first seasons in the NHL, veteran hockey journalists were casting public doubt on his ability. (Dick Beddoes in 1980/81 said he "might just have made third-string centre on one of the good Leaf teams of the past.")

Gretzky's skills were not in any way typical. With his bent-over style, his motion was not outwardly graceful or efficient. He would not win any All Star skills competitions with his skating speed or the power of his shot. And his strength was less than impressive. But when Oilers players were tested by a University of Alberta physiologist in 1980, Gretzky proved to have exceptional recuperative abilities. His stamina was phenomenal.

As a scorer, he followed the example of Maurice Richard, who attributed his goal production to taking as many shots per game as he could. At the height of his scoring prowess, from 1981/82 to 1985/86, Gretzky averaged well over 300 shots on goal per season, while most scorers struggled to approach 300.[5] In 1981/82, when he broke the 200-point barrier with ninety-two goals and 120 assists, he produced 369 shots on goal, or 4.6 per game. That season, Mike Bossy scored sixty-four goals (with eighty-three assists) on 301 shots, or about 3.8 per game. Gretzky's shooting percentage, usually around twenty, was about five points better than Marcel Dionne, Bobby Hull and Phil Esposito, about the same as Bryan Trottier and Mario Lemieux, and a little lower than Bossy, who scored on about 22 percent of his shots.[6]

He did not have Trottier's reputation as a great defensive forward as well as being a scoring star, although he was dangerous as a scorer in shorthanded situations. He was not, at least initially, cast as a team leader. With Gretzky only a teenager when he arrived, the captain's C was worn during his first four seasons by Ron Chipperfield, Blair MacDonald and Lee Fogolin, before Sather recognized he had the maturity to lead and turned it over to him.

His politeness (when he arrived in the NHL, he called older star players "Mister") has grated on cynics, but those who have spent time with him away from the game insist that Gretzky in private is the same person that turns up for a media interview: a decent, patient, respectful man, more than aware of his exceptional skills but never boastful or vain. As someone whose extraordinary abilities have placed him in a spotlight few professional athletes ever know, Gretzky has certainly learned the art of not giving offence. In November 1983, he observed that the New Jersey Devils were a "Mickey Mouse" operation, and was chastised for it from within the league. As an icon of the game, he subsequently made sure such off-the-cuff criticisms were left to others, such as the ever-opinionated Brett Hull in the 1990s. Asked, for example, during the Nagano Olympics about the firing of his New York Rangers coach, Colin Campbell, Gretzky produced a masterpiece of neutral-zone commiseration, expressing his regrets over Campbell's dismissal without sounding a note of umbrage toward general manager Neil Smith. Campbell, he pronounced, was "good people," and things would work out for him. (Gretzky was right. Campbell ended up being hired as the NHL's senior vice-president and director of hockey operations after Brian Burke left to take the general manager's job in Vancouver.)

All attempts to attribute Gretzky's skills to some physiological anomaly come up empty handed. Rather, he seems to have benefited immensely from his upbringing, on and off the ice, in Brantford, Ontario. The role of his father, Walter, cannot be overstated. In addition to spending up to six hours a day on the ice, whether in a local arena or on his backyard rink, Wayne was blessed with his father's common-sense advice on matters of play and personal conduct.

The skill most often cited as uniquely Gretzky's was his ability to see the game as a whole, in motion. It could be argued that his fundamental skills, such as skating (despite outward appearances), shooting and passing (but not body-checking or fighting), were so well honed that his mind was left free to picture the action in several dimensions at once: where he was, where his team-mates were, where his opponents were, where the puck was, where it was going, and where everyone was going. Hockey is much easier to watch than to play, because the viewer's perspective (especially on television) is elevated, making the game unfold like a chalkboard diagram. It's so different when seen from six feet above the ice by one player in motion, but Gretzky excelled at seeing the game, in its entirety, while he was in the midst of it. Glen Sather has noted that Gretzky had the highest panic threshold of any hockey player he'd known, being able to hold onto the puck long after others would have shot or passed it. Gretzky played as if there were invisible lines of tension between himself and opposing players, as if his mind overlaid the ice with a stress map, and opposing players occupied breaking points. With or without the puck, he manipulated the space available—not only moving *into* open ice, but also creating it. He skated with a clear understanding of how his presence shifted spaces, drawing and repelling opponents. This skill is most obvious on the power play, when an attacking player tries to lure a defender out of his corner of the defensive box to create an opening for himself or a team-mate. With Gretzky, every moment of the game—at even strength, four-on-four, shorthanded and on the power play—expressed his ability to rearrange the ice to meet his needs. He didn't have to hit players or skate around them (although he certainly could) to create opportunities. He had a wonderful appreciation of what opponents were likely to do, and consequently of what he could probably make them *want* to do, to his advantage.

Gretzky's skill as a playmaker lay in his ability to lure opponents his way, then move the puck to a team-mate in scoring position with pinpoint passing. "I'm not like a Perreault or a Lafleur, where I'll skate through a whole team," he noted in the spring of 1984. "The secret to our success is moving the puck and going to the holes. If someone backs up on me, I'll keep going. If he comes at me, I'll either go around him or pass it off. When you play against our team, you can't just worry about Wayne Gretzky. Teams that worry only about me never win anything."

It has became a given that, without Wayne Gretzky, the Oilers dynasty would never have happened. In 1984, when the dynasty was scarcely under way, Glen Sather could look back on his decision to persuade Pocklington to buy Gretzky from Skalbania and confidently pinpoint the teenage acquisition as the foundation of success, both for Sather himself and for the team. "Now, when I look back, I ask myself, where would the Oilers be, where would my coaching career be, if I had been wrong about Gretzky. But I was sure I was right. He had that sparkle in his eyes where others have glass."

There is no disputing the enormous role Gretzky played in the Oilers dynasty. Yet it is worth asking not only what the Oilers would have been without Gretzky, but what Gretzky would have been without the Oilers. It might seem almost sacrilege to consider the possibility of Gretzky having turned out to be a gifted player whose potential went unrealized, but the history of the game is filled with can't-miss prospects who never lived up to expectations, and in some cases flopped altogether as professionals. Twenty years after his arrival in the NHL, it should be clear not only that the league was extraordinarily fortunate to be graced by his talent, but also that Gretzky was fortunate to have come to the major league when he did, and where he did. To understand how successful Gretzky was, it helps to appreciate how the careers of other sure bets ended in frustration.

On June 14, 1977, one year before a seventeen-year-old Gretzky signed his first professional contract with the Indianapolis Racers of the WHA, the Detroit Red Wings made twenty-year-old Dale

McCourt the first pick overall in the NHL amateur draft. It was a draft rich in talent—Mike Bossy was passed over by fourteen teams before the New York Islanders selected him, and Rod Langway, who would win two Norris Trophies with Washington, wasn't chosen until 36th (by Montreal) as the last pick in the second round.

McCourt had all the markings of a superstar for the eighties. His uncle was George Armstrong, the long-standing captain of the Toronto Maple Leafs in the 1950s and 1960s, and as such he shared both Armstrong's aboriginal heritage and his nickname "Chief." In three consecutive seasons leading up to the draft, McCourt had demonstrated tremendous ability with Hamilton and St. Catharines in the Ontario Major Junior A, scoring more than fifty goals in each campaign and setting a league scoring record with 139 points in both 1975/76 (when Hamilton won the Memorial Cup) and 1976/77. He was an OHA All Star for both campaigns, a Memorial Cup All Star and tournament MVP in 1975/76 (with twenty goals and eight assists in fourteen games), the Canadian Major Junior Player of the Year in 1977, and a member of the 1977 World Junior tournament All Star team. In the season that followed McCourt's selection by Detroit, his Junior scoring record fell to Gretzky, though while Gretzky also made the World Junior All Star team, in 1978, his Junior career with Sault Ste. Marie never took him to a Memorial Cup tournament or title.

Initially, McCourt showed every promise of fulfilling his potential in the NHL. While he did not win the Calder Trophy—Mike Bossy's fifty-three-goal performance with the Islanders saw to that— McCourt had an excellent rookie season, leading the Red Wings with thirty-three goals and thirty-nine assists and helping them reach the playoffs after a seven-season absence. On August 8, 1978, however, McCourt's career was hobbled by an off-ice setback, just as Gretzky was about to make his professional debut with Indianapolis. In a rare free-agency signing, the Red Wings had acquired goaltender Rogie Vachon from Los Angeles. As compensation, Detroit sent McCourt to the Kings.

McCourt was incensed. He had played his rookie season with the Red Wings under a one-year contract, and had just re-signed with Detroit when they flipped him to Los Angeles. Had he known general manager Ted Lindsay was going trade him he would not have signed in good faith with Detroit. Indeed, McCourt could have followed Gretzky's example and signed for big money in the WHA, and he knew this. He went to court to block his transfer to Los Angeles; to avoid a punitive anti-trust ruling, the NHL arranged to have Los Angeles trade McCourt's playing rights back to Detroit. His continued career as a Red Wing was assured, but it was a Pyrrhic victory that left him playing in a poisoned atmosphere, which did nothing to alleviate the considerable pressures he faced as a top draft pick. McCourt soldiered through three more Red Wing seasons, producing better-than-average offensive numbers (eighty-one points in 1979/80, eighty-six points in 1980/81), but as the Next Big Thing he had been eclipsed by players like Bossy and Trottier in Long Island, and Gretzky in Edmonton.

Unlike his playing rivals, McCourt was toiling in a far from enlightened or supportive environment. The Red Wings were in the last days of the Norris ownership regime, haemorrhaging money and missing the playoffs. Bobby Kromm, who had coached the stylish, European-dominated Winnipeg Jets of the WHA, lasted two seasons in Detroit before Lindsay took over the bench himself in 1979/80, and then ushered in a trail of successors through a revolving door. After Kromm took the Red Wings to the quarter-finals in 1977/78, the team went back to missing the playoffs for five consecutive seasons as Lindsay traded away young prospects for pugilistic veterans. After twenty-six games in 1981/82, McCourt was dealt to Buffalo, where Scotty Bowman was coach and general manager. At five feet, ten inches, McCourt lacked the heft and the two-way game Bowman was looking for in a power forward, and his contract was bought out by the Sabres after five games in 1983/84. He finished the season as a free agent signing with the Leafs, where his uncle worked in the front office, and then departed the NHL for a seven-season stint in Switzerland.

McCourt's true potential was forever obscured by the enmity of the court battle over the Vachon deal and the questionable management of the Red Wings organization during his unhappy tenure there. McCourt's experience in Detroit could not have differed more from Gretzky's in Edmonton, where the ownership treated him from the beginning like a national treasure, and team management, committed to a foundation of youth and high-speed scoring, built a team with his abilities in mind.

McCourt, however, was never a prospect with Gretzky's unique abilities in scoring and playmaking. Gretzky, it is easy to argue, was such an exceptional talent that he would have excelled in the NHL no matter where he ended up playing. Leaving aside how well Gretzky would have fared under Lindsay in Detroit, it is easier to understand the importance of time and place to Gretzky's stardom by looking into the past—to a predecessor who showed tantalizing suggestions of The Great One's innate skills, yet who was doomed to stumble through an entirely star-crossed career.

When asked to name a scoring star of the NHL of the 1950s, most fans will readily cite Gordie Howe (Gretzky's childhood hero), Jean Beliveau or Maurice "Rocket" Richard. They would be hard-pressed to even recognize the name Dan Lewicki. Yet Lewicki was one of the most gifted players the Canadian amateur system ever produced, a prolific scorer and intelligent playmaker. He was unfortunate, however, to have been born thirty years before Gretzky, which meant he had to seek employment in a six-team NHL that was indifferent, even hostile, to the gifts of his game.[7]

Like Gretzky, Lewicki was a teenage sensation. Growing up in the twin city of Port Arthur-Fort William (now Thunder Bay), Ontario, Lewicki was only fifteen when he began his first full season of Junior hockey, with the local Knights of Columbus club in the Thunder Bay League. In sixteen games in 1946/47, Lewicki produced a league-leading fourteen goals and eighteen points, as well as a league-leading seven goals in four playoff games. It was just the beginning of a stellar Junior career in which he routinely set the offensive pace in the regular season and the playoffs. In 1947/48, he was picked up by the Port Arthur West End Bruins for the Memorial Cup playdowns. In a hard-fought and bloody seventeen-game campaign, Lewicki's offensive output led the Bruins to the national Junior Championship, with the most goals (twenty-one) and points (forty) of any player.

By then, Lewicki had attracted the belated attention of Toronto Maple Leafs scout Squib Walker, who was based in Thunder Bay. In 1947, team impresario Conn Smythe wanted Lewicki badly enough that he agreed to pay the Providence Reds of the American Hockey League $10,000 plus the rights to Jackie Hamilton—a deal worth about $20,000 in Smythe's estimation—just to get his negotiating rights. (The Reds had acquired Lewicki's rights in 1946 when Lewicki's coach, Leo Barbini, secured them for Providence on his sixteenth birthday.) This was, at the time, one of the largest deals Smythe had ever cut for any player, amateur or professional. It can be argued that, like the Gretzky trade to Los Angeles of 1988, the Lewicki rights sale of 1947 helped establish a new threshold of player worth. In December 1948, the Reds would set an NHL record for a minor-league player deal by securing $60,000 plus the rights to Ed Kullman from the New York Rangers in exchange for defenceman Allan Stanley.

Having secured Lewicki's negotiating rights, Walker then offered Lewicki a C-form. In return for an annual signing fee (generally $100), a C-form secured an NHL club the exclusive right to call upon an amateur player to sign a professional contract at age eighteen. It was the standard recruitment tool of the Original Six era. There was no WHA, no free-spending entrepreneur offering a lucrative personal services contract in a rival league in lieu of indentured servitude in the NHL. Through Squib Walker's entreaties, Dan Lewicki became, to his everlasting misfortune, the property of the Toronto Maple Leafs.

His amateur career was marred by squabbles with Smythe over

where he would play his Junior hockey. Barbini, Lewicki's coach in Thunder Bay, had just been hired by the Stratford Kroehlers of the OHA for 1948/49, and Lewicki wanted to follow him there. The Leafs, however, wanted him to join the Toronto Marlboros. His amateur playing rights were still held by the Fort William Columbus club, and Stratford actually outbid the Leafs for his amateur services, paying Fort William $3,500 to get him. Lewicki produced forty-eight points in twenty-nine games, reinforcing his status as one of the game's brightest young prospects. Thereafter, his career was a near-endless series of controversies.

After Lewicki turned eighteen in the spring of 1949, the Leafs were positioned to execute a contractual squeeze play. While they had no legal right to force an amateur to change Junior teams, they could compel Lewicki to switch to the Marlies by enforcing the C-form and threatening to make him turn pro. This the Leafs did in August 1949, requesting Lewicki to report to their American Hockey League farm team, the Pittsburgh Hornets. They hoped Lewicki would accept the Marlies assignment as an alternative.

But Lewicki wanted neither to join the Marlies nor to report to Pittsburgh. He felt he'd been bamboozled by Squib Walker when he signed the C-form at seventeen (the age at which Wayne Gretzky signed his first professional contract with Nelson Skalbania), thinking it meant nothing more than agreeing to a tryout with the Leafs. Refusing to report to the Hornets, Lewicki was suspended by the Canadian Amateur Hockey Association for defying the C-form. After sitting out two months of hockey, Lewicki relented and signed what amounted to a one-way minor pro contract to play for the Junior Marlies. In thirty-two games in 1949/50, Lewicki racked up seventy-two points. That spring, he was added to the lineup of the Senior Marlboros, and won the national Senior title, the Allan Cup.

Interviewed by this writer nearly half a century later, Lewicki said he felt his relationship with the Maple Leafs organization never really recovered from the C-form debacle. The season after winning an

Allan Cup, Lewicki was a Maple Leaf. After a modest start to his NHL career (thirty-four points in sixty-one games), Lewicki appeared in nine playoff games nursing an injured knee. Assigned to a checking role, he didn't record a single point as the Leafs defeated the Canadiens for the Stanley Cup. In four seasons, Dan Lewicki had managed to win three major hockey championships: the Memorial, Allan and Stanley cups. He was twenty years old, and his career was about to nosedive.

Lewicki was more than a highly promising prospect whose professional misadventures invite comparison with the smooth ascent of Gretzky. One can also argue that he was to a substantial degree the Gretzky of his day in actual playing style. Lewicki was said by teammates to think his way around the rink, and to this writer Lewicki equated the game with chess in terms of its positional strategy. These echoes of Gretzky's visualization of the game have not gone unnoticed. Ted Kennedy, captain of the Leafs during Lewicki's troubled tenure with the team, is explicit about the parallel skills of the two men who were separated by several decades. "Danny was a very talented hockey player," Kennedy told this writer. "He wasn't very big, you know, and in the rough going he wasn't at his best. But in this era, he'd be as effective around the net as Gretzky. He was that talented. Offensively tremendous, but in playing for the Leafs then you had to be a two-way player."

Lewicki came to the Leafs when the NHL played a tough, close-checking game, in which every man fought his own fights—and there were many, complete with bench-clearing brawls. There were no enforcers, no one like a Marty McSorley to ride shotgun for the team's offensive star. The choreography of play had not been liberalized by the influence of the European game. Goaltenders weren't supposed to leave their crease, defencemen weren't supposed to cross their own blueline, and wingers were supposed to skate ruts up and down one side of the ice—joining in on a rush, then picking up their check on the way back. No criss-crossing, no drop passes. No chess. The game was a low-scoring one: teams averaged about 2.5 goals per game, compared to about 4.0 in Gretzky's heyday. The league did not have twenty-one teams and a diluted talent pool. It had six teams, about a hundred starting jobs, a rigid mindset about how the game was played, and, without a players' union, a tight grip exercised by the coaches and general managers on who got to play in it.

In 1951/52, Lewicki made a cardinal error for a Maple Leaf. He got married in midseason. In a team run on regimental lines by Smythe, marriage at any time was an annoyance. In midseason, it was a guaranteed ticket to the minors. Lewicki was banished to Pittsburgh. In 1952/53 and 1953/54, he resurfaced for a total of eleven Toronto games. Even though he managed a goal and three assists in just four appearances in 1952/53, even though the Leafs were beginning to slide in the standings, Lewicki was kept down on the farm. Finally, Smythe sold Lewicki's contract to the New York Rangers.

There followed one brief, bright glimpse of the star that could have been. After being shut out of the NHL for the better part of two seasons by the Leafs, with the Rangers Lewicki was suddenly a star. He finished 10th in the NHL scoring race, with the fifth-highest number of goals (twenty-nine), as many as Gordie Howe produced. He outscored every Maple Leaf but Sid Smith, who was the only left winger in the league to score more goals than him. The performance earned him the second All Star team berth, behind Smith on the first team. And by doing it all with only eight penalty minutes, he was runner-up to Smith in Lady Byng voting.

Lewicki's resurgence after several seasons in the Maple Leaf doghouse was regrettably short. Phil Watson arrived as the new coach of the Rangers for 1955/56, and the two men could not see eye to eye on how a left winger was supposed to do his job. Watson was an old-school ruts man, and over the next few seasons under Watson, Lewicki's scoring stats steadily eroded. He was finally claimed in the 1958 intra-league draft by Chicago, where he says he earned the wrath of management by advising rookie Stan Mikita to ask for a scoring bonus in his contract. The Blackhawks didn't even ask him back for 1959/60, and sent his rights to Montreal. Four seasons in the American league rounded out his playing career. After trying his hand at coaching Junior hockey in Hamilton for one season, he gave up the game entirely and embarked on a new career selling auto parts.

The history of the game is rife with stories of talents who were derailed by the vicious politics of league owners, particularly of talents who were deliberately buried in the minors and never came up for air. Not everyone subscribes to these stories. Dick Duff, best remembered for his six Stanley Cup wins with Toronto and Montreal in the 1960s, has a succinct way of sweeping away the might-have-been lore: "Everyone who should have made it, made it." Still, the Lewicki saga is a "There but for the grace of God" warning to those who feel great careers are preordained for great talents. There is certainly little doubt that, had Wayne Gretzky come of age in the late 1940s instead of the late 1970s, an NHL career might not have been a sure thing. Billy Harris, who played for Conn Smythe as a Maple Leaf in the late 1950s and early 1960s, and who coached Gretzky as an assistant with Edmonton in the early 1980s, has said to this writer, "Gretzky would have driven Conn Smythe nuts." One is tempted to play a parlour game of swapped lives. Had Gretzky been born in 1931, not 1961, would he have found his playing genius thwarted by the rigidity and mendacity of the 1950s NHL? And had Lewicki been born in 1961, not 1931, might he have found himself hoisting the Stanley Cup four times in the 1980s?

It is hardly fair to Gretzky to temper the enormous successes he deservedly enjoyed in the 1980s and 1990s with speculation that he might have failed utterly at the game in the 1950s. Yet at the least we should appreciate the fact that talent itself must be properly appreciated, and exploited, for it to find success. And in Edmonton, in Glen Sather, Gretzky found a coach and manager who was not only smart enough to let him play the way he knew best, but was willing to shape an entire team lineup around the kind of game Gretzky made possible.

PART Two

CHAPTER SIX

THE NHL OILERS were an instant hit in Edmonton. Playing to sellout crowds of 15,423 at Northlands, with the highest ticket prices in the league (an average of $10.12), the Oilers finished second to the New York Rangers in gate revenue for 1979/80, and would pass them the next season as 1,500 new seats were added to the Coliseum. The Oilers might have won the gate-revenue race in 1979/80 had the team been able to sell concourse box seats, but a dispute between Pocklington and Northlands left them empty for the season. The regular-season gate was worth more than $6 million, and the Oilers provided what turned out to be a one-game bonus at Northlands in qualifying for the postseason. The 1979 expansion plan had called for sixteen of twenty-one teams to advance to the playoffs, and the Oilers squeezed into the final spot, with twenty-eight wins. They were paired in the preliminary round with the first-place Philadelphia Flyers, who had gone a record thirty-five games without a loss that season. The Oilers twice extended Philadelphia into overtime, but were swept 3-0. The Flyers went on to lose the Stanley Cup finals to the New York Islanders.

Despite the club's apparent success at the gate, Pocklington asserted that he had lost $750,000. "I've owned this club for five years, and we've lost money every single year," he said. "This past year, our costs were $7 million." Pocklington pegged his operating costs at $4.5

million. "It cost another million for rent. Another $400,000 for league dues. The rest of the costs include the front office, public relations, advertising and World Hockey Association cleanup." He placed his total investment in the Oilers to date at $14 million.

"I should make money for the first time next year," he proposed. "I think I have a right to break even and maybe even shoot for the moon and try to make whatever the interest rate happens to be as a profit. I'm not saying I'm going to. I want to have a team that's still in the Stanley Cup playoffs in May, and I'm going to spend money until I get one. I think the fans know that."

Still, Pocklington chafed at the wages his players commanded. "We've got ridiculous salaries," he complained, calling Pat Price's US$120,000 salary "insanity." In March 1981, Sather would trade Price to Pittsburgh to get back Pat Hughes, whom he'd lost in the 1979 reclamation draft. Pocklington's umbrage over player costs did not prevent him from lavishing attention on his young star, Wayne Gretzky, as he rewarded him for his rookie NHL season with a black Porsche. (The NHL, however, decided he wasn't really a rookie, having played in the WHA, and ruled him ineligible for the Calder Trophy, which went to Boston's Ray Bourque.) The Great One had rapidly deflected most criticism that he couldn't stand up to the rigours of the NHL. Only nineteen years old, he would have won the Art Ross Trophy as the league's leading scorer on his first try, had Marcel Dionne of the Los Angeles Kings not outscored him, fifty-three to fifty-one, as they finished tied on points, with 137. Leading the league with eighty-six assists (he tied Bill Taylor's 1947 record for most assists in one game, seven, in an 8-2 defeat of Washington at Northlands on February 15), Gretzky won the Hart Trophy as the player most valuable to his team—his first of eight consecutive wins. He also earned the Lady Byng as the league's most gentlemanly player, and made the first of seven consecutive All Star game appearances. Only Mario Lemieux would interrupt his string of MVP and All Star accolades in the 1980s, in 1986/87. Off the ice, Gretzky worked tirelessly to promote the team and himself, making weekly appearances in Edmonton at banquets and shopping malls, and appearing at charity golf tournaments in the off-season.

After Gretzky, Peter Pocklington's most important hockey asset was Glen Sather. It was clear that Larry Gordon's long-term prospects as team general manager were not high, and Gordon deftly removed himself from Sather's career path in the fall of 1979 by telling Pocklington he would buy the Wichita Wind of the Central league if the Oilers transferred their sponsorship there from Houston. Pocklington agreed, and after the 1979/80 season Sather was given complete control of the Oilers as coach, general manager and president. It was suggested in the press that Sather could earn more than $200,000 in 1980/81 if the Oilers met a number of performance criteria.

"I admit he's being very highly paid," said Pocklington. "But I think I've got the right guy for the job. I think he's one of the greatest guys in hockey. I love him. I'm convinced he'll do a better job as general manager than Larry, although I don't mean that as a knock on Larry. And he's a president because that's the way I run my businesses. I find a first rate young man, give him a couple of years to learn the ropes and make him a president." He predicted Sather would "bring the Stanley Cup to Edmonton within five years."

Getting to the Cup finals would require more than routine superlative seasons from Gretzky. Sather already had a few key components. Kevin Lowe, who roomed with Gretzky, lived up to his reputation as an opening-round pick. Messier, the gamble at 48th, was problematic, but had huge potential. Represented in salary negotiations by his father, Doug, Messier was late for his first Oilers training camp as he held out for an escalating contract that paid him about $70,000. He missed a flight to St. Louis in late October, and Sather punished him with a demotion to Houston in the Central league. He had no business being there. After four games, in which he picked up three assists, it was plain he belonged in the NHL, however raw his talent. Sather brought him back, and he recorded twelve goals and twenty-one assists, with 120 penalty minutes. "Sometimes you'd see him on the ice and you'd think his mind was at Newport Beach watching the waves come in," is how Sather would describe Messier in those first seasons as an Oiler.

The real find in the 1979 draft appeared to be Glenn Anderson. His play in the Canadian Olympic team program so impressed scouts in the season following his selection by the Oilers that Sather was regularly fielding offers to cut trade deals for him. Sather tried to convince Anderson to join the Oilers for the end of the 1979/80 season, after the Olympic Games, at which Anderson produced two goals and two assists in six games as the Canadian team finished sixth. But Anderson insisted on maintaining his commitment to the national team program and went to a tournament in Europe instead. He would, however, join the Oilers for 1980/81.

To create a winning lineup, Sather needed more strong performances at the entry draft. Having finished 16th in 1979/80, the Oilers had a much better selection position than in 1979. They could now pick sixth in every round, although they had dealt away their second-round pick to Montreal in 1979 to get Dave Lumley and Dan Newman. Edmonton would choose sixth overall, then 48th, and on down the draft.

After the surviving WHA clubs were folded into the NHL, the first few years of the new NHL entry draft provided opportunities and challenges that would never be seen again. For a few precious years, it was possible for a team not only to do well in the critical first two rounds of selection, but to score with deep picks as their scouting staff explored largely untapped international resources. No team fared better in these early drafts than the Edmonton Oilers. By the same token, few teams did as poorly in the draft as the Oilers in the late 1980s, once the draft pool and improved scouting efforts reduced long-shot opportunities.

The major factors in draft dynamics in the early 1980s were the size of the draft pool, the number of participating teams, the quality of their scouting programs, their prejudices with regard to talent sources, the decreasing age of draftees, and the willingness of teams to commit draft picks to Eastern bloc players who would have to defect to join the lineup.

The 1980 draft saw the eligibility age drop to eighteen, which made the talent pool deeper at the same time that it was getting wider. It also made the talent pool more unpredictable. An eighteen-year-old's talents are still developing, and scouting staffs were now being asked to make draft selection commitments with teens whose ability to play professionally (whether in one year or five) was far from assured. General managers were learning that the U.S. college system (many of whose prospects were Canadians playing on scholarship) was a legitimate source of new talent. Edmonton had helped prove this with the selection of Anderson, who had spent a year at the University of Denver. With the drop in draft age, another American player source came on stream: the powerful high school programs in hockey hotbeds like New England and Minnesota.

Overseas, the Scandinavian and Eastern bloc countries provided unique drafting challenges. Overwhelmingly, Sweden was considered the best source of European players. It had a highly regarded national team program and professional league. Neighbouring Finland was a conundrum. The country showed flashes of brilliance in international play, but generally lagged behind the Soviet Union, Czechoslovakia and Sweden in tournament results. A few Finns had made it into the WHA and NHL, but there was little excitement among NHL general managers for the country's young players.

The Soviet Union and Czechoslovakia had many excellent players, but they were stuck behind the Iron Curtain. Older players whose best years were behind them were occasionally allowed to leave to play in the West, but getting a young player without him defecting was impossible. Teams interested in these players from communist countries either had to be prepared to engage in international intrigue and help arrange a defection,[1] or use a late draft pick to secure a player's rights and hope that the Eastern bloc collapsed or the player made it to the West under his own initiative.

All of these factors created unprecedented risk at the draft, but also unprecedented opportunity. The notion that the best players would be snapped up in the first two rounds would be firmly refuted. For the first few seasons after the 1979 expansion, teams who scouted off the beaten track and played long-shot hunches could find themselves not only with capable journeymen, but with outright stars.

The Oilers paid no real attention to the American high school talent pool, and made minimal efforts to secure American collegiate players after Anderson's selection (which had been due more to the fact that chief scout Barry Fraser was able to study him closely at the Canadian national team camp in Calgary than to the fact that he had attended the University of Denver). Fraser criss-crossed North America, sussing out the Canadian Junior system, which in the late 1970s had begun to expand into cities in the American west.

While centre Doug Wickenheiser was chosen first overall by Montreal, six of the first eight selections in the 1980 draft were defencemen, and Sather (along with 2,500 spectators at the Montreal Forum in the NHL's first entry draft open to public) watched as Winnipeg took Dave Babych second, Los Angeles took Larry Murphy fourth (after Chicago took centre Denis Savard third), and Washington chose Darren Veitch fifth. At sixth, Sather selected Paul Coffey of the Kitchener Rangers.

Coffey had just turned nineteen on June 1, and so qualified as an "underage" Junior—a draft-eligible player who was still of Junior age. With Canadian Junior leagues disturbed by the number of young players being taken from their rosters before they turned twenty-one, the NHL agreed that any underage Junior drafted who did not make the cut at the NHL team's training camp that fall would be returned to his Junior team rather than being sent to the minors. Though he had played only two seasons of Junior hockey, Coffey would not be going back to Kitchener. In his first Junior season, with Gretzky's old Sault

Ste. Marie Greyhounds, Coffey had produced eighty-nine points. Switching to Kitchener early in 1979/80, Coffey completed the season with 102 points and a spot on the league's second All Star team.

Like Glenn Anderson, Coffey had speed and size, standing over six feet tall. He derived his powerful strides from an unusual strategy of sharpening his skate blades flat, like those of a goaltender. He precisely fit the bill for an offensive defenceman on the up-tempo team Sather was striving to create. He was Sather's answer to Sinden's Orr, and although he had a tentative rookie season, with thirty-two points, he was going to become the highest-scoring defenceman in league history. In that first NHL season, he caught the eye of Buffalo general manager Scotty Bowman, who tried to make a trade for him. Sather declined. Like Anderson, Coffey was a keeper.

After having to sit out the draft's second round, the Oilers next picked in the third round, at 48th. It was still possible to find quality players well into the fourth, fifth and sixth rounds, but in the third round the Oilers missed the mark with right winger Shawn Babcock, who never made the NHL, while the next nine selections did. Nine picks after the Oilers took Babcock, the Blackhawks took Troy Murray of Doug Messier's St. Albert Saints, right out from under Sather's nose. The centreman joined the Blackhawks after two seasons at the University of North Dakota, and managed a 915-game NHL career, during which he won the Frank J. Selke Trophy as the league's top defensive forward.

The Oilers redeemed themselves in the fourth round, with the 69th pick. Barry Fraser wanted to try their luck with the Finnish talent pool. Only a dozen Finns had been picked since the NHL's universal draft was introduced in 1969, and none at all had been chosen in 1979, or up to this point in the 1980 draft. Fraser was ready to pick one by the fourth round. He had first seen Jari Kurri play at age seventeen in 1978, while scouting overseas for the Houston Aeros. Already starring in the Finnish Elite League for Jokerit Helsinki, Kurri was a member of the Finnish team at the 1978 European Junior

Championships, and was named best forward of the tournament after scoring in overtime to upset the U.S.S.R. in the Championship game.

At the 1979 World Junior tournament in Karlstad, Sweden, Kurri was a standout, along with Reijo Ruotsalainen, on the fourth-place Finnish team. Fraser visited with Kurri over Christmas 1979 and asked him to keep his playing options open. The Finns were beginning to assemble their team for the 1980 Olympics, and Kurri was a natural candidate. Fraser wanted to choose him in the 1980 draft, and bring him to North America. By the time Kurri became available in the draft, he had won a silver medal at the 1980 World Junior Championships, with eleven points in the tournament, and was edged out by the Soviet Union's Vladimir Krutov (who also had eleven 11 points to tie Kurri for the scoring lead) in voting for the best forward. Kurri's team-mates, Ruotsalainen and Jari Paavola, were named the tournament's top defenceman and goaltender. At the Olympics in Lake Placid, Kurri and his fellow Finns finished fourth.

"We could never have waited until the fourth round [of the 1980 draft] if everybody had known what we knew, that he'd come to the NHL right away," Fraser reflected on Kurri in 1983. "He'd have gone real high."

After the Oilers took Kurri 69th, they ignored Ruotsalainen and Paavola. The Oilers' next pick was at 90th. At 89th, Washington took Timo Blomqvist, a nineteen-year-old defenceman who had been Kurri's team-mate on Jokerit Helsinki and had played in the last two World Junior tournaments. Then came Edmonton's selection of Walt Poddubny, a left winger with the Kingston Canadians who would get a four-game callup from Wichita in 1981/82 before being traded to Toronto in March 1982, along with minor pro Phil Drouillard, for Laurie Boschman.

Ruotsalainen was still available when Edmonton picked next, at 111th. The Oilers went for Mike Winther, a centre with the Brandon Wheat Kings who never made the NHL. Eight picks later, the Rangers spoke for Ruotsalainen. Edmonton would end up making a trade for

Kurri's old team-mate in 1986. (Paavola went 146th, to Buffalo, but never played in the NHL.)

As the draft moved into the hundreds, opportunities thinned considerably, but they still were there. Right after the Rangers claimed Ruotsalainen, Chicago found right winger Steve Larmer of the Niagara Falls Flyers, who went on to play more than 1,000 NHL games. At 128th, Winnipeg took right winger Brian Mullen, a member of the U.S. Junior team, who played more than 800 games. And at 132nd, the Oilers chose goaltender Andy Moog.

Halfway through the Oilers' first NHL season, Dave Dryden, who had played his first professional game in 1961/62, hung up his goaltending equipment, leaving the net to Ed Mio; in March, Sather traded captain Ron Chipperfield to Quebec to get another starting netminder, Ron Low. Dryden was given a scouting job, and went looking at teenage goaltenders. One of them was Grant Fuhr, then seventeen and playing for the Victoria Cougars. The other was Andy Moog, who was from Penticton, B.C., and whose father had been the backup goaltender for the Penticton Vs when they won the World Championship for Canada in 1955.

Moog was a second-team All Star with the Bighorns of Billings, Montana, in the Western Hockey League, as the Western Canadian Junior game was now known. Players like Moog had gone to the United States to play their Junior hockey because the Western Canadian Junior game was going south. Four teams had recently relocated to the United States. Calgary had lost its team to Billings, the Kamloops franchise went to Seattle and Edmonton twice lost the Oil Kings. Struggling in the shadow of the WHA Oilers, the Oil Kings had first left town in 1976 to become the Portland Winter Hawks (with whom Mark Messier made his 1977/78 playoff appearance). Billy Hunter participated in a revival of the Oil Kings for 1978/79 at his Edmonton Gardens, serving as president of a local investment group, but the Oil Kings lost $100,000 after attracting an average of 500 fans per game, and were sold to a Portland group that wanted to put the team in Great Falls, Montana.

Playing in the unlikely location of Billings, Moog impressed both Dryden and Barry Fraser. The Oilers made him their sixth pick of the draft, and with their seventh, at 153rd, chose another goaltender, Rob Polman Tuin of Michigan Tech. Polman Tuin never made the Oilers, but Moog, as late a pick as he was, soon provided an unexpected injection of youthful skill in the Edmonton crease.

With their last pick, at 174th, the Oilers narrowly missed a keeper. Looking to Sweden, they took defenceman Lars-Gunnar Petterson. Petterson never played, but one pick later the Vancouver Canucks took another Swede, centre Patrik Sundstrom, who would log more than nine seasons in the NHL.

As in 1979, the Oilers had turned in a hit and miss performance at the draft, in which the misses were tolerable and the hits were spectacular. With selections like Coffey, Kurri and Moog, no one need dwell on the fact that the Oilers took a Petterson when they could have had a Sundstrom.

Coffey was expected to go high in the draft and Moog was a smart pick, but it was Kurri, taken relatively late, who was the wondrous selection. His dad was part-owner of a gas station in Helsinki, so it was fitting that the youth was going to play professional hockey in a Canadian oil town. One of the challenges in drafting Scandinavian players was to actually convince them to leave home and try the NHL grind. Thinking he would give the NHL two years, Kurri signed a one-year contract with an option year. He spoke hardly a word of English when he arrived in the fall of 1980, but he learned quickly. Kurri was joined on the Oilers by a free agent signing, twenty-six-year-old Matti Hagman, one of those rare early Finnish draft picks when selected 106th overall by Boston in 1975. The centre from Helsinki gave Sinden's Bruins a try for a season and a half in 1976/77 and 1977/78 before being sold to the WHA's Nordiques, for whom he produced fifty-six points in fifty-three games. He returned to Finland for the next two seasons, and gave the Oilers two more before heading back to Finland for a career that lasted another decade.

The Oilers that Kurri and Hagman joined were struggling to improve on their first NHL season. With his new responsibilities as general manager and team president, Glen Sather didn't think he could keep coaching. Like Scotty Bowman, who was wearing all the hats in Buffalo, Sather wanted to be replaced on the bench for 1980/81. With the Sabres, Bowman tried Roger Neilson for the entire season before taking the coaching job back. Sather's attempt to delegate was more short-lived. He promoted his old friend, assistant coach Bryan Watson, and it proved to be a mistake. Over eighteen games, the Oilers won four, lost nine and tied five. Sather made a painful but necessary decision and fired Watson, returning to the bench himself.

In December 1980, the newly arrived Kurri solved a major problem for Sather: finding a winger for Gretzky who could cover for him defensively, and make plays and score goals with him. When he put them together, they clicked almost immediately. In his first NHL season, Kurri scored thirty-two goals, with forty-three assists. His plus-minus of +26 was outstanding on a team that scored only one more goal than it allowed over the season. Gretzky reached new heights. His own plus-minus, which was +15 in his rookie season, reached +41 as he scored fifty-five goals, had a league-leading 109 assists and won the scoring title with 164 points. His season represented the highest points-per-game production (2.05) in league history, and the Canadian Press chose him as Canada's Male Athlete of the Year.

The Oilers were only slightly better in their second NHL campaign —twenty-nine wins versus twenty-eight in 1979/80, with seventy-four points versus sixty-nine, which moved them from 16th to 14th overall. But the Oilers at season's end were a team ready to move to the next level. Andy Moog, who had been called up from Wichita for only seven regular-season games, rose to the occasion of the playoffs, starting every game for the Oilers. Paul Coffey came through with seven points, as did Messier, whose offensive production had improved to sixty-three points in the regular season but had been a defensive liability with a -12 rating. A so-called second-line right winger, Glenn Anderson produced twelve playoff points, including three power-play goals. After shocking third-place Montreal with a three-game sweep in the opening round, the Oilers put up a stiff fight against the Islanders, the defending Cup champions. The Islanders won in six, but as they advanced, they could see a future threat awaiting them.

I F YOU MAKE as many rapid-fire deals as Nelson Skalbania did, a few are bound to backfire, or leave you to rue your decision to buy—or to sell. By his own admission, Skalbania in most deals was selling something before he'd finished buying it. The master of the quick flip had flipped his way right out of what proved to be two enviable properties: the Edmonton Oilers and Wayne Gretzky.

As the Oilers and their young superstar became the toast of Canadian sport, Skalbania made an aggressive return to sports invest-ment. He bought Junior hockey's New Westminster Bruins in 1980 after the team logged a 10-61-1 record. When the team won only sev-enteen games in 1980/81 and missed the playoffs, Skalbania made a customary run for the exit, selling it to Pocklington. Pocklington kept 70 percent of the equity and sold the rest to a group of local business-men, while the team was relocated in Kamloops and renamed the Junior Oilers. (He would keep the team until 1984.) Skalbania was far from finished. Between 1980 and 1981, he also bought baseball's AAA Vancouver Canadians with Jim Pattison, the CFL's Montreal Alouettes, and the North American Soccer League's Memphis Rogues (which he moved to Calgary and renamed the Boomers); above all, he partici-pated—some say meddled—in the arrival of NHL hockey in Calgary.

Skalbania horned in on a deal already under way to buy the Atlanta Flames and move them to Calgary. Local businessmen Doc and B.J. Seaman and Harley Hotchkiss were negotiating to buy and move the Flames when Skalbania crashed the party, waving more money around than anyone could imagine or match. He had presold

THE GLORY BARONS

the local television rights to Molson ($6 million for ten years) and made what was then a record and outlandish offer of $16 million for the team—manna from heaven for principal owner Tom Cousins, who had been prepared to give away the money-losing operation to anyone who would keep it in Atlanta. A rift opened between Skalbania and the Calgary group that had been pursuing the team, and Skalbania brought in Norman Green as an investor and intermediary. Skalbania ended up with half the team, the Calgary investors with the other half. After the Flames' first season in Calgary, 1980/81, Skalbania was bought out in a two-step deal. For 1981/82, as the league adopted an unbalanced schedule with an emphasis on divisional play, the Flames were moved into the Smythe Division with the Oilers, and the foundations of the Battle of Alberta were set.

While Skalbania was on his franchise acquisition binge, Pocklington was making every effort to keep pace. In addition to his Junior hockey investment picked up from Skalbania, he bought the Oakland Stompers' NASL franchise and turned it into the Edmonton Drillers, and brought AAA baseball to Edmonton by acquiring the Pacific Coast League's defunct Ogden, Utah franchise, renaming it the Trappers. He also diversified his investments, making two fateful moves. In late 1979, he went after Winnipeg-based Fidelity Trust, the largest trust company in western Canada. The Canadian Deposit Insurance Corporation allowed as much as 10 percent of a trust company's capital reserves to be held in real estate, and, because there were tax advantages to trust ownership, Pocklington acquired Fidelity for $25 million and folded into it his Patrician Land Corporation Ltd. He also went into the meat packing business, first acquiring Gainers in 1978 from Ben Torchinsky of Agra Industries in Saskatoon, swapping him 550 apartment units under construction in Calgary for the beef and hog processing business. Then he swallowed the Canadian operations of Chicago-based Swift and Company (which he folded into Gainers) for $50 million, using money borrowed from Canadian Commercial Bank and some Ontario pension funds.

119

Pocklington had realized that Swift's Edmonton hog processing operation was underpriced because its valuation didn't reflect the land the
plant sat on. He sold the property to Alberta Housing, and built a new
plant on cheaper land in Edmonton. But what seemed like good deals
at the time—the Fidelity Trust takeover and the venture into hog processing—proved fundamental to Pocklington's eventual downfall. As
the fortunes of his Oilers began to soar, Pocklington's began to dip,
and at some point their trajectories were doomed to cross, and knock
the Oilers out of the sky.

AFTER SATHER returned to coaching and the 1980/81 season was
over, he still didn't have the staff he wanted. He had tried different
assistant coaches: Bryan Watson, Dave Dryden, Billy Harris. Dryden
left and tried his hand at Junior coaching in Ontario before becoming
a high school principal. Harris would be dropped by Sather, and
left on bitter terms. The former utility forward for the Stanley Cup-
winning Maple Leafs of the 1960s was a soft-spoken gentleman, a stylish player in his day, who would have been better off playing in the
1980s than the 1960s. He had coached in the WHA (he was in charge
of the All Star squad that played the Soviets in 1974), as well as
coaching the Swedish national team at the World Championship
and Olympic level. Harris understood what Sather was trying to
accomplish with the run-and-gun Oilers, but Sather would let Harris
go before he got to see the Oilers reach the finals.

Sather got pointed in the right direction in the summer of 1981,
when he made the surprising choice of Ted Green as an assistant
coach to work alongside Harris. Green had been a stalwart blueliner
with the Bruins in the 1960s, playing under Sinden and with Sather.
He may have been best known for losing a horrifying stick-swinging
duel with Chicago's Wayne Maki in a preseason exhibition game in
Ottawa in 1969. The fractured skull Green suffered required a steel
plate to repair, and kept him out of hockey for Boston's 1969/70

Stanley Cup-winning season. After returning to the lineup and winning the Cup in 1971/72, Green made the jump to the new WHA. After three seasons in New England, he was traded in May 1975 to Winnipeg, where he played out his career in 1978/79.

Green returned home to Manitoba to run a hotel in Carmen, and found himself gravitating toward coaching. He took on the Carmen Beavers, an Intermediate team, and they won the provincial championship in 1980/81. That was all the coaching experience Green had when Sather vaulted him into the ranks of NHL professionals.

"Our hockey club doesn't have a winning heritage," Sather explained. "We need somebody to tell the kids what it takes, the sacrifices that have to be made in order to win." Green had done it all. Picked up from the St. Boniface Canadians for the 1958/59 playoffs, he won a Memorial Cup with the Winnipeg Braves. After his Stanley Cup win with Boston in 1971/72, he won the WHA's Avco Cup with both the Whalers and the Jets.

It was Green's experience with the Jets that may have sealed his hiring in Sather's mind, for in Winnipeg Green had played the high-flying offensive game Sather so admired. More importantly, he had been a dependable blueliner, tending to defensive duties on a team that prioritized goal scoring. He was the right person to instil some defensive discipline.

THE OILERS were well positioned for the 1981 amateur draft. Their impressive playoff performance against the Canadiens and Islanders showed the team's enormous potential, but having finished only 14th overall in the twenty-one-team league, they got another shot at the draft pool with a high pick. In picking up Don "Murder" Murdoch (Mark Messier's cousin) from the Rangers in March 1980, the Oilers had surrendered Cam Connor and the third-round pick[2] in 1981. But they still had their picks in the other rounds, as well as the sixth-round pick acquired from Toronto in 1979 for Reg Thomas.

The draft was spotty this year. Six first-round picks in 1981 would play one season or less in the NHL, although the first dozen chosen would all have long careers. The Oilers risked their opening-round selection being a washout by using it for a goaltender.

Several very good goaltenders were available in the 1981 draft, but they went relatively late in the proceedings. Mike Vernon wasn't spoken for by Calgary until 56th, and the Rangers waited until the 72nd pick before choosing John Vanbiesbrouck. But rather than take Vernon or Vanbiesbrouck, Minnesota and Montreal had used the 31st and 32nd picks in the second round to get netminders Mike Sands and Lars Eriksson.

Mike and Lars who? This was precisely the problem with drafting goaltenders high. Among all players, their professional potential was the hardest to read, and the lowering of the draft age to eighteen only made it harder. Goaltenders got better as they got older, and many great netminders in their formative years were drafted deep or not at all, left unprotected in an intra-league or expansion draft, or signed as free agents out of college.[3] If asked where great goaltenders came from, an honest general manager would confess: no one knew. It was one of the lesser yet more persistent mysteries of the cosmos.

In 1981, no goaltender had been chosen in the first round of the draft since 1975. The reason was sometimes called the Martyniuk Syndrome, in honour of Ray Martyniuk, who was the netminder for the Flin Flon Bombers when Bobby Clarke played with them. Martyniuk was the fifth pick overall in the 1970 draft by Montreal, but he never made the NHL. Thereafter, it has been said, general managers were leery of squandering a first-round pick on a goaltender.[4]

The most promising goaltenders became at best second-round selections who went in the thirties. Detroit took Al Jensen 31st in 1978. In 1979, Atlanta took Pat Riggin 33rd and the Flyers chose Pelle Lindbergh 35th. And in 1980, Don Beaupre went 37th to Minnesota and Kelly Hrudey was selected 38th by the Islanders.

Thus, the Oilers' decision to use the eighth pick overall for a goaltender in 1981 was a daring one. But if they didn't take him then, they would have to wait until 29th, in the second round, and Sather didn't think he'd last that long.

Grant Fuhr had been studied long and hard by the Oilers. He'd grown up just outside Edmonton, in Spruce Grove, and while playing Pee Wee there he was coached by former NHL netminding great Glenn Hall, who saw poise and skill before Fuhr was even a teenager. Fuhr moved to Victoria at seventeen in 1979 to play Major Junior A for the Cougars. He was the WHL's first-team All Star in 1979/80 and 1980/81, and in 1980/81 led the league in shutouts and goals against in the regular season and the playoffs, as the Cougars won the WHL title. Scouts talked him up as the greatest Junior netminding prospect since Bernie Parent in the mid-1960s. Edmonton's second-round pick, at 29th, Saskatoon left winger Todd Strueby, only played five NHL games. With the 30th pick, the Rangers secured Sweden's Jan Erixon, who played more than 500 games.

At last, a first-round goaltending pick wouldn't prove a letdown. Though only nineteen at the start of the 1981/82 season, Fuhr was so impressive in training camp that he knocked Andy Moog right back to Wichita in the Central league as Low stuck around to relieve Fuhr for twenty-nine games.

The 71st pick got the Oilers right winger Paul Houck, who began four years at the University of Wisconsin after being selected. Though Houck never played for the team, he was the beginning of a chain of trades that greatly increased the Oilers' manpower. Sather swapped his rights for Minnesota goaltender Gilles Meloche on May 31, 1985. On September 11, 1985, Sather flipped Meloche to Pittsburgh for three players: Marty McSorley, Tim Hrynewich and Craig Muni (a future consideration fulfilled in October 1986). And while Phil Drouillard, chosen 92nd, didn't make the NHL, he helped Sather get Laurie Boschman the following spring. The 111th pick (the sixth-round selection acquired from Toronto for Reg Thomas in 1979) reeled in a prize, as defenceman Steve Smith was taken from the London

Knights. At 155th, the Oilers had a curious miss, given their interest in Finnish talent. They took Kelowna defenceman Mike Sturgeon, who didn't reach the NHL, leaving Vancouver free two picks later to select Finnish left winger Petri Skriko, who went on to play 541 NHL games and produce more than sixty points in four seasons, as well as representing Finland in two Canada Cup tournaments, two Olympic Games and three World Championships.

Edmonton's eighth pick, at 176th, was a calculated longshot. Czechoslovakia's Miloslav Horava, not yet twenty, made the All Star team and was voted top defenceman at the 1981 World Junior tournament, but he was untouchable so long as the Eastern bloc was intact. Sather would throw his rights into the 1986 deal that got the Oilers Reijo Ruotsalainen, and Horava joined the Rangers late in 1988/89 as the Cold War thawed. The last Oiler pick, at 197th, was Gord Sherven of Saskatchewan's Weyburn Red Wings, who was about to begin playing at the University of North Dakota. He played intermittently with Edmonton, Minnesota and Hartford before taking his game to Germany in 1988 for almost a decade.

With the 1981 draft, Glen Sather had completed the nucleus of his eighties dynasty and found a few players who proved to be lucrative trade bait. Having come into the league with Gretzky, he had added, with three successive inspired drafts, the lead dogs of the team—the ones he would refer to in 1986 as "untouchables," the players he would never trade. Joining Gretzky in this elite circle were Glenn Anderson, Mark Messier, Kevin Lowe, Paul Coffey, Jari Kurri and Grant Fuhr, with Moog an unexpected bonus. In the season that followed the drafting of Fuhr and the hiring of Ted Green, the team coalesced. Anderson's points production went from fifty-three to 105, Messier's from sixty-three to eighty-eight as he scored fifty goals, Coffey's from thirty-two to eighty-nine as he produced sixty assists. Lowe, in a more defensive role, still produced forty points, with a plus-minus of +46. Kurri, who had already impressed with seventy-five points in 1980/81, reached eighty-six. And Gretzky laid waste the record book. He reached the fifty-goal plateau in thirty-nine games, faster than any player in NHL history, with an empty-net goal against Philadelphia on December 30, 1981. He led the league with a record ninety-two goals, a record 120 assists, a record 212 points. Where Gretzky had been the only Oiler on the All Star team in the previous two seasons, there were now four: Gretzky and Messier on the first team, Fuhr and Coffey on the second team. Fuhr was passed over in Calder voting but was runner-up to Billy Smith in polling for the Vezina.[5] Gretzky won the Art Ross, the Hart and the Pearson, the MVP award voted on by NHLPA members. In Gretzky's first two seasons in the league, his peers had chosen first Marcel Dionne and then Mike Liut for the award. The Pearson would belong to Gretzky for the next four seasons.

And the team went from winning twenty-nine games to winning forty-eight, from finishing fourth in the Smythe Division to first, from 14th in the league to second, behind the Islanders. They became the first team to score more than 400 goals, with 417, and their goals against dropped from 327 to a respectable 295.

But when they advanced to the playoffs and in the opening round met the Los Angeles Kings, the fourth-place team in their division, a team that had won half as many games, scored 103 fewer goals and allowed seventy-four more, the Oilers lost. In six nightmarish days in April they lost three games to a vastly inferior team and won only two, a 3-2 overtime win in game two and a 3-2 squeaker in game four to stay alive in the best-of-five. They were shelled 10-8 at Northlands in the opener, fell against the ropes with a 6-5 overtime loss in game three and surrendered 7-4 in the clincher. The Vancouver Canucks, their division rivals, who had finished eighteen wins behind them in second in the Smythe, defeated the Kings and then Chicago to draw the assignment of dethroning the Islanders. The Islanders swept the Canucks in four games, for their third consecutive championship.

Edmonton had gone so far, so fast, but had also gone too far, too soon.

CHAPTER SEVEN

THEY WOULD board an old DC-3 together in Yellowknife, as many as twenty of them—captains of industry, politicians, movers and shakers of various stripes. George Bush made the pilgrimage, and so did Ken Taylor, the former Canadian ambassador to Iran and hero of the 1979 hostage crisis, in which he helped spirit American embassy employees out of the country. There was generally a core group of about ten men, and they included Glen Sather and Harry Sinden, and Taylor too. Once, in the early 1980s, Wayne Gretzky came along, enduring the trip at a time when he suffered from a fear of flying. The vintage airliner would carry them on a journey of about two and a half hours' duration, above the Arctic Circle, to a lodge where the Tree River drained into the Arctic Ocean. There, for two weeks at the end of July and the beginning of August, Peter Pocklington presided every summer over an elite assault on Arctic char. Taylor was a gentleman angler, seemingly capable of trying his luck in a dress jacket and Gucci shoes, while Sather was a consummate competitor, outfitted in hip waders, glowering over the twenty-pounders less serious members of the annual expedition managed to haul in.

Ralph Lean became one of the regulars on this great northern fishing derby in 1982. He was a corporate lawyer for Pocklington who forged a close friendship with Sather and came to socialize with other members of the Sather/Pocklington circle, including Taylor and Sinden. The trips had begun in the late 1970s, when Pocklington acquired control of the Oilers, and there were similar, though less populated, excursions in the name of golf—to Palm Springs, for example, where both Pocklington and Sather established residences. The golf and the fishing carried on for two decades, and counting. At the 1999 NHL All Star game in Tampa Bay, Ralph Lean teamed up with Ontario Premier Mike Harris to nick Sather and Sinden for thirty bucks each on the golf course owned by Tampa Bay Lightning general manager Jacques Demers.

As a senior partner at Cassels, Brock and Blackwell in Toronto, Lean had an international clientele. As a sports fan and a friend of Sather's, he would take care to schedule business trips to coincide with Oilers road games, doing business by day in New York, for example, and then catching up with Sather and the Oilers at Madison Square Garden for a game against the Rangers. Sather opened the door to a world of champions for him. He got to hold the Stanley Cup and hang out at the NHL annual draft. All the while, Lean advised Pocklington (through whom he met Sather) on his complex and, eventually, troubled business affairs, and sat on the board of Canbra, Pocklington's well-run and profitable canola oil processing business in Lethbridge. It was formerly owned by Burns Foods, which was controlled by Calgary multimillionaire Arthur Child. Pocklington acquired 53 percent of the common stock in 1986 to give him majority control.

Lean was treating Pocklington to lunch at the Albany Club, a conservative bastion in Toronto, in 1982, when the Oilers' owner stunned him with an out-of-left-field statement. As they ate in the shadow of a statue of Sir John A. Macdonald, the country's first prime minister and patron saint of ambitious Tories, Pocklington announced, "I'm going to run for the leadership of the Progressive Conservative party, and you're going to run the campaign."

Pocklington was always ready to talk politics. He was libertarian conservative, advocating as little government as possible. He had been talking in public since 1978 about some day becoming prime minister and took advantage of his notoriety as owner of the Oilers to speak regularly in public on policy issues. "If I ran, I'd win," he had vowed in 1978. In April 1982, he reflected on the quote. "I'd like to temper that by saying a guy would be crazy to run for politics because of the personal and family time it would require. Hell, it would take away five years of my life. The only way I would do it is by making a snap, eleventh-hour decision. Bang. And I'd be there."

Pocklington had apparently made his snap decision. This was the first time he had ever voiced to Lean an ambition to lead the national PCs. And the only reason to lead them, of course, was to become prime minister some day.

"Peter had strong political convictions," says Lean. "He believed that government should run like a business." Lean knew many politicians and bureaucrats, and, despite his conservative stripes, also knew the dream nursed by men like Pocklington, particularly self-made men, was elusive. "You can move government closer to a business model, but business people who get into politics become terribly frustrated, because government will never run like a business."

That wasn't going to stop Pocklington from trying, nor would Lean's firm opinion, offered repeatedly and in all honesty to Pocklington over the next few months, that he had zero chance of winning the party leadership. Besides, at the time Pocklington announced his intentions, the PCs weren't technically looking for a new leader. "Peter," Lean said at lunch, "there's no opening. Joe Clark is there and doesn't appear to want to go anywhere."

Joe Clark, the man from High River, Alberta—hometown of Glen Sather—had won the party leadership in 1976. His minority government, elected in May 1979, lost a non-confidence vote in the House of Commons over its first budget at year-end, and was trounced by the Liberals in the resultant federal election; Clark had been clinging to the party leadership ever since.

Riven by factions even in good times, the Conservatives in the wake of the 1980 election loss were brimming with disparate groups who wanted Clark out. Clark held onto the leadership when only 33.6 percent of delegates at the 1981 annual convention voted for a review. While there was nothing in the party constitution that required anything more than a simple majority for a leader to stay on, the endorsement was less than ringing. Clark campaigned relentlessly among party members from coast to coast for two years and then, at the annual convention in Winnipeg in January 1983, learned he had made almost no progress for his efforts. The call for a leadership review had been reduced by half a percentage point, to 33.1, and Clark had been conspicuously abandoned by delegates in Ontario and his home province of Alberta, who didn't show up to vote. Clark recognized the thinness of his support, and called for a leadership convention in June in Ottawa.

Lean attended the Winnipeg convention, although he was called away by the terminal illness of his mother. Also there were two political pros, Skip Willis, a seasoned campaign organizer, and Peter Regenstreif, a pollster, speech-writer and all-round political operator. A political science professor at the University of Rochester, Regenstreif was also active in Canadian and American political campaigns, working both the left and right sides of the street. In the aftermath of the Winnipeg vote that led Clark to call for a leadership convention, Willis and Regenstreif shook their heads over the spectacle of winning and losing at the same time, and agreed to keep in touch in the event that one of them came up with a leadership candidate.

Soon after the Winnipeg convention, Regenstreif's telephone rang. It was Willis. "I've got a candidate," Willis said.

"Who is it?" asked Regenstreif.

Willis told him.

"Oh my God," said Regenstreif.

NORMALLY, RALPH LEAN didn't take on hopeless campaign causes, and he knew Pocklington's leadership campaign was utterly hopeless. He was working on Art Eggleton's successful mayoral race in Toronto, and helping MPP Dennis Timbrell prepare a leadership campaign for the Ontario PC party that could hit the ground running whenever Premier William Davis retired (which wouldn't happen until 1985.)[1] But he looked at the $300,000 his law firm was billing Pocklington and his companies every year, and made a simple decision. If Peter wants me to run his campaign, I'll run his campaign. He bid his law partners adieu and began putting Pocklington's windmill-tilt together.

Lean was a money man, not a campaign expert, which is why he recruited Willis and Regenstreif to work with Pocklington. Raising money was work enough, however. It was the hardest job Lean ever took on. No matter whom he was trying to raise money for, people were always looking for an excuse not to contribute, and Pocklington gave them two excellent reasons: he had no hope of winning, and if he was so rich, why did he need other people's money? There was a lot of hat passing at public speaking functions by Pocklington, and in the end Lean was able to meet the campaign's $1 million budget target.

Pocklington began his campaign without a shred of grassroots support in the party. He was not a political animal in the sense of being someone to build a power base over years within the party rank and file, the way Brian Mulroney had been. Nor did he exhibit any ambitions of attending the convention as a kingmaker, a candidate who could corral enough delegate votes to influence the choice of the eventual winner. Pocklington was in it for all the marbles, apparently without considering that few marbles could be won without extraordinary groundwork being prepared. Whenever Lean reminded him that he couldn't win, Pocklington would retort, "You're a negative thinker. I don't like negative thinkers."

"He thought he was the right candidate," Lean says. "He thought he had a vision. Peter is very smart, very well read. He's your classic salesman-entrepreneur. He had convinced himself that he could win, and nobody could tell him he had no chance. My goal was to make sure he didn't embarrass himself, that he finished respectably, and that at the end of the day we didn't wind up in debt."

Pocklington was inspired by his own convictions over the need for broad changes in public policy. As Regenstreif notes, the Oilers' owner was a careful reader of policy papers coming out of Stanford University's Hoover Institute, a conservative think tank. The Hoover Institute provided him with a fundamental policy: the idea of an across-the-board flat rate of 20 percent for personal income tax. A similar flat tax would be championed by Steve Forbes in the Republican Party presidential primaries of 1996, and in 1999 Alberta, under the Progressive Conservative government of Premier Ralph Klein, became the first Canadian province to introduce such a flat tax on income. "Prescient," is how Regenstreif describes Pocklington's leadership campaign platform, and Pocklington's long-standing friend Ken Taylor (a Liberal) also argues that on many issues Pocklington has been ahead of his time.

It frustrated Regenstreif that Canadian media pundits were wont to dump Pocklington into the special place they reserved for right-wing wackos, and Lean would feel, looking back on the vote, that if delegates had been able to separate the controversial candidate from the policies and voted on the policies alone, Pocklington would have done even better than he did. By the time the leadership convention came along, Pocklington was in full bloom as a public figure with a slightly flaky aura. In a book published in 1981, he confessed to a near-death experience, having almost drowned while swimming in surf. He participated in death-defying jet-boat racing on wild rivers, and had once been captured by Mexican bandits when his craft broke down in one such race. In 1982, he was the victim of a bizarre hostage taking at his Edmonton home; the kidnapper's intentions or motivation were never completely explained, and Pocklington was wounded by police during the rescue. He admitted to consulting a psychic, and she sued him (unsuccessfully) for sexual harassment. Peter C. Newman's 1981 bestseller, *The Acquisitors,* had captured Pocklington in all his glory, and Peter Gzowski had provided a relatively affectionate, larger-than-life portrait of Pocklington in his 1982 bestseller, *The Game of Our Lives.* By the time Pocklington came to run for the Progressive Conservative leadership, he had national name recognition most politicians would kill for, but a persona to go along with it that they would kill to shed.

As it was, Pocklington ran a credible campaign, even though Lean cringed when he saw the kind of delegates Pocklington tended to attract. He became a magnet for the party's far-right agitators—right-to-lifers, gun enthusiasts and religious fundamentalists—even though Pocklington's platform didn't address any of their heartfelt concerns. In addition to his flat tax proposal, Pocklington called for fiscal accountability and a balanced budget. He wanted Ottawa to sell off all Crown corporations, reduce the size of the civil service, and give the Canadian military back its pride by increasing its funding and doing away with the Liberals' melding of the separate army, navy and air force into one Armed Forces, with its shared drab green uniform. Although he favoured capital punishment, he stayed away from abortion and never made an issue out of free trade, a key policy plank of John Crosbie, the finance minister in the defeated Clark government.

Without any foundation within the party, Pocklington got lucky one day in the campaign leading up to the convention when Lean answered his telephone to find a pc backbencher in the Ontario legislature on the line. It was Bob Runciman, who would become minister of correctional services in the Harris government a decade later. Runciman informed Lean that as a delegate at the forthcoming leadership convention, he was interested in supporting Pocklington. "Where are you?" Lean asked. "I'll be there in five minutes."

The Pocklington campaign was compromised somewhat by Pocklington's self-imposed restrictions on his availability. He didn't want the campaign to interfere with his family life (his wife, Eva, at any rate, was known to be less than enthusiastic about her husband's political ambitions), or with his devotion to the Oilers. If given a choice between flying in his personal jet to see an Oilers road game or speaking to delegates who might support him, Pocklington was on his way to root for the Oilers, who in spring 1983 were in the midst of a Stanley Cup run. Regenstreif made and cancelled three meetings with one Ontario mayor as Pocklington chased his hockey team around North America. Pocklington's campaign staff was, however, able to grab his attention long enough for a meeting with the PC members of the Prince Edward Island legislature. But his basic lack of experience in either the party or national affairs was revealed painfully when he fielded questions from the assembled MLAs. In mulling over one query, Pocklington replied, "That's a good question. What's your name, sir?"

"Jim Lee," said the man.

"And what is it you do?" Pocklington asked.

"I'm the premier," said Lee.

Pocklington has a rich speaking voice, full timbred, not unlike that of Brian Mulroney. (He is also said to sing opera very well.) Pocklington enjoyed public speaking, and Lean felt Pocklington thought he was better at it than he really was. But where Lean saw Pocklington truly excel was in the Q&A sessions of open-line radio. He exhibited the seasoned politician's knack for taking any question and answering it in such a way that he got his platform points across. As a complete political rookie, Pocklington could be impressive on the stump. But he still had zero hope of winning.

SEQUESTERED IN his suite on the 16th floor of Ottawa's Inn of the Provinces on the evening of June 10, 1983, Peter Pocklington was one night's sleep away from learning how many of the 2,952 delegates at the federal Progressive Conservative party's leadership convention would choose to dump Joe Clark and make him—and not Brian

Mulroney, Michael Wilson, John Crosbie, David Crombie, John Gamble or Neil Fraser—their new leader. Befitting his role as the champion of the libertarian right, Pocklington was ten days removed from a session of brinkmanship with organized labour. Pocklington had fingered a profitability puzzle of his Gainers meat packing plant back in Edmonton: the pigs the plant processed were in Alberta, but many of the customers for the end product were several thousand miles to the east, in Ontario. Pocklington had gone to Local 280P of the United Food and Commercial Workers Union to exact wage and benefits rollbacks that would offset the transportation costs his operation incurred in competing with Ontario-based processing plants. Threatening to hire replacement workers if the union didn't ratify the new contract, he placed help-wanted ads in the local newspapers, which caused more than 1,000 people to line up at the plant doors on West 66th. Deeply split by Pocklington's demands, the union voted 52 percent to accept the new contract. The starting wage for new employees immediately dropped from $11.99 to $7.80 an hour, overtime rates were clawed back, and health benefits were scaled down.

The Gainers showdown meant that Pocklington came to Ottawa for the leadership convention with an important personal victory under his belt and his public reputation as a no-nonsense free-enterpriser reinforced. But this victory failed to obscure a recent, more public loss. On May 17, Pocklington's Edmonton Oilers had lost 4-2 to the New York Islanders in Long Island, allowing the Islanders to complete a four-game sweep of the Stanley Cup finals. The Islanders' victory—their fourth consecutive title—had been a stunning repudiation of Pocklington's young team's preparedness. After another sparkling regular season, in which they tied with Philadelphia for the second-best record behind Boston, the Oilers had taken care not to stumble in the first round, the way they had so badly against Los Angeles in 1981/82. They swept Winnipeg in three games and, on the way to the finals, lost only one of twelve playoff games. But they could carry none of that momentum forward into the final series.

Stunned by a 2-0 shutout in the opening game, they never recovered. A team that had been accustomed to scoring more than five goals a game in the regular season was held to just six over four games in the finals.

Walking past the Islanders' dressing room after the deciding game, Glen Sather would take note of all the ice packs being applied to bruises and think: no one on our team looks like that. The Oilers were caught in a nasty flashback. They were in danger of being cast as the eighties version of the Chicago Blackhawks of the sixties, who could rule a regular season and hoard silverware and All Star votes for individual players, but be undone in the playoffs by an experienced, close-checking team, like the Leafs, Red Wings or Canadiens, that was prepared to pay a physical price to win. In what should have been the culminations of their greatest seasons, the Blackhawks were routinely smothered in a defensive wrap and steered well clear of a Stanley Cup victory, or even an appearance in the finals.

The best-of-seven series for the Stanley Cup is unlike any other playoff hockey. Experience here carries tremendous weight, as much or more than the talent at hand. This is why the National Hockey League's history has tended to feature championship streaks: teams that solve the riddle of winning under the most crushing pressure hold onto their hard-won lessons fiercely, and keep winning, even when their regular-season performances begin to suggest that their time has passed. They have the demeanour, the collective will, of champions.

Sport, like politics, is a numbers game. Addition and subtraction are the final measures of success. Politicians succeed by attracting more votes than they repel. Hockey teams succeed by scoring more goals than they allow. The ways and means are complex, arcane and sometimes vicious, but the simple truth of numbers ultimately carries the day. The Edmonton Oilers were deceptively simple to assess in purely numerical terms, as the team and its individual players showered the record books with new standards in offensive production. Certainly the 1982/83 season could be summed up more easily with a spreadsheet than a speech. The Oilers scored many, many goals—424 of them, far more than any other team that season or in the history of the league—and because they allowed substantially fewer goals than they scored—315—they won most of their games. They continued to perform in this manner through the first dozen playoff games that followed the eighty-game season. Then, in the four games of the final series against the New York Islanders, they no longer scored many, many goals. In fact, they allowed almost three times as many goals as they scored—six for, seventeen against—as they lost all four games.

When a team that has been so offensively prolific, so successful at winning more than it loses over the course of ninety-two games, only to score and be scored upon at a rate on par with the very worst teams in the league in its last four outings, something is not right. Provided nothing traumatic happened to the team before the final series, either the first ninety-two games were illusory, or the last four were. Or there was something about those first ninety-two games that left the team ill-equipped to play the last four, the most important ones in the entire campaign.

While the Edmonton Oilers were statistically one of the best teams in 1982/83, they were not ready to be Stanley Cup champions— at least not if that meant defeating the Islanders, who had won the last three Cups. Until the final series against the Islanders, the Oilers appeared to have their reputation for laggardly defensive play licked. Their lack of discipline in their own end had reached a nadir on February 19, when they defeated the Penguins 10-7 in Pittsburgh. Eight nights later, Wayne Gretzky decided that enough was enough: against the Winnipeg Jets that night, the Oilers would have to get a shutout. The team hadn't recorded one in 279 games. It was more than three years since the last shutout, recorded twenty-five games into their first NHL season. The team did Gretzky's bidding and beat the Jets 3-0. "That's ridiculous," Gretzky said of the Pittsburgh game after the Jets were shut out. "The time had come for this team to get it together in our own end. It wasn't funny any more."

The apparent breakthrough had been delivered by Gretzky, where the imprecations of Sather and his assistant coaches Ted Green and John Muckler (who had replaced Billy Harris) had not been taken seriously. It was an important step toward Gretzky assuming the team's captaincy in 1983/84. "The team played so poorly in Pittsburgh that, as coaches, we were supplied with the ammunition needed," Muckler said. "It got the players starting to realize that it was becoming a bit ridiculous . . . Lately, when we've discussed defence, we've been getting the full cooperation of the players . . . It's a matter of getting everyone to think you can't win on offence alone. You have to be solid in all areas of the game."

The Stanley Cup sweep by the Islanders showed that the Oilers had not yet mastered all areas of the game, one of which was desire. The Islanders wanted to win more than they did, as evidenced by the physical punishment to which they subjected themselves to contain the faster, younger Oilers. In taking over as coach of the Boston Bruins in 1966/67, Harry Sinden had said, "I want a team that skates like Montreal, checks like Detroit, and is as mean as Toronto." There was no such magical combination in Edmonton yet. The experience, discipline and commitment of the Islanders had overshadowed the offensive glitter of the young Oilers.

In politics, as in hockey, this same grit is a crucial element in the process of achieving and retaining power. The Progressive Conservatives, whom Pocklington was seeking to lead, had little practical experience with running the country. The last majority PC government had been John Diefenbaker's, elected in 1957. The Liberals had regained power in 1963, and it took sixteen years for them to yield the reins.

The timing of the minority-government election victory of Clark's PCs on May 22, 1979, had been noteworthy for Pocklington, capping the Oilers' final season in the World Hockey Association. That fall, the Oilers crossed over to the National Hockey League as the great seven-season WHA experiment was wound up. Clark's PCs then proved their inexperience by walking wide-eyed into a non-confidence vote ambush seven months later. Creeping inflation, a hall-mark of the Liberal government in the late 1970s, was supposed to be arrested by the Conservatives with a tough-love budget, but an inability to count heads when the budget was tabled stopped that initiative. Clark had failed to ensure he would have enough government members sitting in the House to avoid the defeat, then rashly welcomed a return to the polls, thinking the electorate would punish the Liberals for a winter campaign so soon after the last election. And since Pierre Trudeau had intended to retire, the sudden election would surely leave the Liberal leadership in disarray. But in February 1980, with Trudeau having agreed to stay on, the Liberals were elected with a majority government, leaving Canadian Conservatives like Pocklington infuriatingly out of synch with the Reagan revolution that was formally launched south of the border with the November 1980 presidential election.

The most galling fact for men like Pocklington was that Trudeau's Liberals formed a majority government without winning a single seat west of Winnipeg. There followed the Liberals' National Energy Program—hated in Alberta for its imposition of domestic price ceilings on the province's oil.[2] It was designed to save the hides of central Canadian consumers and businesses as world prices skyrocketed in the wake of the Iranian hostage crisis, but Conservative politicians in Alberta decried its limits on profitability. Premier Peter Lougheed would charge that it cost the provincial economy upwards of $60 billion in revenues.

Joe Clark had had his opportunity in 1979 and had blown it, as an experienced Liberal caucus sent the Conservatives back before the electorate for a thorough thrashing. Likewise, in Nassau Coliseum in Long Island and Northlands Coliseum in Edmonton, experience had counted, as the Oilers were humiliated in those four decisive games between May 10 and 17, 1983. Experience was also about to count profoundly on the floor of the Ottawa Civic Centre, where the arena ice had been thawed and drained away for the assembled delegates who would decide which of eight candidates would lead the federal Progressive Conservatives into the next federal election.

Pocklington had daringly, quixotically and naively declared himself to be one of them. He was up against an incumbent leader and former prime minister, his fellow Albertan Joe Clark; against John Crosbie, Michael Wilson and David Crombie, three cabinet ministers from Clark's short-lived minority government; and, not the least, against Brian Mulroney, an early favourite in the 1976 leadership race who had been bested by Clark and had been waiting for a second chance ever since. As a self-made man, Pocklington's relentless optimism and belief in his own possibilities had set him up for a personal embarrassment even greater than the humiliation so recently suffered by his Oilers. On Friday, June 10, the eve of the leadership vote, the Pocklington campaign's staffers were seriously concerned that their candidate might fall short of 100 first-ballot votes—as good as an opening-round playoff loss. They knew he would ultimately lose, but for Peter's sake they wanted the loss to come with dignity.

Fortunately, dignity was within Pocklington's grasp. Unless Clark surprised everyone with an unassailable performance on the first ballot, the contest was expected to be a three-way race between Clark, Crosbie and Mulroney. Regardless of the amount of lobbying and polling, no one could be absolutely certain of how the delegate voting would split up on that first ballot—who would be within striking distance of a second-ballot victory, who would be forced to turn to whom with a pledge of support. Above all, the contenders and also-rans alike would have to decide which candidate they would band together to block from achieving the party leadership: Clark or Mulroney.

In convention politics, "room to grow" is a fundamental quality of an eventually triumphant candidate if no one emerges with a majority on the opening vote. A strong showing on the first ballot isn't enough, if a candidate can't marshal further support on the second ballot as other candidates fall by the wayside. If too much of the convention floor is opposed to a candidate, he can stall, allowing a candidate with fewer initial votes to overtake him. This had been Mulroney's fate in 1976. He had been second on the first ballot, with 357 delegates, trailing fellow Quebec candidate Claude Wagner, who had 531. Three ballots later, Mulroney had inched up only to 369, while Joe Clark, who had begun with 277 on the first ballot, rode the wave of a stop-Wagner movement to surge to 969, only thirty-four ballots behind Wagner. At that point Mulroney had turned his delegates loose to vote for whomever they chose, and Clark had overtaken Wagner. Mulroney had plateaued early. He had shown no room to grow, while Clark ended up with about five times as many votes as he had started with. Mulroney couldn't let this happen again. If he couldn't win outright on the first ballot—and this was doubtful, given Clark's core following—he had to be able to pick up delegates that had cast their initial support to a rival.

The peculiarities of the leadership race meant Pocklington was positioned to be a kingmaker. Even if he attracted only 100 votes on the first ballot, by delivering some or all of those delegates to whomever he chose, Pocklington could help decide the party leader, and perhaps the country's next prime minister. Convention politics was not always about winning a leadership; for some candidates, it was about controlling a bloc of delegates and using the weight of their votes to help choose a winner—and in the process securing a senior position in the government that might be formed in the future. Pocklington's frame of mind would soon have to shift from the fantasy of becoming a leader on the national and global stage to more familiar territory for the celebrated entrepreneur. It was time to be a deal-maker.

"Room to grow" was not a concept solely on the mind of Brian Mulroney that June. It was also of concern to Peter Pocklington's Oilers organization. If the team's Stanley Cup shortfall three weeks earlier did not represent the peak of its ability, then some concrete potential had to be found. The Islanders, to be sure, had no room to grow. After four consecutive Cup wins, the team was greying. Eleven starters were between twenty-eight and thirty-two years of age. The Oilers, on the other hand, had youth on their side. Kevin Lowe was twenty-four, Jari Kurri, Andy Moog and Glenn Anderson were twenty-three, Wayne Gretzky, Paul Coffey and Mark Messier were twenty-two, and Grant Fuhr was twenty. Sather and his organization had done an almost unerring job of building a contender through draft picks in the team's first seasons in the NHL. They had not squandered any first-round pick, and had done improbably well with deep picks. The Oilers would never have another draft like those from 1979 to 1981, but then, neither would any other club. And three days before Peter Pocklington confronted the first-ballot results of the leadership convention, Sather and chief scout Barry Fraser turned in one more inspired effort at the league draft. With their first pick coming 19th overall in the first round, they scored well with defenceman Jeff Beukeboom of the Sault Ste. Marie Greyhounds, Wayne Gretkzy's old Junior team. Their next two picks were duds—neither Mike Golden (40th) nor Mike Flanagan (60th) made the NHL—but with their fourth pick, down at 82nd, they found a future star. Returning to the Finnish talent pool, which had yielded Kurri in 1980, they chose eighteen-year-old left winger Esa Tikkanen. Tikkanen would be a star of the late-eighties Oilers; he would also be a client of player agent Rich Winter, an Edmonton lawyer whose dogged pursuit of Alan Eagleson would bring down the Players' Association head and help change entirely the economic landscape in which a small-market team like the Oilers had thrived.

With the selection of Tikkanen, the Oilers closed the chapter on their draft-building years. Only Kelly Buchberger, 188th in 1985, and Geoff Smith, 63rd in 1987, would be added thereafter to an Oilers Cup–winning lineup through the draft. Denied top draft picks by his team's league-leading regular-season performances, Sather had to vie for later selections with rival general managers who had sharpened their scouting efforts in the wake of the Oilers' successes. Sather would no longer play the prescient spotter of teenage talent at the annual draft. Instead, he focused on being "Monty"—a nickname inspired by Monty Hall, host of the game show "Let's Make a Deal," and given to him by his players during the Oilers' first days in the NHL. Sather would make trades at an almost frenetic pace, echoing the owner's penchant for deal-making. The Oilers would win five Stanley Cups in seven seasons, and they would do it with forty-nine different players. In a league that permitted a team to dress eighteen skaters and two goaltenders for a game, this represented a player turn-over of 150 percent. In winning four Cups in the early 1950s, Detroit used thirty-eight players; in winning five consecutive Cups in the late 1950s, Montreal used thirty-seven. The Oilers would rule the NHL with a revolving-door roster that would see some of its most celebrated players spun off for cash or fresh talent.

Awaiting Brian Mulroney's arrival in his hotel suite as midnight approached on June 10, Pocklington was about to do some deal-making of his own. Whether or not the Oilers had room to grow would be proved in the next NHL season, which wouldn't start until October. Whether or not Pocklington had room to grow—or, more realistically, whether or not he was inclined to afford Mulroney some room of his own—would be known conclusively before the weekend was out. In both cases, the goal was the same: to build a dynasty that would last for years. If all went well for Peter Puck, the Oilers would rule the NHL and the Progressive Conservatives would rule Canada.

As Mulroney entered Pocklington's hotel suite, the lateness of the hour suggested that time was running out for both of them in their leadership ambitions, but it also promised a new dawning. Mulroney and Pocklington came together as losers that night—Mulroney a failed leadership candidate from 1976, Pocklington the owner of an NHL team that had failed to deliver on its potential in the Stanley Cup finals—but they would be rapidly transformed into two of the country's most spectacular winners.

THE 1982/83 STANLEY CUP finals had played out the blessing and curse of the Oilers' location. When Edmonton joined the NHL from the WHA in 1979, the Vancouver Canucks' approval had been secured with the promise of a balanced schedule that would ensure for at least two seasons Vancouver fans would have regular visits from established NHL clubs out east, and not be saddled with too many uninspiring games featuring the likes of the Oilers. Edmonton had made its NHL debut in the Smythe Division of the Clarence Campbell Conference, along with the Chicago Blackhawks, St. Louis Blues, Vancouver Canucks, Winnipeg Jets and Colorado Rockies. In a balanced schedule, with teams playing opponents in the opposite conference in the opening playoff round, the divisional alignments mattered little beyond playoff qualifications for the marginal teams. After two seasons, the league decided to move to an unbalanced schedule, with each team playing the bulk of its games against its division rivals, fewer games against its fellow conference members and a minimum of games against teams in the opposite conference. The playoffs would also unfold within divisions and conferences, to reinforce and capitalize upon regular-season rivalries. In 1981/82, the season of Edmonton's performance breakout, Edmonton occupied the Smythe Division with Vancouver, Calgary, Los Angeles and Colorado.

Equally important in 1981/82 was the swap between conferences of the Norris and Patrick divisions. When the Patrick was moved out of the Campbell Conference into the Prince of Wales Conference, six of the league's best teams—Montreal, Boston and Buffalo (in the Adams), Philadelphia, the Islanders and the Rangers (in the Patrick)—were located outside of Edmonton's conference, minimizing play between them and the Oilers. And in 1982/83, the Patrick's Washington Capitals greatly improved, making for seven solid franchises far removed from the Oilers. In 1981/82, Edmonton was the only club in the Smythe Division with a winning record. In 1982/83, after the Colorado franchise was moved to New Jersey and became the Devils, Winnipeg took its place in the Smythe, and Edmonton again was the only division team above .500.

Overall, the Campbell Conference was far weaker than the Prince of Wales. In 1981/82, Chicago and Vancouver, a pair of teams with losing records, vied in the conference championships for the right to be swept by the Islanders in the Stanley Cup finals. In 1982/83, seven of ten Campbell teams had losing records. Only Edmonton in the Smythe, and Chicago and Minnesota in the Norris, had records above .500. Over in the Prince of Wales Conference, eight of eleven teams had records of .500 or higher. The top four teams in the Patrick, where the Islanders resided, all had better records than the second-place Flames in the Oilers' Smythe Division.

Noting that teams in the Smythe were "weak" defensively, without recognizing that they were forced to play regularly against the explosive Oilers, is a bit like saying the hens in a particular chicken coop have a high mortality rate without acknowledging they have been locked up with a fox. To be sure, the Oilers represented the fox in the Smythe henhouse. But there was also a different game philosophy behind the statistical differences. The Prince of Wales Conference was home to the defence-first tradition that had been the foundation of the great Montreal Canadiens teams of the 1950s through the 1970s. The Oilers offered a daring and exciting rebuttal to this long tradition, and while their talent certainly preyed upon weaker clubs in the Smythe Division and Campbell Conference, their presence also forced other teams to adjust their games accordingly. When they couldn't check the Oilers into submission, opponents were forced to play a more wide-open game. The mere presence of the Oilers in the division—and ultimately in the league—changed the way the game was played.

While none of the top four Patrick teams in 1982/83 allowed more than 287 goals, none of the Smythe teams allowed less than 309. Overall, seven of eleven Prince of Wales teams allowed fewer than 300 goals; only two Campbell Conference teams (Chicago and

Minnesota) did so. In goals-against, Prince of Wales teams ranked first (Islanders, 226), second (Boston, 228), third (Philadelphia, 240), fifth (Washington, 283), sixth (Buffalo, 285), seventh (Montreal, 286) and eighth (Rangers, 287). In comparison, the Smythe Division teams ranked 10th (Vancouver, 309), 11th (Edmonton, 315), 13th (Calgary, 317), 15th (Winnipeg, 333) and 19th (Los Angeles, 365) out of the league's twenty-one teams. Six of ten Campbell teams allowed more goals than they scored, while only three of eleven Prince of Wales teams had a scoring deficit.

There was an important distinction to be drawn between the teams of the Oilers' Campbell Conference and the Islanders' Prince of Wales Conference when pondering scoring statistics. Such numbers could indicate a team's style of play, but not how they were *capable* of playing. Tight defensive teams like the Islanders were capable of shifting gears, finding an overdrive when necessary and piling up goals when the need or opportunity presented itself. Downshifting—transforming a club in a moment's notice from one that scores six goals while allowing four, to one that scores four goals while allowing two—is often much trickier. A team committed to a freewheeling offensive style relies on solid goaltending to bail it out of two-on-one and three-on-two breaks when defencemen get caught up ice or a backchecking assignment is missed. When such a team has its scoring game taken away from it, the task of regrouping to take care of its own end and launch a tight-checking game of its own can be as difficult as learning a foreign language overnight.

The Oilers had become accustomed to playing wide open in 1982/83, with minimal appearances against the tough, disciplined defensive clubs of the Prince of Wales. Although in the playoffs Edmonton swept Winnipeg, which had a losing record, in three games, games two and three were decided by one goal, each 4-3 decisions. Against Calgary, which also had a losing record, the Oilers were able to run wild, scoring thirty-five times in five games. It wasn't until the conference finals, against Chicago, that the Oilers played a team with a winning record, and the four-game sweep, with scores of 8-4, 8-2, 3-2 and 6-3, against a club with the league's fourth-best record and fourth-best defence, suggested that the Oilers might actually be ready to win a Stanley Cup. They were scoring prolifically—on power plays, at even strength, even when killing penalties. Both Wayne Gretzky (against the Jets) and Jari Kurri (against the Blackhawks) scored a pair of shorthanded goals in one game. (Kurri got both of his in the third period of game one of the conference finals, securing the 8-4 win.)

In the opening game of the Stanley Cup finals at Northlands Coliseum, however, the Islanders abruptly shut down the Oilers' shooting gallery. The Islanders scored early and protected the 1-0 lead all the way to the end of the third period, when an empty-net goal salted the game away. Northlands fans had not seen their Oilers shut out in two seasons, and the last doughnut, 189 games earlier, had as it happened also been served up by the Islanders' Billy Smith. The Oilers scored three goals two nights later, but the Islanders scored six. When the series moved to Long Island, 5-1 and 4-2 wins gave the Islanders their fourth consecutive Cup. It was their second consecutive sweep in the finals; the Islanders had won twelve of their last thirteen Stanley Cup games. For the second playoff season running, the Islanders had more trouble in the rounds leading to the finals than in the finals themselves.[3]

In their run to the 1982/83 finals, the Islanders had to get by three difficult opponents. In the division semi-finals, Washington took them to four games in the best-of-five. In the division finals, the Rangers stretched them to six in the best-of-seven. The conference finals were probably the "real" Stanley Cup, since the Islanders had to confront the Boston Bruins, who had compiled the season's best record with fifty wins and had the second-best defensive record, just behind the Islanders. Like the Rangers, the Bruins took the Islanders to six games. And while the Islanders were well known for their tight defensive game, they had shown themselves capable of unleashing reserve firepower. While lowering their goals-against average, the

Islanders cranked up their offence by about one goal a game in the playoffs against Washington and the Rangers. Against Boston, their scoring reached an average of 5.0 as they won game three 7-3, game four 8-3, and game six 8-4.[4] Their goals-against average was 3.5 as they held the Bruins to three or fewer goals in three of six games. No team had really been able to open up against them: in sixteen games, they had surrendered more than four goals in a game just twice, in a 7-6 loss to the Rangers and a 5-1 loss to Boston. The Islanders had played four more playoff games than the Oilers when they convened for the finals, but the older, bloodied Islanders were the ones who had the desire, skill and experience to win the Cup, which was sealed with a victory on home ice in their 100th game that season.

They outplayed the Oilers, and outfoxed them. Billy Smith, who appeared in seventeen of twenty playoff games, was the consummate money goaltender, his average dropping from 2.87 in the regular season to 2.68 in the postseason, and free-falling to 1.5 in the finals. Smith was closing in on the all-time playoff appearance record for NHL goaltenders in both games and minutes, held by Glenn Hall, and would surpass it in 1983/84. As things stood, he had played in and won more playoff games than any other NHL goaltender in every season since 1979/80. (In 1979/80, he set the record for most playoff wins in one season, with fifteen in twenty games, and would surpass Ken Dryden's career record of eighty playoff wins in 1983/84.) Having shut out the vaunted Oilers in seven of twelve periods, Smith was chosen for the Conn Smythe Trophy over Mike Bossy, who had produced five game-wining goals (four of them against Boston) in nineteen playoff games.

Smith's contribution to the Islanders' victory went beyond stopping pucks. He was also one of the most penalized netminders in the history of the game, slashing viciously at anyone who wandered into or around his crease. The old four-by-eight crease was still in use, and the rules on "running" the goaltender were not as stringent. Smith took it upon himself to protect his territory, challenge opposing players, and through his cantankerousness get a rise out of his own team-mates and unnerve the opposition. Smith's slashes were not love taps. The beating he inflicted on the Vancouver Canucks in the 1981/82 finals moved Tiger Williams to express his desire to "punch Smith in the oesophagus so he has to eat out of a blender for six months." In the 1982/83 finals, he caught Glenn Anderson with a two-hander that sent Glen Sather screaming for a suspension, and later he clipped Gretzky for good measure. Distracted by Smith's antics, the Oilers were not so much knocked off their game as hacked off it.

The Oilers lacked the versatility to deal with a traditional close-checking team that managed to knock them off their game. Wayne Gretzky's league-leading performances in goals (seventy-one), assists (125) and points (196), provided the clue to his team's fundamental vulnerability. Gretzky was involved in almost half his team's scoring. Nullify him, and a five-goal-a-game team suddenly became a two-and-a-half-goal-a-game team with a penchant, even when winning, for allowing four goals a game. The Islanders limited Gretzky to four assists and no goals in the four games of the finals, as the Oilers produced just 1.5 goals per game while permitting 4.25. To win, the Oilers would have to spread the work around.

WHEN BRIAN MULRONEY came calling at the Pocklington suite around eleven o'clock on the Friday night of the leadership convention, he hoped to secure the unequivocal support of the Oilers' owner on the second ballot. If the universe had unfolded slightly differently over the previous seven years, Mulroney might have found himself striving to satisfy the desires of Pocklington the NHL franchise owner at the league annual general meeting, which was taking place at the same time as the leadership convention, in Montreal. After Mulroney failed to secure the PC leadership at the 1976 convention, the well-connected Montreal lawyer had been left to ponder career options. One of the doors apparently open to him was the presidency of the NHL. Clarence Campbell was retiring after holding the post since 1946, and a search committee had been struck to find his replacement. One of the members of the eight-man committee was Jacques Courtois. When the Montreal Canadiens were acquired by the Bronfman empire in 1972, Courtois, a Montreal lawyer influential in local PC politics, was named team president, holding the Canadiens' seat on the NHL board of governors. At the celebrated game between the Canadiens and the Soviet Union's Central Red Army team, played at the Montreal Forum on New Year's Eve, 1975, Mulroney was spotted sitting beside Courtois, right behind the Canadiens' bench. The senior team of Mulroney's 1976 leadership campaign had also included Alan Eagleson, who was president of the Ontario Progressive Conservative party from 1976 to 1980. Eagleson, unusually chummy with league owners for a labour union leader, was in a prime position to promote Mulroney's candidacy for the league presidency.

By the time the 1983 PC leadership convention came along, the race was shot through with a tangle of factions, allegiances and rivalries drawn from the hockey world. Eagleson had abandoned Mulroney and was now working on the Clark campaign, at cross purposes to both Mulroney and Pocklington. The Players' Association president had suffered his first serious career setback in 1980 when Bobby Orr, his star client and personal friend since the former superstar's teenage years in the mid-1960s, publicly broke with Eagleson over the handling of his career and finances. Orr went on the hustings for Mulroney during his 1983 leadership campaign—a move that was controversial not just because Orr was now a bitter enemy of Eagleson, but because he was an American citizen and resident insinuating himself into a Canadian political campaign. Eagleson was a friend of Sather's, but another friend of Sather's was Harry Sinden, the Boston Bruins general manager who had tried in vain to sign Orr to one final Bruins contract (which included 10 percent of the team) in 1975, as Eagleson steered his client into the hands of Chicago's Bill Wirtz.[5]

It was difficult to imagine someone as upwardly mobile as

Mulroney accepting a job that would mean contending with the contrary cast of characters that comprised the NHL's ownership ranks. And as events transpired, the NHL presidency did not go to Mulroney in 1977, though his skills as a labour negotiator would have served the league well. The recruitment of a new president turned out to be an inside job. After engineering the movement of Orr to his Blackhawks, Bill Wirtz teamed up with his fellow member of the league old guard, Bruce Norris of Detroit, to engineer Campbell's retirement. Whatever the eight-man executive search committee was supposed to accomplish, Campbell's replacement by Wirtz and Norris's handpicked candidate, Red Wings counsel John Ziegler, was never in serious doubt.

After the 1976 PC leadership campaign, Mulroney, rather than becoming NHL president, became president of the Iron Ore Company of Canada, a firm actually based in Cleveland, Ohio, that was removing a wealth of natural resources from the ground in northern Quebec and Labrador. Mulroney was settling into his high-paying position just as Pocklington was buying the Oilers. The Wirtz–Norris skulduggery worked to Pocklington's benefit, because Ziegler was absolutely committed to putting an end to the war between the NHL and WHA that was escalating player salaries. With the consent of Eagleson's NHLPA, the WHA was folded and Pocklington got his foot in the door of the NHL brotherhood of franchise owners. An astute labour negotiator, Mulroney might have brought about a truce in the NHL–WHA battle more quickly than did Ziegler, but as fate would have it, Pocklington and Mulroney were still destined to meet. Their coincident desire to become the leader of a small but respected Western democracy brought them together in an Ottawa hotel room, hours before the leadership race's critical first ballots would be cast.

Although rarely directly involved in player trades, Pocklington was by nature a deal-maker and a gambler. He was more prudent in his corporate manoeuvres than his cowboy-capitalist persona suggested. But Pocklington had a craving for the adrenal jolt that came from laying everything on the line. It was what had attracted him to the extraordinarily dangerous sport of racing jet-boats down rapids-torn rivers,[6] and what made him engage in high-stakes backgammon games. During the leadership campaign, Pocklington pollster Peter Regenstreif found himself on Pocklington's private jet, holding a small Monet Pocklington had anted up in a game with Skalbania. He watched Pocklington lose the small treasure, but then win it back on the next flight.

As Brian Mulroney arrived in Pocklington's hotel suite, the Oilers' owner was ready to see what his leadership rival would ante up in order to win control of a political party. The Pocklington camp had already considered pitches from several other candidates. Ralph Lean had been approached by the David Crombie and Michael Wilson camps with the idea of forming an alternative-candidate pact. It had become apparent that about one-quarter of the delegates at the 1983 convention would not support Clark under any circumstances, and that another quarter were equally disdainful of Mulroney. The door was open for a third candidate to come out of the weeds on subse-quent ballots as an alternative to Clark and Mulroney. Michael Wilson was a possibility, but more likely was John Crosbie, the crafty Newfoundlander who as minister of finance under Clark had tabled the budget that invited the non-confidence vote which brought the minority government down in 1979.

For Crombie or Wilson to win, the front runners would have to stall and show little or no room to grow. If, in the process, either Crombie or Wilson came through with about 350 delegates, he could emerge as a compromise choice, as Clark had in 1976, and win on a subsequent ballot. Both the Crombie and Wilson campaigns wanted a deal with Pocklington wherein Pocklington would throw his support behind whichever of them finished higher on the first ballot. According to Lean, however, neither Crombie nor Wilson was willing to extend the same courtesy to Pocklington—to support him if he managed to finish ahead of them on the first ballot—and Lean told both camps that he couldn't even take such a proposal to his candidate.

After the speeches on Friday night, John Crosbie came calling with his advisor, John Lassinger. Lean says Pocklington made no firm commitment to support Crosbie on the second ballot. Then came Mulroney, accompanied by campaign manager Paul Weed, as well as John Bitove Sr. and Metro Toronto chairman Paul Godfrey—both friends of Lean, and whom Lean was sure were chosen to come along because the Mulroney camp believed Lean could influence Pocklington's decision.

Pocklington had high stakes in mind. According to Regenstreif, were Pocklington to cast his support to Mulroney on the second ballot, and were Mulroney to win the leadership and the next federal election, Pocklington wanted to be his minister of finance.

Mulroney declined to hand over the finance post, perhaps the most plum cabinet position and his strongest bargaining tool. He would likely have to deliver it to Michael Wilson to get the Bay Street broker's support. Wilson, it was believed, was unhappy with Clark for having given the position to Crosbie in his short-lived minority government. Mulroney instead proposed that, were the Conservatives to form the next government, Pocklington chair a special committee review of the Canadian taxation system.

Any delusions Pocklington might still have been harbouring of a 600-vote performance on the first ballot were firmly shattered by Mulroney. During his cross-country pre-convention campaign, Mulroney had been careful to stroke Pocklington's ego, on one occasion telephoning him from Lethbridge to tell him that one of the biggest surprises of the convention would be how well Pocklington would do on the first ballot. Now, Mulroney laid out firmly, presciently, with the voice of someone who had been down this road before, how the first vote was going to break down. Mulroney didn't have to say bluntly that Pocklington's campaign for world leadership was about to come to a crashing halt. It was plain that he was not going to be a front runner, or even a dark horse with room to grow.

Pocklington had acquitted himself well in his speech to the delegates and in Q&A sessions; he needed a statesmanlike conclusion as the balloting unfolded. And nothing could be more statesmanlike than playing kingmaker.

Mulroney told Pocklington that Clark would be first on the first ballot. Mulroney himself would be a strong second and Crosbie would be third, substantially behind. That's where Pocklington would have to make his move, Mulroney explained. "And you won't have much time. I've been around these conventions long enough to know that you'll only have about ten minutes to make up your mind."[7]

Pocklington told Mulroney he'd already made up his mind. He'd go with the winner.

Exactly who Pocklington would decide had the makings of a winner—Mulroney or Crosbie—depended on the outcome of the first ballot. Mulroney's camp was predicting it would have about 850 delegates, which would make him Pocklington's most likely choice. But if Mulroney only came through with, say, 650, while Crosbie gathered 600, Pocklington would face a tougher decision.

As to how many delegates Pocklington would collect, Regenstreif was seriously concerned about a blowout. It would be written that Pocklington's delegate support was built on Amway distributors lining up Pocklington delegates by packing delegate-selection meetings at riding associations. Lean, however, didn't feel this was a significant source of Pocklington delegates. "There may have been some, but I don't think there were many," he recalls.

In the midst of the pre-convention campaign, though, the Pocklington camp was approached by individuals who said they had delegates for sale, according to Lean. "We had people coming from Quebec saying, 'We'll deliver X number of delegates for $75,000.' The problem was they'd get to Peter. He's a businessman. I'd say, 'Peter, we're not doing a deal like that.'"

Regenstreif had a modest goal for Pocklington: 100 delegates on the first ballot. If Pocklington could make it into three figures, he could look respectable. The day before the first ballot, Regenstreif says he turned to Peter Lougheed, Alberta's premier. Lougheed had tried scrupulously to avoid taking a public stance against Clark, a fellow Albertan, but it was known that he favoured Mulroney. Lougheed could deliver the twenty-one delegate votes wielded by the province's federal PC MPs, who were expected to go en masse with Mulroney. Regenstreif's pitch was: Lend me those delegates for the first ballot, for Peter. After that, he'll be out of the running, and they can go where they want. Regenstreif says that Lougheed agreed.

On the first ballot, Clark came up well short of victory, with 1,091 delegate votes. Mulroney was right where his polling said he'd be, at 874. Crosbie was a strong third, at 639. Wilson and Crombie were well back, at 144 and 116. And Peter Pocklington had squeaked into the three-figure ranks, with 102, putting him well ahead of fringe candidates Gamble, at seventeen and Fraser, at five.

The brokering that ensued was ferocious. The goal of almost every candidate was to deny Clark victory. It remained to be decided who could assemble a majority from the non-Clark delegates. Each candidate occupied a box, or section, of the arena seats, which were packed with advisors, friends and family, and wired with telephones. The phone in the Pocklington section rang furiously as deals were proposed. Lean could see John Bitove Sr. and his family waving emphatically at him, trying to get Pocklington to make a symbolic walk over to the Mulroney section and help stave off a second-ballot surge by Crosbie.

Pocklington took a call from Crombie's people, who wanted to know what he was going to do. Pocklington told them he wanted to talk with Wilson. After Pocklington compared notes with Wilson, Lean sensed that Wilson personally was tending toward Crosbie. But Dennis Timbrell, for whose provincial leadership ambitions Lean was drumming up financing, was supporting Wilson, and Lean thought it possible Timbrell would tilt Wilson toward Mulroney.

Then Pocklington made up his mind. He would go to Mulroney.

Wilson agreed to go with him. Crombie refused to capitulate and decided to stay on the second ballot, while Gamble and Fraser dropped out. Pocklington and Wilson met on the middle of the convention floor and shook hands. It was on this spot, on October 11, 1972, that the puck was dropped for the first regular-season game in WHA history, between the Alberta Oilers and the Ottawa Nationals. History was being made again as, for the first time, two leadership candidates at a national PC convention were publicly joining forces to throw their weight behind another candidate.

Lean was seconded to lead the parade over to the Mulroney box. If all the delegate votes they had attracted on the first ballot followed, Mulroney would have an extra 246 votes, enough to overcome Clark, 1,120 to 1,091, provided the incumbent picked up no new votes.

The procession of Wilson and Pocklington provided one of the convention's most dramatic moments, as Lean got lost in the churning throng of the arena floor. Mila Mulroney burst into tears as she saw Pocklington and Wilson head right past their box . . . toward Crosbie's.

"I blew it," Lean says. "I overshot Mulroney."

The group regained its bearings and homed in on their relieved target. Mulroney was poised for a second-ballot victory.

It didn't happen. Wilson and Pocklington could not guarantee that the delegates who voted for them on the first ballot would follow them to Mulroney on the second. And on the second ballot, Mulroney came up ninety-nine short on the 246 votes Wilson and Pocklington had attracted. Crosbie, meanwhile, picked up 152, while Clark lost six and Crombie lost forty-nine. Lean is confident that 90 percent of Pocklington's votes went with him to Mulroney, which would suggest about half of Wilson's delegates went to Crosbie.

Clark now had 1,085, Mulroney 1,021 and Crosbie 781. Crombie crossed over to Crosbie, making for a potential emergence of Crosbie as the eventual winner. Clark's support could collapse completely and, for Mulroney, prematurely, in view of the fact that Clark now had only the slightest hope of winning. If Clark's delegates were now turned loose, they might push Crosbie past Mulroney on the third ballot.

But the Clark vote held. The third ballot gave Clark 1,058, Mulroney 1,036 and Crosbie 858. As the last place candidate in the round, Crosbie was out. It all came down to a final, fourth-vote show-down between Clark and Mulroney.

Mulroney got 1,584. Clark got 1,325. And Peter Puck had been right. He had, as he had promised to Mulroney on Friday night, gone with the winner. With his firm decision before the second ballot, he had started the movement toward the man who won the leadership, and soon the prime ministership.

The day after the convention, Brian Mulroney appeared in the House of Commons' spectator gallery to wave at the Progressive Conservative MPs whose leader he now was. Mulroney did not yet hold a seat of his own; he had never been elected to public office. The participation in the leadership campaign of Pocklington, who had also never held elected office, helped defuse the objection that Mulroney couldn't ask to lead a national political party when he'd never even run in an election. Standing at Mulroney's side in the gallery was his kingmaker. Mulroney placed his hand familiarly on Pocklington's shoulder, expressing a bond that proved to be more than a superficial quid pro quo of campaign politics.

A genuine friendship developed between the men; Peter and Eva would regularly socialize with Brian and Mila. On the night of September 3, 1984, the Pocklingtons joined the Mulroneys and a small circle of the PC leader's friends and political associates in the north-shore Quebec town of Baie Comeau, to watch the returns in Mulroney's first federal campaign. Pocklington had indeed chosen a winner. The Mulroney Conservatives crushed the opposition, win-ning 211 of 282 seats. By the time the returns began to roll in from Alberta, the Conservatives already had a majority government, but

Pocklington's province delivered Mulroney his most emphatic success: all twenty-one available seats, with a daunting 70 percent of the popular vote.

The Conservative majority government Pocklington had craved for Canada, a northward extension of America's Reagan revolution, had come to pass. His Oilers had also fulfilled their tremendous promise in the year since the leadership convention. They had achieved a rematch with the Islanders in the finals, and this time the Oilers delivered the rout, winning in five games to bring the Stanley Cup to Edmonton. A Canada Cup tournament was about to begin, with Gretzky, Coffey, Fuhr, Messier, Lowe and Anderson performing for Team Canada. Room to grow? For the Oilers, for Peter Pocklington, the sky seemed the limit.

CHAPTER EIGHT

THEY WERE, in the end, only four games, a hard-earned lesson in the nature of winning that came perhaps at the wrong time and place for fans, but had an indelible effect on the team itself. Being swept by the Islanders in the 1982/83 Stanley Cup finals did not spell the end of the Oilers. They dusted off the defeat and proceeded to have the greatest season in franchise history, and one of the greatest the league has ever seen.

Dynastic teams seldom win the Stanley Cup on their first try, sometimes spending years contending with shortfalls before the right formula, the right attitude, is found. The Red Wings lost back-to-back finals to Toronto, in 1947/48 and 1948/49, before winning the first of four Cups in six seasons in 1949/50. The Leafs lost to Montreal in 1958/59 and 1959/60, then were dumped in five games by Detroit in the 1960/61 semi-finals, before winning three Cups in a row and a fourth three seasons after that. The Bruins that won for Harry Sinden in 1969/70 had spent three seasons gathering playoff experience before they broke through. The Islanders, the four-time winners whom the Oilers were expected to dethrone, almost didn't win a Cup at all. After showing initial promise in 1974/75, the Islanders reeled off a series of playoff disappointments, unable to reach the finals. It wasn't until general manager Bill Torrey engineered a massive reshaping of the team roster, with eight new players joining in 1979/80, that the team was able to achieve its goal.

Glen Sather made no such overhaul following the 1982/83 loss. The team that embarked on the 1983/84 season was essentially the same as the one that had come up short in 1982/83. The only significant new faces in the playoffs of 1983/84 were Pat Conacher and Kevin McClelland. Conacher, an Edmonton native who had played on the Billings Bighorns with Andy Moog, was selected 76th overall by the Rangers in 1979. The left winger was signed as a free agent at the start of the 1983/84 season, and he was used in three playoff games. McClelland was a midseason find by Sather. A pugnacious right winger originally drafted 71st overall by Hartford in 1980, McClelland had been sent to Pittsburgh as part of a free-agency compensation package when Hartford signed Greg Malone in 1981. McClelland was drifting in Pittsburgh, bouncing between the Penguins and their AHL farm club, the Baltimore Skipjacks, when Sather cut what proved to be an entirely one-sided deal. The Penguins wanted Tom Roulston, whom Sather had picked up with Risto Siltanen in the summer of 1979 for Joe Micheletti, and to get him Pittsburgh handed over both McClelland and its sixth-round pick in the 1984 draft. While Roulston played only fifty-eight games for Pittsburgh before taking his business to Europe, McClelland played on four Edmonton Cup winners.

As great as the 1981/82 and 1982/83 seasons had been, Edmonton moved to a new level in 1983/84, winning fifty-seven games—ten more than in 1982/83—to earn its first overall league title. The team received a franchise-high four appointments to the All Star team, with Gretzky making the first team and Coffey, Messier and Kurri getting the nod for the second team. Gretzky won another triple crown of silverware, capturing the Art Ross, Hart and Pearson trophies, while Paul Coffey, who was runner-up to Gretzky for the league scoring title, was also runner-up for the Norris Trophy to Washington's Rod Langway, who won it for the second consecutive season. Gretzky produced more than 200 points for the second time in his career, with 205, on eighty-seven goals and 118 assists (after reaching 212 in 1981/82, he had produced 196 in 1982/83). Gretzky had first surpassed the goal-a-game pace, set by Maurice Richard in 1944/45, in 1981/82, when he scored ninety-two in eighty games for a rate of 1.14. Although his ninety-two goals stood as the league record, his 1983/84 output of eighty-seven in seventy-four games set a new goal-per-game mark of 1.18.

Although Coffey was a distant second to Gretzky in the scoring race with 126 points, it was an extraordinary performance for a defenceman. He had surpassed Bobby Orr's 1973/74 performance of 122 points (although Coffey played eighty games to Orr's seventy-four); only Orr's 139-point mark of 1970/71 remained higher. (Coffey would fall one point short of breaking it in 1985/86.) Coffey had now scored more goals in one season than any defenceman but Orr. His forty goals put him ahead of the thirty-nine scored by Chicago's Doug Wilson in 1981/82, the thirty-seven by Orr in 1970/71 and 1971/72, and well ahead of the thirty-one produced by Denis Potvin in 1978/79 and Ray Bourque of Boston and Phil Housley of Buffalo in 1983/84. Orr's forty-six-goal effort of 1974/75 was the last hurdle in the record book, and it would fall to Coffey when he scored forty-eight in 1985/86.

As Edmonton aged as a franchise, it became younger as a team. The older pros Sather had depended on for playing experience when the Oilers joined the NHL had been falling by the wayside. In the seasons leading up to the 1983/84 win, a number of newer, younger faces appeared.

Randy Gregg, Glenn Anderson's captain on the 1980 Canadian Olympic team, was added on defence as a free agent in 1982 (after his Olympic campaign, Gregg played two seasons in Japan with the Kokudo Bunnies). Ken Linseman—the player whose court actions had ushered in the drafting of teenagers—had played against the Oilers as a Philadelphia Flyer in the 1979/80 preliminary playoff round. Sather gave up Risto Siltanen and minor pro Brent Loney to get Linseman and Don Nachbaur (another former Billings Bighorn) in August 1982.

Sather had given up on an early reclamation project, Don

Murdoch. Having been selected sixth overall by the Rangers in the 1976 draft after scoring more than eighty goals in two consecutive seasons with the Medicine Hat Tigers, Murdoch had produced thirty-two goals in his NHL rookie season, but his production declined thereafter. A conviction for cocaine possession finished him in New York. Sather gave him another chance after acquiring him in March 1980, but it proved an expensive miscalculation. Sather had given up Cam Connor and his third-round pick in the 1981 draft, which the Rangers used to get Peter Sundstrom. Murdoch's scoring touch did not return with the Oilers. He scored fifteen times in fifty games, and in August 1981 Sather handed him over to Lou Nanne in Minnesota in exchange for defenceman Don Jackson. The deal helped balance the books on Murdoch. While Murdoch was immediately sent by Minnesota to Detroit, who fared no better with him than Edmonton, Sather found in Jackson a player who was almost ready to step up from the minors (where he had spent most of the last three seasons) and play regularly with the league's best club. After spending almost all of 1981/82 in Wichita, Jackson came up to the Oilers in 1982/83.

Sather was also able to sign Czech left winger Jaroslav Pouzar, drafted 83rd overall by the Oilers in 1982. The thirty-year-old defensive specialist was considered expendable by the Czechoslovakian national team—he had played in six World Championships, two Olympics and two Canada Cup tournaments—which permitted him to come to North America. Sather used him effectively for three seasons before Pouzar left for Germany in 1985/86, then brought him back for twelve regular season and five playoff games in 1986/87.

Finally, Sather added a former team-mate of Ted Green on the Winnipeg Jets, Swedish right winger Willy Lindstrom. Lindstrom came into the NHL with the Jets, and in March 1983 Sather traded Laurie Boschman to Winnipeg to get him. He was almost thirty-two when Sather made the trade, an old man by Oilers standards, and Sather used him through 1984/85 before letting him go on waivers to Pittsburgh.

The core of the Oilers was untouched: Coffey and Lowe on defence, Messier, Kurri, Greztky and Anderson up front, and Fuhr in goal. After the 1981/82 upset loss to Los Angeles, in which the Oilers had relied on the rookie Fuhr, Moog was given the lion's share of the netminding work for 1982/83, and was in net for all but eleven minutes of the 1982/83 playoff run. Beginning in 1983/84, Sather regularly made Fuhr his first choice in goal during the playoffs.

With the 1983/84 season, the Oilers revolution in playing style began to make its influence felt on the league. The tight defensive style of the Islanders, depending on big players and clutch-and-grab tactics to slow opponents down, was proving ineffective against the Oilers as teams tried to hold them in check. Sather had emphasized speed and finesse in building the team, and the Oilers could not be stopped by trying to stand up to them at the blue line, or clogging up the neutral zone. They played a creative, high-tempo passing game that took the action aggressively to opponents. "Five up" was how the style came to be described: Oilers' forwards were on top of opponents' defencemen, and the Oilers' defenders moved up to engage the forwards. Sather became the first NHL coach to use offensive stars like Gretzky and Kurri as penalty killers, which created a new threat in the Oilers' scoring arsenal: the shorthanded goal. Gretzky got twelve of them in 1983/84, twice as many as in 1982/83, and in 1984/85 he produced more shorthanded goals (eleven) than he did on the power play (eight). In 1983/84, Kurri added another five, while Messier and Anderson scored four each. (In 1985/86, Coffey would get nine.) So effective were the Oilers at turning a shorthanded situation into an offensive opportunity that their reputation alone was enough to make an opposing team play cautiously when enjoying a man advantage.

The four-man attack employed on the penalty kill was equally, if not more, dangerous when the referee awarded matching minor penalties and the Oilers got to play four-on-four. The team's free-wheeling speed was devastating, and in 1986 the league paid them the highest compliment by rewriting the rule book. Just as the Montreal

Canadiens' awesome attack caused the league in 1956 to rule that a man advantage would end if the team with the power play scored,[1] the Oilers' effectiveness in four-on-four play led the league to decree that match penalties would no longer require teams to reduce the number of skaters.

The Oilers began the 1983/84 playoffs with a pasting of the Winnipeg Jets, which had finished fourth in the Smythe with a losing record. Opening the series with a 9-2 win at Northlands, the Oilers survived game two with a 5-4 overtime win, then polished off the Jets 4-1 in Winnipeg to sweep the best-of-five. They had scored eighteen goals and allowed only seven.

The Oilers then ran into the Calgary Flames, who presented a very different reception than they had in the 1982/83 division finals. In that first postseason encounter in what became the Battle of Alberta, the Flames had been smothered in five, losing 9-1 in the deciding game. Calgary in 1983/84 was a far more formidable opponent, even though its regular-season record—eighty-two points—was not much different from the seventy-eight it managed in 1982/83.

The Flames, however, were becoming another team. New to the defence was rookie Al MacInnis, who had one of the hardest point shots in the league; as well, Jamie Macoun played his first full season on defence. The team delivered tenacious checking from veteran forwards Doug Risebrough (a Stanley Cup winner with Montreal in the 1970s) and Jim Peplinski, excellent goaltending from Reggie Lemelin and Don Edwards, and scoring from a pair of old pros, former WHA Jet Kent Nilsson and ex-Leaf Lanny McDonald. The Oilers recorded their fourth straight playoff win with a 5-2 decision in the opening game at Northlands, but when Calgary tied the series with a 6-5 overtime win the next night, Edmonton's cruise to the finals was over. The Oilers took a 3-1 series lead with 3-2 and 5-3 wins, but Calgary came back with two close 5-4 victories (in overtime in game six) to send the series to a seventh game. The Oilers came through, 7-4, and as much as the two teams had established a rivalry that ran to pure hatred,

Edmonton owed Calgary a debt of gratitude. The division finals were the trial by fire that Edmonton had needed to harden them for play-off hockey, to make them understand what was required to win in the postseason. The youthful cockiness, which some blamed for their fail-ure in the 1982/83 finals as much as inexperience, was being tempered by adversity.

After Calgary, the conference finals against Minnesota were an extended practice. The North Stars, who finished first in the Norris, had gotten by the St. Louis Blues with a game-seven overtime win in the division finals. The North Stars had one of the league's better offensive teams, its 345 goals second to the Oilers' 446 in the Campbell Conference and fifth best in the league. But it was defen-sively weak, allowing 344 goals to the Oilers' 314. At the beginning of the decade, the North Stars had had the making of an Oilers-style contender. Glen Sather's friend Lou Nanne had a young, exciting team, and in 1980/81 reached the finals. Nanne quipped, "We're so young that if we don't win the Stanley Cup, we're going to challenge for the Memorial Cup because we have nine players who are eligible." They were taken in five by the Islanders, and since then the Oilers had passed them as the lead pretenders to the Islanders' throne. Minnesota had no real answer to the up-tempo Edmonton game, sur-rendering twenty-two goals as they lost in four straight.

The quick dispatch of the North Stars gave the Oilers nine days in which to prepare for the Cup finals. As the Oilers were rolling over Minnesota, it looked as if they would meet Montreal. The Canadiens had won the first two games of the Wales Conference finals against a tired Islanders team. The Islanders had begun their quest to match the record of five consecutive Cup wins (set by Montreal in the 1950s) with a difficult division semi-final against their cross-town rivals, the Rangers. It took a 3-2 overtime win in the deciding fifth game for the Islanders to advance past the first round, and they then slogged through a closely played best-of-seven division final against Washington, which they nonetheless won in five. On May 1, as

Edmonton finished off Minnesota, the Islanders tied the series against Montreal at two wins apiece. The Islanders went on to eliminate Montreal in six games, with four straight wins, and made possible a rematch of the 1982/83 finals.

The Islanders were older, and hurting, but they were still a dangerous team. They had won fifty games in 1983/84, eight better than in 1982/83, which allowed them to regain the Patrick Division and Wales Conference titles. Only Edmonton had won more games, and the Oilers continued to have no success against Al Arbour's team. When the finals began, the Oilers hadn't beaten the Islanders in ten meetings. Edmonton, which had been resting for four days when the Islanders finally rid themselves of Montreal, used the spare time productively. Sather brought in Roger Neilson, one of the game's most innovative coaches, who had pioneered the use of video replay in the league. Neilson had taken the Vancouver Canucks to the 1981/82 finals against the Islanders, and with his guidance the Oilers coaching staff and players dissected, frame by frame, the tight defensive methodology of Long Island.

The finals were a complete reversal of the shock Edmonton had received the previous season. Where Edmonton had been shut out 2-0 at Northlands in the 1982/83 opening game , the Oilers now shut out the Islanders in Nassau. Edmonton was far from stingy in its own end, relying on Fuhr to turn away thirty-eight shots, but it held off the Islanders' attack and pounced on the only offensive opportunity required. At 1:55 of the third period, Islanders forward Duane Sutter coughed up the puck in his own end. Kevin McClelland, the midseason addition from Pittsburgh who was better known for his penalty minutes (189) than his goals (ten), emerged from his forechecking and troublemaking to bury the puck behind Billy Smith. The lead held and, for once, it was advantage Edmonton.

The Oilers almost let the series get away from them in game two, a brawl-filled contest the Islanders won 6-1 with Roly Melanson taking Smith's place in goal. But when the series moved to Edmonton for the next three games, the Oilers were in complete control, scoring nineteen times as the Islanders managed only six in return.

The series turned the Oilers' way in the final minute of the second period in game three. Tied 2-2, the Oilers got to play four-on-four, and Paul Coffey scored twice in seventeen seconds. Outshooting the Islanders 40-26, the Oilers added three more goals in the third period for a 7-2 romp.

In game four, the Islanders were trailing 2-0 when Edmonton's Ken Linseman was assessed a five-minute major for slashing Bryan Trottier in the face. The Islanders could not produce a goal in the lengthy power play, and went on to lose 7-2. When the Oilers got their sixth goal, Arbour pulled Smith in favour of Melanson. Taking Smith, the ultimate money goalie, out of the series for the second time was as good as a sign of surrender from the Islanders. The Oilers had lost Grant Fuhr in game three with a bruised shoulder, and in his stead Andy Moog was playing terrifically. The Islanders were dispirited and suffering. Dehydrated, Denis Potvin was knocked out of game three with leg cramps, and a viral infection made Mike Bossy completely ineffective in games four and five, in which he didn't get a shot on net.

Game five brought the Oilers within grasp of a Cup victory on home ice. With Moog still in goal, the Oilers built a 4-0 lead, even though they were outshot 25-22 in the game. Smith was pulled in favour of Melanson again, and the Islanders mounted one final, desperate assault in the third period. It wasn't enough, and Edmonton won 5-2.

With the Stanley Cup finally in their grasp (and filled with champagne to pour over the head of Peter Pocklington), the Oilers had achieved the goal they had set themselves six years earlier with the signing of Gretzky. But the victory did not rest on his shoulders alone. It was Mark Messier, not Gretzky, who was awarded the Conn Smythe Trophy as the playoff MVP. Gretzky produced the most assists (twenty-two) and points (thirty-five) of the playoffs, but in the trench warfare of the series against Calgary and especially the Islanders, it was Messier's physical play that carried the Oilers forward, in addition to eight postseason goals and eighteen assists. Messier had turned in the most ornery regular season of his entire career, with 165 penalty minutes, a huge increase from the seventy-two of 1982/83, while gathering 101 points. The weakness of Gretzky's style was revealed in the heavy traffic of an aggressive physical game. Unlike Messier, he could not fight his way through and still contribute to scoring. Gretzky needed a linemate who could ride shotgun for him—at first Dave Semenko, later Mike Krushelnyski, with Marty McSorley lurking back on defence—who could make sure no one ran the scoring star. He had to resort to evasion rather than confrontation—avoid hits, pass the puck to team-mates—and when abused, rather than retaliating the way Messier could, he had to turn to his on-ice bodyguard, or take dives to draw the referee's attention to the abuse he was taking. Gretzky's disinclination to fight elbows with elbows, hooks with hooks, made some people resentful of his special status in the game: protected by team-mates and by those who argued that, as an exceptional talent, he should be given special treatment by on-ice officials and by opponents, who would be endangering the marketability of the game if they ever hurt him. Gretzky, for his part, assured people he took a lot of hits, and devoted a lot of energy to making sure he didn't line himself up for more of them.

The Islanders had neutralized Gretzky in the 1982/83 series and appeared to be on their way to doing it again in the first two games of 1983/84. Gretzky didn't get his first goal in the finals until he opened the scoring in game three. Messier's Conn Smythe win was not a repudiation of Gretzky's skills, but an indication that a championship team needed more than playmaking finesse. It was the first indication that the Oilers might be able to win without Gretkzy, and that they could lose if Messier was not completely effective.

THE OILERS followed the 1983/84 Stanley Cup win with an encore performance in the 1984 Canada Cup in September. Gretzky had been the only member of the Oilers to participate for Canada in the 1981 tournament, in which the Soviet Union laid on an 8-1 humiliation in the one-game final. After leading the tournament with five goals and seven assists, Gretzky couldn't produce a single point in the deciding game. For Gretzky and for hockey nationalists, the 1984 series was an important opportunity to restore pride.

Glen Sather was named the team's coach and general manager, and he loaded the team with Oilers. He took Grant Fuhr, four defencemen (Paul Coffey, Randy Gregg, Charlie Huddy[2] and Kevin Lowe) and forwards Glenn Anderson, Wayne Gretzky and Mark Messier. The ill will between the Oilers and Islanders in the Team Canada dressing room, left over from the Stanley Cup finals, almost tore the team apart. Canada had a poor round-robin, with two wins, two losses (including a 6-3 trouncing by the Soviet Union) and a tie to finish in fourth, behind the Soviet Union, the United States and Sweden. The team was able to resolve its differences long enough to get the job done in the semi-finals. Tied 2-2 at the end of regulation time in its game against the Soviets, Canada advanced with a symbolic bit of cooperation as Mike Bossy deflected a Paul Coffey shot into the Soviet net. The win brought on a best-of-three final against Sweden, which had crushed the United States 9-2 in their semi-final. Canada won 5-2 and 6-5 to regain the trophy.[3]

Only five players had returned to the Canadian team from the 1981 squad. One of the newcomers was Mike Gartner, who had played in three World Championships for Canada since 1981 but, despite a forty-eight-goal effort in 1980/81 with Washington, was cut from the Canadian team at the 1981 Canada Cup training camp. Gartner had played with Messier as a Cincinnati Stinger, and against Messier, Gretzky and company for the past five years in the NHL.

In Edmonton, says Gartner, "Wayne Gretzky was the key to the entire process. Players were able to come in and be part of his whole aura. It made them infinitely better hockey players. It gave them tremendous confidence, and confidence is the key to achieving in any sport. That's why they were considered such a cocky team. They were so confident. Anybody drafted into that system had an automatic confidence that made them a great player. I saw it happen at the training camps for the 1981 and 1984 Canada Cups, and the big changeover in the Canadian team in 1984 from the Islanders to the Oilers. When Gretzky and company came in, they just lifted the whole level of play up. The confidence he exuded helped everybody, even the best players from other teams."

EDMONTON'S PERFORMANCE the next season was not quite as overwhelming as its 1983/84 showing, but was hardly disappointing. Retreating to forty-nine wins, the team finished second in the league to Philadelphia, but still led comfortably in offence with 401 goals, while bringing its goals-against below 300 (to 298) for the first time since 1981/82. Gretzky won another scoring race (with 208 points), with linemate Kurri finishing second with 135 points and Coffey fifth with 121. Gretzky collected the Art Ross, Hart and Pearson trophies again, while Coffey won his first Norris and Kurri earned the Lady Byng. The Oilers dominated the first All Star team, with Gretzky, Kurri and Coffey being named.

The team was entering a transition phase, with Sather beginning to change the lineup around the nucleus, relying on deals with his old friends Lou Nanne in Minnesota and Harry Sinden in Boston. Ken Linseman was sent to Boston for Mike Krushelnyski. While far from being a brawler, Krushelnyski nonetheless could provide muscle for the line of Gretzky and Kurri. After joining them, his points production went from forty-five to eighty-eight in one season. Glenn Anderson and Mark Messier were also given a new linemate in January as Mark Napier, one of the original underage free agents of the WHA, who had won a Stanley Cup with Montreal in 1978/79, was acquired from Minnesota. Larry Melnyk, a defenceman who'd been picked up from Boston the previous March to beef up for the playoffs and who appeared in six playoff games, divided his 1984/85 season between the Oilers and Edmonton's new AHL affiliate, the Nova Scotia Voyageurs (which were renamed the Oilers in 1985/86). And when the Islanders made centre Billy Carroll available in the October 1984 waiver draft, Sather took him. Sather got a season out of him, but when he demoted Carroll to Nova Scotia in 1985/86, Carroll requested a trade, feeling he didn't belong in the AHL when he still had something to offer the NHL. Sather concurred, and sent him to Detroit. Finally, two future Oilers regulars made appearances. Defenceman Steve Smith was called up from Nova Scotia for two games, and Esa Tikkanen joined the lineup for three playoff games after starring for Finland at the World and World Junior championships.

Changes were also afoot in management. Sooner or later, Glen Sather was expected to withdraw from coaching and concentrate on the president's and general manager's jobs. John Muckler made it clear he expected to succeed him as the Oilers' coach. A career minor-league coach, Muckler had taken the head coaching job in Minnesota at the age of thirty-four in 1968/69, before he was ready for the major leagues. The North Stars won only six of thirty-five games under him, and he was fired. He spent the 1970s coaching in the minors, working in the Vancouver Canucks system. Hired by Sather to coach Wichita in the CHL in 1982, he quickly was elevated to Edmonton to replace Billy Harris as an assistant coach. Muckler had assisted Sather with Team Canada in the 1984 Canada Cup, and he had made a solid impression on the players from around the NHL who had participated. "I know when Slats [Sather's nickname] steps down I'm going to be the next coach of the Oilers hockey club and, at this time, I want it," Muckler said in December 1984.

Muckler's contract with Edmonton would be up for renewal in June 1985, and he expected a head coaching job—if not in Edmonton, then somewhere else in the league. Muckler's old organization, the

Canucks, was in the hunt for a head coach. Harry Neale, who had replaced Roger Neilson at the end of 1983/84, was in turn replaced by Bill Laforge after sixty games in 1984/85 in what was viewed as a temporary move.

Compared with the 1983/84 playoff run, the 1984/85 season was anticlimactic. In the first round, however, Los Angeles at times threatened an upset even more colossal than the one the Kings managed in 1981/82. On March 1, Andy Moog was injured in a collision with the Kings' J.P. Kelly, by default making Fuhr, who had been in a slump, the starting netminder for the playoffs. Fuhr had been scalded by the Kings in 1981/82, and in the 1984/85 series was forced to turn away penalty shots in both games two and three. While the Oilers needed overtime wins in games one and three, they swept the Kings. They were spared a gruelling division final when Winnipeg eliminated Calgary in the opening round. Had Winnipeg not defeated Calgary, the series between the Flames and the Oilers probably would have been exceptionally brutal, because Mark Messier had served a ten-game suspension in the regular season for cracking the cheekbone of Jamie Macoun with a high stick. (Messier had also been suspended for six games the previous season, in February 1984, for breaking his stick over the head of Vancouver's Thomas Gradin.) Edmonton took the Jets in four straight, gaining speed as they played on through the spring. After defeating Winnipeg 8-3 in the final game, they moved on to a rollicking shoot-out with Chicago. They ran their playoff streak to nine straight wins with scores of 11-2[4] and 7-3, before the Blackhawks fought back with 5-2 and 8-6 wins. But the Oilers finished them off emphatically, with 10-5 and 8-2 efforts. In six games against the Blackhawks, the Oilers had scored forty-four times.

In the 1984/85 finals, Edmonton faced Philadelphia. The Flyers, the regular-season champions, had a rebuilt lineup with rookie coach Mike Keenan in charge. Much tighter in their own end than Edmonton, they missed having the season's best defensive record by four goals. They surprised the Oilers in game one, winning 4-1, but thereafter the Oilers ran the show, and concluded four straight wins with an 8-3 victory, the largest number of goals scored in a Cup-winning game.

Grant Fuhr's fifteen playoff wins in one season matched the record set by Billy Smith in 1979/80 and 1981/82. The Oilers' scoring set a plethora of new standards. Jari Kurri produced a playoff-season record of nineteen goals. Twelve of them came against Chicago, a record for a playoff series other than the finals, and his fifteen points against the Blackhawks was then the fourth highest for a non-finals playoff series. Kurri also set a record for the most three-or-more-goal games in one playoff year (four) as he recorded one four-goal game and three three-goal games, surpassing the record (three) set by Mark Messier and Mike Bossy in 1982/83. Three of these games came in the Chicago series, which was a record for one playoff series.

Gretzky won the Conn Smythe, as he led on playoff assists (thirty) and points (forty-seven) for the third consecutive season. The thirty assists were a new playoff record, and his seven points in the 8-3 defeat of Winnipeg in game four of the division finals tied his record effort against Calgary in the 10-2 game three division finals win of 1982/83. His eighteen points in the Chicago series was second only to the nineteen points scored by Rick Middleton in 1982/83 in one playoff series other than the finals, and his hat trick in the 4-3 defeat of Philadelphia in game three was a Cup-final rarity. But some felt the Conn Smythe should have gone to Coffey, who was masterful. His six points against Chicago in the 10-5 win in game five set a playoff record for defencemen, and he set new playoff-year records for defencemen in points (thirty-seven), goals (twelve) and assists (twenty-five). His thirty-seven points eclipsed the twenty-five-point standard set by Denis Potvin in as many games (eighteen) in 1980/81. "I've never seen anyone play better, including Himself," said assistant coach Ted Green—who by "Himself" meant his old Bruins team-mate, Bobby Orr, whose playoff assists record of nineteen Coffey had just obliterated.

That summer, the coaching staff underwent important changes. Unwilling to leave the bench just yet, Sather struck a compromise with the ambitious Muckler, agreeing to make him his co-coach. Green announced that he was leaving to tend to a computerized skate sharpening business he owned. In his stead Sather hired Bob McCammon, who two years earlier had been coach and general manager of the Flyers before Bobby Clarke replaced him as GM and hired Mike Keenan as coach. Sather credited McCammon with building the team that had made it to the 1984/85 finals against the Oilers. Esa Tikkanen joined Kurri on Gretzky's line; muscle was added as Steve Smith and Marty McSorley (acquired from Pittsburgh) joined the defence. Sather launched another player revitalization project as he took centre Craig MacTavish from Boston. MacTavish had been ruined by a vehicular manslaughter conviction, which sent him to prison in 1984/85. Sather had helped Harry Sinden get MacTavish out of town to start over again by signing him as free agent in February 1985; he joined the team for 1985/86, and stayed with the Oilers for nine seasons.

The stage was set for a "three-peat," as the Oilers embarked on one of their greatest regular seasons. It ended as few glorious campaigns do: in an apparently innocuous miscue, with no time left do do anything about it.

*Seventeen-year-old Wayne Gretzky enjoys breakfast with
Nelson Skalbania after signing a seven-year personal services
contract with Skalbania, owner of the World Hockey Association's
Indianapolis Racers, on June 12, 1977.* [AP]

*Walter Gretzky looks on as Wayne Gretzky celebrates his eighteenth birthday on
January 26, 1978, by signing a twenty-one-year personal services contract with
Edmonton Oilers owner Peter Pocklington at Northlands Coliseum.* [Canadian Press]

Oilers captain Wayne Gretzky screams with joy as he hoists the
Stanley Cup over his head for the first time, following the team's defeat of the
New York Islanders at Edmonton's Northlands Coliseum on May 19, 1984.
[Canadian Press]

Oilers captain Mark Messier celebrates the team's fifth Stanley Cup victory after defeating the Boston Bruins on May 24, 1990. [Canadian Press]

Oilers coach and general manager Glen Sather addresses the media at the
press conference held on August 11, 1988, to reveal that Wayne Gretzky
(watching teary-eyed in the background) has been dealt to the Los Angeles Kings.
[Canadian Press]

▲ *Rick LeLacheur, president and* CEO *of Economic Development Edmonton, was a key player in efforts to keep the Oilers in Edmonton.* [Canadian Press]

◀ *Peter Pocklington announces the sale of the Edmonton Oilers on June 5, 1997.* [Canadian Press]

An Oilers "untouchable" in the 1980s, Kevin Lowe battles Toronto's Tie Domi for the puck in October 1997 after returning to the Oilers from the New York Rangers. [Canadian Press]

▲ *Would-be Oilers purchaser (and fraud convict) Michael Largue appears before the Edmonton media on March 2, 1998.* [Canadian Press]

◀ *Houston millionaire Les Alexander enters an Edmonton city hall meeting hosted by mayor Bill Smith to discuss his proposed purchase of the Oilers on November 3, 1997.* [Canadian Press]

Bruce Saville, Cal Nichols and Jim Hole, three of the major local investors in the bid to keep the NHL's Oilers in Edmonton, celebrate with champagne at a news conference on March 13, 1998, as they announce they have the money to keep the Oilers in town. [Canadian Press]

Oilers assistant captain Doug Weight and Mike Grier celebrate the first Edmonton goal against the Colorado Avalanche, en route to upsetting the Avalanche in the opening round of the 1997/98 Stanley Cup playoffs. [Canadian Press]

Chapter Nine

No groups of citizens are more polarized in their empowerment than voters and sports fans. The voter has the ability to change governments. The sports fan, while perhaps better informed about the game and its players than the voter is about the politicians and their platforms, has no control over the outcome of the contest. He can only watch helplessly as events unfold, for better or worse.

"Give the masses bread and circuses," went the recipe for civic contentment in ancient Rome—a sensible approach in a metropolis without ballot boxes. The republic gave the people not necessarily what they wanted—power over their own lives—but what they craved. Full stomachs and arenas full of spectacle. These were not games that harboured the possibility of disappointment. The lions were not going to be eaten by the Christians. As an opiate of the masses, a coliseum's excesses were administered in reliable dosages. In modern organized sport, however, there is the ever-present possibility that the paying customers will be let down, that an entire arena full of people will be left dejected by the failure of a team to deliver on their fans' ambitions. The spectator can wish all he may for a championship, even expect it as a matter of course, but there is nothing he can do to actually make it happen. He is as loud, as joyful, as angry, as dejected, as he is powerless.

Edmontonians had developed a complacency about winning. The Edmonton Eskimos of the CFL had inculcated high expectations in the city's sports fans, and when the Edmonton Oilers began winning Stanley Cups, it was naturally expected of them to continue doing so indefinitely. It wasn't unusual for conspicuous numbers of Northlands seats to be empty at an opening-round Oilers playoff game as paying customers chose to skip the initial stages of what was presumed to be another championship drive. In the spring of 1983, 1984 and 1985, the Oilers had reached the Stanley Cup finals, winning on the last two occasions. And after a season like 1985/86, there was every reason to believe that a fourth finals appearance was probable, if not inevitable.

Spectators, it is regularly said, vote with their feet. On the evening of April 30, 1986, 17,498 of them filed out of Northlands Coliseum, the vast majority benumbed by a sporting catastrophe they had been able to do nothing to avert. Winning teams create the sensation of a bond between the players and the fans. A winning team that suddenly loses abruptly finds that bond severed. If the team does not lose the fan altogether, then it at least loses its grip on the fan's unquestioning devotion. An accounting is required. Heads must roll. Even Wayne Gretzky knew this. Before the fateful game, the Oilers' star had allowed that "good guys" would be traded if the team didn't produce another Cup win. The thousands of Oilers fans who made their way out of Northlands that night after the Oilers' shocking loss were primed for change. The same-old, the tried and proven, wasn't good enough.

Unhappily for Don Getty, the premier of Alberta, he was asking these same people to re-elect his Progressive Conservative government in just eight days.

I N EDMONTON, ALBERTA, in the spring of 1986, the bread was in short supply and the circus was in danger of folding its tent, while the public was about to go to the polls to elect another provincial government.

The Edmonton Oilers returned from Calgary for a seventh and deciding game against the Flames in the Smythe Division finals. In the opening round the Oilers had swept the Vancouver Canucks in three games and outscored them 17-5—a performance to be expected from a champion club that had produced a league-leading 426 goals that season, compared to Vancouver's 282, and had won more than twice as many games as the Canucks. The Flames, however, who had finished second to the Oilers in the Smythe and scored seventy-two fewer goals, refused to allow the division finals to play out according to statistical probability. When Edmonton lost game five 4-1 on April 26 at Northlands, to fall behind 3-2 in the series, a seventh game on April 30 was preordained were the Oilers to have a chance of advancing. A 5-2 Edmonton win in Calgary on April 28 brought on the decisive game in the all-Alberta division final. Toronto would play St. Louis in their own game-seven showdown the same night to determine the other conference finalist.

Leaf fans would have to follow their game on television, since the Blues were hosting the deciding game. Oilers fans, in contrast, would be gathering at Northlands to see if Glen Sather's still youthful club (no one was older than twenty-eight) had the makings of a true dynasty, or was already a spent force, a half-realized successor to the New York Islanders. The Oilers had lost only six of forty home games all season, finishing first overall in the league, but had thus far in the series against Calgary lost two of three home games. In five of the six games, the Flames had scored first, forcing the Oilers to play catch-up hockey, and had confounded Edmonton's wide-open style with a tough checking game.

The Edmonton CBC television affiliate faced a seemingly insoluble programming decision. Should the Oilers defeat Calgary on Wednesday night and advance to the conference finals, they would be playing game four on May 8, the same night as the provincial election. Which would the CBC cover more prominently? Could they get by carrying the game and cutting away to the election results during the intermissions? If the game was played in Toronto, two time zones away, the third period might wrap up by 8:30 Edmonton time, freeing up much of prime time for the election returns, but a game in St. Louis wouldn't end until 9:30. And God forbid that the game might go into overtime, wherever it was played. The premier-elect would be trying to make himself heard to his subjects between beer commercials and instant replays.

Anyone who thought this would be an easy programming decision didn't know much about the city. The Oilers occupied centre stage in Edmonton's affections and attention. A provincial election was an important civic event, but in Alberta they tended to be bereft of any drama. Peter Lougheed had presided as the blue-eyed sheik of the premiership for fourteen years of Progressive Conservative rule before retiring in June 1985. Thanks to the Lougheed government's decisive performance in the 1982 election—winning seventy-five of seventy-nine seats—whoever won the ensuing PC leadership convention would inherit a party with a stranglehold on the legislature.

Don Getty, a Grey Cup hero as quarterback of the Edmonton Eskimos in the 1950s, emerged from the convention huddle as the new premier. Getty had been a member of Lougheed's inner circle when the party began its rise from obscurity in the mid-1960s. But Getty was coming to power in times far different than the economic glory years of the 1970s, when oil and gas had made the province tremendously rich. Canadians in Ontario and Quebec had shaken off the short, sharp recession of 1982 to embark on the runaway boom of the eighties. In Alberta, the eighties binge never quite came calling. The 1982 recession was devastating in the west, and it had given Peter Pocklington his first major business reversal. Like so many western trust companies, his Fidelity Trust had significant capital reserves tied up in real estate. As interest rates climbed above 20 percent, real estate values plummetted, taking the trust companies with them. Fidelity staggered forward into 1984, then collapsed. It cost the Canadian Deposit Insurance Corporation $359 million to rescue depositors at

Fidelity alone, as independent trust companies dropped like dominoes. Credit unions were so devastated that the provincial government spent millions propping them up.

Easterners oblivious to the lean years out west could mistakenly equate the dynamic on-ice success of the Oilers, its vibrancy and youth, its threat to the established pecking order, with Alberta itself. But the perception was off by a full decade. The Oilers might prove to be a team for the ages, but at the time it was rewriting record books many of its fans were struggling.

The saga of the Oilers was almost coincident with the saga of modern Alberta: the team's WHA franchise was awarded in November 1971, just after Lougheed's breakthrough election. After the OPEC oil embargo, launched in the wake of the 1973 Middle East War, clobbered the Western world, more than doubling oil prices in January 1974, inflation helped keep prices high for the rest of the decade. Alberta, rich in oil and gas reserves, embarked on a perpetual feud with central Canada and the federal government over just how rich and how independent both the province and the oil industry were going to be. Pierre Trudeau's Liberals had formed a national oil company, Petro Canada, partly at the urging of the leftist New Democratic Party, which was supporting his minority government. Nationalization in the oil patch was not a popular strategy with westerners, but there was worse to come. The Iranian hostage crisis of 1979 set off another oil embargo, quickly doubling the barrel price and sending it above the thirty dollar level. After the federal Liberals defeated Albertan Joe Clark's minority Progressive Conservative government in the 1980 election, the hated National Energy Policy was enacted. Among other things, the NEP placed price limits on Alberta oil for domestic consumption that were well below the world price commanded by OPEC. Lougheed responded with court challenges to Ottawa's resource meddling and launched an intranational embargo by cutting back Alberta's production to force up domestic prices.

The election of Brian Mulroney's majority Progressive

Conservative government in 1984 would begin the dismantling of the NEP, but as the program faded, so did Alberta's opportunity to reap windfalls from sky-high world oil prices. In 1980, when Trudeau's Liberals had returned to power, crude oil prices in U.S. dollars per barrel almost broke through the $40 ceiling. Peter Pocklington, who had sunk some cash into natural resources investments, happily predicted that oil prices could reach $50 to $60 a barrel. But prices began a steady retreat below $30, and in early 1986 the price went into freefall as the U.S. Federal Reserve Board pressed its war on inflation. As the Edmonton Oilers recorded one of its greatest regular seasons, the industry that inspired the team's name imploded, its losses draining away the livelihoods of the fan base.

On December 11, 1985, the Oilers claimed another line in the NHL record book, as they combined with the Chicago Blackhawks to tie the league mark for the most goals in one game (twenty-one in a 12-9 victory for Edmonton) and set a new record for most goals in one period (six each in the second period), with Gretzky notching a record-tying seven assists in the game. But as the Oilers' accomplishment was being duly recorded, oil was lurching downward to $27 a barrel. It slid to $23 in January, then plummetted to $15 in February, when Gretzky equalled his record seven assists in an 8-2 home win against the Nordiques on Valentine's Day. In March, when Paul Coffey registered eight points—two goals and six assists, a record-tying effort for a defenceman—in a 12-3 home defeat of Detroit on the 14th, oil dropped below $13, where it remained to cast a pall over the Oilers' playoff run in April. The more records the Oilers broke in scoring, the more records the beleaguered oil industry seemed to set in lost value. Some industry members were contending they needed $16 a barrel just to break even in their operations. By August, they would be getting less than $12, a price not seen since 1976.

As the Oilers prepared for game seven against the Flames, Brian Mulroney tossed Don Getty an electoral bone. To give a break to western Canadian farmers, prairie grain freight rates would be frozen for a year beginning August 1, and the farm fuel tax rebate would be raised from 3 to 5.5 cents per litre.¹ He also sped up the dismantling of one of the last vestiges of Trudeau's hated NEP. With Finance Minister Michael Wilson determined, come what may, to balance the federal budget, the Petroleum Gas Revenue Tax, a gross tithe assessed at the wellhead, had remained in place after the Liberal defeat in 1984. Scheduled to be phased out by 1988, the PGRT's disappearance was now accelerated slightly. Mulroney exempted Alberta's two commercial oil sands projects, run by Syncrude and Suncor, from the tax for the rest of the year, and raised the maximum PGRT tax credit for oil companies from $500,000 to $2 million. The increased tax credit had the immediate effect of exempting all but forty-five of some 600 oil companies from having to pay the tax at all.

But Mulroney's gesture could not prevent reminders of difficult times from percolating up from the oil patch, into the minds of voters, as the Oilers prepared for game seven. Dome Petroleum, the once-mighty leader in oil field exploration, announced it had won a thirty-day extension from the courts, giving it until May 30 to negotiate a new repayment schedule for its colossal debt load of $5.3 billion.

Despite the Fidelity Trust collapse, Peter Pocklington was still presiding over a business empire with outward good health, but his former Oilers partner Nelson Skalbania was struggling to keep his head above the red ink. No longer a part of the Flames' ownership, Skalbania had a predilection for making lightning-fast real estate flips (some of them to Pocklington) that had caught up with him. Losses in the collapsed Vancouver market, where he was now based, had put him $10 million in the hole. The previous July, Skalbania had picked up half of Ponderosa Ventures Inc. on the Vancouver exchange for 55 cents a share, and was hoping to ratchet up the holding company's value so he could pay off his creditors. Skalbania was using Ponderosa to raise capital for a slew of ventures, including Alberta's Allwest supermarket chain, Western Match Factory in Penticton, B.C., and Columbia Trust Co. in Vancouver. In a recent series of business plays,

Skalbania had folded into Ponderosa a restaurant in Colorado, a sub-division in the ski-resort town of Whistler, B.C., and a large holding in the laser research company Westlake Resources. Beginning the new year with Ponderosa trading at 98 cents, Skalbania had raised $4 million in capital for the shell company by arranging private placements of shares. He had managed to hold on to his 50 percent share of the stock by rolling his own business interests into Ponderosa and promising to devote all of his energies to the company. The day before game seven between the Oilers and Flames, Ponderosa was trading at $4.55. It looked like the man who had given Wayne Gretzky his start in professional hockey and Pocklington the opportunity to own the Oilers just might dig his way out of another hole.

With eight days left to the Alberta provincial election, though, Don Getty was digging himself into a deep one as his campaign sputtered badly. The stolid former gridiron star was no Lougheed. Another PC majority in the legislature in Edmonton seemed almost a given, but there was a real possibility of some measure of upset emerging in the unlikely guise of the New Democrats, who held just two seats. Left-wing labour politics were generally not to the taste of the Alberta electorate, but these were increasingly tough times, and dissatisfaction was growing with the disconcertingly clumsy Getty. He was campaigning in the upbeat mode of Lougheed, yet his off-the-cuff optimism was producing self-inflicted wounds. In its single-minded war on international terrorism, the United States had launched an air strike against Libya, killing and wounding a number of civilians. The campaigning Getty grasped the tragedy as a break-through for Alberta tourism. Who'd want to board a plane with all this terrorist activity? "Would you fly to Europe now, or Athens?" he asked. On the day of game seven, he outdid himself with his spin on the news of the nuclear meltdown at Chernobyl. As citizens crouched in fear of the radioactive miasma predicted to be heading their way over the pole, and as the scale of human tragedy in Ukraine became apparent, Good News Getty saw the prospect of nuclear winter as a boon to the province's flagging oil industry. Nuclear power plant construction was going to dry up after this mishap. Oil demand would increase. The barrel price would go up. Prosperity for the province would result. The editorial page of the *Edmonton Journal* could scarcely contain its distaste for Getty's relentless boosterism.

While it would take a catastrophe on the scale of Chernobyl to prevent the PCs from retaining power, the opposition appeared, as election day approached, to have a genuine opportunity to make a dent in the near-monopoly Getty's government enjoyed. NDP leader Ray Martin was tooling around the 660,000 square kilometres of Alberta's Big Sky country in a rented Greyhound bus plastered with campaign posters. Squirrelled away with him were advisors parachuted in from Manitoba and Saskatchewan, where the NDP had actual experience of winning provincial elections. Ray Martin appeared to have no real hope of forming a government, but he was threatening a certain measure of humiliation for Getty. Edmonton in particular, where Getty had to defend his own seat, was vulnerable. The provincial capital was full of white-collar unionists, government employees who bore no resemblance to the small-*c* conservative stalwarts out on the farms and ranches who were the traditional bedrock of PC support. The very idea that Alberta was a frontier society, populated exclusively by ranchers and oil rig roughnecks, was increasingly the stuff of myth alone. About 80 percent of the province's people were urbanites—as firmly ensconced in the world of pavement, streetlights, and municipal water and sewage as were people in Ontario and Quebec. More than half of Alberta's 2.5 million population was crowded into just two cities, whose hockey teams were trying to advance toward the Stanley Cup finals. Edmonton was a metropolis of 800,000, Calgary of some 700,000; no other urban centre had many more than 60,000 citizens. Martin saw his party's opportunity in the province's changing demographics. There was, he pointed out, "a much more diverse society in

Alberta" than when the Progressive Conservatives first piled up their big majorities.

As Martin's campaign gained momentum, Getty momentarily failed to stick to the proven Lougheed campaign script: he actually acknowledged the existence of the opposition. Getty did, however, turn to the most well-worn page in the Alberta PC political playbook: taking pot-shots at easterners. Martin, he declared, was nothing more than a tool of Toronto. That's where the marching orders were issued for the NDP, Getty opaquely explained. As a native Albertan running in the riding of Edmonton–Norwood, Martin was baffled by Getty's charge, but its inspiration was obvious. The Canadian Labour Congress was holding its annual convention in Toronto, and its 3,000 delegates were welcoming a new leader, Shirley Carr. Carr was something new for the union movement. Since its formation in 1956, the CLC had never had a woman as its head, or anyone from outside the ranks of industrial labour. As a former social worker, Carr represented labour's anticipated next wave of support, the white-collar employee. Her agenda was concerned with such "pink-ghetto" issues as pay equity and child care. But she was also determined to unite the oft-fragmented labour movement, and to do it Carr would choose as a prime target Progressive Conservatives, wherever they ruled. A former NDP candidate, Carr restated the CLC's official support of the party (a support actually delivered fairly unevenly by unions' voters). Among the motions passed at the convention were calls for more public ownership of companies in the financial and natural resources sector.

Carr drew a bead on Prime Minister Mulroney, and in particular on the negotiations for freer trade with the United States, which were set to begin in Ottawa in just a few weeks. A weak Canadian dollar opened the potential for increased exports to the country's main trading partner, and free-trade proponents were further motivated to get a deal to offset protectionist sentiments in the U.S. Senate. But Canadian labour groups and economic nationalists feared an erosion of social policies and a loss of manufacturing jobs. The U.S. dollar was worth $1.31 Canadian when Mulroney came to power in September 1984, but he had not breathed a whisper about free trade in his election campaign—he had actually opposed it during his PC leadership bid in 1983. In the eighteen months since Mulroney's election, however, the dollar had retreated farther, and the U.S. dollar had broken through the $1.40 ceiling in January. "Freer" trade was now on the table, and organized labour was taking dead aim against it. "The prime minister of Canada," Shirley Carr informed the CLC convention, "has to understand he's not going to shove us around anymore."

Brian Mulroney would not have been prime minister without the support of Peter Pocklington at the 1983 leadership convention. For a conservative hardliner like Pocklington, Carr's promise of a more unified, more politicized, more militant labour movement was a gauntlet thrown. Within one month, he was facing a strike vote by workers at his Gainers meat packing plant in Edmonton. Their narrowly ratified two-year agreement, in which Pocklington wrested major wage and benefits concessions, was about to end. Production at Gainers had since tripled, and the Canadian labour movement under Carr was in a fresh fighting mood. The slaughterhouse operation Pocklington had bought in 1978 in part to get its real estate was poised to deliver a potentially fatal blow to his status as one of Canada's highest-flying entrepreneurs.

The game between Calgary and Edmonton began at Northlands on that Wednesday night in an atmosphere of uncertainty that rendered the building's structure virtually transparent; it was as if everything inside and outside the arena was up for grabs. The long-standing rivalry between the two cities found easy expression in sports, but this game was played in a cacophonous din of conflict generated by the impending provincial election and by the national tensions between left and right, labour and capital. The grim economic tidings made foolhardy any attempt to argue that victory in this game would resolve anything of substance. Winning would not bring back jobs, boost commodity prices, or erase an uneasy sense that the province's best years were over. Despite the wont of politicians to ally Alberta's prosperity with the federal/provincial power struggle, its boom years had always rested fundamentally in the hands of distant events beyond its control. An Arab-Israeli war, an Ayatollah ascendant, had allowed the Alberta oil fields to gush phenomenal wealth. Now the U.S. Federal Reserve Board wanted inflation tamed as the American deficit became alarmingly bloated. Too much oil, too little consumption and a tight-fisted monetary policy in the world's largest economy had pushed the commodity's price into the cellar. Almost eighteen thousand people in the arena, and hundreds of thousands of fans tuned in through television and radio, were free to confront the sensation that, however the game ended, when they woke up in the morning they would still be facing grim economic news and an impending election that invited a vote of protest as much as of choice.

About forty young men, clad in their respective bright uniforms—the red, gold and white of Calgary, the orange, blue and white of Edmonton—met for their seventh consecutive game, resolved to play at least sixty minutes of hockey that would rid themselves of each other for another season and allow one side to move on to wage another pitched battle with fresh opponents. Both sets of players had played a best-of-five series in the division semi-finals to get to this round, the last time they would have such a quick ramp-up into the second round. The new collective bargaining agreement that would be finalized that summer between the league and their union, the NHL Players' Association, would see them concede to play yet more playoff hockey, opening the postseason with a best-of-seven series. In the spring of 1986, the eight division semi-finals amounted to twenty-eight games; in the spring of 1987, the eight opening series would produce forty-four games—sixteen more dates in which to sell tickets, concessions, parking and air-time. It was one more in a series of blunders by the players' union in a decade that saw all the breaks go the owners' way.

The Flames could not boast a lineup full of talent the likes of the Oilers. It had strong goaltending from Mike Vernon, a Calgary native, and a relentless work ethic laid down by coach Badger Bob Johnson. The postseason rivalry called the Battle of Alberta, suspended in 1984/85 when Winnipeg eliminated Calgary in the opening round, returned with gritty intensity in the spring of 1986. Calgary had moved into the ranks of clubs with forty-win seasons in 1984/85, but still lagged behind Edmonton in overall and individual performances. The Oilers were a font of superlatives, winning fifty-six games in 1985/86 as they aspired to a third successive Cup win.

The Flames did not inspire complacency in Glen Sather, however. Calgary had entered the playoffs with a bolstered, well-rounded lineup. On February 1, a six-player deal with St. Louis had landed Calgary Joe Mullen, a tough right winger and a former NCAA All Star (whose brother Brian had played for Badger Bob at Wisconsin) who was capable of forty-goal seasons. And on the trade deadline, March 11, the Flames had picked up from the Islanders John Tonelli, a left winger who had participated in all four of New York's Stanley Cup wins, and had been through three critical playoff series against the Oilers—the 1980/81 quarter-final series and the 1982/83 and 1983/84 finals. Sather saw in particular three veterans—Tonelli, Doug Risebrough and Lanny McDonald—who were reaching the ends of their careers and would play with the kind of heart that comes from knowing this season might be their last opportunity to win a Stanley Cup.

Sather, on the other hand, had left the lineup of his club essentially intact. Left winger Esa Tikkanen, who had seen three games of action in the 1984/85 playoffs, had been called up from the Nova Scotia Oilers of the AHL for thirty-five games in 1985/86, and on April 30 was appearing in his eighth postseason game that spring. Defenceman Steve Smith, who at six feet four inches had in Sather's opinion the potential to be another Larry Robinson, was completing his rookie season. Gone was Jaroslav Pouzar, the veteran left winger from Czechoslovakia, now playing in Germany after three seasons with the Oilers. Right winger Pat Hughes, originally acquired late in the 1980/81 season from Pittsburgh, had been sent to Buffalo via Pittsburgh in October for right winger Mike Moller, who spent all but seven games of his time with Edmonton playing for its AHL farm team in Nova Scotia.

Edmonton lived and died by its offensive prowess, and the Flames took away two of Edmonton's three greatest scoring weapons. Neither Jari Kurri nor Paul Coffey could break through the checking game Calgary laid on in the neutral zone, and while Kurri switched his focus to defensive duties, Coffey mystified and infuriated some critics. In the 1984/85 finals against Philadelphia, Coffey had been able to rise above the pestering style of the Flyers and finish with his record thirty-seven points in eighteen playoff games. In the 1985/86 playoffs, however, Coffey did not dominate play in the way many expected of someone who had just won his second consecutive Norris Trophy as the league's top defenceman (with 138 points and a plus-minus of +61, both career-high performances). He would have only one goal and nine assists in ten games, a span in which the Oilers scored forty-one times.

Gretzky was playing to his consistently high standards, and the effort of Tikkanen provided reassurance of still more stellar talent in the Oilers system, but Mark Messier had been almost as disappointing as Coffey. "The Moose" didn't seem to show up against Calgary until game six, but observers were unaware he was playing with an injured shoulder. The team overall turned out for game seven to confront the spectre of its own passing as the league's dominant club. For a team that had just produced one of its greatest regular seasons—a franchise-high 119 points (tying the 1983/84 season), a fifth consecutive division title, a second overall regular-season title, the fewest road losses (eleven) in its history; coach of the year honours for Sather; All Star first-team appearances for Gretzky and Coffey, second-team honours for Kurri; the Art Ross and Hart trophies to Gretzky, the Norris to Coffey, runner-up status in Lady Byng voting for Kurri; a record 163 assists and 215 points for Gretzky, a record forty-eight goals (for a defenceman) for Coffey—it was both remarkable and appalling that not just a great season, but a great run through league history was on the verge of ending on the Northlands ice.

The game began badly; Calgary opened the scoring yet again and carried a 2-0 lead into the first intermission. In the second period, Edmonton's hope was renewed as goals by Messier and Glenn Anderson evened the score. At 5:18 of the final period, the comeback collapsed with a ghastly miscue. Steve Smith marked his twenty-third birthday in a cruelly unforgettable way. Pausing behind his own goal line, Smith casually directed a breakout pass up the middle of the ice . . . and banked the puck into his own net off the skate of Grant Fuhr. Calgary's go-ahead goal was awarded to the last Flame to touch the puck, Edmonton native Perry Berezan, his first of the series. The spectators in Northlands greeted the terrible gaffe with a stunned silence.

The Oilers poured shots on Flames goaltender Mike Vernon for the rest of the period, but he held his ground, and the go-ahead goal Smith had delivered for Calgary held up. In St. Louis, the Blues had edged the Leafs 2-1. The Flames and Blues would begin playing in the conference finals in two days. The CBC in Edmonton no longer had to worry about what to broadcast on May 8.

After the game, Wayne Gretzky spoke with the voice of a man whose team had just passed the torch to a new dynasty. "We've always looked up to the Islanders and saw how they were as champions," he told reporters. "We tried to emulate them. We took it away from them fair and square, just as Calgary did to us. We know how tough it is to win two Cups, we know how tough it is to win four. I'll tell you what: it's awfully hard just to win the first one."

The harsher world around the Oilers began to close in on the fans just as Gretzky contemplated the sobering defeat. At midnight, Suncor's tar sands operation in Fort McMurray was hit simultaneously by a strike and a lockout. The Independent Oil Workers Union, whose members were making $17 to $18 dollars an hour, had hoped to secure an extension of their existing contract for another year in light of the tax relief Brian Mulroney had just delivered the industry, but with tumbling prices management wanted overtime rates cut, and seniority clauses and severance pay benefits for layoffs dropped from the agreement. The day after the Oilers' loss, it was learned that Syncrude, the other commercial player in the oil sands, was cutting 300 of 4,500 white-collar jobs, 100 through immediate termination, the rest through programs such as early retirement. At the same time, Nova head Bob Blair informed company shareholders that pay cuts of eight to fifteen percent were being introduced for senior executives, with a merit pay increase of five percent cancelled. Also, 300 jobs were being slashed at subsidiary Husky Oil.

An Oilers fan, NDP leader Ray Martin nonetheless succumbed to Getty's affection for silver linings as he contemplated Edmonton's loss to Calgary. "It shows that with hard work, the underdogs come up from time to time," he ventured. Just like the mighty Oilers, he suggested, Getty's Conservatives were capable of scoring the winning goal on themselves.

And with no Stanley Cup run by the Oilers to distract them, the people of Edmonton, and much of the rest of Alberta, were left to contemplate the continuing flow of discouraging economic news for their province, and their voting options for election night. "Edmonton will certainly have a lot more interest in the election than they would have, obviously, with the Oilers not there," Martin said. "I'm not sure about Calgary."

On May 8, the New Democrats pulled off an unprecedented electoral rout in Edmonton, winning eleven seats. In all, the NDP won sixteen seats, while the previously phantom Liberal party (not seen in the legislature for twenty years) corralled four. With sixty-three seats, Getty had preserved a Conservative majority government, but the province's ruling elite had been put on notice. Three weeks later, the 1,080 unionized employees of Pocklington's Gainers plant walked off the job in what became one of the ugliest, most prolonged strikes in

Canadian labour history. Pocklington's defiance of the strike would so tax him financially that he would lose Gainers, a galaxy of Oilers stars, and finally the Oilers themselves.

The dismemberment of the Oilers dynasty had begun, appropriately enough, in a slaughterhouse. Two years after the 1986 playoff loss to the Flames, as Peter Puck peddled Wayne Gretzky to Bruce McNall and the Los Angeles Kings, Coffey (who by then had been shipped down the road to Pittsburgh) would acerbically note that Gretzky was sold "like a piece of meat." They had been two of the seven players Sather categorized as "untouchable" in 1986. None would remain in Edmonton for their entire careers. While Gretzky had predicted that "good guys" would be traded if the Oilers lost game seven of the 1985/86 Smythe Division finals to the Flames, he could not have imagined he would be one of them, or that the trades would come not because of a failure on the ice, but because of the failure of a group of hog butchers across town to secure a wage and benefits package they felt they deserved.

CHAPTER TEN

FTER THE TRAUMATIC loss to Calgary in the 1985/86 division finals, the Edmonton Oilers rebounded to win two consecutive Stanley Cups. These were noteworthy accomplishments, but in hindsight, from the perspective of the game as an enterprise and as a national institution, the events that unfolded off the ice in Edmonton in the late 1980s would hold equal if not greater significance in the history of the sport. What happened in Edmonton in those critical years had a profound impact on where the game was headed—on relations between management and labour, and ultimately on whether the entire game would leave the country.

In the midst of devastating events that were visited upon the Oilers and Peter Pocklington in the space of one month—the loss to Calgary on April 30, the strike at Gainers on June 1—came an incendiary article in *Sports Illustrated* on May 12, alleging that at least five members of the Oilers had "substantial" cocaine problems. One non-Oilers player said he had used cocaine with three Oilers during the past season. No offending players were named in the piece, and the Oilers organization and the NHL were infuriated by the unsubstantiated allegations. The team's defenders scored some points when it was revealed that one of the article's co-authors had been successfully sued for libel by a Canadian cabinet minister while at the *Toronto Sun*, but the article's timing, coming on the heels of the playoff disaster, seemed fortuitous for the magazine. Perhaps a reckless off-ice lifestyle had been the cause of the Oilers' playoff collapse?

The Oilers were a young team, with disposable income and a predilection for partying. When they won their first championship in 1983/84, the Stanley Cup was taken on a tour of Edmonton strip bars. A famous anecdote holds that rush-hour drivers on an Edmonton thoroughfare the morning after the Cup win encountered one hung-over Oiler seated at the side of the road, his arm draped familiarly around the trophy. Meanwhile, Mark Messier was courting notoriety with his driving escapades. Messier had failed a breathalyzer test in December 1981, was fined for refusing another one, and had once run his car into three parked vehicles. Edmontonians became accustomed to seeing Oilers zipping around in the black Porsches that Peter Pocklington handed out as playoff and contract bonuses.

But it was a big leap from a team marked by the typical off-ice tomfoolery of young professional athletes to one debilitated by drug abuse among its major players. And while the broad swath of accusation levelled by *Sports Illustrated* would never be proved (or disproved), in at least one case the problem would turn out to be very real.

For Pocklington, the PR problems of the *Sports Illustrated* article rapidly paled beside the public relations disaster of the Gainers strike, which became one of the longest and ugliest in Canadian labour history. Pocklington was primed for a showdown. He ran his first advertisement for replacement workers in the *Edmonton Sun* on May 13—the day after the *Sports Illustrated* article appeared and two weeks before the union had even voted to strike. Gainers offered the replacement workers $8 an hour—a dollar more than the existing contract specified.

The day before the union struck on June 1, Pocklington had made a preemptive move, suspending company contributions to the employee pension plan. He was made to restore them. On the first day of the strike, Pocklington was quoted as saying he'd never negotiate with a union again, though he later sent a letter to the union and media denying the statement.

The strike quickly became vicious. Pocklington hired strikebreakers and non-union hands to drive their buses through the picket lines. Five hundred police officers were on hand on the fourth day of the strike to get the replacement workers into the plant. Gainers secured court injunctions to address alleged picket-line violations and interference with other businesses through boycotts of Gainers products. On September 11, the union was found guilty of criminal contempt and fined $12,500.

An alarmed Premier Don Getty had attempted to clean up the mess by appointing Alex Dubensky as an Industry Disputes Inquiry Commissioner on June 11, in the hope that he could broker a settlement. Two months later, Dubensky took to the union a settlement proposal that fell far short of its demands, and the Union rejected it by a margin of almost 95 percent.

For the participants in Pocklington's annual fishing trip to Tree River, the controversy of the Gainers strike provided a raucous reception on their return to Edmonton in early August. The members of the fishing party, who included Ken Taylor and Ralph Lean, had to run a crushing gauntlet of media at Edmonton International Airport when they returned. Watching the news that night, Lean was amused to see himself identified as Taylor's bodyguard.

On September 4 and 5, Gainers management and its union met across the bargaining table for the first time since June, but the issue of replacement workers caused the talks to break down. Pocklington proposed a merit system of hiring in which worker would be pitted against worker, just like hockey players at training camp, in an effort to reduce the size of the payroll. The wage and benefits costs for the displaced workers would be shared equally by Gainers and the remaining employees.

The strike churned forward, a cause célèbre of both the Canadian labour movement and captains of industry, who felt it was time to draw a line in the sand for a labour movement that was becoming increasingly agitated over the federal government's free trade negotiations. The Gainers strike became too big for either side to back down. The union volunteered that there was more to the strike than wages and pension benefits at a hog butchering factory. Ed Seymour, the union rep responsible for media relations in the strike, wrote in the October 1986 issue of *Canadian Labour* (the magazine of the Canadian Labour Congress) that the Gainers action was "more than a strike by a union against an employer. It is a struggle against an anti-labour bias which exists throughout the province, within the ranks of the Conservative government of Alberta, the courts, the police and the business community. It symbolizes labour's efforts to put an end to concessions and unreasonable demands placed on workers by employers in the province."

"It was a brutal, brutal strike," says Lean. "Peter was not afraid to take on unions if he thought it was right. I got a lot of calls from very prominent businesspeople from across the country, saying, 'Tell Peter to keep it up. We support him.'" These callers, however, wouldn't say so publicly. In addition to his own convictions about the rightness of his cause, Pocklington was bearing the expectations of his fellow members of the corporate elite, and the entire strike was being played out against the battle his friend Brian Mulroney was waging against the left over the free trade agreement.

"Sometimes Peter is his own worst enemy," says Lean. "He wants to grab every nickel. He's always bought low and sold high, and he likes to use other people's money. But Peter is very smart and very tough. I represent a lot of Peter Pocklingtons. These are guys who sign on the dotted line, take risks, and employ people."

Pocklington felt he was fighting a war on two fronts: against the union, which had what he saw as an unrealistic ambition to bring wage and benefit levels up to parity with Ontario workers, and against the Alberta Pork Producers Development Corporation, which was driving up costs. "The problem," the Oilers' owner/entrepreneur proposed in an interview with *Alberta Report* in August 1998, "was the hog marketing board, which the government had legislated as the monopoly supplier in Alberta. Companies were forced out because the hog monopoly was formed to serve farmers. They raised the price of hogs so high that everyone was squeezed out of the business. It's no accident that today the only pork processing plant in this province is Fletcher's in Red Deer. And it belongs to—guess who?—the hog board! They've always said they would integrate upward and they succeeded."

Pocklington, and the friends who have stood by him, ultimately would feel he was vindicated in the Gainers strike by the eventual failure of the Edmonton plant in 1998 (as well as the failure of other western hog processing operations). The labour costs and hog prices rendered the business unprofitable. But if Pocklington's stand at Gainers was solely on principle—inviting an extended showdown rather than settling, selling the operation or closing it down as unprofitable—it was an enormously costly strategy.

IN ADDITION to the Gainers workers' vote to strike on June 1, Pocklington and the Oilers were impacted by another decision that summer, made by the membership of the NHLPA. It wasn't the new collective bargaining agreement, which was a win for Pocklington and his fellow team owners, with the players giving up liberalized free agency for new pension benefits. It was the majority decision of the NHLPA membership that Wayne Gretzky wasn't the league's most valuable player anymore.

NHL players are singled out for excellence by two different MVP awards: the Hart Memorial Trophy, which the league has been handing out since 1926, and the Lester B. Pearson Award, introduced in 1971. The Hart (voted on by professional hockey writers) honours the player "adjudged to be the most valuable to his team." The Pearson, donated by the NHLPA and voted upon by the players, honours the league's outstanding player. The Hart is the more subjective prize. The recipient isn't necessarily the best player in the league (which the Pearson presumes to recognize), only the player who is most valuable to his team, above and beyond all other players who are valuable to their teams.

The perception of Wayne Gretzky's excellence as exhibited by sportswriters and fellow players, each working to slightly different criteria, is informative. Gretzky was in his third season in the league before the NHLPA membership decided in 1982, after the Oilers' breakthrough season, that, yes, he's the best there is—holding off judgment while they voted for a second consecutive season for Marcel Dionne (who nipped Gretzky in the scoring race) in 1980, and then for goaltender Mike Liut in 1981.

The sportswriters, however, chose Gretzky as the MVP at the first opportunity, selecting him ahead of Dionne in 1980. From 1982 to 1985, the Hart and Pearson were in lock step: Gretzky was it. Then, in 1986, after the horrible finale to the 1985/86 season, the writers and the players broke ranks. The writers still thought Gretzky was the most valuable player to his team. The players, on the other hand, had decided he was no longer the league's outstanding player. They anointed a newcomer, Mario Lemieux of the Pittsburgh Penguins, whom the writers had made runner-up for the Hart. Super Mario had arrived, and the very stability of the Oilers dynasty was placed in question.

The writers remained loyal to Gretzky, awarding him the Hart again in 1987, as the NHLPA members returned the Pearson to him. But after 1987, Gretzky's fellow players never gave him the Pearson again, while he was awarded the Hart one more time, in 1989, when the NHLPA was choosing Steve Yzerman as the league's top player.

From the perspective of the Oilers' future and Gretzky's role in it, what mattered most was that in 1986, for the first time in four years, the Hart and Pearson did not agree that Gretzky was The Great One, and that after a return to consensus in 1987, the writers and the players parted ways on the subject of Gretzky's importance. And this crumbling of consensus came just as Peter Pocklington was heading into financial difficulty.

As a player, Gretzky was still extraordinary. Though denied the Art Ross Trophy (for the highest points total) by Lemieux in 1987/88 and 1988/89, Gretzky would win it three more times, as late as 1993/94. But in 1986, Pocklington could no longer be assured that he owned the greatest player in the league. Gretzky was getting older. Younger stars were emerging, and as an asset his value could only decline. Gretzky was still enormously talented and still a blue chip investment. But in 1986, with the announcement of the Pearson Award recipient, it must have seemed as if IBM had just shed twenty points.

Two factors impacting on Gretzky's future in Edmonton were more than plain to see after the 1986/87 season. Gretzky was not getting any younger, and Peter Pocklington was painting himself into a financial corner with the Gainers strike. During the 1986/87 season, Pocklington explored the possibility of taking the team public, inspired by the successful public offering on the New York Stock Exchange in 1986 of the limited partnership that owned the Boston Celtics of the NBA. Pocklington held discussions with the investment bank that put together the Celtics deal, with the idea of trying the same thing with the Oilers. He had considered such a share issue for all his sports investments back in 1981, but it didn't go forward then, and neither did the Celtics-inspired public offering. Ken Taylor feels that Pocklington ran into problems with the share-offering concept at the NHL board of governors level, although Harry Sinden of the Boston Bruins (who was abundantly aware of the Celtics share issue) doesn't recall the Oilers share issue plan ever getting to a vote before the board of governors.

Pocklington's exploration of taking the team public made his need for cash fully evident. After the Oilers rebounded from the 1985/86 playoff upset to win their third Cup in 1986/87, the time was right for Gretzky to secure a new contract—one that would replace the twenty-one-year personal services deal he had signed at eighteen, back when being taken care of by Peter Pocklington until he turned thirty-nine had seemed a great idea.

Since 1981, Gretzky had been represented by Mike Barnett, a former collegiate hockey player who had earned bachelor's degrees in physical education from St. Lawrence College in upstate New York in 1971 and in education from the University of Calgary in 1973. After spending five years in the minor pro system of the WHA's Houston Aeros, Barnett had turned to the agent business; one of his first clients, secured in 1979, was Lanny McDonald.

The new deal Barnett structured for Gretzky was for four years, with an option year that could extend the contract to five. While it did not have a no-trade clause, the contract would allow Gretzky to retire after three years. The logic was that, since it was very possible that Gretzky would eventually be traded to an American team with a big payroll, the presence of the retirement clause would give him some leverage in cutting a deal with the new team. Any team trading for him before the retirement clause kicked in would have to be prepared to present handsome terms to keep him active.

The retirement clause in the 1987 contract demonstrated that Gretzky was preparing for a trade in the near future. Gretzky may have wanted to finish his career in Edmonton, but Pocklington's circumstances made it imperative for Gretzky to sign a new deal that put him in the best possible position for a relocation. But the retirement clause also made it imperative for Pocklington to trade Gretzky within three years, as his market value would decrease steadily as his retirement option approached. And if Pocklington did not trade Gretzky and he did choose to retire, Pocklington would be left with nothing of value.

Having Gretzky around since 1978 had provided Pocklington with an enormous source of cash flow. But from a cold and practical business perspective, Gretzky was like an apartment building bringing in a steady flow of revenue, but which might suddenly be demolished. Pocklington would be mad not to try to sell his asset before the dynamite went off.

BESIEGED FROM outside his hockey operations by the Gainers workers, Peter Pocklington's ability to continue running the Oilers in relative comfort was also being threatened from within the NHL's power structure. NHL owners had been blessed by a complacent players' union, run by owner-friendly Alan Eagleson. But the movement to depose Eagleson, which would eventually rewrite the league's cost structure in the 1990s, was gathering momentum on Pocklington's own turf, in a small law office right in Edmonton.

Rich Winter was a kid growing up in Drumheller, Alberta, in the early 1970s when he took Alan Eagleson as a role model. Most boys keen on hockey want to play it for money some day; Winter wanted to do the deals. "I didn't know what he was," Winter remembers, "but what he looked like he was, was something I wanted to be."

The WHA was in its infancy; Eagleson was an off-ice hero of the 1972 summit series between Canada and the Soviet Union. Winter would grow up to be what Eagleson looked like he was, and from his base in Edmonton during the height of the Oilers' NHL success, he helped marshal the movement that brought Eagleson down and transformed the game. The Oilers were an extreme manifestation of the pre-downfall NHL economic climate, and when Eagleson was gone, it was no coincidence that the Oilers' greatest seasons would be gone, too. Rich Winter did not end the Oilers' reign, but had he not pursued so doggedly the controversial and powerful head of the NHLPA, the profound changes in the game's financial climate might never have occurred, and the Oilers might have rolled on, for at least a few more years, as a championship club. But the price would have been a players' union still under the control of a boss who was not simply owner-friendly, but corrupt.

None of the upheavals would have come to pass had not Winter, an idealistic Mormon law student, made his way to Los Angeles in 1982 in a third-year special study program of his own devising. Having already completed a commerce degree, Winter had turned to law at the University of Calgary. The third year of study presented the opportunity for a practicum, in which for a semester the student attended one course while gaining practical experience in the field. The practicum was normally conducted in a traditional pursuit like administrative or criminal law, but Winter, who was hooked on the idea of law as it applied to the entertainment and sports industries, proposed his own custom-designed program to take place in Los Angeles, home of Hollywood, recording stars and professional athletes of all stripes.

Winter had already made some connections in the film industry during a summer away from his law studies, when he insinuated himself into a job on a film starring veteran actor Darrin McGavin that was shooting around Drumheller. He helped McGavin out with some pointers on legal matters in a script the actor was working on. Knowing Winter was interested in entertainment and sports law, McGavin encouraged him to come to L.A. The following summer, Winter did so, making contacts through which he was able to set up his practicum. He ended up working with Ted Steinberg, one of whose clients was Kareem Abdul-Jabar of the NBA's Lakers; Steinberg's partner counted NFL quarterbacks John Elway and Dan Marino among his clients.

With a law school colleague, Winter staged a seminar in Malibu Beach on protecting the athlete from unscrupulous agents. Winter had seen his first agents as a high school student, when he tagged along to watch a few friends from around Drumheller (including future NHLer Jim Nill) at the training camp of Major Junior hockey's Medicine Hat Tigers. There he saw a number of future NHL players, and the agents hanging around them. "They just looked like sleaze," he says. "They were buying the players cars . . . it didn't make sense to me. I felt I could do the job then as well as those guys, and I was about sixteen."

At the Malibu Beach seminar in 1982, Winter met Ron Salcer. Salcer represented clients on the Los Angeles Kings like Jimmy Fox and Dave Taylor, who were already complaining to him about the way Eagleson was running the players' union. It would take nine years for Winter and Salcer to dethrone Eagleson, but the first tentative step had been taken. "Had I not met Salcer at Malibu Beach," Winter says, "Eagleson might still be in business today."

After he returned to Edmonton and completed his law degree, Winter was temporarily sidetracked into corporate law. His mother was the secretary to a senior partner at a prominent Edmonton firm, and the partner gave Winter a job. He hated it, and struck out on his own, setting up practice in the city's university neighbourhood, committing himself to what he'd always wanted to pursue: sports and entertainment law.

His first NHL client was Frantisek (Frank) Musil, referred to him through a California contact. Musil was a less than routine vehicle for breaking into the NHL agents' ranks. A star of the Czechoslovakian national team, Musil was behind the Iron Curtain when the Minnesota North Stars selected the defenceman 38th overall at age eighteen in the 1983 draft. The North Stars were gambling on the possibility that, like those of the Stastny brothers before him, Musil's defection could be arranged. Musil wanted to come to the West, but was afraid that if he was caught trying to leave before completing his compulsory military service, he would be shot for desertion. A member of the 1985 World Championship team, Musil's fortunes dimmed in the spring of 1986 when he was suspended from the national team after refusing to sign a five-year contract. His opportunity to escape came that June, when he was able to travel to a seaside resort in Umag, Yugoslavia, with his girlfriend after completing his military service.

Winter got a call one morning at home in Edmonton and turned to his girlfriend. "You're going to have to get a ride home," he informed her. "I've got to go to Yugoslavia. Some guy there who's a hockey player wants to defect."

Teaming up with North Stars general manager Lou Nanne, Winter spirited Musil out of the Cold War's clutches and into the United States. Musil's plans to defect were so secretive that he didn't tell his parents or even his girlfriend that he was leaving. Today, Winter admits to his own naivety, having had little idea of the dangers involved. Musil is still a client—he joined the Oilers at the end of the 1997/98 season—and the services Winter provided to a young defector led to other Czech clients like Dominik Hasek and David Volek.

As Winter's business grew, he took on several clients from the championship Oilers: Craig Muni, who became an Oiler in October 1986 in a numbingly complex deal; Esa Tikkanen, the 1983 draft pick who played his first Oilers games in the 1984/85 playoffs; and their star goaltender, Grant Fuhr. Winter had entered the agent business just as the Oilers were encountering their first serious turbulence. The shocking playoff loss to Calgary the previous spring had been followed by the *Sports Illustrated* cocaine-story scandal, right after which came the Gainers strike. The new five-year collective bargaining agreement between the NHL and NHLPA was also struck, in which Eagleson convinced his union membership to abandon hope for a better free agency deal in return for a revised pension plan.

The failure to secure proper free agency, the NHLPA's less than aggressive approach to securing details of pension plan funding and surpluses from the league, and the unclear picture of how the Eagleson-run Canada Cup tournament fit into it all, sowed increasing dissatisfaction with Eagleson's union leadership. Winter risked Eagleson's ire by taking Tikkanen's and Muni's contracts before the Alberta Labour Relations Board in an attempt to have them declared invalid on the grounds that "the union was basically a non-entity." He also began working with Salcer to plan a formal assault on Eagleson's leadership. From his Los Angeles base, Salcer had contacts with NHL players that went beyond his own client list. In organizing meetings, he helped deflect Eagleson's attacks away from Winter alone. Several hundred mutinous NHL players banded together to hire Ed Garvey, the former head of the NFL players' association, to work in concert with Salcer, Winter and lawyers John Agro, Bill Dermody and David Dempster to prepare a report on Eagleson's performance as union leader. The dump-Eagleson campaign was building toward a showdown at the NHLPA annual meeting in Palm Beach, Florida, in June 1989.

In Edmonton, the relationship between players and management was unusual in the league, if not in sport itself. This was partly because the team was so isolated in Edmonton, but more because the team was so unusually young. "In Edmonton," says Winter, "there was such a large number of kids. It was a unique situation not only in hockey, but in all of professional sports. You'd be hard pressed to find a dynasty in the history of any sport where the core of six to eight players were under the age of twenty-five."

It is difficult to encourage young players—not just in Edmonton in the 1980s, but even today, with multimillion-dollar contracts— to think about career spans and the consequences of poorly managed finances. "There is a tendency of athletes to think for the moment," says Winter. "What makes them great is their ability to focus on the faceoff, on the last minute of play, on defending the guy right in front of them. Those strengths are also the things that get them into trouble off the ice. You talk to young players about long-range planning. Some of them have grown up with doctors and lawyers—professionals—as parents. They don't get it, but they understand they should be considering it. The rest of them to a large degree have to be pushed to understand that.

"Guys were eighteen, nineteen when they started in Edmonton, making two hundred, three hundred grand. They were having a blast. Everywhere they went, people bought them beers. They didn't have much in the way of expenses, they all bought nice little condos downtown, they had everything they needed. I don't think it was much more [to them] than an extension of minor-league hockey. They were a bunch of guys who didn't give a lot of thought to the draft, to the business around it. It was like, 'In Juniors we had a really good team and we won the Memorial Cup. And then we went to Edmonton and we had a really good team, we had a lot of fun and it was really great.'"

Winter looks to Gretzky, whom he never represented, as a player whose attitude changed considerably with his circumstances. "Gretzky now is a lot older, more experienced, not as naive as he was. I remember Gretzky at centre ice, eighteen years old, and Pocklington signing him until 1999. It's hard to imagine that if that contract had been enforceable and stayed in place, in 1998/99 Gretzky would be playing his last season under that contract. How dumb was that? But that was the kind of thing the players felt. It was like, 'Wow, Peter's going to take care of me until I retire.'"

There was a father–son dynamic in the relationship between Oilers management and players. Pocklington was wont to speak about the players in the team's first NHL seasons as if they were his children. After the first NHL season in 1979/80, Pocklington noted, "I've become involved with the fellows on the team to a point where they've become like thirty sons to me. In Wayne's case, I've watched a seventeen-year-old boy grow into a mature young man." Pocklington would take players on golf excursions to Palm Springs and Pebble Beach, where Ralph Lean would play rounds with them. "The majority were a nice bunch of young kids who you'd be proud to be a father of," says Lean. He was especially impressed with Gretzky, whom he found bright, thoughtful, polite and no different in private than in public.

Gretzky was especially close to Glen Sather, who had built a team around him, encouraged his growth as a player and admired him enormously. Sather was a father figure to the team as a whole. "They loved him, they hated him," Lean says of the players and Sather. "But most of all they respected him."

"It's less the case now," says Winter, "but with a lot of players, when they played minor-league hockey, their coach was their friend.

He was like their mom's insurance agent, who came regularly over to the house. He really cared about them, about all aspects of what they did. There was a perception among the young players on the Oilers that that was just continuing. What they didn't understand was that in negotiating their salaries, their interests were diametrically opposed [to those of the owner]. They didn't really get that. They got it later. On top of that, there was no disclosure of salaries, no understanding of the business situation—and then, all of a sudden, they were winning all those Stanley Cups. If you or I tried to point things out to them, it was like, 'Who cares? Shut up! Whatever! Who needs it?' Then, if they did go to Glen with questions, he'd say, 'Don't worry. You're making a ton of money.'"

"The Oilers did a great job of having everybody in that mind-set, that this was a great job and they were winning Stanley Cups," says Mike Gartner, now the NHLPA's director of business relations. "And teams had the collective bargaining agreement on their side. 'If you don't like things, you're not going anywhere, ever. We'll bury you in the minors' . . . Now a player has to go through real waivers, where someone can actually pick them up."

Rich Winter feels the Oilers lacked the presence of the older, savvier players usually found on other teams, who could lift the young eyes above the here-and-now and make them think more about their lives after hockey. "On another team with older guys, you'd have someone who was planning to be a stockbroker, helping team-mates, saying, 'Maybe you should see this person and get a budget organized, some investments, because the end comes pretty quickly.'"

Sather sometimes took on that role himself, with entirely good intentions, trying to keep players with reckless spending habits out of trouble. In Winter's view, however, Sather's interventions complicated contract negotiations. The NHL Oilers have always been Sather's show, but Winter has seen two different Sathers in contract negotiations: the one in charge before Eagleson's downfall, and the one after. "In the early days, Glen was much more willing to use clandestine tactics. He was much more intimidating. He would talk directly to the players [when agents were negotiating their contracts]. He would berate or belittle agents, when certain salaries were actually realistic. He had a large desire to have control, because control got him better results. He worked hard on the relationship with the players, so they were as likely to believe him as their agent. He'd say, 'Grant, five or six hundred thousand is fair for you. Look, Kevin Lowe's been here longer than you, and he's only making two hundred fifty thousand.' But maybe he was really making four hundred thousand. We never really knew, because there was no salary disclosure.

"I don't think Glen thought agents really had a place in the game. In the early stages I think he thought of these kids a little bit as his family. Because he had been a borderline player, he found the salaries obscene. He felt the players should be playing more for the satisfaction of the game and the result than for the money, and because of that perception he genuinely believed what he was doing in negotiations and offering to the players were reasonable. He'd become a bit of a businessman. He saw that Pocklington needed a return on his money, and felt he was doing the right thing."

Ralph Lean places Sather and Harry Sinden in the same camp, as presidents and general managers who to this day do not spend their team owners' money casually. "They treat the owner's money like it's their own. They're bothered [by] paying crazy amounts for players." On the current fragile state of small-market teams like Edmonton, Sinden believes the problems "could have been avoided if the rest of us could have avoided being so idiotic about paying players."

Sather, however, has changed, says Winter. "The post-Eagleson Sather is more businesslike, more accepting of the circumstances and more willing to work within the confines of the system. Glen is more accepting than a lot of the general managers in what he has to pay. He doesn't like what he has to pay in some cases, especially with rookies, despite the rookie salary cap, but he's more willing to accept it."

It could be argued that the Oilers helped to perpetuate the

Eagleson reign, if only because the paternalistic management model of Sather and Pocklington, and the sheer youth of the lineup, drunk on success, did not lead a challenge to Eagleson's entrenched control. Gretzky's inability to assume a front-line role on behalf of fellow players in the Eagleson drama was unfortunate. When the critical NHLPA meeting was held in June 1989, and Ed Garvey's devastating report on Eagleson's behaviour was tabled, Gretzky didn't even attend, opting for the no man's land between the warring camps. After being sold in 1988 to Bruce McNall, the Los Angeles Kings owner later convicted of fraud, Gretzky had struck up a new close relationship with management, buying the Toronto Argonauts of the Canadian Football League with McNall and Canadian actor John Candy, and investing in a vintage Honus Wagner baseball card with McNall. As a clean-cut spokesman for the game itself, who went to great lengths not to offend anyone, Gretzky steered clear of the whole Eagleson mess, declining to lend his considerable voice in 1989 to the cause of his fellow players.[2] It took two-and-a-half more years to bring Eagleson down.

CHAPTER ELEVEN

O NE OF THE FIRST signs that the Oilers dynasty might be in trouble was the rift between Paul Coffey and Glen Sather. Coffey's play had drawn comment during the playoff loss to Calgary in April 1986, and in 1986/87 he was publicly criticized by Sather and had his ice time reduced. Dressed for fifty-nine games, the Norris Trophy winner and first-team All Star for the past two seasons saw his offensive output fall drastically. In one season, his goals fell from forty-eight to seventeen, assists from ninety to fifty. No awards came his way; 1986/87 was one of only two seasons from 1981/82 to 1996/97 in which Coffey did not participate in the All Star game.

The Oilers won another Stanley Cup that spring, after Ted Green returned from his personal business hiatus to tend to defensive duties again as an assistant coach. The team had a first-rate season, with fifty wins, as it captured another regular-season title. The playoff run was one of the most uneventful in the team's history. Los Angeles was pushed aside in five games in the division semi-final's best-of-seven series, which included a 13-3 walloping in game two that set a record for most goals by one team in a playoff game.[1] The Winnipeg Jets had eliminated Calgary in their division semi-final, and against Edmonton in the division finals the Jets went down, four straight. The conference finals brought on the Detroit Red Wings, who had just completed a draining seven-game division finals against Toronto two nights earlier, while the Oilers had been resting for eight days. The Red Wings were moved aside in five.

The finals also promised an easy series, as the Philadelphia Flyers fell behind three games to one. But with superlative goaltending from rookie Ron Hextall, the Flyers came back to force a seventh game. The Oilers won 3-1 but Hextall had been so impressive in his league-leading twenty-six playoff appearances[2] that he was awarded the Conn Smythe Trophy.

Gretzky and company formed the nucleus of Team Canada in the 1987 Canada Cup that September. After Canada traded 6-5 wins with the Soviet Union in the best-of-three finals, Gretzky set up one of hockey's most memorable goals in game three. With 1:12 left to play in the third period and the score tied 5-5, Gretzky led a three-on-one break across the Soviet blue line. His neat drop pass to Mario Lemieux resulted in the game-winning blast from the NHL's new superstar. Gretzky set a tournament record with twenty-one points on three goals and eighteen assists.

The Oilers' players in the tournament returned to a team facing mounting dissension. Messier had played in the Canada Cup under the shadow of a paternity suit filed by a New York fashion model on August 17, and both he and Paul Coffey were suspended after failing to report to training camp following the Canada Cup. Gretzky had signed his new contract that summer, and both Messier and Coffey were looking for new deals. Andy Moog was also a holdout; he was beginning to chafe under the backup role Sather had assigned him, behind Grant Fuhr.

The star holdouts came as Pocklington was trying to clean up the financial mess left by the lengthy Gainers strike. He had finally resolved it, he would later allege, at the behest of Premier Don Getty, who said he had felt the strike was embarrassing the province. As Pocklington described it for *Alberta Report* in August 1998, "Getty called me into his office for a one-on-one meeting because the television news footage of the strike made Alberta look bad. Getty called me, I didn't call him. He wanted to know what would patch things up. I said Gainers needed an interest-free loan of $50 million and, more fundamentally, I begged him again for a fair hog pricing system. He agreed but it didn't work out that way."

According to Pocklington, the government, through Alberta Treasury Branches, agreed to lend Gainers Properties Inc. (GPI) $55 million, with a further $2 million every six months to cover interest costs. Government financial records show that on September 25, 1987, ATB and Pocklington entered into a master agreement to cover a term loan facility and loan guarantee. For collateral, Pocklington's Gainers Properties Inc. provided a demand debenture worth $67 million, which effectively constituted all of Gainers: its properties, equipment, chattels and the preferred shares of Gainers held by GPI. In other words, if Gainers defaulted on loan repayments, the government could seize the entire company. The deal between Gainers and the ATB came on top of other loans made by ATB to Pocklington's enterprises (including, it is believed, the Oilers) since the early 1980s.

Messier came to a new six-year deal with Sather, but Coffey could not be placated. Already angry about his treatment in 1986/87, Coffey also felt grossly underpaid. He had learned that Rod Langway, who had held the Norris Trophy before Coffey won it in 1984/85 and 1985/86, was making about US$500,000, while Coffey was being paid $320,000 Canadian. Pocklington tried to appease Coffey with a new package that included some land holdings, but Coffey and his team were at an impasse. On November 24, Sather traded Coffey to Pittsburgh with left wingers Dave Hunter and Wayne Van Dorp for left winger Craig Simpson, centre Dave Hannan, and defencemen Moe Mantha and Chris Joseph. Coffey was the first of Sather's "untouchables" to be touched.

Andy Moog was also lost. When it was decided a few months before the 1988 Winter Olympics in Calgary that hockey teams could use professional players, Moog, unhappy with his secondary role in the Oilers goaltending stable, left the Oilers to join the Canadian team. Oilers team-mate Randy Gregg, who had played for Canada at the 1980 Olympics, joined him. Gregg returned to the Oilers after the Olympics, at which Canada finished fourth, but Moog (who won four starts, with a 2.25 average) was finished as an Oiler. Sather turned to Harry Sinden for a deal on March 8 to relieve himself of the unhappy netminder. In addition to a new goaltender, Bill Ranford, Sather received left winger Geoff Courtnall and Boston's second-round pick in the upcoming draft. Moog became the Bruins' main goaltender, compiling the best winning percentage of any active NHL netminder during more than five seasons there.

As the 1987/88 postseason transpired, Moog ended up facing Fuhr in the Stanley Cup finals, as Sather and Sinden finally confronted each other in a championship tilt. (Sinden, however, wasn't on the Bruins bench. His coach was Terry O'Reilly.) Edmonton had sagged in the regular season, falling to forty-four wins and to second in the Smythe behind the rapidly improving Calgary Flames. The once-dominant Oilers scoring machine was in retreat. Goal production, which in 1986/87 had fallen below 400 for the first time since 1981/82 (to 372), dipped again to 363 in 1987/88. Edmonton had still been the league's top offensive club in 1986/87, but in 1987/88 fell behind Calgary, which produced 397 in finishing first overall in the league, while the Oilers settled for third, behind Montreal. The Oilers' domination of the All Star ranks was also over. Gretzky and Kurri had made the first team in 1986/87, but in 1987/88 only Fuhr made the first team, as Gretzky was finally displaced to the second team (for the first time since 1979/80) by Mario Lemieux. And Fuhr replaced Gretzky in Hart Trophy polling, finishing runner-up to Lemieux.

But Gretzky, who had also finished second to Lemieux in the scoring race (and to Mats Naslund in Lady Byng voting[3]) could still lead a team to a championship. Edmonton made perfunctory work of Winnipeg, moving them aside in five, to deliver the hyped Flames a lesson in postseason grit. The Oilers swept Calgary in four, giving Edmonton its second consecutive meeting with Detroit in the

conference finals. It was another dominating Oilers performance, the
five-game series victory capped with an 8-4 win at home.

Boston had survived the seven-game conference finals against
New Jersey, and the showdown between Fuhr and Moog fizzled. Fuhr
had played a record seventy-five of eighty regular-season games for
the Oilers (with forty wins), and won the Vezina in addition to earning his first-team All Star appearance and finishing second to Lemieux
in Hart voting. He held the Bruins to nine goals in Edmonton's four-
game sweep. The most excitement in the series came when game
four had to be abandoned at 16:37 of the second period with the teams
tied at 3-3, after the power failed in the ancient Boston Gardens. Two
nights later Edmonton won the replay 6-3 to earn a fourth Cup.

In the playoffs, Fuhr won a record sixteen games, surpassing Billy
Smith's fifteen in 1979/80 and 1981/82 and his own fifteen in 1984/85,
while the Oilers won a record eleven playoff games at home, surpassing the mark of ten they had set in 1984/85. The Conn Smythe Trophy
went to Gretzky, after he set a Cup finals record with thirteen points
(three goals, ten assists) in the four games.

T HE NEW CONTRACT for Gretzky, negotiated in 1987 with a retirement option three years ahead, might have seemed to provide
Pocklington with breathing room, but he was being squeezed from
two directions: the evidence in the Hart and Pearson voting of
Gretzky's declining worth, and Pocklington's own financial straits,
arising from the Gainers strike settlement. Pocklington would assert
that the deal he agreed to with the union was costing him an extra $8
million a year. "I should have just closed the plant and sold the labels,
which were worth maybe $30 million," he told *Alberta Report*. "But I
kept hoping the government would keep its word about reforming
the hog pricing system. If that had happened, Gainers would be here
today and Edmonton would be 1,200 jobs richer. From 1987 to 1989,
we lost about $1 million a month."

Buy low, sell high is the creed of all investors. Pocklington had bought Gretzky in the fall of 1978, when he was only seventeen, and paid a few hundred thousand dollars. As the captain of a Stanley Cup winner in 1988, he was worth millions, easily more than $10 million. Having just borrowed heavily from the Alberta Treasury Branches to clean up the Gainers mess, Pocklington was in a mood to liquidate assets. And when you begin liquidating assets, you always unload the ones that are declining in value before the ones that are appreciating. Gretzky was worth a small fortune in 1988, possibly nothing in 1990, and in between—who knew? Like Bobby Orr, a knee injury could finish him. Or the rising tide of new talents could further erode his worth.

Gretzky might not have been at that stage as superlative a talent as Mario Lemieux—for in addition to Gretzky's deftness Lemieux had considerable size, which gave him a Messier-like ability to fend for himself and power past opponents—but Gretzky had the intangibles of celebrity and personality in spades. Lemieux was considered moody, uncommunicative, and hot and cold rather than playing at full RPM every game. Gretzky was also a proven winner, an outstanding hockey player and an outstanding person, someone who could always be counted on to do whatever was required for the good of the game. In 1988, after he had led the Oilers to a fourth Cup win and earned his second Conn Smythe in the process, Wayne Gretzky was worth a mint.

Nelson Skalbania resurfaced in Gretzky's life, proposing to buy the Gretzky contract for $20 million. His playing rights would be sold to Frank Griffiths of the Canucks, and marketing rights would go in a separate deal to Jim Pattison.

On May 27, the day after Gretzky led the Oilers to their game-four defeat of Boston in the 1987/88 Stanley Cup, Gretzky apparently learned from Pocklington of the Skalbania scheme. Gretzky was appalled by the timing. "I can't believe you coming to me with this the day after we won the Cup," he said.

Without a no-trade clause, Gretzky couldn't prevent himself from being shipped out of town. But he could at least use the consequences to lever himself some influence. He asked Pocklington for the right to approve the team to which he was dealt. In return, he would bear the brunt of the public fallout, saying it was his own idea, and spare Pocklington the backlash that could hurt ticket sales and Oilers revenues in general.

Pocklington's decision to trade Gretzky was further complicated by the fact that Gretzky was to be married in Edmonton on July 16, in one of the most ornate weddings ever staged in Canada, which only increased the emotional pitch of the summer's events.

"Canada's Royal Wedding," as it was proclaimed, was either the social event of the decade in Edmonton or a tad over the top, depending on one's perspective. Never had an athlete's marriage vows warranted such lavish public attention. Sensing the scale of his own union, Gretzky invited Edmonton's mayor and Alberta's premier, who came, and the country's prime minister, who did not. The use of Edmonton's largest Roman Catholic church for the ceremony offended some, given that neither Gretzky nor his bride was of the faith. But overall the event was a major celebration, followed nationally. As things turned out, it preceded a trauma of equally national proportions.

Gretzky had broken off a long-standing relationship with Edmonton nightclub singer Vicki Moss in 1987. Moss would later tell *Macleans* that Gretzky had become upset with her intentions to move to Los Angeles and pursue her singing career; he wanted her to stay in Edmonton, settle down and begin a family. Gretzky met actress Janet Jones at an L.A. Lakers game that year. A whirlwind romance ensued, and soon there were wedding plans.

At the wedding, Gretzky told Paul Coffey, who was one of his ushers, that Pocklington was trying to trade him. It was later revealed that Sather had reluctantly been trying to cut a deal with the Rangers before the draft in June. Five days after the wedding, Gretzky got a call from Bruce McNall, owner of the Los Angeles Kings. McNall told Gretzky that Pocklington had given him permission to call. "Peter had told him, 'If you can swing him over, you've got him,'" Janet Jones would recall.

The deal called for Gretzky to tell the press that the trade was his idea, and that he and Janet were happy to be moving to her home town. Ironically, after breaking off with Moss, supposedly because she wanted to pursue a career in L.A., Gretzky was now marrying an L.A. starlet and moving there himself. (Jones, however, intended to stop working and raise a family, and did so.)

Gretzky would tell Peter Gzowski in a television interview shortly before his retirement in 1999 that Sather spent an hour trying to talk Gretzky out of accepting the trade, even offering to tell Pocklington he'd quit if the deal wasn't killed. But Gretzky went ahead with it. He probably understood a deal was inevitable, and he could not have failed to recognize that the trade to Los Angeles would make him very rich and take his career to an entirely new level. He might not ever win a Stanley Cup again, but in L.A. he could reach a superstar status in the American media that playing in Edmonton could never make possible. Gretzky would become a major sporting celebrity, rising far above his own sport's profile, and garner the endorsements that went with it. Sanyo would break new ground for Gretzky by hiring him to do a television commercial for their video camera, without even identifying him onscreen as a hockey player or an L.A. King. It testified to how beneficial leaving Edmonton was for Gretzky.

The deal, which was cut on August 9, was structured as a trade, with three other players and four first-round draft picks involved. But at its heart, the trade was a sale, pure and simple. Pocklington got US$15 million for his star. Gretzky got $5 million for going along with it, in addition to his US$1.4 million salary and a cut from the Kings' ticket sales.

While Pocklington got his $15 million, Sather worked the player exchange. Gretzky took along with him two bodyguards, Marty

McSorley and Mike Krushelnyski. In return, Sather got Jimmy Carson, whom he hoped would be a new centre to work with Jari Kurri and Esa Tikkanen. Sather also got four of the Kings' first-round draft picks. They handed over their 1988 pick, left winger Martin Gelinas (who remained with the Hull Olympiques for most of 1988/89), and promised the team's first-round picks in 1989, 1991 and 1993.

The press conference called in Edmonton to announce the trade of the century did not proceed matter-of-factly. One press report described it as an exhibition worthy of the World Wrestling Federation. It was hard to tell what was real and what wasn't. Pocklington sat at Gretzky's right while Bruce McNall watched from behind and to Gretzky's right. The public seemed to need a villain in this set piece, and it wasn't clear who to pick. Was it Gretzky, fleeing his native land and his team-mates for American dollars and the lush life of L.A.? Was it Pocklington, selling Gretzky (as Paul Coffey had so perfectly put it, given the Gainers mess) "like a piece of meat"? Was it the new Mrs Gretzky, the American ingenue, making her husband leave dreary, dumpy Edmonton for La La Land? Or how about McNall, waving crude sums of cash around to steal a national treasure?

There was no way to sort this out, although Janet Jones Gretzky felt like the most hated woman in Canada after the deal was announced, and she clearly should not be blamed for it. Gretzky cranked up the emotional decibel level by revealing that his new bride was pregnant, and that going to L.A. was in the best interest of his family-to-be. He also cried a fair amount, as McNall looked on poker-faced and Pocklington tried to contain his exasperation.

When it was over, Pocklington told the *Edmonton Journal* that Gretzky had "an ego the size of Manhattan," and that he was a "great actor" in crying at the press conference. "I thought he pulled it off beautifully when he showed how upset he was. I think he was upset, but he wants the big dream."

Gretzky did seem to make a bit of a show of requesting Kleenex and daubing his eyes, but the tears were genuine. Perhaps, deep down, what Gretzky was feeling was guilt. He later admitted he'd been terrified to tell Messier (who succeeded him as captain) that he was leaving the Oilers. Gretzky, the player who always did the right thing, was doing something that was undoubtedly, as always, for the good of the game. Going to the Kings could only help raise the NHL's profile south of the border. But it was also a move that was good for him. He was giving up on the Oilers, perhaps not by choice, but ultimately to his own benefit.

"I'll be back," he promised the assembled press. He didn't say exactly how, or when, but the following spring he returned with the Kings to knock the Oilers out of the playoffs.

THE OILERS season that followed Gretzky's trade was an awful one for a team accustomed to winning. The team slipped to thirty-eight wins, to third in the Smythe division, behind Calgary, which amassed a stupendous fifty-four wins, and Gretzky's Kings, with forty-two wins—twelve more than in 1987/88, before The Great One arrived. (The Oilers hadn't won fewer than forty-four games since 1980/81.) Offensive output fell to an ordinary 325 goals, and a slumping Fuhr forced Sather to go with Bill Ranford for twenty-nine regular-season games, though he switched back to Fuhr for the playoffs.

Jari Kurri, whose skills had always been discounted because of his proximity to Gretzky, was one of the Oilers' few bright spots, as his output actually improved. His points production rose from ninety-six in 1987/88 to 102 in 1988/89 as his new centre, Jimmy Carson, produced 100. Kurri was the only Oiler to make the All Star list, being voted to the second team, while his linemate, Esa Tikkanen, was runner-up for the Selke as the league's top defensive forward.

In the playoffs the deal of the century boomeranged on Pocklington, as Gretzky inspired his Kings to down his former team-mates in the opening round. Down three games to one, the Kings rallied to win two games 4-2 and 4-1, before polishing off the Oilers, now led by captain Mark Messier, 6-3 in Los Angeles.

Edmonton fans who might have switched their playoff allegiance to Gretzky's Kings at this point then had to watch his team be swept by the Oilers' hated rivals to the south, the Calgary Flames, in the division finals. When the Oilers were upset by the Flames in 1985/86, Calgary had gone on to reach the Cup finals, where they lost to the Canadiens. In a rematch with Montreal in the 1988/89 finals, though, Calgary won in six. Edmontonians circulated a derisive joke—How do you spell dynasty in Calgary? O-N-E—but it couldn't mask the sensation that the Oilers' own dynasty was over.

It got worse. In June, Grant Fuhr filed his retirement papers with the league, and talked about selling cars and golfing for a living. His agent, Rich Winter, had begun to suspect Fuhr was having drug problems, and when he failed a test Winter made him take, he agreed to enter the Straight Center in St. Petersburg, Florida, in August. When he came out, he made a flurry of changes in his life. He dropped Winter as his agent, separated from his wife Corrine, changed his mind about retiring, and negotiated a new contract with Sather, who was turning over the coaching job to John Muckler, with Ted Green serving as co-coach.

Fuhr's problems, which were long-standing, clearly had been part of the inspiration for the *Sports Illustrated* article of May 1986. His ex-wife Corrine told all in an interview with the *Edmonton Journal* in 1990. She related how drug dealers had come to the house during the 1983/84 playoffs, threatening to "kneecap" him if he didn't pay off debts. Corrine's revelations angered Fuhr, who had remarried. He said he'd been clean since the Straight Center visit (Corrine justified her interview by saying she wanted Fuhr to confront his problems), and that the exposé had been especially hurtful to the eldest of his and Corrine's two daughters. Agreeing to be interviewed by the *Journal,* Fuhr explained that "I was trying to get my life straightened out. I wasn't happy."

Fuhr never used the word "cocaine," preferring to discuss his use of a "substance," although Corrine revealed that he had been using the drug. His abuse of drugs and alcohol seemed to have begun around 1983. His outward persona was a what-me-worry casualness. "Life is too short to get tense about anything," he said during the 1984/85 playoffs. Gretzky chimed in, "Nothing ever seems to bother Grant, or if it does, he's able to keep it disguised. He never gets excited when things are going good or down in the dumps when they're bad. He just stays on a steady, even keel. No matter how many mistakes are made in front of him or how badly a guy goofs up on a play, he never blames anyone else for a goal against him." When Fuhr signed a new eight-year deal in February 1988 worth about $400,000 a season, Sather offered that "He doesn't get uptight about a lot of things. He's very relaxed emotionally, and he's a confident, level-headed guy. He's got the right attitude to play goal."

How much Sather knew about Fuhr's problems is not known, although he was fully aware of his problems with money, according to Rich Winter. "Glen had a pretty iron-fisted control of Fuhr, largely because of his off-ice shenanigans," says Winter. "Glen wanted to control his life, and some of it was well placed. He was concerned about Grant. He got Grant a pretty good deal."

Fuhr was the classic star goaltender, able to keep his emotions in check, his attention on the job at hand. But what was good for the Oilers was disastrous for Fuhr. "I basically self-destructed," he said in January 1991.

The drug problem he'd sought help for at the Straight Center was a closely guarded secret when he returned to the Oilers for the 1989/90 season. He lost the starting job to Ranford, who played fifty-six regular-season games and then all twenty-two playoff games. Yet Edmontonians had another scandal to distract them while Fuhr tried to resurrect his career. Peter Pocklington's Gainers had defaulted on loan payments due under the 1987 master agreement with the Alberta Treasury Branches, and on October 6, 1989, the government moved to

take the business away from him. It also sued Pocklington, claiming
he had improperly transferred funds out of Gainers.[4] There came a
flurry of suits and countersuits between Pocklington and the government over his indebtedness and their seizure of his assets.

Nine days after the ATB made its move on Gainers, Wayne Gretzky
made another visit to Northlands as a King. He scored on Ranford
late in the game to tie the score and record his 1,851st NHL regular-
season point, one more than record-holder Gordie Howe. It was the
first NHL record Gretzky broke without wearing an Oilers uniform.
While Gretzky was reminding Edmonton fans of what they had lost,
Jimmy Carson, who had been a key acquisition from Los Angeles in
the 1988 Gretzky trade and had contributed 100 points in 1988/89,
announced he was retiring four games into his fourth NHL season,
saying he couldn't "get mentally up for the games." After being suspended by Sather, Carson was traded in November to Detroit (along
with Kevin McClelland and Edmonton's fifth-round choice in the
1991 entry draft) for Joe Murphy, Jeff Sharples, Adam Graves and Petr
Klima. When the Oilers visited the Kings in Los Angeles on February
28, 1990, the teams combined for a record eighty-five penalties and
356 penalty minutes, with the Oilers setting a record of their own
with forty-four penalties—twenty-six minors, seven majors, six ten-
minute misconducts, four game misconducts and one match penalty.
The Oilers' days of setting scoring records were behind them.

As Pocklington lost Gainers, Alan Eagleson began to lose his grip
on the Players' Association. At the June 1989 NHLPA meeting in
Florida, Ed Garvey had presented a fifty-five-page report based on the
investigation he had conducted in concert with Rich Winter. It was a
devastating, depressing litany of allegations of improper spending,
including loans of NHLPA funds to Eagleson's friends and business
associates (including a few sports journalists) and conflicts of interest
in which Eagleson did business with league owners while representing the union membership. Eagleson fought the charges strenuously
but, as an FBI investigation picked up speed with subpoenas being

issued for grand jury testimony, Eagleson had no choice but to resign as head of the NHLPA in January 1992.[5]

THE OILERS did have a slightly better season in 1989/90. While wins remained at thirty-eight, points improved from eighty-four to ninety as they moved past Los Angeles (who slumped to fourth) into second place in the Smythe, behind the Flames. Mario Lemieux, who had won the 1988/89 scoring race with 199 points, was limited by back problems to fifty-nine games for Pittsburgh, and Gretzky, with 142 points, became the first King to win the scoring title since Marcel Dionne edged him a decade earlier. Messier surged forward with 129 points to finish second, then rose to the leadership opportunity Gretzky's trade had presented him by taking the Oilers on one last great playoff run.

While Gretzky's Kings eliminated Calgary in six, the Oilers fought past the Winnipeg Jets in seven, bringing on a dream series meeting between Los Angeles and Edmonton in the division finals. The series was a dramatic letdown. Messier's Oilers clobbered Los Angeles 7-0 and 6-1 in the first two games at Northlands, then hung on to win the next two games in Los Angeles 5-4 and 6-5 (in overtime). Then Chicago was eliminated in six, setting up another final between Edmonton and Boston.

The first game, in Boston, was a marathon. The score was tied at two when overtime began, and it took almost an entire second game to settle matters. At 55:13 of overtime, Petr Klima scored on Andy Moog to end the longest game in Stanley Cup finals history. He had been riding the bench for most of the game, and got onto the ice when most of the regular Oilers were exhausted. The goal echoed the feat of benchwarmer Ken Doraty, who won a semi-final game for Toronto against Boston in 1932/33 at 104:46 of overtime.

Thereafter, the Oilers were almost entirely in charge. They won the second game 7-2, dropped game three at Northlands 2-1, then racked up 5-1 and 4-1 wins to make it five Cups in seven seasons. Bill Ranford, who had played every postseason game for Edmonton and won sixteen of them (matching the mark set by Grant Fuhr in 1988 and Calgary's Mike Vernon in 1989), was awarded the Conn Smythe. The Canadian Press named the Oilers Canada's sports team of the year.

Over the course of winning five Cups in seven seasons, Glen Sather had run through more than sixty different players (including the ones used in 1985/86 and 1988/89). But even without Gretzky, he had been able to reach the fifth Cup win with seven players who had been around for all of them: Grant Fuhr, Glenn Anderson, Randy Gregg, Charlie Huddy, Jari Kurri, Kevin Lowe and Mark Messier. Five of them belonged to his list of "untouchables" from 1986. But the Gretzky trade hadn't cost him only the most celebrated player of the modern game. Gretzky's departure also helped trigger a boom in player salaries. Sather, hampered by the personal financial difficulties of Pocklington and the inequalities in league revenues that would consign Edmonton to the "small-market" basket of also-ran franchises, would no longer be able to afford the team he had built.

THEY GAVE IT another try in 1990/91, and strove mightily in doing so, but when the underdog Minnesota North Stars edged the Oilers 3-2 at Northlands in game five of the conference finals, the dynasty was finally over. The North Stars went on to lose in six to Mario Lemieux and the Pittsburgh Penguins. Just to get to play Minnesota, the Oilers had battled through two epic series. The Flames had taken them to seven games, the last two ending in overtime, in a bloody division semi-finals, before they met Gretzky's Kings in the division finals. The Oilers won that match in six, but four of the games had gone into overtime, including the clincher, and the Oilers had won three of them. To then lose to the North Stars, who had won ten fewer regular-season games than Edmonton, was a dispiriting defeat.

The playoff run had truly been a last gasp effort, for Edmonton's regular season had been the least Oilers-like its fans could remember seeing. The team scored only 272 goals, about 150 less than in its glory years. No Oiler made the top-ten scorers list. No Oiler was an All Star. The fans and the team also had to contend with the Fuhr drug scandal, which finally blew wide open when his ex-wife granted her interview to the *Edmonton Journal* at the start of the season. Citing the league's Reaganesque "just say no," zero-tolerance drug policy, league president John Ziegler hit Fuhr with a one-year suspension.

The NHL's drug policy was widely criticized. Rather than try to help players with substance abuse problems (and with hundreds of players in the league, surely there were a few), it chose draconian punishment, which would only serve to drive the problem underground. Fuhr's suspension was the most severe the league had ever handed out. Don Murdoch's 1978 conviction for cocaine possession had netted him a forty-game suspension by Ziegler. In 1982/83, Rick Nattrass of Montreal was suspended for thirty days in his rookie season after being found guilty of marijuana possession (hence the nickname "Stash" cited in the NHL's official encyclopedia)—an offence he committed while still in Juniors with the Brantford Alexanders.

Ziegler took the criticism of the league policy to heart and lifted Fuhr's suspension after sixty days; Fuhr returned to the ice in February 1991 to shut out the New Jersey Devils, and went on to play successfully through the next decade. But like all of his fellow "untouchables," he ended up playing somewhere other than Edmonton.

THE THREE most important events in the modern history of the NHL are considered to be the Gretzky trade, the fall of Alan Eagleson and the institution of salary disclosure by the NHLPA under his successor, Bob Goodenow. All three events made possible the rapid increase in player salaries that changed the game's economics and helped create the distinction between "have" and "have-not" franchises.

Salary disclosure was discussed by players during Eagleson's reign, but he didn't encourage it and players were unsure of its consequences. Apart from privacy issues, players were afraid that if salaries became public knowledge, every time they missed a pass or a check they'd be open to extra criticism as a result of their large salary. Sports columnists would make their compensation figures as important in their game stories as the numbers on their jerseys. But without disclosure, the players were at an obvious disadvantage in salary negotiations. The general managers, who spoke with each other constantly, knew what everyone was making, but the players didn't. It was difficult for a player to know if a contract offer was fair when neither he nor his agent knew what a player of comparable skill on another team was making. And not disclosing all salaries was in the best interest of some agents, who could keep their clients in the dark about how good a job they were doing for them.

The Gretzky trade is usually cited as a watershed event because debatably the game's greatest player in 1988 (Mario Lemieux's supporters might disagree) was assigned an open-market price. No longer negotiating his pay package in secret with Pocklington, Gretzky was sold in full view of the league's owners, managers, fans and players. In 1961 Frank Mahovlich was almost sold by the Toronto Maple Leafs to the Chicago Blackhawks in a cocktail-party deal between Harold Ballard and Bill Wirtz. The Maple Leaf Gardens board of directors had the deal killed, not only to keep Mahovlich in Toronto, but also to prevent such an astronomical sale tipping off other players to their potential worth. The Gretzky deal was as close as players could get to a free-agency deal in the labour climate of the 1980s. (Gretzky wouldn't exercise free agency in the NHL until July 1996, when he signed with the New York Rangers—eighteen seasons after he began his professional career as an underage free agent in Indianapolis.)

Rich Winter, however, believes the significance of the Gretzky deal shouldn't be measured in raw dollars. Rather, the deal presented to players (especially the Oilers) the reality that no one was immune to trades, that everyone could be, or should be, mobile in his career and, moreover, that for all the talk about players being like sons to an owner such as Pocklington, they were ultimately no different than an apartment building he might swap for a meat packing plant. "It was the beginning of players seeing themselves as assets," Winter says. "Gordie Howe never got traded. Bobby Orr's trade [to Chicago] was injury related. Gretzky was the greatest player of all time, and he wasn't just traded. He was sold outright for cash."

After dealing away Gretzky in 1988, Pocklington was so disturbed by the public backlash that he made a rare intervention in salary negotiations, bypassing Sather to deal directly with Winter on the contract of Esa Tikkanen. "Pocklington lived in the town and he was concerned that he'd lost Gretzky and was about to lose Messier [who did sign a new contract]," explains Winter. "He was a salesman. He recognized the value of the marquee guy. Tikkanen had been the big playoff hero that year [with twenty-seven points in nineteen games] and he was concerned that if he lost Gretzky, Messier and Tikkanen, they were done." Pocklington informed Sather, whom he otherwise trusted completely, that he would do the deal directly with Winter. "Glen would have been willing to wait it out, but Pocklington wanted to get it done." Tikkanen got a lush six-season, $7 million deal, which Winter believes made his client the third highest-paid player in the league. Soon after, Craig Muni, who had originally walked onto the Oilers as a free agent in August 1986 after a four-season minor-league career with Toronto, received about $3 million over five years—"phenomenal for a defensive defenceman in hockey," notes Winter. These were the players whose contracts he was trying to have declared invalid by the Alberta Labour Relations Board. The sudden eruption of cash after Gretzky left town, before Peter Puck's money dried up and Eagleson was dethroned, stunned Winter. "I started to realize the depths of the problems in hockey."

After the 1990/91 playoff loss to Minnesota, the Oilers, almost en masse, began treating themselves as assets. The fun had gone out of the team, and money in Edmonton was tight as Pocklington battled the Alberta Treasury Branches. Pocklington was happy to treat the players as assets, for by now he needed not just cash, or at least a smaller payroll, but new players.

CONCEALED BENEATH the financial misadventures of Pocklington as the Oilers dynasty broke up is the fact that, for several seasons, the Oilers' track record at the annual draft bordered on dismal. The Oilers were no longer finding the new young talents they needed to roll the lineup over. Scouting overall in the league had improved greatly since the Oilers' first few heady drafts, in which Sather had come away with Coffey, Lowe Anderson, Messier, Kurri, Fuhr and Moog. After Tikkanen's selection in 1983, Edmonton's draft efforts for at least seven years were largely forgettable. As the team moved up in the standings, its draft selection opportunities correspondingly moved downward. But low opening-round picks cannot explain away Edmonton's poor showing in the entry draft. There was plenty of talent available every year in the second and third rounds, and even lower. Time and again, Edmonton made forgettable selections, only to have a number of NHL regulars and even stars chosen later in the same round.

In 1984, the Oilers' draft was a disaster. Selmar Odelein, the first Oilers pick (21st overall) played only eighteen NHL games; the second pick, Darryl Reaugh (42nd), played only twenty-seven; the third pick, Todd Norman (63rd) never played at all. Nor did the fourth (Rich Novak, 84th), the fifth (Richard Lambert, 105th), the seventh (Ivan Domic, 126th), the eighth (Heikki Rihijarvi, 147th) or the 10th (Joel Curtis, 209th). The sixth pick, Emanuel Viveiros (106th) lasted twenty-nine games, the 11th (Simon Wheeldon, 229th) fifteen games. Sather scored well deep in the selections with Todd Ewen, his ninth pick at 168th. Ewen had played 518 NHL games on right wing as of

1997/98, but none of them with Edmonton. Sather traded him before he reached the NHL to St. Louis for Shawn Evans, a seven-game NHLer when Sather got him. Evans proved to be a strictly minor-league talent. He never played with the Oilers, and his only subsequent NHL games were two with the Islanders in 1989/90.

The 1985 draft was almost as disastrous as 1984. Only the selection of Kelly Buchberger, down at 188th, redeemed it. The first pick, left winger Scott Metcalfe (20th overall) played nineteen NHL games. After the Oilers picked Metcalfe in the first round, teams in the second round took Sean Burke, Joe Nieuwendyk, Mike Richter, Ed Weinrich and Benoit Hogue, among others. Edmonton then took defenceman Todd Carnelley, at 41st. He never played in the NHL. After him, in the third round, teams took a number of NHL starters, including goaltender Bill Ranford, whom Sather would trade for. Edmonton then came in at second-last in the third round, at 62nd, to take Michael Ware, who played five NHL games. Then in the fourth came selections of a half-dozen NHL regulars. At 104th, Edmonton took Tomas Kapusta of Czechoslovakia, who never played in the NHL. Again, after him came at least six NHL regulars. At 125th Edmonton took Brian Tessier. He never played in the NHL. Again, after Tessier came Pat Jablonski and Stu Grimson. Edmonton took Shawn Tyers 146th. He never played in the NHL. One pick later, Philadelphia got Tony Horacek. At 167th, Edmonton took Tony Fairchild and at 209th, Mario Barbe, neither of whom played in the NHL. The Oilers salvaged the draft with Kelly Buchberger at 188th. But one pick after Barbe, Boston got Bob Beers, who played 258 NHL games; Vancouver then got Igor Larionov. At 230th, Edmonton took Peter Headon. He never played in the NHL. Four NHL regulars followed him.[6]

A year later, the 1986 draft was a complete disaster for Edmonton. Picking last in the first round, the Oilers took right winger Kim Issel, who played four NHL games. Right after Edmonton, to open the second round, Detroit took Adam Graves, whom Sather had to cut a trade to get in November 1989. At 42nd at the end of the second round, Edmonton took Jamie Nichols, who never played in the NHL, thereby missing out on Bob Corkum, Rob Zettler, Jyrki Lumme and Bill Berg. At 63rd the Oilers took Ron Shudra, who played ten NHL games. Right after Shudra, a swath of NHL starters were chosen, including Ron Tugnutt (another player Edmonton would trade for).[7] Edmonton chose Dan Currie 84th. He played twenty-two NHL games. At 85th, Detroit got Johan Garpenlov. He had played 536 NHL games by 1998/99. At 105th, Edmonton took David Haas, who played seven times in the NHL; he was followed by future NHLers Troy Crowder, Jeff Daniels and Darren Turcotte. At 126th, Edmonton took Jim Ennis, who played five NHL games. After Ennis came league regulars Kevin Todd, Mike Hartman, Mike Hudson, Lyle Odelein and Richard Pilon. Of Edmonton's next six picks, only one, goaltender Mike Greenlay, showed up in the NHL, and that was for two games in 1989/90. Through the course of those remaining selections, Murray Baron, Dave McLlwain, Lance Pitlick, Dan Keczmer and Greg Hawgood were claimed.

In 1987, the Oilers continued to miss the boat with early selections. Peter Soberlak, taken 21st at the end of the first round, never played in the NHL. After him in the second round came Stephane Matteau, Rick Tabaracci, Mark Fitzpatrick, Daniel Marois, Daniel Lacroix, John LeClair, Jeff Hackett, Eric Desjardins and Adam Burt. At 42nd the Oilers at last found someone capable of playing in the NHL, defenceman Brad Werenka, but they didn't keep him. He played only intermittently in the big league before breaking in with Pittsburgh in 1997/98. Sather had traded Werenka to Quebec in March 1994 for goalie Steve Passmore, who was not seen in the NHL until 1998/99, when he played six regular-season games for the Oilers. Two picks after Werenka, Montreal got defenceman Mathieu Schneider, and later in the third round Chicago got blueliner Cam Russell. Edmonton finally scored well, with defenceman Geoff Smith at 63rd and centre Shaun Van Allen at 105th. But Sather would have to trade Smith in 1993 to get draft picks from Florida, and Van Allen would only play twenty-three games with Edmonton over three seasons before Anaheim signed him as a free agent in 1993 and made him an NHL starter. The rest of the draft effort by Edmonton was forgettable, but the pool overall was well depleted after about 120th.[8]

In 1988, Edmonton had another largely wasted draft effort. Francois Leroux, chosen 19th, had a future in the NHL, but not with the Oilers. He played eleven games over five seasons with the Oilers, was let go on waivers in October 1993, and after being picked up by Ottawa began building an NHL career.

It was another case of Edmonton missing what proved to be stronger choices coming up in the second round. Troy Mallette went 22nd, and after him came Stephane Fiset, Tie Domi, Adrian Plavsic and Tim Taylor. Edmonton's next three picks, at 39th, 53rd and 61st, were washouts who combined for three NHL games. Sather thus missed out on a flurry of what proved to be outstanding picks: Darin Kimble (66th), Mark Recchi (67th), Tony Amonte (68th) and Rob Blake (70th). Edmonton salvaged the draft effort with one inspired choice, left winger Shjon Podein, down at 166th, but after partial seasons with Edmonton in 1992/93 and 1993/94, he was lost to Philadelphia through free agency.

In 1989, Edmonton made the only first-round selection that didn't reach the NHL by 1997/98 (three others played one game each), as they took defenceman Jason Soules 15th, thereby throwing away one of the first-round picks gained from Los Angeles in the Gretzky trade. There followed an all-too familiar roll call of quality players taken by other teams before Edmonton could choose next: Olaf Kolzig, Steven Rice (later traded for by Edmonton), Adam Foote, Travis Green, Kent Manderville, Mike Craig, Patrice Brisebois and Greg Johnson, to name a few.

Given who was chosen next, the Oilers' decision to take goaltender Richard Borgo 36th proved to be the Martyniuk Syndrome writ large. Borgo didn't reach the NHL, and between Borgo and Edmonton's next pick at 78th, the following players were chosen: Paul Laus, Ted Drury, Rob Zamuner, Scott Pellerin, Louie DeBrusk (yet another future Oiler through trading), Nicklas Lidstrom, Jason Woolley, Kris Draper, Jim Cummins, Robert Reichel, Jim McKenzie and Sergei Fedorov. Sather's choice at 78th, Josef Beranek, would play in the NHL, but he was yet another acquisition with no real Edmonton future. The Czech left winger joined the team in 1991 after playing in the Canada Cup that September. In January 1993 Sather gave him up (along with Greg Hawgood, who had been acquired from Boston for Vladimir Ruzicka in October 1990) to get Brian Benning from Philadelphia. Sather had Benning for eighteen games before he went to Florida as a free agent.

At 120th, Sather got Anatoli Semenov, a Moscow dynamo forward. Sather had him for two seasons, then left him unprotected in the 1992 expansion draft in which he was taken by Tampa Bay. The rest of the 1989 draft was forgettable for the Oilers.

Even by Edmonton's recent standards, the 1990 draft was a remarkably bad effort by the Oilers. Every pick (17th, 38th, 59th, 67th, 101st, 122nd, 143rd, 164th, 185th, 206th, 227th and 248th) was a miss— not one NHLer resulted. Scott Allison was the opening Edmonton pick at 17th, and following him in the first round were such selections as Keith Tkachuk, Martin Brodeur and Bryan Smolinski. Among other players the Oilers managed to miss out on were Jiri Slegr, Felix Potvin, Doug Weight (whom Sather would surrender Esa Tikkanen to get in March 1993), Geoff Sanderson, Mikael Renberg, Vyacheslav Kozlov, Paul Kruse, Sergei Zubov, Gino Odjick, Richard Smehlik, Alexander Godynyuk, Eric Lacroix, Andrei Kovalenko, Peter Bondra, Alexander Karpovtsev, Valeri Zelepukin and Sergei Nemchinov.

Finally, in 1991, Edmonton found someone who could play in the NHL with their first-round pick, although Tyler Wright, at 12th, was not as strong a pick as others who followed in the round, including Alexei Kovalev and Markus Naslund. Fortunately, Sather had an additional first-round pick from Los Angeles, acquired in the Gretzky trade, and he used it at 20th to take Martin Rucinsky. But Rucinsky played just two games as an Oiler before being dealt to Quebec in

March 1992 to get Ron Tugnutt and Brad Zavisha. While Rucinsky established an NHL career (and won an Olympic gold medal with the Czech Republic in 1998), Zavisha played only two NHL games after the trade, and Tugnutt went to Anaheim in the 1993 expansion draft.

After the first round in 1991, Edmonton went back to racking up misses. The Oilers didn't find an NHL player with any of their next four picks, while other teams secured (to name a few) Jason Dawe, Jozef Stumpel, Yanic Perreault, Sandy McCarthy, Steve Konowalchuk, Michael Nylander, Dave Karpa, Igor Kravchuk and Mariusz Czerkawski (whom the Oilers would make a trade to get), Alexei Zhitnik, Bill Lindsay, and Dimitri Yushkevich. At 144th, Edmonton took David Oliver, a right winger who gave the Oilers 139 games before being claimed on waivers by the Rangers. Edmonton's next three picks produced nothing.

THE FIRST "UNTOUCHABLE" to go after the 1990/91 playoffs was Jari Kurri, who hadn't been seen in an Oilers uniform since 1989/90, as a contract dispute saw him play in Italy instead. On May 30, Sather packaged Kurri with Dave Brown and Corey Foster and sent them to Philadelphia for Craig Fisher, Scott Mellanby and Craig Berube. (The Flyers immediately sent Kurri to Los Angeles, where he was reunited with Gretzky and reached the 1992/93 Stanley Cup finals with him.)

Fisher and Foster cancelled each other out as minor pro exchanges. Dave Brown was a combative right winger who had been acquired from Philadelphia in February 1989 in exchange for veteran centre Keith Acton (acquired from Minnesota in January 1988) and Edmonton's fifth-round choice in 1991 as the Oilers beefed up for the playoffs.[9]

Mellanby was an NHL regular, but not of Kurri's star quality. After he produced thirty-two points in 1992/93, Sather made him available in the 1993 expansion draft, and he became more productive as a Florida Panther than he ever was as an Oiler.

Berube never made it to the Oilers, as Sather included him in his next big "untouchables" trade. On September 19, 1991, Berube was tossed in with Glenn Anderson and Grant Fuhr in a supertrade with Toronto that netted Edmonton four desperately needed new players in return (as well as future consideration and cash). Sather got Vincent Damphousse, Peter Ing, Scott Thornton and Luke Richardson. One year later, Sather used Damphousse (and Edmonton's fourth-round pick in the 1993 draft) to scare up more players in a deal with Montreal that got him Shayne Corson, Brent Gilchrist and Vladimir Vujtek.

While the trades of Kurri, Anderson and Fuhr were momentous events in the dismantling of the Oilers dynasty after the Gretzky deal, the most significant one was still to come. On October 4, Sather sent his captain, Mark Messier, to the New York Rangers (who had already signed Adam Graves as a free agent in September) in exchange for Bernie Nicholls, Steven Rice and Louie DeBrusk, plus a provision for future considerations that apparently amounted to millions of dollars—possibly more than $5 million. Sather could have had Rice and DeBrusk already in the draft, but the Oilers had missed the opportunity while making choices that didn't pan out. Rice was lost to free agency as Hartford signed him in August 1994; DeBrusk was an enforcer who never played a full season in Edmonton before going to Tampa Bay as a free agent in September 1997. Nicholls had produced 150 points on Gretzky's wing in Los Angeles in 1988/89, but after being acquired by New York and then Edmonton, he returned to life as a point-a-game centre. In January 1993 Sather sent him to New Jersey for Zdeno Ciger and Kevin Todd.

The draft failures from 1984 to 1991 were a largely unrecognized counterpoint to the successes Edmonton enjoyed in the draft from 1979 to 1983. When the Oilers were ruling the NHL, and few thought Pocklington might be forced to auction off one of the greatest lineups in the history of the game, it was possible to overlook the lack of new stars emerging from within the team's development system. And once

Pocklington's financial straits spurred on the decimation of the winning lineup in the early 1990s, public enmity toward the team's owner and sympathy for Sather's circumstances obscured Sather's own culpability in the resulting lean years. The Oilers teams of the mid-1990s weren't poor just because the stars of the 1980s had left town. They were poor because in seven entry drafts the Oilers secured almost no NHL-calibre players to take the place of the aging and expensive stars.

By the time the 1990/91 season and the 1991 draft were over, the Oilers organization was in serious trouble. Not only was Pocklington strapped for cash, but also Glen Sather and his scouting staff had missed out on an entire generation of new stars at the same time as the existing stars were decamping, either because they were unable to get the money they wanted from the Oilers or because they just wanted out of town. And the crisis in the Oilers roster struck just as the NHL was undergoing a major change in its economic environment. A more militant players' union was on the horizon, and the business was being transformed by a fresh league enthusiasm for expansion—an enthusiasm shared by Peter Pocklington. Expansion brought not only new teams but also new owners, with new business priorities. Self-made entrepreneurs like Pocklington were giving way to media conglomerates who saw professional sports franchises not as ego trips, but as key assets in a portfolio that integrated the team, its arena and its television rights. There is never an ideal time for any enterprise to encounter hard times, but the Oilers were weakening at the worst possible moment in the league's modern history.

PART THREE

Chapter Twelve

T HE REAGAN REVOLUTION—launched by the eponymous president in 1980, perpetuated by the Bush administration into the 1990s, then carried forward under the Clinton Democrats and Republican-dominated Congress—changed professional sport by changing the industries around it. Broadcasting, which since the 1960s had been fundamental to the business's growth and profitability, was transformed by deregulation of network ownership. Through the binge of mergers and acquisitions begun in the 1980s came the rise of media megaproperties, with cross-ownership in network broadcasting, cable television, print media, direct-to-household satellite service and any other communications and entertainment ventures one could name. Professional sports franchises, which were the ready-made content for content-hungry airwaves, became a natural part of the media property portfolio. Media investors, once feared by some old-guard franchise owners as interlopers in their arena-centric business plans, became A-list potential franchisees—especially in professional hockey, which was so desperate to attract interest in its product from the American television industry.

The NHL wanted strong nationwide television coverage in the United States, and in coveting this long-elusive grail, it began to reshape itself into a facsimile of the networks whose cameras it wished to have trained upon itself. If a network required affiliated stations spaced throughout the union in every significant urban market, then a sports league needed similar distribution in its franchises. Without this mimicry of the network, there was no network audience for the game to sell. The rise of specialty channels and "superstations" like Ted Turner's TBS Atlanta may have meant a diminished role for traditional network broadcasting, but it did not change the network-mimicking imperative of the NHL. A specialty sports channel like ESPN is carried by individual local cable services, creating a pseudo-national network when households around the country tune in. (A superstation like TBS is a UHF-broadcasting station which makes its feed freely available to individual cable services. The station makes its money by charging advertising rates that reflect the viewer boost of cable subscribers.)

While the NHL waited for a national breakthrough in its media presence, the profitability of many of its teams relied heavily upon local cable audiences, and the league made a special effort in the 1980s to increase its television presence through cable distribution. Teams with strong local cable audiences were much more profitable than ones without. Proceeds from national television contracts negotiated by the league with networks and specialty sports channels are shared equally among teams; local broadcast rights are the properties of individual teams. Cable systems require strong regional product, and broadcasts of local sports teams provide it. As media empires have grown through deregulation, particularly since the U.S. Telecom Act of 1996,[1] it has made increasing sense in major markets for the cable company or its parent to own the team (and its arena) rather than pay broadcast rights fees.[2]

And so, two clear trends emerged in the NHL in the 1990s:

1. Expansion and franchise relocation were designed to increase the league's "electronic footprint," leading the league into regions (i.e., the American sunbelt) that might not know much about hockey, but that added new

television markets to the league's electronic presence.

2. Teams, whether existing ones or new franchises, were sought by media companies as captive content. The league in turn looked favourably upon major media players who were interested in acquiring a team.

The sum of this pair of trends was the following: In attempting to attract more American television attention, the NHL increasingly became the outright property of the American television industry.

Some of the NHL's strongest franchises have turned into chattels of major media and entertainment interests. In July 1996, the Philadelphia-based cable TV monolith Comcast Corp. took a 66 percent interest in a limited partnership with Ed Snider's Spectacor, the largest arena and convention facility management company in the United States (with about sixty clients), which also owned the Philadelphia Flyers, the 76ers of the NBA, and the arenas in which both teams play, the CoreStates Center and CoreStates Spectrum. In October 1997, Comcast Spectacor teamed up with the Phillies of major-league baseball to launch Comcast SportsNet, a twenty-four-hour regional sports programming network carrying Flyers, 76ers and Phillies games to an audience of about 2.6 million.

Another NHL team entwined in the cable television business is the Buffalo Sabres. Thirty-four percent of the limited partnership Niagara Frontier Hockey, which owns the Sabres, is held by cable giant Adelphia Cable Communications, which has the 10th largest cable subscriber base in the United States.

In 1995, the Quebec Nordiques were purchased by COMSAT Corporation and moved to Denver, to begin playing as the Avalanche; COMSAT already owned the Denver Nuggets of the NBA, which it had acquired in a series of transactions from 1989 to 1992 at a total cost of $60.2 million. The year of the Nordiques purchase, COMSAT placed its multimedia and entertainments assets (including the sports properties) within one management group, called Ascent Entertainment

Group Inc., for which COMSAT completed an initial public offering of stock on NASDAQ in December 1995, trading under the symbol GOAL. (COMSAT retained about 80 percent of the shares.) Among Ascent's holdings was Ascent Network Services, the primary provider of satellite distribution services linking NBC with its 170 affiliate television stations. Ascent also owned 57 percent of a publicly traded subsidiary, On Command Corporation, which (by room count) was the largest provider of on-demand in-room video entertainment in the U.S. lodging industry. Ascent was also involved in feature film and television production through its subsidiary Beacon Communications Corp., and in 1997 had a summer box office hit, *Air Force One*, starring Harrison Ford. (Beacon's president, producer Marc Abraham, was a former sportswriter.) Ascent forged ahead with a plan to replace the publicly owned McNichols Arena with a new facility in downtown Denver, the Pepsi Center, which was slated to open in 1999/2000. An agreement was struck with the city in November 1997 under which Ascent would build, own and manage the new facility. The city would release Ascent from its McNichols lease, in return for sales tax revenues of at least $1 million annually and title to the arena land for twenty-three years. At the same time, Ascent received property tax concessions.[3]

Most of the production funding for Beacon's *Air Force One* had come from Buena Vista, an arm of the Disney empire, which had joined the NHL ownership ranks just ahead of Beacon's parent, Ascent. The Mighty Ducks of Anaheim, which began playing in 1993/94, are owned and operated by Anaheim Sports Inc., a Disney subsidiary. Anaheim Sports is also the managing general partner in the limited partnership that owns major-league baseball's Anaheim Angels. In February 1996, Disney completed its acquisition of ABC, which operates national radio and television networks. Disney already had extensive holdings in specialty cable channels, including an 80 percent share of the cable sports enterprise ESPN. In turn, ESPN owned 32 percent of NetStar, which owned The Sports Network (TSN) and Les Reseau des Sports, among other Canadian media properties.

The glittering prize for media companies has been the New York Rangers. When Mark Messier and six other former Edmonton Oilers won the Rangers the 1993/94 Stanley Cup, the championship helped solidify the franchise's market value while boosting the NHL's profile in a major media centre.

The New York Rangers were part of the sports entertainment company MSG, which also owned Madison Square Garden, the adjoining Paramount (now MSG) Theater, the Knicks of the NBA, and two broadcasting properties, the Madison Square Garden Network and SportsChannel Associates (also known as SportsChannel New York). In March 1995, MSG commanded one billion American dollars when sold by media giant Viacom to a limited partnership (MSG Holding) owned by ITT and Rainbow Media Holdings, a company controlled by Cablevision Systems Corp. (In 1997, 25 percent of Rainbow Media was acquired by NBC subsidiary NBC Cable Holdings.) Rainbow Media increased its share of MSG Holding from 26.6 percent to 50 percent in February 1997.

Meanwhile, an aggressive new force was emerging on the U.S. television scene: Rupert Murdoch's Fox empire. In 1994, the upstart Fox (a subsidiary of The News Corporation) had delivered the NHL its first national television contract for the United States since the 1970s. When impediments to cross-ownership between cable and broadcast networks were removed by U.S. legislators with the Telecom Act of 1996, Fox moved quickly to dominate sports broadcasting on the two main fronts: national and regional broadcasting. In April 1996 Fox entered into a fifty/fifty joint venture with Liberty Media Corporation, a wholly owned subsidiary of Tele-Communications Inc. (TCI), creating Fox/Liberty Networks.[4] Fox/Liberty combined the reach of regional sports networks (RSNs) with a twenty-four-hour national sports programming service, Fox SportsNet, which included Fox Sports News. (Fox/Liberty also provided general entertainment programming through its FX Network).

Fox/Liberty owned twelve RSNs and had direct or indirect equity

243

(ranging from 12 to 70 percent) in another nine; with affiliate agreements, Fox had a healthy stable of twenty-six RSNs, boasting local tele-vision rights to seventy of seventy-five NHL, NBA and major-league baseball teams in the United States.

As a direct or indirect majority RSN owner, Fox held local television rights for the NHL's Dallas Stars, Los Angeles Kings, Mighty Ducks of Anaheim, Pittsburgh Penguins, Colorado Avalanche,[5] St. Louis Blues, Phoenix Coyotes, Detroit Red Wings, Carolina Hurricanes, Tampa Bay Lightning, Chicago Blackhawks and San Jose Sharks. As the minority investor in an RSN, it had local rights for the Washington Capitals, Florida Panthers, New York Rangers and (in New York City) New York Islanders. Through third-party RSN affiliates with Fox SportsNet, Fox/Liberty had access to games of the Boston Bruins, Philadelphia Flyers and Buffalo Sabres.

While Fox was expanding its electronic sporting empire, Rainbow Media was increasing its control of the New York Rangers and affiliated MSG properties (which grew to include the New York Liberty of professional women's basketball, the New England Seawolves of arena football, and the Hartford Wolf Pack of the American Hockey League). In June 1997, Rainbow Media began a two-year buyout of ITT's share of MSG, increasing its holding to 89.8 percent by folding its SportsChannel regional sports networks into MSG and paying ITT $500 million.

In December 1997, Fox/Liberty made an aggressive play for greater control of the NHL product by buying 40 percent of Rainbow Media's interest in MSG, which included seven RSNs. Regional Programming Partners (RPP) was thus created; it is owned 60 percent by Rainbow Media and 40 percent by Fox/Liberty. In addition to a minority interest (through MSG) in the New York Rangers and other sports teams, Fox now had a piece of SportsChannel Chicago, SportsChannel Pacific, SportsChannel New England, SportsChannel Ohio, SportsChannel Cincinnati, SportsChannel Florida and Metro Channel LLC. By 1998, Fox/Liberty was the largest regional sports network programmer in the United States. The 1997 deal with Rainbow Media had also created a joint venture, National Sports Partners, dedicated to national broadcasting services, of which Fox Sports became the managing partner.

Fox's rise was a direct threat to Disney, which, as noted, in addition to owning the Mighty Ducks franchise possessed the ABC network and 80 percent of the national cable sports service ESPN. In 1998, Disney made two major plays for dominance in American sport broadcasting. For $9 billion, it secured an eight-year contract with the National Football League to carry Monday Night Football on ABC and Sunday afternoon games on ESPN. Disney also cut Fox out of the NHL's national television rights by making a five-year national rights deal with the NHL through ABC and ESPN, to begin in 1999/2000. The deal was worth an aggregate $600 million. The NHL's previous five-year contracts for both network rights (with Fox) and cable rights (with ESPN) had totalled only $220 million.[6] The Disney deal meant that the Mighty Ducks of Anaheim franchise essentially was writing a cheque for about $4 million every year to each of its fellow league members. It gave one team implicit leverage in league affairs not seen since Bill Wirtz ran half the NHL during the Original Six era through his ownership of the Blackhawks, a controlling block of shares in Madison Square Garden (owner of the Rangers) and a bailout loan to the Boston Bruins.

Integration with media properties was far less common in the Canadian NHL market, and in fact began running counter to the American trend in team ownership. Following the 1997/98 season, Molson Companies, owner of the Montreal Canadiens and the Molson Centre, made what it called a "heart wrenching decision" to end a forty-year tradition and not bid for national English broadcast rights for Canadian NHL games, although it would continue both to hold French language broadcast rights in Quebec and to pursue involvement with Canadian NHL clubs on a regional (i.e., cable) basis. Molson fully expected it would have to pay a higher price for the national television rights, which had been the foundation of its longstanding participation in CBC's "Hockey Night in Canada" broadcasts, but cited declining ratings for choosing not to spend more money on what had been a flagship marketing venue for the brewery. Molson's commitment to sports entertainment in general was weakening. Revenues from the Canadiens and their arena were down 5.6 percent in 1998, while profits had diminished from $17.3 to $2.9 million that year. The company protested the high annual realty tax it paid the city of Montreal on its new Molson Centre. In its 1998 annual report, the company said the rate of about $10 million was three times the amount paid by the Corel Centre, home of the Ottawa Senators, which in turn was higher than the taxes paid by all of the U.S. NHL teams combined.

With Molson backing out of the bidding for national English Canadian broadcast rights in 1998, the NHL concluded a new four-year deal with the CBC for network television and with the new SportsNet service for cable, worth a total of about US$190 million over four years. SportsNet was owned by the CTV network (40 percent), the cable firm Rogers Broadcasting (20 percent), the British information services firm LMC International (20 percent) and Molson Companies (20 percent). Before the NHL deal was even signed with SportsNet, however, Molson applied to the CRTC (on May 19, 1998) for permission to sell its share in the cable channel to Rogers. The request was denied by the CRTC on October 23, 1998, on the grounds that it would give Rogers yet more power in a market in which its parent company, Rogers Communications, was already the single largest cable service in the country. This made Molson a strangely reluctant participant in the televising of NHL games in 1998/99 as it sought another buyer for its SportsNet share. Meanwhile, CTV took over the new service's main rival, TSN. In February 1999 it outbid CanWest Global Communications for the piece of NetStar, the parent of TSN, not owned by Disney's ESPN.[7] The deal was subject to CRTC approval, and if it passed muster, CTV would change the name of TSN to ESPN Canada.[8]

Because the major untapped media markets for the NHL at the beginning of the 1990s were in the American sunbelt, and because major media players were American, it followed that the league's expansionary momentum was southward. The southerly movement of the NHL was further assured by the shift in financial power from the Canadian to the American NHL franchises. Before 1984, from which time national television revenues in Canada and the United States have been pooled and shared equally among all franchises, the Canadian franchises enjoyed a disproportionate windfall from the Canadian television rights.[9] For almost a decade, there had been no U.S. national television revenues at all. After 1984, it was share and share alike. In the 1990s, as national U.S. deals were struck with Fox and ESPN in 1994, and then with ABC and ESPN in 1998, revenues from U.S. national rights came to far surpass the monies flowing in from Canadian national rights. As of 1998, three times as much revenue was coming into the league pool from the U.S. as from Canada, and any hope for further revenue growth lay in the U.S.

Not only was it probable that no Canadian city would receive a new NHL franchise after Ottawa achieved the miracle in 1991, but it was also more than likely that many (if not most) existing Canadian franchises would end up heading south. It was partly due to the law of supply and demand. More American cities and American media businesses wanted NHL franchises in the 1990s than the league was able to supply through expansion. This meant owners of struggling Canadian teams could fetch top prices in lucrative American dollars. And because cities wanted these attractions as part of grandiose downtown revitalization projects, to get a team into a new, civic-funded building, they were willing to make sweetheart deals on arena rent (like eliminating it completely) and ancillary profit streams like parking and concessions.

In the early 1990s, the Edmonton Oilers, Calgary Flames, Winnipeg Jets and Quebec Nordiques were all in danger of being written off as small-market casualties of the modern sporting economy, their cash flow problems exacerbated by the crippling exchange rate with the U.S. dollar—and the Jets and Nordiques would duly head south. But "small market" was a misleading label for the malaise affecting tier I professional sports franchises like the Oilers, because it wasn't based simply on raw numbers of potential fans. There were more than enough people in a metropolis the size of Edmonton (800,000) to buy enough season tickets and fill the rest of the seats with walk-in customers. The profitability of modern sports franchises, however, was dependent on factors far beyond traditional gate receipts, with broadcast revenues the most obvious. A weak local television market became a problem shared by the Oilers and the Flames. Despite having a relatively large regional audience from which to draw, a lack of cable television service in the rural markets surrounding Calgary and Edmonton suppressed audience numbers and so the value of those rights.[10]

With the momentum of NHL expansion overwhelmingly directed at the American sunbelt, a bigger league was, in hindsight, not in the best interest of Canadian teams like the Oilers. The new teams generally were not going to be much of a draw on the road or on the tube, and their presence made for a diluted product. And yet, most Canadian teams were wholeheartedly committed to "growing" the league, if for no other reason than that the one sure source of extra revenue in the hard-pressed 1990s was expansion franchise fees, which were shared among the existing teams. For a struggling operation like the Oilers, it seemed to make economic sense to keep pressing for a bigger and bigger league.

After the admission of the Oilers and their three fellow WHA survivors in 1979, the NHL had turned away from further expansion for a decade. At the board of governors' meeting in December 1989, nineteen of twenty-one teams voted in favour of adding three teams, with eleven of them willing to consider more later in the nineties. Toronto and Minnesota, on the other hand, wanted only one new team, as they were concerned that existing franchises should be operating profitably before more were added.

Gil Stein, who served as league president from 1992 to 1993, attributed the league's expansion ambitions in 1989 to short-term greed. New arenas were being built in North America, and the NBA had just been through an expansion that commanded a $32 million franchise fee. Peter Pocklington, according to Stein, was probably the most aggressive team owner on NHL expansion. At the 1989 meeting, he argued for three more teams to be added in 1992/93, with four more later, secured with option fees. Only the New York Islanders (arguing like Edmonton for three plus four) were so expansion-minded. The board resolved to expand by seven teams, reaching twenty-eight by the year 2000, with an initial expansion of one or more teams in 1992/93. The league ended up being even more expansionist than Pocklington had initially envisioned. The NHL added five teams between 1991/92 and 1993/94 and approved four more in 1997, to be added from 1998/99 to 2000/01, which would bring the league to thirty teams.

Pocklington was also one of the most aggressive owners on expansion fees. At the 1989 meeting, Stein has written, the well-financed New York Rangers thought $40 million was about right, which was the lowest estimate. Eleven teams preferred $50 million. The Oilers, along with Boston, New Jersey and the Islanders, argued for $60 million. Only Pittsburgh went higher, at $65 million. The league began its 1990s expansion with a price tag of $50 million, paid by Ottawa, Tampa Bay, Florida, San Jose and Anaheim. (Disney was allowed to use half of its $50 million fee as an indemnification payment to the Los Angeles Kings for encroaching on the territory with the Mighty Ducks franchise, thereby reducing the fee shared by teams to $25 million.) The fee leapt to $80 million in 1997 for Nashville, Atlanta, Minnesota and Columbus. Total revenues shared by teams from this expansion bonanza were $545 million.

It looked like a windfall, but there was a dangerous flaw in the expansion concept. As the league became bigger, the player talent pool thinned. The law of supply and demand for an industry reliant on a

relatively limited pool of highly skilled labour dictated that players in
general, even with increasing imports from Europe (especially players
once held back by the Iron Curtain), would become more expensive,
and good players disproportionately so, as teams found it difficult to
secure even two first-class centres. New clubs struggling to establish a
fan base would be particularly prone to making record-breaking signings to get fans into the building.

Even as the NHL was creating the potential for explosive growth in
salaries through its aggressive expansion plans, the league had little
real control over the growth of team payrolls. The NHL was not a
single corporate entity, negotiating with a union to set basic wage
rates, benefits and seniority standards. It was an ungainly cartel
formed from individual businesses who were wont to pay whatever
they thought was fair as they negotiated contracts individually with
employees. The collective bargaining agreement between the league
and the Players' Association was simply a framework for player compensation and mobility. As the nineties dawned, the CBA had a minimum salary, but no maximum, for either individual players or team
payrolls. The owners could try to rein in the potential for spiralling
wages by pressing for tight restrictions on free agency, but they had no
way of preventing their fellow franchisees, who were ultimately business rivals, from spending whatever they felt like.

Back in the days of the WHA, some NHL owners, like Toronto's
Harold Ballard and the Bronfman family's Edper group in Montreal,
tried to hold the line on salaries by refusing to get into bidding wars.
The elimination of the WHA in 1979 was supposed to put an end to
such player bargaining power, and for about a decade, it did. But
expansion—in what should have been no surprise—helped fuel an
internal bidding war among NHL owners for top players.

The Detroit Red Wings and free agent Sergei Fedorov were at an
impasse in 1997/98, with Fedorov exercising his Group II restricted
free agency by refusing to report until Detroit made a favourable
offer. The Red Wings were determined to let him sit for the entire

season if necessary when, in February, the Carolina Hurricanes, Peter Karmanos's relocated Hartford franchise, made a surprising six-year, $38 million offer. While technically not an expansion team, the Hurricanes looked, smelled and tasted like one. They were in a new hockey market, trying to put fans in seats in Greensboro Coliseum, their temporary home, while they waited for a new facility to be built in Raleigh. The Hurricanes needed a player of Fedorov's stature to build a season-ticket base, and with a sweetheart deal from Raleigh to lay on a new arena, the team had a cost structure that suggested it could afford a Fedorov over the long haul. The Red Wings were forced to match the Carolina offer to hang on to their centre, a past winner of the Hart, Pearson and Selke awards.

While Red Wings coach Scotty Bowman excoriated the Hurricanes for making Fedorov such an enormous offer, the incident proved that there was little the league could do to stop runaway labour costs once the players' union threw off the self-administered shackles of the Eagleson years and the ownership ranks were revealed to harbour damn-the-expense team builders. The have-not franchises like the Oilers were doomed to lose talent to the haves as free agency siphoned stars from their rosters.

If owners of NHL franchises did not see the skyrocketing costs of labour coming in the 1990s, then they were fools, for there was no way an increase in total franchises of almost 50 percent could withstand inflationary salary pressures without rigorous controls. Alan Eagleson had allowed a large amount of such control in the eighties by not fighting for greater free agency, but it should have been clear by the time expansion was voted on in December 1989 that his reign was almost over. Some kind of salary or payroll cap was the only solution, but the prospect of achieving anything like this rapidly proved doubtful as the union decided, for the first time, to stand its ground. Eagleson had always been close to league president John Ziegler, and as salaries began to increase in the early 1990s, Pocklington was among those owners who wanted Ziegler fired for failing to ensure labour costs were held in check. Ziegler negotiated with Eagleson's successor, Bob Goodenow, to end the ten-day walkout in April that threatened to scrap the 1991/92 postseason. The new collective bargaining agreement mainly gave the players licensing rights for products like hockey trading cards, but Ziegler was ousted that June for not figuring out how to contain salaries. After Gil Stein served on an interim basis as president, Gary Bettman became the league's first commissioner in February 1993.

Bettman had helped bring a salary cap to professional basketball as an executive with the NBA, and the NHL's owners clearly were looking to him as a saviour in their negotiations with an uncharacteristically hard-nosed NHLPA. The league and its fans endured a pseudo-lockout that almost wiped out the 1994/95 season, and the best the NHL could manage was a cap on rookie salaries, while the NHLPA in return gained liberalized free-agency regulations that gave players true mobility for the first time in league history.

The NHLPA had embarked on a crusade to determine who actually owned the game: the players, or the team owners. By the raw measure of salaries, the players were winning. Despite all their complaints about profitability, owners could not resist cutting precedent-setting deals for key players that affected salary structures all around the league. With the union having adopted full salary disclosure, everyone knew what everyone else was making: the "comparables" era had come to the NHL labour market.

Pocklington could complain about the cost of icing a team in the 1990s, but he had laid the groundwork for soaring player salaries by selling Gretzky to the Los Angeles Kings. Once he had auctioned off the game's greatest player on the open market, Pocklington had made possible everything that followed. The Gretzky sale alone set a market value on top talent that every player agent could use as a measuring stick (and which, as Rich Winter has noted, reminded players that owners considered them assets, and that the players should begin thinking in the same vein).

Pocklington further fuelled the salary fire, however unintention-
ally, by turning loose virtually all the Oilers stars (when he no longer
could afford them) in a labour pool thin on talent. Back in 1926, the
player contracts of the Edmonton Eskimos of the just-folded Western
Hockey League were snapped up en masse to create the new NHL
franchise in Chicago, the Blackhawks. In the early 1990s, the New
York Rangers were rebuilt in a similar vein using the human resources
suddenly available from the Oilers. In winning the 1993/94 Stanley
Cup, the Rangers used former Oilers Mark Messier, Kevin Lowe,
Glenn Anderson, Esa Tikkanen, Craig MacTavish, Jeff Beukeboom
and Adam Graves. (Later, they would also acquire Wayne Gretzky and
Jari Kurri.)

Following the Rangers' victory in 1993/94, the St. Louis Blues'
owners, the limited partnership Clark Enterprises, became the bad
boys of the league's ownership ranks by running amok in the free-
agency market. The Rangers had shown that shrewdly building a
winning club through careful drafting and development of young
talent, as the Oilers had done, could be bypassed by allowing the
general manager access to the corporate safe. The Rangers' excesses
were tolerated because they brought a league title to New York,
America's media capital. St. Louis's excesses were bemoaned for their
crassness and inflationary salary effect. Having swiped coach
Mike Keenan from the Rangers within days of New York's Cup win,
the Blues proceeded to try to build their own version of the Oilers,
with seven former Edmonton Cup winners—Esa Tikkanen, Wayne
Gretzky, Charlie Huddy, Glenn Anderson, Grant Fuhr, Craig
MacTavish and Joe Murphy—employed at different times from
1994/95 to 1996/97.

Neither the Rangers nor the Blues operated in a manner
Pocklington approved of, and when the Vancouver Canucks signed
Mark Messier with a three-year, $22 million deal in July 1997,
Pocklington declined to conceal his contempt for the free-spending
ways of the Canucks' owner, Seattle's cell-phone billionaire John

McCaw. Pocklington felt that, at this stage of his career, Messier was worth $2 million a year. But the outlandishly high salaries suddenly enjoyed by NHL players was a genie Pocklington had helped loose from the bottle.

The league further fuelled higher wages by allowing weak franchises to move to stronger markets. It could be argued that, when three of the four WHA refugees of 1979 were permitted to relocate, operating expense burdens were sure to accelerate for the league as a whole. Keeping teams in small markets might actually serve as a brake on inflationary costs, were these operations to be supported and nurtured by the league through greater revenue sharing. But in a business context in which the pursuit of profitability is foremost, it would be difficult to argue that the collective good of owners required some of them to remain mired in the have-not ranks. Every owner wants to maximize his return, even if that means cashing in the capital value of the franchise by selling it to someone who thinks he can get an operating bargain in a big American city.

The league's business structure had become burdened by the runaway use of comparables by players and owners, a trend that drove labour costs ever higher and threatened overall stability as owners strove to force operating costs ever lower. A left winger with sixty points who signed for $4 million a season naturally made every other sixty-point left winger in the league want the same money. Similarly, when one franchise owner got a tax-free deal or cheap arena rent, the other owners were eager to claim they deserved the same perks. Operating overheads became the next comparable to haunt the league. As new franchises were practically given taxpayer-funded buildings to use for their own profit, owners like Peter Pocklington wanted similar deals for their leases of public facilities. (And those team owners who owned their building could still play the comparables game by arguing for municipal taxation breaks—like the Montreal Canadiens, who would claim to pay more in property taxes than all the American NHL teams combined.)

Perversely, while high labour costs provoked owners to seek even lower operating costs, low operating costs freed up money to drive labour costs higher. It was a vicious circle with no real resolution. The illogic of the league's fiscal dilemma was that, despite constant assurances from owners that they couldn't make money, franchises kept increasing in value. The price of an NHL expansion franchise had grown from $2 million in 1967 to the $6 million paid in 1979 by the former WHA teams, to $50 million in 1991 and up to $80 million in 1997, with established clubs capable of commanding far higher prices. This hyperinflation of an asset's value, coinciding with consistent assertions that operations were drowning in red ink, would normally suggest an impending implosion to correct gross overvaluation, but there seemed little real concern that NHL franchises were en route to a league-wide Black Monday. A team like the Oilers might be losing money, but that didn't mean it wasn't worth much. The escalating value of franchises helped exacerbate Peter Pocklington's financial crisis, as the increasing collateral the value represented allowed him to carry more borrowings from the Alberta Treasury Branches, even though the operating revenues couldn't service the debt. On the open market a struggling franchise like the Oilers could fetch a handsome dollar, provided whoever bought it was allowed to move it where revenues, and not just expenses, were in American dollars, and where the comparables were either more favourable or simply not an issue for a deep-pockets owner. A place, for starters, like Oklahoma City.

CHAPTER THIRTEEN

THE WALL STREET equities binge, the enormous fees generated by mergers, acquisitions and hostile takeovers, the frenetic activity injected into erstwhile staid industries like transportation and energy by government deregulation, the coincident boom in high technology industries and the transformation of the twelve-channel television industry into a 500-channel cacophony dominated by satellite and cable transmission . . . all of these things contributed in the late 1980s and 1990s to the creation of a new social and economic order in the higher tax brackets, and to dramatic shifts in the urban landscape. Cities like Denver and Phoenix sprawled; other established addresses reinvented themselves with ambitious urban renewal projects, to make amends for lax zoning regulations and a flight to the suburbs by industry and citizen alike that in the previous decades had gutted the city centre. By the late 1980s, publicly funded entertainment facilities, particularly arenas, were springing up all over America, often without a major private tenant—i.e., a major-league sports franchise. Michael Eisner, chairman and CEO of the Disney Corporation, set off down the road to acquiring an NHL franchise for Anaheim when he drove by the city's new arena one day and wondered what it was being used for. Not, as it happened, for hockey. Enter the Mighty Ducks.

Publicly funded buildings began to change the traditional

economic structure of sports, particularly hockey. In the Original Six era, it was a given that the team's owner was also supposed to own the arena. Few politicians were interested in building enormous structures to rent out to entrepreneurs, and the entrepreneurs themselves wanted to own the building anyway so they could collect the revenues not just from the gate, but also from concessions and parking, as well as the rent that could be charged on the three-hundred-odd nights every year the hockey team wasn't in the building.

As the NHL began to expand, aspiring franchisees who would have to pay rent to use a community-owned building were looked upon with some dubiousness. But by the 1990s a revolution was changing the relationship between tenant and landlord in professional sport. As affluent new metropolises arose, they began to desire the accoutrements of civic status. A major-league sports franchise was at least as desirable (if not more so) than a traditional right of bragging, such as a symphony orchestra or an art gallery. Sometimes the cities built the building and then waited for the teams to materialize, à la Shoeless Joe on a baseball diamond hewn from a cornfield. Sometimes the city worked in partnership with local investors, hatching a plan to acquire a franchise, with the civic-funded arena the enticement. These potential new franchise sites were thrown into competition with two other types of city: those that were attempting to revitalize their city core with an anchor attraction (in some cases by seeking a league franchise after one had been lost), and those like Edmonton that were struggling to hang on to a franchise in the face of the siren call of these new facilities.

It always came down to the building. How new, how expansive, how diverse in revenues. Edmonton had lost the Eskimos of the old Western Hockey League when, in 1926, the WHL died because the league's rinks could not generate the revenues to match the salaries being paid by the new NHL franchises out east. The Eskimos were playing in the 6,000–seat Edmonton Stock Pavilion, built in 1913, while NHL teams were playing in new facilities capable of seating

more than 10,000. The rink since the Eskimos' demise had remained
essentially the same: 200 feet long, 85 feet wide. The season, by the
nineties, had grown about as long as it could grow: eighty-two games
beginning in early October, with four rounds of playoffs dragging on
into June. Owners kept finding new ways to squeeze revenues from
the architecture surrounding the ice. More seats, more luxury boxes,
more concession and parking revenue. An entire building could be
rendered obsolete in a decade, requiring expensive renovations and
ultimately outright replacement. Increasingly, franchises turned their
backs on the Original Six model of the team owner as arena operator—or at least an arena operator who paid for the building. Let the
community build the thing. We'll give them professional sports in
return. And we get to keep the money.

It was a potent twist on the boosterism of the Canadian prairies,
an attitude that predated the First World War and lived on in Edmonton—which held that civic leaders and businessmen could and
should band together to erect buildings to attract events that would
put the town on the global map. As the same proactive civic attitude
took hold on new urban frontiers, Oilers fans watched as other cities,
minor in the American topography but populated by more citizens
with far greater wealth, brought the same determination, by intent or
consequence, to erasing Edmonton from the map.

On the evening of Sunday, December 13, 1992, the Edmonton
Oilers met up with an old nemesis, the New York Islanders, in a
game that showcased the sorry decline of the two dynastic clubs of the
1980s.

Between them they had won nine of the last thirteen Stanley
Cups, and the Oilers had been in eight of the last ten "final four" playoff rounds. But the Islanders had missed the playoffs in three of the
last four seasons, and were currently in last place in the Patrick
Division. While Al Arbour, who would win his 700th NHL game this

season, was still behind the Islanders' bench, Bill Torrey, who had served as general manager since the team's creation in 1972, had left to run another NHL team—a new one in Florida.

Three days before the Islanders–Oilers game, the NHL had announced that it was awarding two new franchises. In a break from the customary process of inviting franchise applications, the NHL had actively courted two major players in corporate America: Wayne Huizenga, who had made his fortune with Blockbuster Video, and Michael Eisner of the Disney Corporation. Huizenga and Disney (through Eisner) were successfully wooed. Huizenga was granted the Miami-area franchise, which became the Florida Panthers, to be operated on Huizenga's behalf by Torrey, while Disney got Anaheim (home of Disneyland), which became the first major-league sports franchise to operate as a movie spinoff when it was named after *The Mighty Ducks*. (Disney's California Angels at least already existed before the company made *Angels in the Outfield*.)

Of the five franchises awarded since 1990, four—Anaheim, Miami, Tampa Bay and San Jose—were in the American sunbelt (Ottawa was the lone exception). It was the hothouse of the new, affluent suburbia, ready-built with cable television. With the Gund brothers having been allowed in 1990 to set up shop in San Jose, and with approval for the Minnesota North Stars to relocate to Dallas about to be granted in March 1993, the NHL was leaving its northernmost franchise, the Edmonton Oilers, ever more isolated.

The Oilers had become prima facie evidence that the game's economic momentum was rapidly heading south. The team was either in the throes of a debilitating dismantling, or on the way back to the top through an aggressive rebuilding. Even with the loss of so many stars of the 1980s, the Oilers' decline had not been immediately apparent. The team had finished third in the Smythe again in 1991/92 and had made another admirable playoff run—eliminating Gretzky's Kings in six in the division semi-finals and overcoming the Canucks in six in the division finals, only to be swept by the Blackhawks for the conference championship. But as the 1992/93 season began, the decline became precipitous, and the exodus of talent that had accelerated after the 1990/91 playoffs was not abating. The team's captain, Kevin Lowe, the last of the core members of the original championship team, had just been lost two days before the game against the Islanders. Injuries had kept him out of the lineup for the entire season to date, and on December 11, Glen Sather dealt him to the New York Rangers. In July 1992, Neil Smith of the Rangers had become Sather's corporate equal when he was named New York's president as well as general manager (a job he had held since July 1989). Backed by the media giant Viacom, Smith was continuing to build a Cup contender out of star players whom Peter Pocklington could no longer afford. Smith already had Mark Messier, Jeff Beukeboom and Adam Graves. By giving up Roman Oksiuta and his third-round pick in the 1993 entry draft, Smith now had Lowe as well.

The loss of Lowe was a grievous blow to Oilers fans who were mourning the passing of the eighties dynasty. The dependable blue-liner, articulate and gentlemanly, was a class act as well as a valued athlete. Sather had not dispensed with Lowe entirely—he had long seen him playing a role in the Oilers organization after his playing career ended. Sather essentially was doing Lowe a favour by sending him to New York, where he could earn top dollar and win another Stanley Cup in the final seasons of his career before returning to Edmonton. Sather would get him back for the 1996/97 season through free agency, and after chronic injuries limited his 1997/98 season to seven games, Lowe would retire and become an Oilers assistant coach and would then replace Ron Low as coach for 1999/2000.

In December 1992, though, Lowe's eventual return to Edmonton was far from certain and in any event well over the horizon. His trade to New York closed the books on the Oilers' greatest years. The Oilers were known for starting the season slowly, but the 1992/93 campaign was showing no sign of a turnaround. Having lost 3-1 to Tampa Bay on Saturday, December 12, they dropped the Sunday game 4-1 to the

struggling Islanders, and surrendered one more token of their celebrated years. The Islanders had not beaten the Oilers since February
14, 1989, when they prevailed 5-3 in Long Island.

Behind the bench that Sunday night, registering the Oilers' loss,
was Ted Green. The co-coach had been promoted by Sather to the full
coaching position in 1991/92; John Muckler moved on to Buffalo to
take over as head coach from Rick Dudley, and was promoted to general manager in 1993. Sather began deal-making in an attempt to sal-
vage Green's sophomore coaching season. He had already sent a
prized centre, Vincent Damphousse (acquired from Toronto in the
Fuhr/Anderson/Berube blockbuster of September 1991) to Montreal
(along with Edmonton's fourth-round pick in the 1992 entry draft) in
August to load up on fresh talent. He had received in return a trio of
left wingers: Shayne Corson; Brent Gilchrist, who had recorded a
career-high fifty points with the Canadiens in 1991/92; and Czech
Vladimir Vujtek. Corson was a keeper, but the other two players
received for Damphousse (who became the Canadiens' captain) provided minimal gain. In March, Gilchrist, who would produce only
twenty points in sixty games in 1992/93, was sent to Minnesota for
Todd Elik. (Gilchrist would win a Stanley Cup with Detroit in
1997/98.) Elik would be allowed to go to San Jose on waivers four
games into the 1993/94 season, and he responded to the change by
contributing sixty-six points in seventy-five games, a career best.
Vujtek split the 1992/93 season between Edmonton and the AHL farm
team in Cape Breton, then went back to Europe after 1993/94. Sather
would trade his rights to Tampa Bay in 1997.

Before Gilchrist was dealt to Minnesota for Elik, Sather tried other
trades to rejuvenate the lineup. Bernie Nicholls went to New Jersey in
January for left winger Zdeno Ciger and centre Kevin Todd. Ciger
would stay in Edmonton through 1995/96, but Todd would be traded
the following October to Chicago for Adam Bennett. To strengthen
the defence, a veteran, Brian Benning, was brought in from Philadelphia in January; Sather surrendered left winger Josef Beranek and

defenceman Greg Hawgood, who was just emerging as an NHL regular. Both Beranek and Hawgood had more seasons left in them than Benning, who in July 1993 was lost to Florida through free agency.

In February, Sather sent holdout Joe Murphy, who had not played all season, to the Blackhawks for Russian defenceman Igor Kravchuk and and a promising young centre, Dean McAmmond. In March, with the Oilers' hopes for a playoff appearance dimming, Sather dumped a few more former Stanley Cup winners as other teams bulked up for a Cup charge of their own. The Rangers' Neil Smith was back for more, collecting Esa Tikkanen in exchange for Doug Weight. Tikkanen had scored only fourteen times in sixty-six games with the Oilers in 1992/93. Sather had always regretted the generous contract Rich Winter had negotiated for Tikkanen directly with Pocklington in the wake of the Gretzky trade. "Sather still gets frustrated with that," Winter notes. "He says, 'You got me there. You went around me to get to Pocklington and he paid too much.' He feels that was part of Esa's downfall, that early on Esa needed more incentive, in Glen's mind. 'You got him a big cushy contract and look what you did to him.'" In addition to dealing away Tikkanen, Sather sent Winter's other Edmonton client, Craig Muni, to Chicago for Mike Hudson.

Having won thirty-six games and reached the conference championship finals the previous spring, the Oilers won only twenty-six games in 1992/93—the worst regular-season performance in their history as an NHL franchise—as they missed the playoffs for the first time.

Perhaps the most noteworthy fact about the telling loss to the Islanders back in December was that it did not come at Northlands Coliseum in Edmonton or at Nassau Coliseum in Long Island. With two new franchises beginning to play in Ottawa and Tampa Bay, the NHL had decided to permit a taste of its product in a plethora of as-yet unserviced markets. Twenty-four regular-season games in 1992/93 were scheduled at neutral sites: Saskatoon, Hamilton, Indianapolis, Milwaukee, Birmingham, Phoenix, Miami, Sacramento, Atlanta,

Cincinnati, Cleveland, Halifax, Providence, Dallas and—on December 13—Oklahoma City. The Oilers had performed poorly before 11,110 fans at Oklahoma's Myriad Convention Center, home ice to the state capital's brand new Central Hockey League franchise, the Blazers.

Having the Oilers play on the Blazers' home ice was a masterpiece of both retrospection and foreshadowing, for Oklahoma City was where Glen Sather had begun his professional hockey career, and it was where his Oilers might ultimately end up. Sather had played for the Blazers of the old Central Hockey League[2]; the Oilers lost to the Islanders before a house full of fans who had taken enthusiastically to the Blazers and the reborn CHL, which had just gone back into business that fall.

The CHL in which Sather had played had been a development league wholly owned by the NHL. As the WHA ran out of steam in the late 1970s, the CHL took in a few WHA teams as it tried to carve out a viable place in the minor pro market.[3] Oklahoma City had its own considerable problems. Its successes in the late 1960s, of which Sather had been such an important part, were due to the team's sponsorship by the Boston Bruins. In 1972, after the Bruins won their second Stanley Cup in three years, Boston decided to place its best minor pro prospects closer to home, with the Boston Braves of the AHL, and the Blazers didn't play in 1972/73. The Tulsa Oilers, sponsored by the Maple Leafs, played a few regular-season games in Oklahoma City, some of them at the new Myriad Center facility downtown. For 1973/74, the Leafs moved their CHL sponsorship to Oklahoma City outright, and the Blazers were reborn, dropping the gold and black livery of the Bruins in favour of the blue and white of Toronto. After three seasons though, and a debilitating move from the Myriad Center to the old State Fair Arena, Toronto cancelled its sponsorship. A group of local investors stepped in to run the team for 1976/77. Picking up a number of former WHA players, the team won only fifteen of seventy-six games. As *The Oklahoman* newspaper would summarize, "there were fifty-one players on the roster and several CHL records set for futility." When a sponsorship arrangement with the Detroit Red Wings fell through, the Blazers sat out the 1977/78 season, but returned in 1978/79 with new sponsorship by the Minnesota North Stars. The name was changed to the Stars and the uniform recast in the parent club's green, white and gold.

The team struggled on the ice and at the box office; the local consortium sold the operation to local insurance executive John Hail. Minnesota pulled out after 1980/81, and new sponsorship was arranged with the Calgary Flames. By the end of the 1981/82 season, the Oklahoma City Stars were filing for bankruptcy protection.

The CHL's president in the early 1980s was Bud Poile, the former coach of the WHL's Edmonton Flyers of the 1960s, who had served in Philadelphia as the general manager of the new (coincidentally named) Flyers franchise from 1967 to 1969 before being replaced by Keith Allen. Poile had already left Edmonton in 1963, when the city felt the consequences of the Red Wings' withdrawal of support for the WHL Flyers, but he was running the CHL in 1982 when the league was staggered by a mass withdrawal of support by NHL franchises. The Calgary Flames had shouldered an estimated US$700,000 of the Oklahoma City team's $1.2 million in losses in 1981/82, even after waiving the $110,000 fee a sponsoring club normally received for the players it supplied. With the bankruptcy of the Stars, Calgary moved its sponsorship to Denver, where a new team would play as the Colorado Flames. Winnipeg, meanwhile, withdrew its support for the Tulsa Oilers, Toronto dumped the Cincinnati Tigers (a one-season wonder) and Minnesota pulled out of Nashville. The CHL managed an eighty-game season with six teams in 1982/83, then folded.

For a decade, a hole was left for professional hockey to fill in the American Midwest, a task that was finally accomplished by Chicago businessman Horn Chen. Chen envisioned a bus league in which he'd own all the franchises and no player would make more than $100,000. He wanted to replicate the success of the East Coast Hockey

League, which had begun play in 1988/89 with five teams, and had grown to fifteen with its low-budget razzle-dazzle product.

Actually, it was Ray Miron, a veteran minor pro executive, who dreamed up the revived CHL and sold Chen on the idea. Miron and a friend, Bill Levins, had conceived of a league owned by a partnership group that would operate at a level below the American Hockey League and the International Hockey League. Miron was representing the NHL's Vancouver Canucks at the IHL annual meeting in 1991 when he pitched Chen, the owner of the IHL's Indianapolis Ice, on the concept. Chen had made a fortune in real estate and restaurants, and by becoming the largest American importer of bamboo through his Eastern Trading Company. Chen gave Miron $800,000 to create a league, and immediately became its majority owner.

In Oklahoma City, Allen Coles, chief executive officer of W&W Steel Co., led local efforts to roll out the red carpet for Horn Chen's new enterprise. In June 1992, Oklahoma City's city council approved about $360,000 in public spending to make the Myriad Center more hockey-friendly and to underwrite the costs of regularly switching its configuration from a hockey rink to other uses. (It was also home to a Continental Basketball Association franchise, the Cavalry.) The CHL was a success, and the Oklahoma City Blazers were by far its most successful franchise. Playing at the 12,500–seat Myriad Center, the Blazers drew an average 8,356 fans a game in the inaugural season as the team produced the league's best regular-season record. With tickets in the $6 to $9 range, the gate was far above the CHL's break-even target of 3,500.

When they played the Islanders at the Myriad Center in December 1992, the Edmonton Oilers were painfully familiar with the size of the audience in the minor-league facility. The 11,110 fans who turned out to watch them lose approached the size of the dwindling gates in Edmonton. And while the crowd of Blazers enthusiasts the Oilers played before in Oklahoma City may have been a little smaller than the recent crowds at Northlands, it felt like Oilers crowds of old—excited about the game and the possibilities of the home team.

Oklahoma City was also a southern cousin of Edmonton. Both were capitals and oil towns; with about one million people, Oklahoma City was slightly larger than Edmonton. Both cities occupied prairie vistas and were sited on rivers—and the one that flowed through Oklahoma City was called the Canadian. They had shared the pain of the economic downturn caused by the plunge in oil prices in 1986. The world of the oil industry made it inevitable that more than a few links were forged between the cities over the years. Their respective oil patches had converged spectacularly in 1981, when Oklahoma's Conoco swallowed Hudson's Bay Oil and Gas Co. (HBOG), an enterprise that controlled 13.6 million acres of Canada and had assets of more than US$1.2 billion. Conoco was immediately the subject of a hostile takeover bid by Calgary's Dome Petroleum, which it successfully fought off.[4] In 1985, Conoco's Canadian subsidiary spent US$35 million to acquire four oil fields and one natural gas field around Edmonton from Calgary's Ocelot Industries. And when Peter Pocklington wanted a senior executive to oversee his food industry investments in 1985, he hired away Robert Autry, senior vice-president of sales and marketing for Wilson Foods Corp. of Oklahoma City.[5]

If Oklahoma City was so much like Edmonton, then surely it could support an NHL franchise, too. The city rapidly caught major-league fever as it embraced the success of the CHL's Blazers. After only one season, the Blazers ignited the notion that the city was ready to attract an NHL team. In fact, it had begun to challenge the weakest NHL operations in terms of fan support. Although Blazers tickets were far cheaper than those for NHL games, the turnstile figures were still impressive. In the fall of 1993, the start of their second season, Blazers attendance was averaging 10,371 (it would be 10,438 over the entire season, the best of any minor pro hockey team in North America). The Hartford Whalers were drawing fewer than 10,200 fans, the

Oilers about 12,500, and New Jersey was doing so poorly the team wouldn't even release gate figures.

If Oklahoma City did attract an NHL team, it would be the first major-league sports team in the city. Oklahoma City was well down the list of major-league demographics. As the 27th largest metropolitan area in the United States, it was poor in electronic spectators, representing only the country's 45th largest television market. (In this aspect, at least, it was similar to Edmonton—both suffered from the lack of a large cable audience in their rural settings.) Among television markets without any major-league team, it ranked 10th. And among cities without either an NBA or NHL franchise, it ranked just 11th in population.

But no matter. The burghers of Oklahoma City were quick studies of the nuts and bolts of landing a professional sports franchise. For such a so-called small market, there was a surprising amount of experience in the business of major-league sports. Oklahoma City could boast of something its oil-patch cousins up north sorely lacked: a set of local deep pockets that could give an NHL franchise financial stability.

Oklahoma City was home to the Gaylord family, who, in addition to owning the local newspaper, *The Oklahoman*, operated a Nashville-based media empire called Gaylord Entertainment. Founder Edward K. Gaylord had established the newspaper in 1903, when Oklahoma was still a territory. His media business embraced radio with the purchase of Oklahoma City's WKY in 1928, then entered television by establishing the city's WKY-TV in 1949. Eschewing network affiliations (affiliates in Tampa and New Orleans were bought and then sold), Gaylord became one of the largest private owners of independent television operations, with stations in Seattle, Houston, Dallas–Fort Worth, Cleveland and Milwaukee. Gaylord was broadcasting to more than 13 percent of American television households by 1989.

A significant part of the company's programming was sports. Gaylord had made a specialty of carrying the away games of major-league baseball teams in its markets. Dallas–Fort Worth's KTVT carried the Texas Rangers (as well as the NBA Mavericks), Cleveland's WUAB the Indians, Seattle's KSTW the Mariners, and Milwaukee's WVTV the Brewers (as well as the NBA Bucks, and University of Wisconsin basketball and hockey).

The Gaylord media empire's great leap forward came in 1983, when Gaylord Entertainment acquired Opryland USA, an agglomeration of country music entertainment properties based in Nashville.[6] With Opryland USA as a core asset, Gaylord immediately entered national cable television broadcasting with The Nashville Network (TNN), whose programming featured "country lifestyles, entertainment and sports." In 1991, it also acquired a 67 percent interest in Country Music Television, a twenty-four-hour video cable network aimed at the eighteen-to-thirty-four age bracket. In 1992, the company took country music global with the launch of the first of its CMT International cable networks in Europe; expansion followed into Asia, the South Pacific and Latin America. (In 1994, the company acquired an option to purchase 95 percent of the outstanding common stock of Z Music, Inc., a cable network broadcasting contemporary Christian music videos.) In 1994, Gaylord Entertainment's revenues surpassed $700 million.

Edward K. Gaylord ran the show until 1974, when he made way for his son, Edward L. As he entered his seventies, Edward L. began to transfer some authority to his own son, Edward K. II, granting him the presidency of The Oklahoman Publishing Co. (OPUBCO) in June 1994. Edward K. II's sister, Christine Gaylord Everest, was also involved in the family business at the director level. And managing OPUBCO's real estate holdings and other investments was Clayton Bennett, brother-in-law of Edward K. II and Christine.

The Gaylord family was consistently enthusiastic about country music and professional sports. In the 1980s, Edward L. Gaylord was a repeatedly rebuffed suitor for major-league baseball's Texas Rangers. The Rangers had been purchased in 1980 by Eddie Chiles, a

University of Oklahoma graduate who ran a Fort Worth–based oil services business, The Western Co. As the oil industry downturn rocked Chiles, Gaylord came through with financial support for the team, securing a one-third interest in 1985. The sale required the approval of ten other American League owners. Gaylord came up one short. In an important test of his authority, the new baseball commissioner, Peter Ueberroth, cast a 10th vote, using the authority invested in him under "the best interests of baseball" clause, and allowed the minority acquisition to proceed.

The dissenting owners feared Gaylord's broadcasting power. The deal gave him a ten-year right to broadcast Rangers games through KTVT, and in Gaylord's independent Dallas–Fort Worth operation they saw the makings of a superstation—a local television station which, through cable distribution, broadcasts on a national level. They were already smarting from market intrusions by Ted Turner, who owned the Braves and superstation TBS in Atlanta, and by *The Tribune*, which owned the Cubs and superstation WGN in Chicago. Owners who beamed their teams' games into other markets, cutting into local market share of other franchises, were pariahs in some circles.

Ueberroth's triumph over the ownership ranks was brief. In February 1986, when oil prices were plummeting and Chiles was being tapped out, Gaylord offered to buy the team (including Arlington Stadium) outright. The superstation issue resurfaced—even though Gaylord said this wasn't his ambition with KTVT—and this time he fell far short of the necessary support among AL owners to get the purchase approved. In August 1988, when it appeared that Chiles would sell his share of the Rangers to a group that wanted to establish major-league baseball in Tampa (but said they wouldn't move the Rangers), Gaylord exercised his right of refusal and made another bid. In March 1989 his bid was again turned down by other owners, who were still fearful of the superstation factor (as well as of the possible role TNN could play). Chiles then sold the 58 percent of the club he still controlled to a local Texas group led by George W.

Bush, son of the serving president and a future state governor and presidential candidate. The Bush-fronted group proved to be pioneers in wresting major financial concessions from local government in getting a new stadium built for the Rangers. Having lost his purchase bid, Edward L. Gaylord reduced his holding in the Rangers, retaining a 10 percent interest through Gaylord Entertainment.

Thwarted by major-league baseball, the Gaylord family tried professional basketball. In February 1993, OPUBCO was one of about ten members of a limited partnership that acquired outright the San Antonio Spurs of the NBA for $75 million. With no growth opportunity for them in the Spurs ownership, the Gaylords, through Gaylord Entertainment, decided to get a team for Nashville. In April, the Minnesota Timberwolves made public their intention to follow the Minnesota North Stars out of their home in the St. Paul suburb of Bloomington. The North Stars were headed to Dallas, and Gaylord Entertainment wanted to steer the Timberwolves toward Opryland, immediately tendering a $100 million bid ($80 million of its own money, $20 million from the city of Nashville in the form of a relocation payment to the current team owners). They were promptly outbid by a New Orleans offer; in the end, the Timberwolves stayed in Minnesota. That May, Gaylord Entertainment placed a $100,000 deposit as it filed a bid for an NBA expansion franchise, pitting itself (unsuccessfully) against Toronto and Vancouver.

Though the Gaylord family was left empty-handed in its efforts to secure the NBA's Timberwolves, the relocation of the NHL's North Stars shone a glimmer of hope that they might acquire an NHL team. After the Florida and Anaheim franchises were awarded, further NHL expansion plans were unclear. However, by permitting the North Stars to go to Dallas, the NHL had showed that relocating an existing franchise was possible.

In the Gaylord family, Oklahoma City had the potential nucleus of a well-funded NHL ownership group. OPUBCO, as it happened, had played a leading role in convincing the NHL to schedule its neutral-site game between the Islanders and Oilers in Oklahoma City. But whether a Gaylord-led group was to secure an NHL team by applying for an expansion franchise or by buying an existing club, Oklahoma City needed a modern arena.

Building multimillion-dollar facilities with public money requires considerable political will, and in Oklahoma City, there was plenty on hand. The city's mayor, Ron Norick, was a self-confessed hockey nut. From 1977 to 1980, Norick had been a member of the limited partnership that tried to keep the local CHL franchise afloat, even serving as its general manager for a time. One of his partners had been his father, Jim, a former mayor who had been a booster of the Blazers when Sather played for them in the 1960s, promoting ticket sales that made the team viable. The younger Norick had followed his father's example by securing the mayoralty in 1987. Their family-owned company, Norick Brothers, which specialized in auto dealer-ship business forms, made it possible for Ron Norick to seek election to a public office that paid only $2,000 annually. In April 1992, a few months before the CHL returned to town, an eighty-two-year tradition ended when the family sold Norick Brothers, which generated $33.8 million in annual sales, to principal rival Reynolds and Reynolds. Ron Norick was free to focus his mayoral enthusiasm on a major urban renewal initiative that had professional sports at its core.

In December 1993, Oklahoma City citizens were asked to vote on a proposal to fund a $285 million infrastructure initiative called Metropolitan Area Projects (MAPS) with a five-year, one-cent sales tax. Included in the development was a 20,000-seat arena that could hold about 18,100 fans when configured for hockey. The arena alone would cost about $80 million and would be completed by 2000. The yeas on the tax proposal vote carried, 55 percent to 45 percent.

Driven forward by Norick's enthusiasm and conviction, Okla-homa City was on its way to boasting an NHL-quality arena that would surpass the one the Oilers played in—and which, in the summer of 1993, Peter Pocklington had been trying to get his Oilers out of, by proposing first to move them to Hamilton, then to Minneapolis–St. Paul, which the North Stars had just vacated. The Gaylords, meanwhile, kept plugging away at sports property opportunities. Mayor Norick's MAPS plan included a $22 million baseball stadium. In October 1993, OPUBCO helped to assemble a local investment group to acquire the Texas Rangers' AAA affiliate, the 89ers (which were renamed the Redhawks), for Oklahoma City. The $8 million price, paid to New York art dealer Jeffrey Loria (who had paid $4.6 million for the club in 1989) was a record for a minor pro operation.

In December it was revealed that, even before the results of the MAPS tax plebiscite were in, an unspecified group of Oklahoma City citizens, led by OPUBCO, were taking the first steps toward acquiring an NHL team. Contact had been made with NHL commissioner Gary Bettman. "We're very interested in the NHL and are interested in beginning the process to attract a team, either through expansion or relocation," Edward K. II's brother-in-law, Clayton Bennett, told *The Oklahoman* on December 18. "Relocation makes more sense to me. We're just now looking at what's available."

Prominent on the list of available clubs was the Edmonton Oilers.

CHAPTER FOURTEEN

ICK LELACHEUR believed in the synergy of sport, community and general prosperity. As a teenager, he had played for Billy Hunter's Edmonton Oil Kings from 1967 to 1969, in the seasons that followed the team's unprecedented string of appearances in the Memorial Cup finals—a twilight period for hockey in Edmonton before Hunter brought the WHA to town. As a young man, he served as vice-president of the organizing committee of the 1978 Commonwealth Games, which was the biggest thing to hit Edmonton until the Oilers won their first Stanley Cup in 1984. In the 1980s, during the Gretzky glory years, LeLacheur played a leading role in the affairs of the city's other beloved team, the municipally owned Eskimos of the CFL. LeLacheur joined the team's board of directors in 1983, was chairman of the Grey Cup committee in 1984, and served as team president in 1986 and 1987. LeLacheur developed a reputation as a doer, showing a knack for pulling off daunting tasks in the sporting forum that showed no sign of abating in the 1990s. When Montreal backed out of hosting the 1997 Grey Cup at the last minute, LeLacheur did an outstanding job of saving the event by having it played at Commonwealth Stadium. When Winnipeg reneged on hosting the 1995 NHL annual draft, LeLacheur was there to quickly relocate it to Northlands and bring it off flawlessly. And when Edmonton decided to go after the 2001 world track and field championships in

1997, LeLacheur was also there, helping spearhead the successful pitch and then assuming the chief executive officer's role for the event, which became known as Edmonton 2001.

His role in fighting to keep the Oilers in Edmonton developed early. In 1990, his family's business, Western Moving and Storage, was sold, making LeLacheur, not yet forty, a man of relatively independent means. He stayed on with the business for the new owners under a two-year management contract, becoming a free man in 1992, just as the Oilers were beginning to falter.

LeLacheur did perhaps more than anyone short of a local purchaser to keep the Oilers from leaving town. His influence was felt as a networker, mediator and instigator. He was able to exert this influence from a position of considerable authority after his management contract at Western Moving and Storage ended, because the city's lawyer, Bob Turner, had just done some instigating of his own, creating a new super-corporation where four separate municipal entities had existed. Edmonton's Convention and Tourism Authority, Convention Centre Authority, Economic Development Authority and Research Park Authority were being folded into one city-owned enterprise, called Economic Development Edmonton. In August 1992, LeLacheur was tapped to serve as EDE's first chief executive officer, effective January 1, 1993.

While waiting to formally take on the new assignment, LeLacheur could watch Peter Pocklington and Colin Forbes, general manager of Northlands Park, engage in a public slanging match in the fall of 1992 over what Pocklington viewed as the unfavourable terms of the Oilers' lease at Northlands. All of the 1980s stars, save Tikkanen (whose departure was imminent), were now gone, dealt away by Glen Sather. The team was off to a slow start in 1992/93, and the open sparring between Pocklington and Forbes threatened a disastrous outcome. Pocklington had showed with the Gainers strike that he was not for bluffing. If he became sufficiently dissatisfied with the Northlands terms, he could very well try to take the team out of Edmonton.

All professional sports leagues were in expansion mode in the United States, as investors and municipalities alike caught the sports entertainment bug. Why did so many cities want professional sports teams? Beyond civic bragging rights (and the desire of local cable companies to have product to sell advertising around in the lucrative 5:00 p.m. to 12:00 a.m. slot, targeting men aged eighteen to forty-nine), teams were being hailed as economic turbochargers, encouraging spending in the local economy. Beyond jobs created within the arena, if the facility was well placed it could anchor an urban revitalization by encouraging the growth of bars, restaurants, hotels and the like. The arena might not pay property taxes, but the surrounding businesses that benefitted from its presence certainly would. Not every politician and economist bought into the spinoff benefits argument. It was often pointed out that the benefits cited were frequently illusory. If people in the local economy didn't spend their money on drinks and season tickets, they would end up spending the money elsewhere—on stereo systems, lawn tractors and movie tickets. But there was no question that an NHL team could put seventeen thousand people downtown two nights a week, and that out-of-town fans—particularly supporters of the visiting team during the playoffs—injected money into the local economy that otherwise would never be spent.

Rick LeLacheur did not doubt the economic benefits of sporting events, and the importance of the Oilers to the Edmonton economy. As soon as LeLacheur was in place as EDE's CEO on January 1, 1993, he called a press conference to discuss the importance of sport to the city. Before going before the media, he contacted both Forbes and Pocklington and told them what he was about to do. He expected the two men to get together and work out their differences. If they needed him, LeLacheur would work as an unofficial mediator to bring the dispute to an end.

It didn't go well. Pocklington called his existing lease for Northlands, which he had signed in 1986 and ran until June 1999, the worst in the league. It required him to pay $2.3 million annually and gave him no share of parking or concessions. In February Forbes offered to have Northlands buy the team from Pocklington for $65 million Canadian. On April 7, Pocklington came up with a better idea. He wanted $105 million Canadian for the team. Northlands could spend $55 million through a newly formed company to buy the team, with Pocklington willing to front $15 million of that sum for five years at an interest rate of 10 percent. The remaining $50 million would be assumed by Northlands as bank debt. According to Pocklington's suggestion, Northlands could then put together a limited partnership of investors to retire most of that debt. The net result was that Pocklington would take $40 million up front, have $50 million worth of ATB debts retired and make 10 percent in interest a year for five years off the $15 million of the purchase price that he allowed Northlands to defer.

On April 16, Northlands rejected Pocklington's proposal, where-upon Pocklington put the gun to Northlands' head. The City of Hamilton was willing to practically give Copps Coliseum away to get the Oilers in town. On April 27, Pocklington announced he would take the team to Hamilton if Northlands didn't agree to a new deal in which he received all revenues from parking and concessions. Pocklington said he could make $20 million a year with the Hamilton Oilers, but that he was willing to make $7 million a year with the Edmonton Oilers if Northlands agreed to his terms. He gave Northlands and the city until midnight on May 14 to comply.

Forbes was outraged. He didn't want to allow Pocklington to take control of the civic arena, and considered that the city might be better off without the Oilers. "The clear thinking people of this city have to say, 'At what cost do we succumb to the demands that have been placed upon the city?' I don't think anyone should attempt to hold a city hostage. Regardless of what's been said, that's exactly what's happening today." On May 4 Forbes added, "I've thought a lot about how much Northlands might lose temporarily if the Oilers leave. But I've also though a great deal about the other things we can do within this building that will generate just as much money and a whole lot less heartache than the Oilers staying here."

Forbes did have the law on his side. Pocklington had an enforceable lease: he couldn't just move somewhere else without major legal consequences. Forbes wrote Bob Morrow, the mayor of Hamilton, effectively telling the city to butt out by pointing out the present Oilers lease at Northlands, which would not expire for six years. Hamilton would be risking a lawsuit if it appeared to be tampering with the Oilers, a Northlands tenant with a binding lease.

On May 12, as Pocklington's deadline approached, the newly elected premier of Alberta, Ralph Klein, wrote to Bruce McNall, the Los Angeles Kings owner who had bought Wayne Gretzky and was serving as the chairman of the league expansion committee. Klein was a friend of Glen Sather (who had personally paid for some of Klein's election campaign advertising). While the province wasn't interested in investing in the Oilers, given the active lawsuits between Pocklington and the ATB (and Pocklington vowed he didn't want provincial money), Klein asked McNall to consider using his influence on the board of governors to ensure that no Oilers move was approved.[1]

It seemed that Pocklington would have difficulty getting the Oilers out of town, since the league's by-laws contained a long list of criteria a team had to meet before being allowed to abandon a market. But in the turbid politics of the NHL, anything was possible. And on May 13, Rick LeLacheur, working with John Ramsey, an ATB staffer who had been appointed by the bank to oversee Pocklington's sports properties, came together with Forbes and Pocklington in the hope of getting a new deal that would ensure the Oilers stayed in town.

They emerged with what looked like something workable. A sublease agreement was mapped out wherein LeLacheur shoehorned Economic Development Edmonton between Northlands and Pocklington. EDE would lease Northlands, then sublet it to Pocklington on the terms he desired. Everyone was happy—for a while.

Northlands began to get cold feet. It wanted written assurances that the Oilers would stay in town, as well as some way to gain $3.5 million in revenues annually for Pocklington's use of the building. The deal collapsed only weeks after it was struck, on July 21. Gary Bettman, who thought the anxieties over the future of the Oilers had ended, was livid, and said publicly that Northlands had "reneged" on the deal. It was too late for Pocklington to have the Oilers play anywhere but in Edmonton for 1993/94, but he had until November 15 to file a proposal with the league to relocate for 1994/95.

The failure of Pocklington and Northlands Park to reach a deal could not have been more badly timed. The Oilers had just missed the playoffs for the first time in their NHL history. There were no playoff receipts from tickets or television for Pocklington at a time when he couldn't afford cash flow shortfalls. He was determined to take the Oilers out of town, and the league was showing its willingness to allow franchises to up stakes and head for warmer and sunnier pastures. The Minnesota North Stars had just become the first NHL franchise in eleven years to be allowed to move. Surely the league would allow the Oilers to hit the road as well.

The North Stars' move was the final act in a complex and controversial campaign by George and Gordon Gund to get their Minnesota franchise to the San Francisco Bay area. In 1989, the Gunds had secretly hoped to move their money-losing North Stars to San Jose. Their plan, however, was coincident with the NHL's first expansion since the absorption of four WHA teams in 1979, and San Jose was considered a prime candidate for a new team. Howard Baldwin, who had sold his minority interest in the Hartford Whalers, was planning to secure the San Jose franchise, with league president John Ziegler's approval. The Gund plan presented a major problem. If the brothers were able to move the North Stars to San Jose, the league would miss out on a $50 million expansion fee and be left without a team in Minneapolis–St. Paul. Although the Gunds were losing money there, Minnesota was one of America's few bona fide grassroots hockey hotbeds. If the league tried to prevent the Gunds from moving their team to San Jose, it risked inviting a lawsuit from them reminiscent of Al Davis's successful action against the National Football League, which had tried to stop him from moving his AFC Oakland Raiders to Los Angeles, where the Rams were already playing.

A compromise was brokered, with the help of Calgary ownership partner Norman Green—a boyhood friend of Baldwin's partner, Morris Belzberg. There was some question of whether Baldwin would be able to raise the $50 million necessary for an expansion team in San Jose, so Green proposed that the Gunds sell Baldwin the North Stars for $30 million and pay the league $50 million for a new team in San Jose. The Gunds' net cost would be just $20 million.

Everyone liked the idea except the Gunds, who had developed a promising young team in Minnesota and weren't prepared to walk away from it. An extremely complex compromise was reached. Baldwin and Green (who left the Calgary ownership to replace Belzberg as Baldwin's partner) would be awarded a San Jose franchise for 1991/92. They would immediately trade the franchise to the Gunds for the North Stars and $19 million. To that $19 million, Baldwin and Green would add $31 million, turning over $50 million to the league. This $50 million represented the expansion fee for the San Jose franchise that Baldwin and Green had traded to the Gunds. The Gunds would also receive the North Stars' share of expansion fees from the next round of league growth. The North Stars would trade all their players and their 1991 entry draft picks to San Jose, thereby allowing the Gunds to take their lineup with them, in exchange for San Jose's draft rights in the 1991 expansion draft. In other words, what had been the roster of the North Stars became the expansion of the San Jose Sharks, and the North Stars were replenished with the expansion draft rights of San Jose.

And that is how the Gunds got the North Stars team to San Jose, while leaving the North Stars franchise back in Minnesota. Baldwin subsequently purchased the Pittsburgh Penguins in 1991; Green then moved the North Stars to Dallas, and in 1995 sold the team to Ted Hicks.[2]

Gary Bettman, who had just become the NHL's first commissioner on February 1, 1993, made blessing the move of the North Stars to Dallas one of his first items of business; the move was announced on March 10, as the battle between Pocklington and Northlands was beginning to heat up. Pocklington discovered that the state of Minnesota, having lost the North Stars to Dallas, was willing to extend attractive terms to get the Oilers into Minneapolis–St. Paul, and in the fall he made plans to relocate. But Northlands secured a court injunction that enforced the existing lease agreement, however odious its terms were to Pocklington. Like it or not, the Oilers would have to show up at Northlands for all their home games in 1993/94.

For the fans, there wasn't much to like. With the superstars long gone after the dismal 1992/93 season, Sather began dealing fiercely toward a lineup that could get the team back in the playoffs. Forty-three different players wore the Oilers uniform in 1993/94. Sather executed a series of trades before the new season, some of which had future draft opportunities in mind. In June, Petr Klima, who had failed to live up to his offensive billing (forcing the Oilers to use defensive specialists like Kelly Buchberger on the power play), was sent to Tampa Bay for the Lightning's third-round pick in the 1994 draft, while Martin Gelinas (acquired from Los Angeles in the Gretzky trade) was packaged with Edmonton's sixth-round pick in the 1993 draft to get Scott Pearson from Quebec. Craig Simpson was sent to Buffalo in September for Joseph Cierny and the Sabres' fourth-round pick in the 1994 draft. In October, Kevin Todd went to Chicago for Adam Bennett; in November, Chris Joseph went to Tampa Bay for Bob Beers. In December, Geoff Smith was shipped to Florida, along with Edmonton's fourth-round choice in the 1994 draft, in exchange for the Panthers' third-round pick in the 1994 draft and the sixth-round pick of St. Louis in the same draft. (This pick, which Florida had previously acquired from the Blues, was then dealt to Winnipeg.)

Into this maelstrom of new faces came Edmonton's first-round pick in the 1993 draft, Oshawa Generals centre Jason Arnott, who had been chosen seventh overall. Arnott skated into a starting role, and provided a welcome reprieve from the Oilers' lengthy history of poor draft efforts. The 1992 draft had provided yet another confounding performance by Edmonton. Its first-round pick, American left winger Joel Hulbig, taken 13th overall, only played twenty-three NHL games, and the team's next picks, at 37th (Germany's Martin Reichel) and 61st (Quebec defenceman Simon Roy) didn't make the league. The Oilers had connected, however, with Owen Sound Plater right winger Kirk Maltby at 65th, and he came to the Oilers with Arnott in 1993/94.

After Arnott's selection, the 1993 draft provided more Oilers misses, although the picks generally became far less reliable once past the first fifteen selections. At 16th, Edmonton took London Knights defenceman Nick Stajduhar, who only played two NHL games. The Oilers' second-round pick, Czech centre David Vyborny, didn't make the NHL. Deep in the draft, Sather had some success. At 111th he found a young Czech centre, Miroslav Satan, who became a starter in 1995/96 and was traded to Buffalo for Barrie Moore and Craig Millar in March 1997. Sather also chose Ilja Byakin, a thirty-year-old former Spartak Moscow defenceman, 267th overall. Sather got forty-four games and twenty-eight points out of him in 1993/94 before he went to San Jose as a free agent in September 1994 (and played his last thirteen NHL games there).

Arnott's sixty-eight-point rookie performance was one of the few highlights of the 1993/94 season as the Oilers charted new lows. Twenty-four games into the season, Edmonton had won only three times, while tying three and losing eighteen. Sather returned to the bench for the first time since 1988/89, replacing Ted Green, who remained in the organization as Sather's assistant. Sather kept dealing, trying to snap the team out of its tailspin. To get points-producing defenceman Fredrik Olausson from Winnipeg (along with the Jets' seventh-round pick in 1994), Sather gave up Edmonton's third-round pick in the same draft. But Olausson's offensive game didn't follow him to Edmonton, and in January 1996 he would be allowed to go to Anaheim on waivers. More deal-making couldn't rescue the season. Rookie left winger Brent Grieve was acquired from the Islanders for Marc Laforge in December, then lost to free agency in July. Centre Mike Stapleton was picked up on waivers from Pittsburgh in February. In March, Brad Werenka, an Alberta native whom Sather had made the Oilers' second pick (42nd overall) in the 1987 draft as he was beginning a five-season college career at Northern Michigan University, was sent to Quebec for Steve Passmore.

With hopes of making the playoffs fading, Sather made a deal for the future on March 15. He sent the Winnipeg Jets an experienced defenceman, Dave Manson, along with St. Louis' sixth-round pick in 1994, in exchange for the Jets' first-round pick in 1994, Florida's fourth-round pick in 1994, Swedish centre Mats Lindgren (who had been Winnipeg's first choice, 15th overall, in 1993) and Russian defenceman Boris Mironov, whom Winnipeg had chosen 27th overall with its second pick in 1992. Mironov completed his rookie season in Edmonton in 1993/94 and was named to the NHL/Upper Deck All Rookie Team. Lindgren, who was named rookie of the year in the Swedish elite league in 1993/94, joined the Oilers in 1996/97. The draft picks netted them Jason Bonsignore in the first round and Adam Copeland in the fourth round. While neither was a franchise player— Copeland didn't make the team, while a disappointing Bonsignore was dealt to Tampa Bay in December 1997 after spending the better part of three seasons in the minors—the eventual success of both Mironov and Lindgren made the deal one of Sather's better ones in recent years.

He had cut the deal for Mironov and Lindgren with a team almost as troubled as the Oilers. The Jets won only twenty-four games in 1993/94 and finished last in the Western Conference's Central Division, while the Oilers, in winning only twenty-five games, finished last in the conference's Pacific Division. The only teams in the NHL worse than Winnipeg and Edmonton were Ottawa, stumbling through its second season with fourteen wins, and Hartford, which had two more wins than Edmonton but one less point. The Oilers' arch-rivals, the Calgary Flames, earned the division title with forty-two wins. Though his team, the Kings, were suffering, with only twenty-seven wins, Wayne Gretzky was winning his last NHL scoring title. In New York, Mark Messier was leading the Rangers to their first Stanley Cup since 1941/42, and he was doing it with one more surplus champion Oiler. In March, Sather had sent New York Craig MacTavish for U.S. Olympian Todd Marchant. For the sixth time, Sather had traded an Oilers captain. It had happened to Ron Chipperfield in 1980, to Blair MacDonald in 1981, to Wayne Gretzky in 1988, to Mark Messier in 1991 and to Kevin Lowe in 1992. Only Lee Fogolin had escaped the indignity, handing over the captain's C to Gretzky while still with the team in 1983. Still, the MacTavish trade was another good deal by Sather. Marchant, whom New York had chosen 164th overall in 1993, had only played one NHL game when Sather got him. He became an Oilers regular in 1994/95.

But while Sather was trying to fashion a future contender amid the chaos of the 1993/94 season, the prospect of the Oilers remaining in Edmonton had reached a veritable crisis point. Oklahoma City, for one, was building a brand new arena that it would allow any NHL club that wished to relocate to use essentially for free. Sweetheart lease deals were now par for the course, as the civic arena business took a strange turn. If a city wanted a major-league franchise, generally it needed needed a major-league arena. Communities that built those expensive coliseums without a secure tenant were wont to allow a prospective franchise to use it at no cost at all, just to get them in the building so they could start spinning off the purported economic benefits throughout the rest of the city. Cities like Oklahoma City that had caught the major-league bug needed talent to put on a show. The talent just had to name its price. In Edmonton, they had to start listening seriously to what Peter Puck wanted, or the Oilers would be lost. Something had to be done to dissolve the enmity between Northlands and Pocklington, between landlord and tenant, to ensure that the team was part of the city's economic future.

The key to a new deal was a new government in Ottawa. The 1993 federal election had brought the Conservative reign to a crashing halt. With Brian Mulroney having worn out his welcome with the Canadian electorate and retired, successor Kim Campbell led the PCs to one of the worst reversals in electoral history, being reduced to two seats in the House of Commons as Jean Chrétien's Liberals formed a majority government. In Alberta, the Conservatives were decimated by the right-of-centre protest party, Reform (led by Preston Manning, son of former Social Credit provincial premier Ernest Manning), which took twenty-two of twenty-six seats. That the Liberals were able to boast four MPs from Alberta showed how much politics had changed in the once arch-Conservative province.

For Pocklington, though, the Conservative defeat in Ottawa, which wrote an appalling epitaph for the career of the politician he had helped make prime minister, provided one pragmatic bonus. The newly elected Liberals rolled out a federal infrastructure funding program, pouring money into capital projects across the land. The first project given the green light was a new convention centre for Quebec City. When Rick LeLacheur read about the Quebec City windfall, he realized he had the makings of a new deal between Pocklington and the city.

Approaching its 20th anniversary, Northlands Coliseum was getting tired and behind the times. It needed sprucing up, which included improved facilities for corporate clients. The lack of revenue-enhancing corporate boxes was a consistent shortcoming among arenas built in the 1970s, as the look and feel of the new facilities changed from one of poured concrete and painted steel railings to one of theatre-like indulgence. If money from Ottawa could be harnessed, the city could create a more profitable Northlands, but

Edmonton would also have to practically give it away to Pocklington to maintain parity with deals available from other cities.

Besides the city's lawyer, Bob Turner, and Rick LeLacheur, two men played critical roles in coming up with a formula for refurbishing Northlands and allowing Pocklington its virtually unfettered use, as well as essentially building a whole new ballpark for Pocklington's AAA Trappers. One was John Butler, a lawyer active in the community who had no formal ties to any of the parties. He helped form the deal that brought about the new Trappers' home, called Telus Field for its corporate sponsor, the provincial telephone company. The other was Bob Ardiel, the general manager of finance for the City of Edmonton, who worked out a formula for the infrastructure funding involving the city, the province and the federal government.

The Oilers had again missed the playoffs in the spring of 1994, and the Alberta Treasury Branches was overseeing Pocklington's every move as his principal secured creditor. Pocklington needed a deal to keep his teetering business empire upright, and the city needed a deal to avoid the very real possibility of both the Oilers and the Trappers leaving town. Pocklington's taking the teams elsewhere wasn't the only potential scenario: the ATB could force him to sell one or both of the teams to the highest bidder—which would almost certainly be an American buyer—or could proceed with the sales itself after pressing Pocklington into personal bankruptcy. The deal that avoided these outcomes was one of the most ambitious ever reached between a sports entrepreneur and a city.

It was agreed that a new baseball stadium with seating for 9,200 would be built at the city's John Ducey Park, at a cost of about $11.5 million, and that about $35 million would be spent renovating Northlands Coliseum. The city received a federal infrastructure grant of $15 million, and the bill for the baseball stadium and the Northlands renovation was split three ways, between the federal, provincial and municipal governments. This split became a source of some confusion, because the city's contribution was often cited as the

$15 million it had received from the federal government. That grant in fact represented the federal contribution. Most of the city's contribution under the funding scheme was provided by Peter Pocklington personally, and in the process he likely deepened his ATB debts. (The deal called for him to spend at least $4 million to install a new giant video screen and build new luxury boxes in the Coliseum, for each of which he could charge seasonal rent of up to $100,000.)

At Telus Field, Pocklington's Trappers were required to pay a base rent of $100,000 per season under a twenty-five-year lease, and turn over a 25-cent ticket tax to a maximum of $30,000 per season. The Trappers were also required to shoulder all maintenance and utility costs, which ran to between $600,000 and $700,000 a year, according to Mel Kowalchuk, Pocklington's minority partner and the team's president (who had been part of the Trappers since Pocklington bought the team in 1981). The team was also permitted to stage up to six additional events (such as concerts) per year, at no additional rental charge. The Trappers began playing at the new park in May 1995.

The Northlands Coliseum deal was far more favourable to Pocklington, giving him everything he could hope for. The basic structure of the failed 1993 deal was revived. Economic Development Edmonton leased the facility from Northlands Park, then sublet it to Pocklington for a ten-year period. Allowed to break an enforceable lease, Pocklington replaced it with a new arrangement that gave him Northlands to run for his own profit. With the exception of a few events, such as the city's annual Klondike Days, any event at Northlands became Pocklington's to promote or charge rent for. He got the concessions and the parking revenues as well. Rather than having to pay rent to Northlands, Pocklington now had the arena as a profit centre. The city wasn't completely bereft of benefits. A ticket surcharge contributed about $2.8 million a season to the city coffers. The three-way split of funding, between the federal government, the province and the city, was also followed, and again Pocklington may have personally provided most of the the city's share. All told, he is thought to have borrowed about $15 million from the ATB for the Telus Field and Northlands Coliseum revitalizations.

The fact that the city had come to a new agreement with Pocklington for the use of Northlands Coliseum was no guarantee that the team would actually stay put. NHL commissioner Gary Bettman had attended several meetings in Edmonton to encourage a resolution during the lease negotiations, and it had become the NHL's general policy, where new or existing franchises wrested major concessions in public arena leases, to assure the city that the team would stick around. For a team to do otherwise—to negotiate the best possible deal, only to leave at the first sign of a better opportunity—smacked of carpet-bagging. Assurances of goodwill weren't enough, however. As the city's lawyer and the corporate counsel for, and special advisor to, the EDE board, Bob Turner wanted tangible legal controls on the Oilers' future in exchange for the Northlands giveaway. (This had been a sticking point in the failed 1993 deal.) It wasn't just Pocklington whom Turner was worried about; he also had to contend with the owner's banker. Because such a significant amount of secured credit was attached to the team, it was entirely possible that the ATB could sell the Oilers out from under Pocklington to recoup its loans. Pocklington might pledge to keep the Oilers in town until eternity, but banks were a different breed of animal. Their main fiscal responsibility was to recover the funds of their shareholders, in the ATB's case the people of Alberta. That meant getting the highest possible price for the team, should they choose to sell it. And that could well mean selling it to someone in Oklahoma City. Or, as it would turn out, someone in Houston.

And so, under Turner's direction, the parties arrived in 1994 at what was known as the Location Agreement. Its basic principle was that the Oilers could not be sold without the approval of EDE and Northlands Park. EDE and Northlands Park were granted a special "golden" share in Oilers Hockey Inc., through which they could exercise a veto. (Implicitly, it was the city that had the veto, since EDE was a wholly owned enterprise.) The Location Agreement bound the Oilers to Northlands until 2004. Should Pocklington or the ATB decide to sell the team before then, they first had to notify EDE and Northlands Park, which would have the opportunity to buy the team or assemble an ownership group. Were Pocklington or the ATB to find a buyer who didn't want to sign the Location Agreement—in other words, someone who wanted to move the team elsewhere—EDE and Northlands Park would have thirty days in which to come up with its own purchaser. In any case, the new owner would have to be approved by the NHL.

A similar arrangement was made for the Trappers' use of Telus Field. If ATB demanded payment on the portion of Pocklington's debts secured by the Trappers, the city had twenty days to pay off the ATB and take over the financing. And if the ATB decided to sell the team, it had to give the city ninety days' notice. (This period could be extended if the ATB and the city so decided.) At the end of the ninety-day period, the city would have another thirty days in which to decide if it wanted to buy the team. If the city declined, the team could be sold to an out-of-town buyer.

A major difference between the master agreement for the Trappers' use of Telus Field and the Oilers' use of Northlands Coliseum was that, in the case of the Trappers, there was no maximum purchase price set for the city. Triple-A baseball clubs at the time could be had for a few million dollars, and avoiding a runaway market price over the course of the twenty-five-year lease wasn't addressed. With the Oilers, however, it was felt that the right of EDE and Northlands Park to match any outside offer needed a price structure. In exchange for handing over almost all revenue flowing through Northlands Coliseum, EDE and Northlands Park wanted a maximum price they or their chosen buyer would have to pay for the team to keep it in Edmonton. There was no practical way to index such a price to either inflation or projected appreciation; it had to have a firm value. Under the agreement, EDE and Northlands Park had the right to line up a local buyer who would only have to match the price of an outside buyer to keep the team in Edmonton. But Turner wanted a ceiling on the price the locals would have to pay. After all, they would continue to operate the team in Edmonton, not in some enormous American market with an entirely different cost and revenue structure. An outside buyer in the new millennium might think $140 million was a bargain for the Oilers if the team were to play in Seattle, but it would be exorbitant for Edmonton. The challenge was to determine a maximum local buyer's price in 1994 for a team that might be sold at any point over the next ten years.

What was a typical NHL team worth? The 1991 franchise fee of US$50 million had seemed awfully steep to some people, as existing franchises sold for far less (Minnesota for just US$31 million in 1991), but it would prove to hold up. And picking a value for the Oilers' Location Agreement that proved, over time, to be too low would have dire consequences for the cause of keeping the team in town. What proved to be a bargain for a local buyer might only make Pocklington or the ATB more determined to sell the team to someone who was willing to pay full market value in order to relocate it.

The Winnipeg Jets had been seriously undervalued in the buyout agreement struck between the ownership group and the provincial and municipal governments in 1991. The Barry Shenkarow ownership group, which wanted out of the money-losing enterprise, was required in return for government support to sell its 64 percent share for $32 million Canadian to a qualified local buyer by 1996. This would put the total capitalization of the Jets at $50 million Canadian.

Meanwhile, on July 1, 1995—Canada Day—the Quebec Nordiques' owners spoiled the national birthday party. Unable to secure from the local and provincial governments either tax breaks or a promise to build the team a new arena (from which they would receive parking and concession revenues), the ownership consortium announced it had agreed to sell the Nordiques to new owners in Denver, where they would play as the Colorado Avalanche. The price: a tidy

US$75 million, the equivalent of $102 million Canadian. The Nordiques had a lineup strong enough to win the Stanley Cup in the team's first season as the Avalanche, but even discounting for the relative quality of the Jets, the Jets' $50 million "local" Canadian price—equivalent in 1995 to US$36 million—was a steal.

Conscious of the potential for local investors to snap up a bargain and then flip it to an American buyer at a substantial profit, Gary Bettman required any local buyer of the Jets to post a US$10 million bond with the league to help ensure that the team in fact stayed put. When no local deal came together, the team was sold to Richard Burke and Steven Gluckstern for US$68 million and moved to Phoenix for 1996/97.

In 1994, Bob Turner sat in Peter Pocklington's office in Edmonton's Suncor building as the Oilers' owner mulled over a figure for the local purchase price on the telephone with Gary Bettman. Pocklington and Bettman finally made what amounted to an educated guess and came up with US$70 million, which Turner accepted.

With that agreement, a cost structure was set for owning the Oilers in the event of a sale. If Pocklington and the ATB (or the ATB alone, in the event of it having pressed the Oilers into receivership) decided to sell the the team, EDE and Northlands Park first had to be notified. A local buyer could immediately offer whatever it felt was fair, but neither Pocklington nor the ATB was likely to go along with a low local bid before shopping the team around. Anything less than a reasonable price would not receive Pocklington's approval. If the ATB for some reason tried to force a low-ball sale, it would be open to a suit by Pocklington, who (as he did in the Gainers case) could allege that the ATB had not made a reasonable effort to get full value for his asset. If nothing else, getting outside buyers in the bid process would likely raise the final sale price. A local buyer inclined to offer $50 million would have to come up with $65 million if that was the outside offer.

The only flaw in the sales process was the relationship between the maximum local buyout price of $70 million and the likely open-market price. If the open-market price was substantially higher than the local buyout price, an outside buyer might be reluctant to even bid, realizing it was only serving as a stalking horse to get the local bid up to its maximum of $70 million. (Under the Location Agreement, even if an outside bidder offered $100 million, the local buyer had only to come up with $70 million. And under the agreement, a "local buyer" was anyone willing to sign the Location Agreement and keep the team in Edmonton. It didn't matter where the new ownership was based.)

Despite the new arena deal struck in the summer of 1994, Pocklington's Oilers investment was anything but healthy. The league was shut down by a player lockout that fall, leaving Pocklington without any revenues for almost four months of the traditional season. After 103 days of inactivity, a new collective bargaining agreement was reached (retroactive to 1993, when the last one had expired) and a forty-eight-game schedule was begun on January 20, 1995. Glen Sather gave the coaching job to George Burnett, the thirty-three-year-old coach of Edmonton's AHL farm team in Cape Breton. Burnett had taken the Cape Breton Oilers to a Calder Cup title in 1992/93, but he could do nothing with the NHL Oilers. He feuded with the team's captain, Shayne Corson, and the Oilers won only twelve of their first thirty-five games. On April 6, while the Oilers were in San Jose, Sather telephoned from Palm Springs to fire Burnett and promote assistant Ron Low in his stead.

While the Oilers again missed the playoffs, there was some measure of improvement under Low as they won five of their last thirteen games. The team at last had some stability in its coaching. Low had come to the organization as a backup goaltender in March 1980, and while Sather traded him to New Jersey in February 1983, Low returned to serve as an assistant playing coach with the AHL Oilers in 1985/86. After another season as an assistant coach, he became the AHL Oilers' coach in 1987/88. In the summer of 1989, Sather had made him an assistant coach with the NHL Oilers. Having passed him over for the head coaching job in favour of Burnett, Sather now made a sound selection in Low. Though never a star, Low, like Sather, was a journeyman whose experience in the trenches of the game made him an effective bench manager.

The team improved under Low to thirty wins in 1995/96, strengthened by the arrival in January of one of the league's better goaltenders, Curtis Joseph, from St. Louis. The Blues took back its first-round picks for 1996 and 1997 that Sather had previously acquired, and surrendered Joseph and the rights to Mike Grier, an NCAA All Star right winger it had drafted down at 229th in 1993. Grier would join the Oilers in 1996/97. The deal was actually cut in August 1995, but Joseph held out on contract terms until January, biding his time with the Las Vegas Thunder of the IHL. The acquisition of Joseph allowed Sather to send Bill Ranford (who had starred for Canada in the 1991 Canada Cup and was named top goaltender at the 1994 World Championships) to Boston. In return, Sather received right winger Mariusz Czerkawski, defensive prospect Sean Brown, and the Bruins' first-round pick in the upcoming entry draft.

The team was still not good enough to return to the postseason. It was the fourth consecutive campaign that left Pocklington without playoff revenues, and he could no longer service his ATB debts. The Oilers were being pounded financially on all fronts. While payroll costs were minimized by employing largely young and middling players, the team was as a result uncompetitive on the ice and in revenue generation. It didn't have the substantial local cable market of a team like Toronto, and so the rights values were suppressed. It was collecting most of its revenues in cheap Canadian dollars, and servicing most of its critical costs (such as player salaries and travel) in expensive American ones.

Robert Kallir, ATB's general counsel, was named to the board of Oilers Hockey Inc. and ATB staff member John Ramsey (already involved in Pocklington's affairs) was appointed chief operating officer. With a window seat on Pocklington's troubled empire, it was clear to the ATB that the only way it was going to get its money back was to have Pocklington sell off some or all of his various business holdings, and have the proceeds sent directly to ATB.

Pocklington's principal business assets were the Oilers, various real estate holdings, the Edmonton Trappers and 53 percent of Canbra Foods Ltd. In his last acquisition as a sports entrepreneur, Pocklington had also been able to acquire the Chicago Power of the National Professional Soccer League (his third such professional soccer team) in August 1996 and move them to Edmonton, where they played as the Drillers. (The previous Drillers had died with their league, the NASL.)

Beginning in early 1997, the ATB embarked on an escalating pursuit of every last shred of Pocklington's business and personal assets, from the Oilers to the contents of his wine cellar, in an effort to clear away the mountain of debt he'd accumulated. Initially, Pocklington publicly expressed only goodwill and appreciation to the ATB for standing by him. Pocklington would later charge that he was a victim of a politically motivated witch hunt; that Premier Ralph Klein's PC government wanted all outstanding ATB loans off the books so it could privatize the ATB at maximum value.

The government would reject this accusation as the ATB pressed forward against Pocklington, but unquestionably he had become a target of the ATB at a critical moment in the provincial lending institution's history. Recommendations to change the ATB from a branch of the Treasury department to a stand-alone bank had first been made in 1993 by the province's Financial Review Commission, and were endorsed in 1994 by the auditor general. Amendments to the Treasury Branches Act, begun in 1995, would convert the ATB into a provincial Crown corporation with its own board of directors, and the powers and procedures of a normal financial institution. The government would strongly deny that it aimed to privatize the ATB, but as its October 1997 launch date as a Crown corporation drew near, the pressure was certainly on to tidy the books as much as possible. And a large part of the mess in the books was directly attributable to loans to Peter Pocklington.

The ATB's asset-stripping war against Pocklington began modestly. On February 5, 1997, Pocklington, with the obvious encouragement of the ATB, attempted to extend to Oilers fans an opportunity to help themselves to equity in his sporting and entertainment enterprises, which would be rolled into one publicly traded company in a share offering handled by Midland Walwyn Capital Inc. The company would include the Oilers, its AHL farm team the Hamilton Bulldogs,[3] the Drillers, the Trappers and Coliseum Management Inc., the company to which Pocklington had assigned the show promotion and event management business produced by his 1994 sublease agreement for Northlands. Under the share offering, Pocklington would hold a controlling interest, consistent with his long-standing credo: own the company and work with other people's money.

Wayne Huizenga, the billionaire owner of the NHL's Panthers, had just taken his team public through Florida Panthers Holdings Inc., and his coup gave hope to Pocklington's proposal. This was at least the third time Pocklington had tried to take the Oilers public in one way or another but, like the previous efforts, it would go nowhere.

Though the Panthers share issue was successful, enthusiasm in the equities market was generally subdued for professional sports properties, and on closer inspection the Panthers issue bore little resemblance to what Pocklington was proposing. After Huizenga made an initial public offering on NASDAQ of Class A common stock on November 13, 1996 (trading under the symbol "PUCK"), his holding company expanded into "high-end destination luxury resorts," which formed the core of a new business segment for the company that it called "Leisure and Recreation."[4] On July 11, 1997, a second issue of Class A common stock began trading on the New York Stock Exchange under the symbol "PAW." The holding company's business strategy became focused not on NHL hockey, but on expanding its leisure and recreation holdings. Without the push into resort properties, the losses associated with the Panthers (hopefully to be offset by the impending completion of a new arena, the National Car Rental

Center in Broward County, paid for by the county) would have dragged down the stock. Where Pocklington was mainly offering a piece of a troubled NHL team and a grab bag of minor pro enterprises, Huizenga's venture was reinventing itself as a high-end resort operator that happened to have an NHL team tucked away in its portfolio.

A Pocklington share issue likely would be subject to the same restrictions that the NHL had placed on Florida Panthers Holdings. The league forbade Huizenga's company to issue cash dividends in order to ensure it had sufficient operating reserves. And there were implicit restrictions on its trading. The league has the right to approve any individual or group that holds more than five percent of a franchise; when applied to a public company, this limits stock accumulation by an investor on the open market, and can impact unfavourably on share value. And unless granted league permission otherwise, Huizenga had to retain voting control of the Panthers' holding company at all times. Pocklington's share issue proposal also kept him in the driver's seat, but the prospect of him continuing to control the operation did not strike everyone as an investment incentive. Too much had happened over the years for people to relish jumping into the equities market with him.

While badly timed as a share issue, the proposed partial sale was perfectly timed with respect to the league's expansion efforts. Two weeks after Pocklington revealed his proposal to divest 49 percent of the Oilers, the NHL's expansion committee announced its selection of finalist candidates for the next growth phase, which would take the league from twenty-six to thirty teams by the millennium. Eleven bidders were reduced to six; come June, they would be cut again, to the final four. Anyone who didn't make the cut and was serious about getting an NHL team would be looking for one that was for sale.

THE OILERS dynasty had scarcely gotten under way when the U.S. economy began to lay a yellow brick road the Oilers could eventually follow out of town and right out of the country. The road was a path of riches in the energy industry that created new members of the merely, the moderately and the profoundly wealthy, who would grasp professional sports enterprises as worthy baubles. By the late nineties, the economic elite could be good corporate citizens simply by bringing a sports team to town, to occupy a facility built with public money. And as Peter Pocklington was discovering, you could become a social pariah by threatening to take a sports team away, no matter how much of your own money you were losing keeping it in town.

In 1985, when the Oilers won their second Stanley Cup and the Canadian oil patch was perched on the brink of crude price implosion, the Federal Energy Regulatory Commission (FERC) in the United States began deregulating the natural gas business. As the regulator of pricing for the storage and transportation of natural gas across state lines through pipelines, FERC wanted to see pipeline operators give natural gas companies better breaks on costs. Deregulation in this industry, in combination with the Free Trade Agreement between Canada and the United States, ultimately would prove a boon to the Alberta economy, as the resultant natural gas exports helped lessen the provincial economy's dependence on the slumping oil market. FERC's regulatory changes began transforming the natural gas business across North America, and one of the most noteworthy changes was the rise of Natural Gas Clearinghouse (NGC) Inc., a Houston-based natural gas marketer founded in 1984 that dominated Oklahoma's natural gas supplies. Beginning in 1990, NGC expanded into an array of other energy fields (liquid natural gas, electricity and crude oil) and activities (processing and generation). Among its many acquisitions was Pan Alberta Gas in 1995. With investment by British Gas, Nova Chemicals of Calgary and Chevron,[5] NGC became a global player. In 1996, NGC merged with the "midstream" assets of Chevron to create a new energy powerhouse, Dynegy, which ranked 107th in the Fortune 500 list of top corporations in 1997.

Leading the way for Dynegy was Chuck Watson, a University of Oklahoma alumnus who had been in charge of oil giant Conoco's natural gas sales in the western U.S. when he joined NGC in 1985 as president. He rose to become chairman and CEO in 1989. With the Chevron assets merger, Watson became chairman and CEO of the new megacompany. Revenues, which had been a formidable $2.8 billion in 1993 (as NGC), rocketed to $13.4 billion in 1997 after the merger that created Dynegy.

In 1995, Watson brought professional hockey back to Houston as he secured an International Hockey League franchise, named the Aeros in honour of the WHA team of the 1970s. One of North America's oldest pro hockey leagues, the IHL's roots reached back to the Canadian Professional League of the 1920s, although it wasn't formally instituted as the IHL until 1945. Then it was a four-team loop centered on Detroit, and in the 1980s was still mainly a Michigan phenomenon. Beginning in 1990, the IHL changed dramatically, undergoing an aggressive expansion into new markets in a sometimes fractious foot-race with the NHL. From nine teams in 1987/88, the IHL reached seventeen teams in 1994/95; one year later, when Houston joined, the league was nineteen franchises strong.

For Watson, the Aeros were but a springboard into the major league, as he set his sights on an NHL franchise for Houston. His partner in the franchise bid was a Houstonite even wealthier than him, Robert McNair. Like Watson, McNair had profited enormously from deregulation of the energy industry. The Energy Policy Act of 1992 created new opportunities for private power producers, and as Watson diversified Dynegy with generating facility investments, McNair became one of America's richest men through his company Cogen Technologies Inc. Cogen specialized in cogeneration—plants that simultaneously produce two forms of energy, such as electricity and heat—and owned three major facilities in New Jersey. Sales of over $100 million a year paled in comparison to the billions generated by Dynegy, but as Cogen's majority owner McNair was worth a fortune. In 1996 McNair cracked the Forbes 500 ranks, reaching 217th with an estimated net worth of $800 million in 1997. Through his personal investment company Palmetto Partners, McNair became seriously involved in thoroughbred racing. He bought the brood mares of the Elmendorf Farm stable, owned by Washington Redskins owner Jack Kent Cooke, shortly before Cooke's death in April 1997, and McNair's Touch Gold won the Belmont Stakes that year. A North Carolina native, McNair had maintained a Houston residence since 1960, and spent much of his time in Washington, keeping tabs on energy politics and moving in influential Republican circles. When President Bush's son, George W. Bush, ran for the Texas governorship, McNair was one of his major supporters, making a personal campaign donation of $25,000.

For McNair, an NHL franchise bid with Watson was a small change pursuit: his principal enthusiasm was getting an NFL franchise back in Houston, as the NFL Oilers were leaving town to become the Tennessee Titans. The NFL was preparing to add two more teams, for which the franchisee would have to pay about $500 million—a sum that could buy an entire division in the NHL. The three leading bids were all from cities that had lost a franchise: Cleveland, Los Angeles and Houston. In September 1998, the NFL would award one of the available franchises to Cleveland, leaving McNair up against two Los Angeles bids. (In March 1999 the NFL made an interim award of the new franchise to Los Angeles. That fall, however, the franchise was re-awarded to McNair's Houston bid.) McNair made it known that if he didn't win the bid selection, he would buy an existing NFL team and move it to Houston.[6] A new $315 million retractable-roof stadium was being built by the city and Harris County next door to the Astrodome, and McNair would sign a memorandum of understanding to commit funds to the project.

The McNair/Watson partnership met an always-persuasive criterion for an NHL franchise owner—impressive net worth—and Houston was regarded as a strong candidate for league expansion. As the field assembled for the expansion round that would add four more teams to the NHL by the millennium, pundits ranked Houston as one of four can't-miss expansion sites, the others being St. Paul, Minnesota; Nashville, Tennessee; and Atlanta, Georgia.

The shoo-in was Atlanta, which had lost the Flames to Calgary in 1980. Since then, R.W. (Ted) Turner had built a media empire, Turner Broadcasting System, through such properties as the cable news organization CNN, Atlanta-based superstation TBS, Turner Network Tele-vision (TNT), the Cartoon Network, Turner Classic Movies, and motion picture fixtures MGM and Castle Rock Entertainment. The company already owned baseball's Atlanta Braves and 96 percent of basketball's Atlanta Hawks. In 1990, its subsidiary, Turner Sports Programming, had participated in the creation of SportSouth, a regional network serving the American southeast, enhancing the company's sports broadcasting presence in a region the NHL viewed as an expansion frontier.

Already formidable in its own right, Turner Broadcasting System became part of a greater media colossus when, in October 1996, Time Warner completed the acquisition of the 80 percent of the company it didn't already own. With a board of governors increasingly domi-nated by media interests, it was inconceivable that the NHL would pass on the opportunity to bring Time Warner and Turner Broadcasting System into the fold.

For any sports league serious about conquering the eastern sun-belt, Nashville had to be breached. What had once been a U.S. cultural backwater had been transformed into another brave demographic frontier for the sports and entertainment business. Country music had reinvented itself as New Country and taken middle-of-the-road America by storm; Tennessee had aggressively courted industrial relo-cation with corporate tax giveaways in the 1980s and built a new bandwidth of affluence between Kentucky and Alabama. Consistent with the NHL's enthusiasm for media investment and major broad-casting centres, Nashville was home to the country music media

empire of the Gaylords of Oklahoma City. The Gaylords' TNN had
a wide-open approach to sports broadcasting, embracing the full
spectrum from bass fishing to roller derby. While the Nashville NHL
bid was not fronted by the Gaylords, who were more closely associated with the Oklahoma City initiative, they were on the periphery of
the bid led by Craig Leopold, an outerwear magnate from Wisconsin.
Nashville didn't have any kind of professional sports franchise, but
the notion that a city had to prove itself with one kind of major-
league team before being considered for another was losing credence,
particularly since the NFL, America's blue chip sports franchise entity,
expanded to hitherto unserviced Jacksonville, Florida. Nashville qualified as what sports biz know-it-alls called a "breakthrough" location.
America's general economic good health was producing affluent
urban centres that might lack the cachet of a major city, but had the
wherewithal and enthusiasm to make a major-league team a great
success. After Atlanta, Nashville was the most likely bid to win NHL
expansion approval in the summer of 1997.

By allowing the Minnesota North Stars to move to Dallas in 1993,
the league had abandoned one of the few corners of the United States
that had vital support at the grassroots level. The state had been producing NHL players since before the Second World War; the North
Stars franchise, however, had been beset with location problems. They
had been playing in the aging Met Center in suburban Bloomington,
and were unable to arrange a move to the new Target Center in downtown Minneapolis. By allowing the team to go to Dallas, the league
had permitted a temporary withdrawal from a strong market while
establishing another toehold in the American sunbelt. A new ownership consortium proposed renovating the St. Paul Civic Center as a
way of getting the NHL back in a city that was rife with knowledgeable
fans and represented the country's 14th-largest television market. The
Minnesota bid also boasted the important component of a broadcasting magnate on board. Stanley Hubbard's family-controlled
Hubbard Broadcasting, headquartered in St. Paul, had made him a

billionaire through its ten television and two radio stations, as well as its direct-to-home digital satellite broadcasting startup, United States Satellite Broadcasting Inc. (USSB). Hubbard Broadcasting had just made a Class A share offering in February 1996, and in December 1998 USSB would be merged into Hughes Electronics, parent of DIRECTV.

Houston, rounding out the top four candidates, was so strong that the McNair/Watson group had to contend with two other competing, well-heeled bids from the city with links to the NBA: the Maloof family and Leslie Alexander.

The Maloofs, one of the most powerful families in New Mexico (one son, Philip J., was a state senator), had once owned the Houston Rockets of the NBA, but sold the club when patriarch George Sr. died in 1983. George's four sons oversaw an empire that included the Fiesta Casino Hotel in North Las Vegas, a beer distributorship in Albuquerque and several banks. They had tried to get back into the NBA by purchasing the San Antonio Spurs, but had been rebuffed in several attempts. (The Gaylords were among the Spurs' minority owners.) The Maloofs would succeed in acquiring one-quarter of the Sacramento Kings in January 1998.

Leslie (Les) Alexander was a former Wall Street trader who had moved to California in 1973 after making his fortune, and there both he and his wife earned law degrees. Resettling in Houston, he concluded a ten-year pursuit of the Houston Rockets by acquiring them in 1994. The team proceeded to win back-to-back NBA titles, and Alexander added an Arena Football team, the Thunder Bears, in 1995, and a Women's NBA team, the Comets, in 1996, to his sporting stable housed at the facility known as The Summit (later renamed the Compaq Center). Unless he opted for indoor soccer or box lacrosse, however, Alexander's sporting empire could expand no farther at The Summit, for the municipal building's hockey rights were held by Chuck Watson, whose IHL Aeros played there. The two men were open rivals, and neither one, for that matter, was going to cooperate with a

Maloof NHL bid. If Alexander secured the NHL franchise, Watson could prevent him from playing at The Summit, which meant a new facility would have to be built. If Watson and McNair won the franchise, they would likewise probably have to get a new building of their own, for Alexander made it clear his Rockets weren't interested in sharing a building with an NHL team that he didn't own. (A similar standoff over sharing a building in Toronto, between the Leafs of the NHL and the Raptors of the NBA, ended when the Leafs bought the Raptors and took over the construction of their new arena, the Air Canada Centre.) Whichever way the cards were cut, a new arena was a prerequisite for Houston getting an NHL team.

As it happened, Houston was in the midst of a downtown renovation scheme called the Cotswold Project, which envisioned a more pedestrian-friendly streetscape and a new arena and baseball stadium. Among the civic leaders on the project's board of directors when the plan was announced on January 20, 1997, was Chuck Watson's NHL bid partner, Robert McNair.

On February 19, 1997, the NHL board of governors' eleven-member executive committee whittled the list of franchise applicants down from eleven to six, with a final decision to be made in June. Atlanta, to no one's surprise, had made the cut, and so had St. Paul, Nashville and Houston. Sliding into the final two positions were Oklahoma City and Columbus, Ohio. Left in their wake were Hamilton, Ontario; Hampton Roads, Virginia; Raleigh, North Carolina; and two of the three Houston bidders: Les Alexander and the Maloofs were cut adrift by the league in favour of Chuck Watson and Robert McNair.

Raleigh rebounded quickly. One month after being refused consideration for expansion, Raleigh was on a fast track into the league when Peter Karmanos, owner of the Hartford Whalers, announced he was moving the team to North Carolina for 1997/98. The team, renamed the Hurricanes, would play in Greensboro while a new arena was completed eighty miles away in Raleigh, the state capital.

With the Whalers' move, five new NHL teams had been created in the past six years by moving existing ones. Minnesota had created both San Jose in 1991 and Dallas in 1993, the Quebec Nordiques had become the Colorado Avalanche in 1995 and the Winnipeg Jets had turned into the Phoenix Coyotes in 1996. Moving an existing franchise was almost as effective as bidding for a new one. And as the final expansion decision from the league approached in the spring of 1997, one existing NHL team openly for sale was the Edmonton Oilers.

EDMONTONIANS WERE wearying of the Oilers under Peter Puck, having been through another round of brinkmanship a few months before his share proposal. After the Oilers missed the playoffs for the fourth straight season in 1995/96, Pocklington again hinted at finding a fresh address. Unless the citizens of Edmonton bought at least 13,000 season tickets for the 1996/97 season, the NHL informed the fans, it wouldn't stand in the way of any effort to move the franchise. The fans responded, the tickets were snapped up, and the Oilers drama paused for a brief intermission as a young team made a welcome return to the playoffs.

Youth and speed were returning to Edmonton. Left winger Ryan Smyth, taken sixth overall by Sather in the 1994 draft, had played his first season in 1995/96. In 1996/97, he emerged as the team's second-highest scorer, behind Doug Weight. An experienced right winger, Andrei Kovalenko, had been added in September, during the first World Cup (the replacement tournament for the Canada Cup). Sather, who was coaching the Canadian team, sent Scott Thornton to Montreal for Kovalenko, who was playing on the Russian squad.

Sather took along two Oilers for the Canadian team: goaltender Curtis Joseph and centre Dean McAmmond. In addition, Doug Weight played for the Americans, Boris Mironov for the Russians and Miroslav Satan for Slovakia. Weight was a standout for the Americans, with seven points in as many games, and shared in the upset victory by the U.S. as a late Brett Hull goal downed Canada in the third game of the best-of-three tournament final.

The final period of the third game had seen Sather's personal stock rise and fall like an Alberta Exchange penny share. Canada began the period with a 2-1 lead, and the CBC's play-by-play crew were talking Sather up as the leading candidate to assemble Canada's Olympic team for 1998, when the NHL would shut down for two weeks to allow its stars to participate. But as the Canadians fell back into a defensive shell, the opportunistic Americans rebounded to take the game and the tournament. In twenty minutes, Sather went from celebrated sage to yesterday's man. As the groundwork was laid for the Canadian Olympic team (which proved to be far less successful than Sather's World Cup effort), it was decided that fresh blood was required in Canada's international tournament management. Sather was out and Marc Crawford, coach of the Colorado Avalanche, the 1995/96 Stanley Cup winners, was in. So were Bob Gainey, president of the Dallas Stars, and Bob Clarke, general manager of the Philadelphia Flyers. When the best efforts of this new generation failed to get Canada a medal, Sather's skills no longer appeared so diminished by time.

As it happened, the presence of six Oilers (including Kovalenko) in the 1996 World Cup tournament hinted there was more talent in the struggling team than its recent efforts suggested. And 1996/97 did prove to be a breakthrough year. Kevin Lowe was brought back to steady the defence, and a fast-skating team that could also hit, backed by Joseph's strong netminding, moved up to third in the Pacific Division with thirty-six wins, then upset the Dallas Stars in a thrilling opening-round tilt that was capped by a 4-3 overtime win in game seven in Dallas.

On May 11, 1997, the Oilers lost game five of their next round, the Western Conference semi-finals, 4-3 to the Colorado Avalanche in Denver, ending their season. The return to respectability of the team was a double-edged sword for Edmonton fans. Its success made concerned civic leaders more determined that the team should remain in

Edmonton. But the success also made the team a more appealing purchase for anyone wanting to take it out of town. When Ascent Entertainment purchased the Quebec Nordiques in 1995, they were acquiring a club that was poised to win a Stanley Cup in its first season in Denver as the Avalanche. In turning the Oilers around, Sather had turned them into another potential Avalanche. They might not be ready to win the Stanley Cup, but a buyer would be getting a strong on-ice product right out of the box—more competitive than a new franchise would be, and with youth on its side.

Less than a month after the playoff loss to Colorado, Pocklington announced the team was on the auction block. Not part of it this time—all of it. Just when the Oilers seemed to be back, they seemed to be leaving, with no chance of ever returning. On June 5, 1997, Pocklington announced that Midland Walwyn was working on his behalf to find an outright new owner for the Oilers. "All final bids will be reviewed and a decision on the successful bid is expected sometime in the fall of 1997," Midland Walwyn stated on June 17.

Fortuitously, the same day that Pocklington announced the Oiler's availability, the NHL's expansion committee formally recommended the league's four new franchise sites. The board of governors approved the recommendation and granted the franchises eight days later. The approval of Atlanta, St. Paul and Nashville were no surprise. The shocker was which of the three remaining cities snagged the fourth spot—or, more precisely, which one didn't.

Houston's failure was a stunner. Only days before the league announcement, bid insiders had allowed to the *Houston Chronicle* that they were 75 percent sure of getting a team. But despite having impeccable owners and a highly desirable market, the Houston franchise had come up short on an arena. Municipal voters had approved a publicly funded building the previous November, but the financing required the approval of the state government, and the necessary bill had become stalled in the Texas legislature. When the bill passed later in June, however, a close associate of Governor George W. Bush,

Dallas Stars owner Ted Hicks, was able to take advantage of state approval for use of public funds in arena construction to build new training facilities for his team.

Without an unequivocal arena plan in place, whether publicly or privately funded, the NHL was reluctant to approve a new franchise. It had learned its lesson with the Tampa Bay Lightning, which it approved for the 1992/93 season despite no clear plans for a major-league building and a vague ownership structure. The team began playing in the inadequate, 10,400-seat Expo Hall before shifting to the 28,000-seat Suncoast Dome, a baseball stadium reconfigured for hockey. The team finally got a proper arena with the opening of the Ice Palace in 1996/97. The league was also mildly embarrassed by the poor facilities used by the Colorado Avalanche. The league had allowed the Quebec Nordiques to relocate to Denver in 1995 to play in the ill-equipped McNichols Sports Arena while the team's new owners and the city wrangled over who would pay for a new facility. A new arena, the Pepsi Center, was finally announced by the Avalanche's owners, Ascent Entertainment, for 1999/2000.

Houston also posed a problem in its unusual rivalry between bid groups, which had forced the NHL to reduce the city's bidders from three to one in February. With no state approval for the new public arena scheme, a Houston NHL team would, at least for the short term, have to use The Summit, where spurned bidder Les Alexander's Houston Rockets of the NBA played. And Alexander had made it clear he wasn't keen on working out the logistics of sharing The Summit with an NHL team he didn't own.

Nashville, by comparison, was a dream expansion site. There was a brand new, 19,000-seat civic arena without a major-league tenant of any kind, and a $20 million public inducement to anyone who wanted to bring one to it. (Raleigh, in concert with North Carolina University, had plans to build a 20,000-seat arena when its franchise bid missed the short list in February 1997, but in passing on Charlotte businessman Felix Sabates's bid, the league conveniently left the door open for Peter Karmanos to move the Hartford Whalers there and take advantage of the new arena plan.)

In bid politics, Columbus and Oklahoma City were fall-back franchise sites—contenders that could pull through (as Ottawa and Tampa Bay did, in 1991) when more promising bids came up short in the final measure of criteria. Once the league had allowed these cities into the final six, it had given them its blessing as viable sites. Of the two, Columbus was more appealing. It was much larger, with 3.4 million people in the greater city area to Oklahoma City's one million, and was far less isolated. Home to Ohio State University, Columbus was positioned in the heart of a lucrative fan market with strong cable television potential. Detroit and Pittsburgh were both about 180 miles away and, as the state capital, Columbus sat in virtually the centre of Ohio, with Toledo, Dayton, Cincinnati, Cleveland, Akron, Canton and Youngstown within about a 130-mile radius. Oklahoma City, in comparison, could point only to Tulsa, about 90 miles away, as another major urban centre from which to draw fans.

When the six finalists were chosen, however, Oklahoma City had one major advantage over Columbus: public approval for a civic-funded arena, gained in a plebiscite in December 1996. Oklahoma City's bid effort was then shaken by controversies surrounding the mayor, Ron Norick. The former CHL Blazers investor, who made only $2,000 a year as mayor, raised eyebrows by refusing to rule out the possibility, when it was announced that Oklahoma City had made the final six in February, that he might end up being one of the NHL franchise's investors. The optics were terrible. Norick had been a hands-on hizzoner in steering through the MAPS downtown rejuvenation program, which included a new NHL-quality arena. If the franchise bid was successful and Norick became a part-owner of the team, he would be wide open to accusations that he had used the mayor's office to press for the public funding of a facility he had not at the time declared he could personally benefit from. It was also revealed that a NASCAR Craftsman Cup Ford 150 racing truck he owned with his son Lance (who was the driver), through their company L&R Motor-sports, was being sponsored by the NHL. This was hard to miss: the truck was painted in the orange and black livery of the league. How cozy was the relationship between Norick and the league he was trying to attract to his city with a publicly funded arena—a taxpayer-footed facility that could play host to a professional team he may end up owning part of?

In an article in *The Oklahoman,* Lance Norick explained the NHL sponsorship of his NASCAR truck as "a business decision by the National Hockey League." Norick noted that 56 percent of NASCAR fans are also NHL fans. "When the National Hockey League lets you use their logo, that's a big deal, just like it is with Coca-Cola or anyone else. They simply saw potential, knowing how brand-loyal NASCAR fans are." (Brand-loyal or not, the apparently significant crossover between NASCAR and the NHL did not move the league to consider the Raleigh bid in its list of six franchise bid finalists, even though bidder Felix Sabates owned a NASCAR team.)

On the issue of investing in any future Oklahoma City NHL team, Ron Norick quickly retreated, and announced formally that he would not be part of any ownership group. And as the June final announcement approached, Oklahoma City had the looks of a genuine dark horse. Houston was troubled by the lack of a firm public arena deal, and in May the Columbus bid imploded on the same issue.

The lead investor in the Columbus bid (called Columbus Hockey Ltd.) was Lamar Hunt, a millionaire Texas oilman who owned the NFL's Kansas City Chiefs. (His brothers Nelson and Bunker had made a notorious attempt to corner the world silver market in the 1970s.) Hunt's family venture, Hunt Sports Enterprises, also owned the Kansas City Wiz and the Columbus Crew of Major League Soccer, the same league in which Pocklington's Drillers now played, and in 1998 would become a leading candidate to purchase the Kansas City Royals of baseball's American League.

Columbus Hockey Ltd.'s bid was anchored in an arena and stadium complex that would house an NHL team and soccer's Crew under a twenty-five-year, $3 million-a-year lease, and would be paid for through a special sales tax. But on May 6, with the league's final decision on new franchises only a month away, voters in Franklin County killed the proposal in a plebiscite.

What happened next became the subject of countersuits between Hunt and his fellow investors in Columbus Hockey Ltd. After the plebiscite failure, bid participants John McConnell and John Wolfe (publisher of the local newspaper, the *Columbus Dispatch*)[7] broke away from Hunt to create a new bid company, COLHOC Limited Partnership. COLHOC's members and Hunt ended up filing countersuits for alleged breach of contract. Hunt claimed he was improperly shut out of the Columbus bid after the plebiscite failed. McConnell and Wolfe's suit asserted that while Hunt was participating in the bid to bring an NHL team to Columbus, he was secretly working on a deal to get an NHL team in Cincinnati. The McConnell/Wolfe case argued through letters it had obtained that Hunt was considering a deal to have an NHL team in Cincinnati with a ten-year rent-free deal, and that he had also been negotiating to put a team in Newport, Kentucky, at a new facility envisioned by promoter Skip Korb. For his part, Korb said what he had in mind was Hunt buying the Edmonton Oilers and moving them to the grandiose building he planned for Newport. Korb was offering ten years of free rent and a $10 million inducement to bring in an NHL team. Hunt defended himself by saying that the Cincinnati and Newport plans were simply unsolicited proposals. In May 1998, a two-week jury trial ended with the judge ruling that McConnell and Wolfe were allowed by Columbus Hockey Ltd.'s operating agreement to participate in COLHOC Limited Partnership. (Hunt's appeal of the judgment reached court in July 1999.)

That the Oilers should be caught up in this maelstrom was far from unlikely because, by the spring of 1997, any city or investor who coveted an NHL team was taking a serious look at the Oilers, who were (officially at least) partly for sale. Oklahoma City, the rival Houston groups of Watson/McNair and Alexander, and an outsider like Korb, were all making enquiries as to the Oilers' availability. Pocklington was already doing business with the core of the Oklahoma City bid through his baseball investment. At the same time as the NHL was considering the expansion bids, AAA baseball was undergoing a complete realignment of its individual leagues. As a result, Pocklington's Trappers and the Oklahoma City Redhawks were placed in the same league.

On June 5, 1997, with the league's announcement of four selected expansion sites, the Oilers became a wild card in the NHL's future. If the Oilers moved in the post-selection scramble, they would not be going to Columbus, for the city's bid had pulled off an eleventh-hour miracle. Over the weekend of May 31–June 1, Columbus's mayor marshaled a marathon of meetings with local developers to find a privately funded solution to the NHL arena dilemma. By Sunday night, Nationwide Mutual Insurance Co. had agreed to fund 90 percent of the proposed $125 million arena's cost, with the rest coming from Dispatch Printing Co., the publisher of the local newspaper. The NHL franchise, should the league award it, would pay a hefty $4 million in annual rent. Columbus City Council approved the deal on Monday, June 2. On June 4, COLHOC presented the new Columus bid and its arena deal to the NHL. It was what the NHL selection committee wanted to hear. The next day, the selection committee announced Columbus, Atlanta, Nashville and St. Paul as the sites that would expand the league to thirty teams. With Houston and Oklahoma City out in the cold, and with Pocklington now announcing that the team was entirely for sale, two likely roads out of town were mapped for the Oilers.

CHAPTER FIFTEEN

THE FOUR LUCKY winners of the NHL expansion sweepstakes on June 5, 1997, would each pay US$80 million to enter the league. The Oilers' share of those fees would be about $12.3 million. Nothing was going to be simple in a deal involving Peter Pocklington, who announced he was selling the Oilers outright on exactly the same day as the expansion teams were revealed. The question of who would be entitled to the Oilers' share of the expansion fees—Pocklington or the new owners of the team—was just one of many complications in the planned sale. Foremost among the issues were: If a buyer wanted to take the team out of Edmonton, would the city let it? And if someone bought the team and kept it in Edmonton, did he have any hope of not losing money the way Pocklington said he had? Much hinged on conflicting readings of the 1994 sublease agreement, in which six parties had been involved.

Pocklington and the ATB needed to push forward the Oilers' sale when there was maximum open-market interest in acquiring an NHL franchise. More than one buyer would be likely to come forward, forcing the local bid up to the US$70 million maximum under the Location Agreement. And if no local bidder arose with the ability to raise $70 million, the team would be sold for top dollar as it left Edmonton. In the name of retiring debt, that was the outcome of utmost benefit to Pocklington and the ATB.

The decision in June 1997 to sell the Oilers thus was impeccably timed, for the winnowing process the NHL had just completed to determine the four new franchise sites had left seven applicants (three in Houston) by the wayside. A number of them were still hungry to get into the league; some were thought to have had a purchase of the Oilers as their Plan B all along. It was doubtful the NHL would consider expanding past thirty teams any time soon, so the only recourse for those left empty-handed was to buy an existing franchise and move it to the site of their choice, with the league's approval.

In 1997, *Financial World Magazine* estimated the Oilers' value at US$52 million, well under the maximum local purchase price in the 1994 Location Agreement. But the magazine grossly underestimated the inflationary effect the latest phase of expansion would have on any existing franchise's value. Having been willing to pay US$80 million for the right to start a team, aspiring franchise owners turned down by the league in June were certainly ready to pay at least that much for one that already existed.

Pocklington and the ATB had reason to be optimistic that they quickly would have at least US$80 million to apply against Pocklington's debts. At the press conference announcing the sale, Pocklington said he was looking for US$85 million. As they relished the thought of a seller's market in the wake of the NHL's expansion announcement, Pocklington's and the ATB's optimism for a top-dollar sale was muted by the terms of the three-year-old Location Agreement. A local buyer could step in and steal Pocklington's greatest asset.

From the perspective of "saving" the Oilers, of keeping them in Edmonton to entertain future generations, buying the team for US$70 million was anything but stealing. From the perspective of Pocklington and the ATB, however, a sale that fell below market value by at least US$10 million when they were trying to settle debts on the public accounts could well be called a steal. The public would not have stood for any other Pocklington asset being sold for less than what it would fetch on the open market, when the proceeds were directly earmarked for cleaning up loans from a government-owned bank.

The ATB held conflicting allegiances in the sale. On the one hand, its fiduciary duty to both Pocklington and the bank's shareholders called upon it to get as much money as it could for the team, and that would lead to a sale to an American buyer. On the other hand, this duty was complicated by the fact that the ATB's shareholders were the people of Alberta, who were not keen to see the team leave Edmonton. The ATB would do what it could to sell to a local buyer, but it would neither give the team away to local interests nor turn its nose up at an outside buyer with a blank cheque. As well, because of the confidential relationship between the ATB and Pocklington, the bank would not share with the city, EDE or Northlands the details of interest voiced by outside buyers before receiving a formal offer.

When announcing the sale on June 5, Pocklington had been upbeat about finding new owners locally. "I really believe we'll get a large corporation plus some smaller investors, or eight or ten investors who want to get involved and have some fun." After the league made its new franchise announcements, however, Pocklington was careful to downplay the fun, doing his best to dissuade local interest with friendly, fatherly advice. "Owning an NHL franchise is not a money-making proposition. There are more than a few bad mufflers," he noted in mid-August, betraying his origins as a used-car dealer in London, Ontario. "I sincerely hope someone does pick it up and keep it here. But I'm just trying to be forthright. I don't want to see anyone get into the position where they spend a lot of money and a lot of energy and a year from now or two years from now—crunch." He added, "The only problems I've ever had with the Oilers are money problems. The money problems have taken the fun out of the business."

Back in February, when trying to convince investors to join him in owning the Oilers and Coliseum Management Inc., Pocklington had been upbeat about the earnings potential. "We're on a roll," he crowed, and compared the investment opportunity with the long-term bonanza enjoyed by people who had bought Maple Leaf Gardens stock in 1931. Now, however, with the entire team on the block and a need to maximize his return from the sale to pay down his ATB debts, Pocklington was almost discouraging, speaking of losses of $6 million to $7 million, and a need for any investor to ride out negative cash flow over the short term.

People weren't sure which version of Oilers fiscal reality to believe. Whenever a professional sports franchise owner cries poor, journalists reach for a handy statement made to the *Wall Street Journal* by Paul Beeston when he was president of the Toronto Blue Jays. "Under generally accepted accounting principles," the man in charge of a two-time World Series winner had boasted, "I can turn a $4 million profit into a $2 million loss and I can get every national accounting firm to agree with me."

It was revealed that the Oilers had lost about $3.5 million in 1996/97, while Coliseum Management had earned about $500,000. Pocklington had assigned the sublease agreement for Northlands to Coliseum Management, jointly managed by himself and ATB, thereby appearing to cleave away from the Oilers the critical rights to the arena and creating a new and profitable entity which now, in his mind, had substantial capital value. Although the details of the management group's operations were not known, Pocklington likely stayed true to the *modus operandi* he demonstrated with Canbra and the Oilers, and paid himself a consulting fee from Coliseum Management's revenues. (This is a typical arrangement for an owner with management duties. His consulting fee for Oilers Hockey Inc., however, had stopped by the time the share offering proposal was made in February 1997. At Canbra, the consulting fee was worth about $40,000 a month.)

Pocklington was now trying to sell Coliseum Management as a going concern separate from the Oilers, with its own market value of about US$15 million. Pocklington in effect was saying that if local buyers wanted the Oilers, they needed Coliseum Management as well. This scheme had the effect of boosting the local buyer price, specified for the Oilers alone, above the US$70 million ceiling, into the realm of the open market price—if Pocklington could get away with it. Bob Turner didn't think he could. Northlands Park had termination rights to the sublease held by Coliseum Management if the hockey team was no longer owned by Pocklington. Pocklington therefore didn't have much of a business to sell in Coliseum Management if, the moment the Oilers were sold, Coliseum Management's entire *raison d'être*—unfettered access to staging events at Northlands Coliseum—evaporated.

The substantial differences of opinion between Pocklington and Turner over what, if any, value could be assigned to Coliseum Management and whether the team was stuck in Edmonton under-lined a fundamental dispute over the essence of the Location Agreement. Pocklington clearly did not view it as an impediment to his selling the club to an outside buyer, while Turner most certainly did. Pocklington did not believe the Oilers were stuck in Edmonton. At the June press conference announcing the sale, the continued enforceability of the 1993 court injunction was raised. Northlands Park had secured the injunction to prevent the team from moving to Minnesota by having the courts enforce the team's obligation under its active lease to play all home games at the Coliseum. The injunction had no expiration date, and appeared to buttress the Location Agreement's requirement that the team remain in town. Pocklington, however, felt the injunction was dead, as the lease it enforced had been replaced by the 1994 sublease agreement. He also believed the 1994 sublease and for that matter, its Location Agreement, couldn't keep the team in Edmonton once it was sold. He argued the only thing that could prevent a new buyer from taking the team out of Edmonton was a bankruptcy.

In Bob Turner's mind, there were only three ways in which the Oilers could leave town. In the first scenario, Pocklington (or the ATB, in the event that the bank pushed the Oilers into receivership) gave the city its opportunity to acquire the team or find it a new local owner, but when no credible offer arose, the city had no recourse but to allow the team to be sold to an outside buyer. In the second scenario, a local buyer would make an offer, but that offer would be vetoed by the NHL, which had the right to approve the ownership of any franchise. (One stumbling block, for example, might be the league's insistence that any franchise owner borrow no more than half the selling price. The NHL also frowned on government ownership of franchises, so even if the city agreed to buy all or part of the team, the league was unlikely to go along with the deal.) The third scenario was for a new local owner to come along and attempt to continue operating the Oilers under the Location Agreement, only to find its losses so burdensome that it asked to be released from the agreement so the team could be sold out of town.

Whatever transpired, Turner was prepared to stand firm on the enforceability of the Location Agreement. He wouldn't argue for pressing the Oilers into bankruptcy rather than see them sold to an outside buyer, but he was determined, working with Rick LeLacheur, to do whatever he could to ensure the team stayed in Edmonton.

In the sale of a team like the Oilers, however, rational fiscal behaviour is often subservient to the tug of heartstrings. Teams are often seen as quasi-public properties by fans, who interpret their emotional investment as a tangible equity position. In western Canada, franchises in the Canadian Football League, like Edmonton's own Eskimos, are owned by community groups. Civic pride and athletic entertainment are tightly bound. Although public support had not been unanimous for a local buyout of the Winnipeg Jets to prevent them from moving to Phoenix, those who did attempt to block the sale participated in a near-hysterical, albeit ultimately unsuccessful, fund-raising drive. The emotionalism tended to be cloaked in debatable assertions of how much spending would dry up in the local economy if the team were lost. In Winnipeg, the Jets were lost, and the city did not blow away like a tumbleweed in a prairie dust storm. Some people were prepared to let the Oilers move on, but others—those who saw genuine economic benefits in the team's presence, felt vulnerability in their own businesses without the spin-off effect of the Oilers, or subscribed sincerely to the idea that the Oilers were an irreplaceable source of civic pride and stature—were prepared to fight to keep the team in town.

ELACHEUR'S CAREER was in transition as the Oilers came up for sale. He tendered his resignation as head of the EDE in August 1997, and would be leaving at the end of March 1998. Looking for fresh challenges, he would be named the new chair of the province's Workers Compensation Board in February. In the meantime, he was helping steer Edmonton's bid for the 2001 world track and field championships, which it would win in November. And with Turner, he was hoping to round up enough local investors to keep the Oilers in Edmonton.

But the search for a hometown saviour for the team was not going well. Edmonton was a white-collar capital, and while there were a few corporate head offices in town, like Suncor, most of the big oil-patch businesses were based in Calgary. The city lacked a person or a business with sufficient financial heft to go it alone in a team purchase. Even the Calgary Flames, for that matter, were owned by a consortium of nine owners. Turner and LeLacheur made the rounds of the most likely potential investors, but came up empty-handed.

Watching the unfolding crisis was the man most responsible for the wonderful years the Oilers had given the city's hockey fans. As president, general manager and (for most of its successes) coach, Glen Sather was the architect of one of the greatest dynasties in NHL history. He had built an exciting offensive machine around the talents of Wayne Gretzky, and was acknowledged to be one of the brightest minds in the league. Rumoured to hold as much as five percent of the

Oilers, Sather in fact had no equity in the team. He had suffered more than anyone when Pocklington began dismantling his lineup, and it had been especially painful in the early 1990s to see his former players bring a Stanley Cup to New York while his own team began a string of playoff absences. No one had more of a right to be angry with Pocklington than Sather, yet Sather was the embattled owner's most ardent supporter. He had known Pocklington for more than twenty years, and saw past the public caricature of Peter Puck the gonzo capitalist. Like other good friends of Pocklington, he saw in him a savvy businessman who was going through rough times, who had kept the Oilers alive in Edmonton at personal cost, to no credit from the public.

While it was true that Pocklington had unloaded all the team's marquee players, there was no way, in the new climate of stars earning $5 to $8 million a season, to keep those players in a small market like Edmonton. Mark Messier, past his prime, was now making more money in one season in Vancouver than the entire Oilers lineup had been paid in the late 1980s. If local investors wanted to keep the Oilers in town, they had better realize what they were getting themselves into. If a new local ownership was found, it seemed doubtful that Sather would stick around. His loss would be as great as that of Gretzky.

Two separate local groups did step forward in late September 1997, with curiously secretive proposals. One was led by local developer and restaurateur Robert Proznick; the other included Cathy Roozen, whose father, Dr Charles Allard, had owned the Oilers back in its WHA days. Neither group, however, had a credible proposal or anything close to a firm offer. Each was contemplating a purchase at the $70 million level. Neither the ATB nor Pocklington was happy with the prospect of settling for the first local offer that came along. They needed some out-of-town action to breath life into their sales effort.

On October 24, Pocklington's efforts produced a banner headline in the *Edmonton Journal*: "SOLD!" The Oilers had found new ownership in a Texas oil town. Oddly, it wasn't the same group from Houston that had just been denied a franchise in the June expansion selection. Instead, Leslie Alexander, owner of the NBA's Houston Rockets, who hadn't made the final cut of expansion franchise applicants in February 1997, was coming to town to save the Oilers and let them keep playing in Edmonton—for a couple years, anyway, while they proved themselves to be profitable. And as long as they made money, they were staying put. If they weren't profitable, it was off to Texas with them.

As in real estate, the three most important factors in a sports franchise sale are location, location and location. Bob Turner had the perfect location for the Oilers, and he was sure he had it in writing, with Peter Pocklington's own signature at the bottom. Was Mr Alexander thinking of keeping the Oilers in Edmonton? Well, what other choice did he have? But if Mr Alexander wanted to take the team to Houston, and nobody else came up with US$70 million to send in the direction of the ATB, what other choice did Bob Turner really have, but to let him? The Oilers exodus, which had begun with Paul Coffey in 1987, had rocked the hockey world with Wayne Gretzky in 1988 and thereafter gathered locomotive momentum, was accelerating toward a final, emphatic departure. The only thing Turner had to toss in its way, in the hope of derailing it, was the Location Agreement, a piece of paper signed by Pocklington back in 1994.

MAYOR BILL SMITH wasn't elected until 1995, after the struggles with Peter Pocklington over the Northlands Coliseum lease were through, but he was now facing a much more complex set of circumstances. The Oilers' ownership was on the verge of changing. Maybe the team was leaving town, and maybe it wasn't; maybe the city could stop the team from going, and maybe it couldn't. The picture surrounding the Alexander offer, particularly his intentions, was far from clear. Bob Turner was called in to address the mayor and city council on the city's rights with regard to the team. Turner was confident: he told them the Location Agreement would "knock him [Alexander] out of the box" if his intention was to buy the team and move it to Houston.

The agreement into which Alexander had entered with Pocklington, says Turner, was "a brutally flawed document." The way Turner read it, Alexander could move the team at his pleasure, and the three-year timeline of profitability didn't mean the team was guaranteed to stay in Edmonton for at least three years. The timeline was backdated, and Turner could see the team leaving town under its parameters in less than a year.

Leslie Alexander came to Edmonton to discuss the proposed purchase with the mayor and a select group in the mayor's office on November 3. He drove in from the airport with Pocklington. Pocklington did not attend the meeting, but Turner (who participated, along with Rick LeLacheur) believed Pocklington had assured Alexander that the locals were onside over the rigidity of the Location Agreement: nobody was going to force him to keep the team at Northlands until 2004. But someone plainly had said something to Alexander before he entered the office that ruined his day. "He was visibly upset when he walked into the office," Smith recalls. "Very tense, to the point of being almost aggressive."

Mayor Smith tried to break the ice by doing the mayoral thing, expressing the hope that Alexander's purchase would lead to a bright new relationship between the people of Edmonton and Houston. Alexander made it clear he was not there to negotiate; he wanted to know the city's position on the Location Agreement. The reasons for the Location Agreement were explained to him: after all the revenues for concessions, parking and other events had been handed over to Pocklington, they couldn't have him walking away from an enforceable lease. Alexander would not be allowed to walk away from it, either. Alexander was astonished. "I have no intention of signing it," he told the mayor.[1]

That was it for the meeting. Mayor Smith clocked it in at twenty-two minutes.

Leslie Alexander left town, and left the future of the team under a cloud of uncertainty.

There were no other outside bidders. The Oklahoma City group had considered the Oilers, but were dissuaded by the Location Agreement. The Gaylords instead took the opportunity to acquire a 20 percent stake in the new Nashville Predators franchise. And now that it had missed the cut in the NHL expansion selection and had passed on the Oilers, the city came to reflect on life without a major-league franchise of any kind. Maybe that was okay. The new arena was going ahead anyway, and they had a new baseball field for the AAA Redhawks. Maybe Oklahoma City's destiny was as a first class minor pro centre, with college sports to go along with it. The city could go after the NCAA basketball tournament. It could go on cheering the Sooners of college football, and it still had the Blazers of the CHL. Maybe Oklahoma City was doing exactly what it was supposed to. Edmonton, meanwhile, was trying hard not to become what Oklahoma City realized it was suited to be.

T HE CLOSER THE Oilers came to being sold, it seemed, the better the team became. Leslie Alexander went home to Houston, but he did not go away. In the lull before the next storm, Glen Sather went on a trade and acquisition spree, with four deals in ten days. He began on December 30, sending Bryan Marchment, Steve Kelly and Jason Bonsignore to Tampa Bay to get defenceman Roman Hamrlik, who had played for the Czech Republic in the 1996 World Cup. (Sather also received Paul Comrie.)

On January 4, 1998, Sather sent Jason Arnott and Bryan Muir to New Jersey to get Russian left winger Valeri Zelepukin and American right winger Bill Guerin, both of whom had also played in the recent World Cup; two days later, he picked up centre Tony Hrkac on waivers from Dallas. And on January 9, veteran defenceman Bobby Dollas was collected from Anaheim in exchange for Drew Bannister, as nagging injuries kept Kevin Lowe out of the lineup.

Off the ice in Edmonton, efforts were made to bring together a local ownership group more credible than the half-formed efforts that had come up with purchase proposals in September. LeLacheur and others were trying to coax the group forward.

Then Leslie Alexander boomeranged. Having read the lay of the land in his November visit, he returned with a formal offer for the Oilers on February 10, 1998. Alexander would pay US$82.5 million cash. The offer included a $5 million non-refundable deposit. If it was accepted, the Oilers could be out of Edmonton at the end of the season. The Alberta Treasury Branches started the thirty-day clock ticking on the Location Agreement's local buyer option. Somebody had to come forward with US$70 million by March 13, or Alexander got the team, subject to the NHL's approval.

Although LeLacheur had left his post at EDE, he remained committed to the cause of making sure the Oilers didn't leave town. He had prepared a report on the Oilers' impact on the local economy, using the Conference Board of Canada's software program called the Tourism Economic Assessment Model (TEAM). The program quantified the impact of tourism events, festivals, conventions and the like on local employment, wages and salaries, gross domestic product, tax revenues and about fifty other spin-offs. Using data from 1996/97, the TEAM program showed the Oilers had contributed $74.7 million to the provincial economy that season, with $62.9 falling in Edmonton. Taxes generated to all levels of government by the Oilers' presence in the economy totalled almost $20 million. The TEAM program also placed an economic benefits figure of about $20 million on the Edmonton Eskimos, and about $5 million on Pocklington's AAA Trappers.

To save the team, a local ownership group had to come up with US$35 million, since the NHL by-laws would allow a franchise owner to finance the other half of the team's equity. After the Alexander offer was received and the city received notification of the running clock, city council debated beginning a huge pass-the-hat program to allow local citizens to contribute their nickels, dimes and dollars to the cause of saving the team. It was a nice idea, but it would run afoul of the law. A partnership group could consist of a maximum of fifty people; after that, provincial securities laws required a prospectus to be issued. LeLacheur felt both the city and the province should be prepared to contribute money, but that wasn't going to happen—not directly, anyway. Ultimately, as he understood and said publicly, people or businesses with millions to spare had to come forward. The mom, dad and kids scheme of chucking coins into the wishing well gave one a warm feeling, but "it's not going to be done that way," LeLacheur said on February 13. "We're kidding ourselves. It's going to be done by major investors."

LeLacheur did, however, speak with Turner, and a foundation to which citizens could contribute, called the Edmonton Oilers Forever Fund, was set up by EDE. Within a week, the fund had collected $31,000.

It was an impressive burst of public generosity, but it wouldn't put the Oilers over the top. Much legwork was required to determine who would or could come forward to form an ownership group. Edmonton was not Houston, with multi-multimillionaires like Robert McNair, Chuck Watson and Les Alexander on call. Edmonton wasn't even Calgary, for that matter, which had the lion's share of head offices in the energy industry. There were successful people in Edmonton, but their investment level potential was down in the single digits of millions, and they would have to be convinced to sink what money they had into an investment that could bleed losses— just the way Peter Pocklington said it could.

Local lawyer and investor participant Cal Nichols took the lead in working the phones and trying to scare up money. The would-be local investment group came up with the idea of selling licensing rights to Northlands Coliseum, plastering its exterior with the corporate logos of the province's energy giants. After all, if the oil industry wouldn't save the Oilers, who would? But the oil industry reacted largely with stony indifference, and the scheme fell flat.

The clock ticked. Investors did appear but after a week of bush-beating, the local investment group, which stood at thirteen, was short by about $7 million of the US$35 million it would need to pull off a purchase, with financing providing the other half. No knight in shining armour emerged from the city. And then a miracle happened. An international investment pro named Michael Largue called from New York City, with US$100 million to burn, proposing to buy the team, sign the Location Agreement, and *leave the Oilers in Edmonton.*

"HE NEVER DID look like the right thing," Bob Turner remembers. But he kept sounding like it, just enough to keep things moving forward in the short time-span available, which allowed little opportunity for the city to give him a full shakedown. Largue presented himself as an investor who could buy the team himself, but had a Swiss friend, a retired president of Credit Suisse, who would be happy to finance the deal alone. And he didn't want to move the Oilers anywhere. Edmonton was just fine. If this former Swiss banker bought the team and signed the Location Agreement, he was the local buyer the city needed to knock Alexander out of the running.

"Rick LeLacheur and I looked at each other," says Turner. "Why, we wondered, would a real candidate be coming out of the woods now?" But time was running out, and they couldn't leave a stone unturned. As it happened, both men had to be in New York on business, so they arranged to stay an extra day, meet Largue and discuss his purchase proposal.

Largue talked the talk. He knew all the right names in and around the NHL, and dropped them as if they were acquaintances. He provided a list of references, which Turner checked. One was his lawyer, another an investment banker at a major New York firm. They both vouched for him. "We didn't do a Dun & Bradstreet [credit check], because there was no time," says Turner. "But he knew all the buzz words and names, and had good references."

Largue spoke with the *Edmonton Journal* and, with a bravura that was almost galling given what transpired, allowed in a report published on February 18, "At this point I'm not really prepared to talk to anybody about it because I want to do some due diligence first."

Cal Nichols had yet to speak with Largue or offer any financial information, and was cautious about an outsider securing a controlling interest in his group. Someone like Largue (or his Swiss banker friend) could end up moving the team out of town. "I don't see any upside or any longevity for the community," he warned.

The mayor invited Largue to Edmonton to meet with the local investment group. He would have to come at his own expense, though, and he agreed. The itinerary called for him to meet with the local group at its office, and then tour Northlands before catching a noon flight back home.

The news that Largue was on his way set off a media frenzy. The white knight was coming! The *Edmonton Sun* published an editorial chastising the locals for not rolling out the red carpet.

Largue's story was elaborate and readily verifiable—or, as it turned out, unverifiable. He had studied for four years at Northeastern University in Boston, earning a degree in political science and playing college hockey. He had gone to Switzerland and played for the Bern Bears of the Swiss Premier League in 1988/89. The team was owned by Lester Mittendorf, the man who now wanted to invest in the Oilers.

It was left to the *Edmonton Journal* to do some old-fashioned reportorial digging and start blowing holes in Largue's C.V. before he showed up. Northeastern had no record of him ever attending the university, never mind playing hockey. And his story of playing in Bern was problematic on many fronts. First, there was no record of him ever being on the team. (When the *Journal* asked him, once he was in Edmonton, how the team finished in his season, he said third, when in fact they won the league championship.) Swiss Premier League rules allowed only two foreign players on the roster at the time, and in 1988/89 they were Alan Haworth and former Oiler Reijo Ruotsalainen.

There were other troubles with Bern. As a literal "club" team, it had no private owner, not now or in 1988/89. Lester Mittendorf could never have owned it. As for Mr. Mittendorf himself, the *Journal* contacted the Zurich financial publication *Redaktion Cash*; a reporter there said he'd never heard of Lester Mittendorf and could find no trace of him in Teledata, the country's authoritative electronic commercial register of investors. Mittendorf appeared to be as real as Santa Claus.

When Largue arrived in Edmonton, the fun began. At the investor group's office, a *Journal* reporter stood out from the media scrum to ask pointed questions about the inconsistencies in every aspect of Largue's story. The other media members picked up on the *Journal's* queries, and by the time the group reached Northlands Coliseum, the tour was in a shambles and Largue was fleeing for the airport. Which was a good thing, because in being outside the United States, Largue was in violation of his probation.

The previous March, Michael Largue, financier and white knight, had been charged with fraud over misappropriation of funds at his apartment co-op. Convicted and sentenced in the fall, Largue was living at home with his parents when he took it upon himself to bail out the Oilers by means only he understood.

Largue was a phony, and a convicted one at that, but he'd been around the NHL since at least 1994, when he mounted a campaign through his purported company, MAL Investment, to buy the Hartford Whalers, a bid he lost to Peter Karmanos. After being hit with his fraud charge in March 1997, Largue had the nerve to pop up in Hartford in April, trying to organize local businessmen in a bid to buy the team from Karmanos to stop him from moving it to North

Carolina. He met with Pittsburgh Penguins co-owner Thomas Ruta to try to enlist his participation in a purchase. Karmanos would report he never heard from Largue. After the team left Hartford, Largue fired at the departing Karmanos: "We anticipated this all would happen. We made an offer to stay for seven years minimum. We were willing to pay more money for the franchise. Silly us. I knew Lowell Weicker [the governor of Connecticut] was a big political wheel, but I didn't know he was a computer expert, too. [Karmanos owns Compuware.] Maybe if he had spent more time on the sale of the Whalers and less time on his PC, the Whalers wouldn't be moving today."

One month after his would-be attempt to keep the Whalers in Hartford, Largue phoned Steve Oto, chief executive officer of the Tampa Bay Lightning, saying he was interested in buying the team. According to a report in the *Tampa Bay Tribune* (which initially reported favourably that Largue was "the leader of an international investment group expressing interest in buying the franchise") Largue was stopped cold when team president Phil Esposito checked his credentials.

And the Edmonton boondoggle was not his first appearance in Canada. The *Edmonton Journal* learned he had earlier tried to buy the Calgary Stampeders of the CFL, but that league commissioner Larry Smith turned him away as less than credible.[2]

For about one week, the excitement surrounding Largue caused the local buyer group to lose precious momentum, as people assumed the white knight was riding into town. Having done a brilliant job of unmasking Largue, the *Edmonton Journal* stepped up to make a $1 million investment with eight days to go to the deadline. It preferred to stay in the reporting business, pledging not to participate in the management of the team, and would endeavour to sell its share once the team was established under new owners.

The effort to raise the cash to save the team went down to the wire, right down to the night of March 12, with the group having to present a credible offer the next day or fold. Car dealer Ron Hodgson had come in at the same time as the *Journal*, and they joined the initial investment group of Cal Nichols, Cathy Roozen, Jim Hole of Hole Engineering (well known to the community as a former Edmonton Eskimos president), Ed Bean (who had once promoted a heavyweight fight between Donovan "Razor" Ruddock and Mike Tyson at Northlands that fell through when Tyson begged off with a vague ailment) and Bruce Saville (whose Saville Systems PLC markets billing and customer-service software for the telecommunications industry[3]). St. Albert businessman Barry Weaver, who owned Skyreach Equipment Ltd., also joined, and is believed to have invested more than $1 million. (Initial investments ranged from $500,000 to $5 million.) Late in the game, Calgary native Todd McFarlane, the comic book artist who created the character Spawn, joined the group, and other investors included a group of five businessmen from Lloydminster, Saskatchewan, who took a partnership block together.

The group[4] emerged from the night of March 12–13 with enough money to finance half the US$70 million local bid price. There was still a challenge, however, in raising the financing for the rest of the purchase. And here, the Houstonites resurfaced.

It is believed that at least two members of the local buyer group flew to Houston to meet with Chuck Watson, to discuss a possible private placement of financing to close the deal. The dynamics between Alexander and the Watson/McNair partnership were fascinating to witness. It was an all-out turf war to see who could do the most for Houston sports-wise. Houston reporters regularly contacted Edmontonians in the know to keep track of the Alexander bid. They were as much interested in whether or not the Oilers would come to Houston as in what Alexander's success or failure would mean for the ongoing one-upmanship between Alexander and Watson/McNair. "The real story," says Bob Turner, "was the chess match each side was playing to block the other."

Funding from the Watson/McNair camp would have allowed the

Edmonton group to close the deal in comfort; it also would have ensured that Alexander wouldn't bring NHL hockey to Houston, which would have been a triumph for Alexander after he had lost the right to bid for an NHL expansion team in 1997 to Watson and McNair. But however tempting the Houston money might have been, the local investor group turned away from it. The optics would have been terrible if word got out that the local buyers had been able to squeeze out Alexander with money from his Houston rivals. Instead, money was found domestically, with help from the Bank of Nova Scotia. (On October 23, 1997, Bruce Saville's Saville Systems PLC had secured a multi-currency operating line of credit of US$15 million from the bank.)

The purchase received the ATB's blessing on March 18, 1998, and Sather celebrated by making another trade six days later, sending Dan McGillis and Edmonton's second-round pick in 1998 to Philadelphia for a young, points-producing defenceman, Janne Niinimaa. As the playoffs approached, the Oilers hadn't demonstrated so much youth, speed, experience and physical toughness in years. Yet there was no guarantee that the forthcoming playoff tilt wouldn't be the Oilers' last in Edmonton, for the purchase deal was far from done.

Jim Hole travelled to New York the week of April 20 to discuss the purchase with NHL executives, and returned home optimistic that the league would give its approval. But a major hurdle was still to be cleared at home. Hole and his fellow buyers wanted a new lease agreement for Northlands Coliseum, which would require a subsidy from the city of Edmonton. The old arrangement, under which Peter Pocklington had effective control of the Coliseum and the revenues from virtually all events, parking and concessions, would be scrapped. Instead, the new owners would lease the Coliseum under the Location Agreement until 2004 for one dollar a year, for Oilers games only. The team would still get the concession revenues for these games, and parking revenues north of 118th Avenue. It also wanted $2.2 million of the $2.8 million ticket surcharge that had previously flowed to the city. In addition to the naming rights for Northlands (which were sold to investor Barry Weaver, who rechristened the building the Skyreach Centre after his equipment company), these additional revenues were projected to be worth about $5 million to the team. While the proposed new deal gave Northlands Park, the Coliseum's operator, annual revenues of about $12 million from non-hockey events that Pocklington had previously controlled, it also delivered Northlands Park about $17 million in expenses. The operator would get the remaining $600,000 of the ticket surcharge revenue the city had once enjoyed. This left Northlands Park about $4.8 million in the hole. The Park would absorb half of it; the city would provide the other half, in the form of a $2.4 million annual operating grant.

It was a tough pill to swallow. Giving Northlands Coliseum to Pocklington to run for his own profit had been tough enough in 1994; now, in 1998, the new owners were asking the city to actually subsidize the team. Edmonton had to give up the $2.8 million ticket surcharge revenue, and send $2.4 million Northland Park's way to help it deal with its own revenue loss.

The board of directors of Northlands Park cast a near-unanimous vote on Wednesday, April 22, to approve the investor plan. Mayor Bill Smith, as one of the Park's board members, cast an affirmative vote. The twelve-member city council then gathered for a special meeting on Friday, April 25, to vote on the city's side of the funding proposal, the terms of which Bruce Saville called "a deal breaker." It was a sometimes acrimonious debate; councillors resisting the proposal could sense the impending free-fall into a perpetual civic subsidy of the business, in the name of keeping a major tenant in the city-owned arena.

Councillor Robert Noce withdrew from the vote over a conflict of interest. His law firm did business with the Bank of Nova Scotia, which he had just learned that morning was involved in raising the financing for the purchase, and he had also spotted his firm's name on the new Location Agreement. Noce's participation in the debate and vote might have made a big difference in the outcome, because afterwards he told the *Edmonton Journal*, "It would have been very difficult for me to support this."

Without Noce, the deal needed six votes to pass. It got seven. One of the dissenting councillors was Brian Mason, who had proposed back in February that the public be allowed to contribute their nickels, dimes and dollars. After the voted, he rued, "They'll be back, and we'll have to dig into our wallets once more."

The following Monday, April 27, the NHL approved the sale. The Oilers were in the middle of their opening-round playoff series against the Colorado Avalanche. The team had come a long way back from the 1995/96 season, when only 6,800 fans bought season tickets to watch the Oilers miss the playoffs for the fourth consecutive time. The day after the NHL approved the Oilers' sale, Edmonton fell behind three games to one against Colorado at Northlands Coliseum. On the ropes, the club fought back to win three straight and record its second consecutive opening-round upset.

The playoff run was over quickly, though. Dallas bounced the Oilers in five games in the next round, but fan enthusiasm allowed the Oilers to reach the 13,000 plateau in season ticket sales in May to qualify for the league's Canadian currency assistance plan, which was worth about $3 million to the new owners.

Edmonton still had its Oilers, but it was not clear if the city would still have Glen Sather to run them. Sather and Pocklington had always been close. Pocklington trusted him completely, and Sather's term as a manager with an NHL team, stretching back to 1978/79, was exceeded only by his friend Harry Sinden's management term with the Bruins, which had begun in 1972/73. Both Sather and Sinden had enjoyed long relationships not only with one team, but also with one owner. For Sather, it had been Pocklington; for Sinden, Jeremy Jacobs, a hands-off billionaire for whom the Bruins and their new home, the Fleet Center, were just one small corner of his Delaware North Companies empire.

Pocklington is intensely loyal to friends, many of whom he has held onto for decades, and they to him. No one expected Sather to leave the Oilers out of simple loyalty to Pocklington, but it was hard to see him staying with a club where money was tight and where he would now have to deal with an ownership consortium of eighteen partnerships in which as many as thirty-five people were involved. Sather was facing the loss of Doug Weight and Curtis Joseph to free agency that summer; there was not enough money in the budget to keep both of them. (Jason Arnott had been traded in January 1998 rather than risk losing him to free agency.) The Oilers would lose Joseph to the Toronto Maple Leafs, who also showed interest in bringing Sather along with him.

"I frankly thought he'd go to San Jose," Ralph Lean says of Sather. The Sharks are owned by the Gund brothers; Sather had played for the Gunds when they owned the North Stars, in his last season in the NHL. "Gordie Gund's another guy who comes fishing with us and is a friend of ours. There's a big budget in San Jose, and the team has not been doing as well as it should. Glen has a place in Palm Springs that's just an hour away. For a challenge, I thought he might come to Toronto."

Instead, Sather chose to stay in Edmonton, for the new owners' first year at least. Sinden and Sather attribute the decision partly to quality of life—Sather and his wife, Anne, both enjoy their home in Banff and life in Edmonton—and partly to loyalty to the city. As for 1999/2000, Sather knew the way to San Jose. It was a matter of whether he would choose to follow it.

IN THE TWILIGHT seasons of their careers, the "untouchables" and their former Oilers team-mates moved through the rosters of the NHL's wealthier teams together. In 1994/95, Wayne Gretzky was playing in Los Angeles with Marty McSorley, who had gone to Pittsburgh and back to the Kings since the 1988 trade-of-all-trades. Los Angeles had picked up Jari Kurri and Charlie Huddy as well, and in February 1995 the Kings sent Huddy to Buffalo in a deal that netted them Grant Fuhr. In St. Louis, the Blues had acquired Esa Tikkanen from New York, and in February signed Glenn Anderson.

When the playoffs ended in disappointment for both the Kings and Blues in the spring of 1995, managers shuffled their Oilers assets. Anderson left St. Louis to play in Europe. Tikkanen was traded to New Jersey, which quickly sent him to Vancouver. The Blues started collecting old Oilers all over again, acquiring Grant Fuhr as their starting netminder. Before the 1995/96 playoffs, Gretzky and Huddy joined Fuhr as Blues, and Craig MacTavish came over from the Rangers. Having sent Gretzky and Huddy to St. Louis, the Kings dispatched Kurri and McSorley to New York to play with Mark Messier, Kevin Lowe, Jeff Beukeboom and Adam Graves.

The Vancouver Canucks signed Glenn Anderson as a free agent on January 22, 1996, having already acquired Esa Tikkanen in mid-season from New Jersey, but let Anderson go on waivers three days later. Glen Sather picked up Anderson for old time's sake as an Oiler for seventeen games, then let him go on waivers to St. Louis, to play with Gretzky, Huddy, Fuhr and MacTavish.

St. Louis's attempt to buy a Stanley Cup in the Rangers' manner by collecting a stable of champion Oilers didn't work, as the Blues lost in seven games to Detroit in the 1995/96 conference semi-finals. Fuhr and MacTavish stayed for 1996/97, but Gretzky signed his first free-agent contract to go to New York to play with Messier, Beukeboom and Graves, as Kurri left for Anaheim as a free agent and Lowe became an Edmonton Oiler again.

The 1996/97 campaign was Kevin Lowe's 18th NHL season. Sather had brought Lowe home to steady a young team behind the blue line, and to groom him for a coaching position. After injuries limited him to seven games in 1997/98 as Edmonton endured the cliff-hanger events of the team's sale, Sather moved to add Lowe to a team staff that had changed little over the years. Barry Fraser was still chief scout. Bob McCammon was still an assistant coach. Ted Green had become an assistant to Sather after trying to coach the Oilers in their bleakest seasons in the 1990s. Now Lowe joined the staff as an assistant coach.

At the press conference announcing his appointment after the team had been sold to the new local investment group, Kevin Lowe was asked to name the most memorable event in his long career. Without hesitation, he said, "May 19, 1984."

It was the day of the Oilers' 5-2 victory over the Islanders in game five at Northlands Coliseum, when Edmonton won its first Stanley Cup.

Kevin Lowe began to weep.

NOTES

PROLOGUE

1. Minnesota held the expansion draft selections of San Jose due to the complex franchise swap engineered by the Gund brothers. See Chapter 14.

2. The CSCAP is designed to compensate Canadian franchises for increased operating costs due to the strong American dollar. The compensation takes two forms: a subsidy based on fiscal performance, and one that assists in signing Group II free agents. To qualify for the subsidies, teams first must rank in the bottom half of the league in revenues and then meet other criteria, which can include minimum season-ticket sales. Subsidies distributed under CSCAP come from the pool of national broadcasting rights sold by the NHL in Canada and the United States. Montreal and Toronto have been too profitable to qualify for CSCAP, while Ottawa, Calgary and Edmonton have regularly received subsidies of about US$3 million each.

CHAPTER 1

1. A star with the Cup-winning Maple Leafs of the 1940s, Poile was part of a six-player blockbuster deal between Toronto and Chicago in November 1947 that landed the Leafs star centre Max Bentley. Poile played most of the 1948/49 season in Detroit after being sent there in a five-player deal, then split the 1949/50 season between Boston and New York before heading into the minor pro ranks, where he played in the short-lived development loop, the Maritime Major Hockey League.

CHAPTER 2

1. Essential details of Pocklington's fledgling business career are related by Peter C. Newman in *The Acquisitors*.

CHAPTER 3

1. The NHL secured a national television contract with CBS, which carried games from 1968 to 1972. NBC then tried the NHL from 1973 to 1975, but did not renew the contract because of unimpressive ratings.

2. The effect of the WHA on individual NHL clubs varied. The Detroit Red Wings were in an awful period of on-ice performance, but the Michigan Stags were only briefly on hand to lure fans away, and Red Wings owner Bruce Norris was intransigent about any capitulation. And while the Chicago Blackhawks had the pesky Cougars to face down, Bill Wirtz was

equally opposed to reconciliation. Boston ostensibly had shaken off the Whalers after two seasons, as the franchise moved to Hartford, Connecticut, to play in the city's new convention centre. But the Whalers were still in the Bruins' backyard, and were winning hockey games and fans. The Minnesota North Stars continued to be hobbled by the presence of the Fighting Saints. While the Quebec Nordiques were about 150 miles from the Montreal Canadiens, the team was popular in the province, cutting into the Canadiens' provincial Francophone fan base as it made off with some of Montreal's top players. The WHA was clinging with perverse tenacity to Ed Snider's backyard. The Philadelphia Blazers remained in town for only one season before decamping for Vancouver, but no sooner was Snider rid of them than he was forced to contend with the wandering New York WHA franchise. Leaving a trail of bad debts, the New York Raiders had become the Golden Blades, and then abandoned the Big Apple altogether to camp just across the Delaware River from the Flyers in the Philadelphia suburb of Cherry Hill, New Jersey, where they played the 1973/74 season as the Jersey Knights. While the Knights, like the Blazers, lasted only one season, heading to San Diego to become the Mariners, Snider's Flyers were not free and clear. As the Knights lit out for California, the Los Angeles Sharks migrated eastward. After trying their luck in Detroit as the Michigan Stags in 1974/75, they made a midseason switch to Baltimore, some sixty miles southwest of Philadelphia, and changed their name to the Blades. They, too, lasted one season.

3. The details of the intrigue on the WHA issue within the NHL's ownership ranks are detailed by Gil Stein in his book *Power Plays*.

4. Full details of this proposal are contained in Gil Stein's *Power Plays*.

5. In *The Game of Our Lives*, Peter Gzowski breaks the four-year, $1.125 million deal down into a $250,000 bonus and $875,000 to be paid over four years.

6. Gzowski discusses the above terms of the Gretzky deal in *The Game of Our Lives*, but makes no mention of Mio or Driscoll.

CHAPTER 4

1. Eagleson's eventual downfall was partly due to misappropriation of rink board advertising revenues from Canada Cup tournaments.

2. The Cincinnati Stingers and Birmingham Bulls joined the Central Hockey League, and became minor pro affiliates of the Hartford Whalers and Atlanta Flames respectively.

3. NHLPA players participated in Canada Cup tournaments believing that they were topping up their pension plan contributions. In fact, the NHL was responsible for all contributions to the pension plan. The players' contributions merely gave the league a contribution holiday. The league further reduced its contributions by helping itself to the surplus from veteran players' contributions. A successful lawsuit by retired players ordered the league to pay them back $50 million in 1998.

4. The official encyclopedia of the NHL records him as a free-agent signing by Birmingham in May 1978, but Gartner says he never signed with the Bulls.

5. Another was Bill Goldsworthy, who had been traded by the New York Rangers of the NHL to the Indianapolis Racers of the WHA for Frank Spring in December 1977.

6. The official NHL record book records that Hunter was claimed from Montreal in the expansion draft, but he was not one of Edmonton's formal selections.

7. The Soviet Union won the gold medal, Czechoslovakia the silver. Finland was fourth and Canada fifth.

8. Kevin Maxwell was chosen highest, 63rd overall, by Minnesota. Don Spring was passed over and signed as a free agent by Winnipeg in 1980. Kevin Primeau, who had played seven games with the Oilers as an underage free agent in 1977/78 while in his last year at the University of Alberta, was a free-agent signing by Vancouver in 1980. Pageau was not selected, and never played in the NHL. As later noted, Randy Gregg, who became captain of Canada's 1980 Olympic team, was a free-agent signing by Edmonton in 1982.

9. Steen was known to have one year of compulsory military service before him, and this may have tempered enthusiasm for drafting him. The NHL had also not yet fully embraced European talent. The Jets, who had done so well in the WHA with Swedish players, were rewarded for their late pick of Steen with a player who joined the team in 1981/82 and played all 950 games of his NHL career in Winnipeg.

CHAPTER 5

1. Another cause of the scoring run-up, related to the arrival of the WHA and more generous player contracts, was the advent of the generous scoring bonus. Star players needed to score plenty of goals to make money, and some people (particularly goaltenders like Ed Giacomin of New York) came to feel that this pressure for goal production caused players to neglect defensive duties.

2. In setting a new playoff points record for defencemen, Potvin came within two points of matching Orr's record nineteen playoff assists in 1971/72. Orr, however, set his marks in fifteen games; Potvin took eighteen.

3. Ulf Nilsson, Anders Hedberg, Willy Lindstrom, Thommie Bergman, Lars-Erik Sjoberg, Mats Lindh and Curt Larsson were from Sweden, and Veli-Pekka Ketola and Heikki Riihiranta were from Finland.

4. They were Ulf Nilsson, Anders Hedberg, Kent Nilsson, Willy Lindstrom, Lars-Erik Sjoberg, Thommie Bergman, Dan Labraaten and Markus Mattsson.

5. A shot on goal is defined as a shot that would result in a goal if the goaltender or another player did not block it. Not included are shots that hit the

post or the crossbar, or dump-in shots from beyond centre ice, unless made at an empty net. The statistic is at best an approximation of offensive effort and of shooting accuracy (when used to calculate shooting percentage, which is the proportion of goals to shots on goal). Players who take a lot of shots but miss the net or hit the post trying to pick corners will have a lower shot total than someone who regularly hits the goaltender square in the chest. The NHL began amassing shots-on-goal and shooting percentage statistics in 1967/68.

6. Gretzky's shooting percentage during his Edmonton years reached highs of 24.9 in 1981/82 and 26.9 in 1983/84—excellent figures. His shooting percentage dropped with goal production in the 1990s, falling as low as 7.7 in 1994/95 in Los Angeles. Top scorers generally hit the mark on about one in five shots, although the statistic varies widely with playing styles. Phil Esposito, who took a lot of his shots from the slot, picking up rebounds or being fed the puck, had a percentage that changed considerably. His seventy-six goals in 1970/71 were achieved with a percentage of just 13.8, while in 1979/80 in New York, his third-last season, he produced a career high percentage of 19.5 on forty-two goals. Mike Bossy was remarkably consistent, scoring on more than 20 percent of his shots in every season he played except the last, which was also the only season he didn't score more than fifty goals. Defencemen tend to have lower shooting percentages because they take a lot of shots from the point, which result in assists through rebounds or tip-ins. Denis Potvin scored on about 10 percent of his shots, with a career-high of 14.2 in 1981/82. Bobby Orr's percentage was never better than 12.0 (in 1974/75), and usually below 9.0, a performance on par with that of Al MacInnis. Paul Coffey scored on more than 10 percent of his shots in every season from 1981/82 to 1986/87, with highs of 15.5 in 1983/84 and 1985/86, when he scored forty and forty-eight goals respectively.

7. Lewicki's career is discussed in greater detail in my book *Open Ice*.

CHAPTER 6

1. The Quebec Nordiques in particular were proactive in helping prospects escape to the West. Peter and Anton Stastny came from Czechoslovakia in 1980, and their brother Marion followed (along with another Nordiques draftee, Miroslav Frycer) in 1981.

2. By strange coincidence, having missed out on Patrik Sundstrom at 175th in 1980 when they chose Lars-Gunnar Petterson 174th, the 50th pick Edmonton surrendered to New York for the 1981 draft was used by the Rangers to choose Patrik's brother, Peter.

3. Ken Dryden, the dominant goaltender of the 1970s, never had his rights acquired in the traditional Original Six manner of getting his signature on a C-form. Playing Junior B in Toronto, he had his rights acquired by Boston in 1964 as a third pick, 14th overall in the annual NHL amateur draft of talent

hitherto unsecured. Boston immediately included him in a four-player rights swap with Montreal, and Dryden was the only one of the group ever to reach the NHL. Tony Esposito, who vied with Dryden for goaltending accolades in the 1970s, skipped Canadian Junior hockey, played four seasons at Michigan Tech, was signed as a free agent by Montreal in 1967, and landed in Chicago in June 1969 when Montreal left him unprotected in the intra-league draft. In 1969/70 he registered fifteen shutouts (a modern-era record) and won the Vezina and the Calder.

Besides Dryden and Esposito, there was the textbook example of the New York Islanders tag team of Billy Smith and Chico Resch. Chosen 59th overall in the 1970 amateur draft by Los Angeles, Smith was left unprotected in the 1972 expansion draft that created the Islanders. Resch was a lowly free-agent signing by Montreal after his college career with the University of Minnesota (Duluth). He was then sold to the Islanders with five other unwanted players in 1972.

4. In deference to poor Mr. Martyniuk, the phenomenon should be renamed the New Westminster Syndrome. Montreal was not scared off goaltenders (at least not right away) by Martyniuk, for in 1972 they did well in choosing Ken Dryden's backup, Michel Larocque, sixth overall. The real damage appears to have been done in 1973 and 1975, when two different NHL teams decided the goaltender of the New Westminster Bruins was worthy of their first-round pick. Detroit, pleased by the success of Jim Rutherford, chosen 10th overall in 1969, chose Terry Richardson 11th in 1973; Pittsburgh took Gord Laxton 13th in 1975. In the year between those two drafts, the Toronto Marlboros won the 1973/74 Memorial Cup with Mike Palmateer in net. He had been playing in Maple Leaf Gardens, in plain sight of the Leaf brass, but they didn't bother with him until they came to their fifth pick, 85th overall, in the draft that followed the Memorial Cup win. The Leafs were rewarded with one of the best goaltenders of the late 1970s; Detroit and Pittsburgh got little for their first-round efforts, Richardson playing twenty NHL games and Laxton seventeen. While Bob Sauve, chosen 17th by Buffalo in 1975, proved a sound pick, after the Laxton selection in 1975 no team could bring themselves to use their opening-round pick for a goaltender until Edmonton in 1981.

5. It was the first season the Vezina Trophy was awarded through a vote by league general managers, rather than being based on goals-against average.

CHAPTER 7

1. Eggleton later became a cabinet minister in the federal Liberal government of Jean Chrétien. Although Lean is a card-carrying Progressive Conservative, politics at the municipal level are less marked by party affiliations, as open party-backed candidacies are not allowed. Timbrell's leadership bid proved unsuccessful.

2. The NEP wasn't unanimously despised. Its nationalist principles helped many domestic oil sector businesses grow in Alberta.

3. In 1981/82, the Islanders needed overtime to earn a game-five win against Pittsburgh in the division semi-finals, then outlasted their local rivals, the Rangers, in six games in the division finals. A sweep of Quebec in the conference finals led to the sweep of Vancouver in the finals.

4. The scores against Boston were 5-2, 1-4, 7-3, 8-3, 1-5, 8-4.

5. The deal that delivered Orr to Chicago was concluded at the home of Reynolds Tobacco chairman Ross Johnson, a former Winnipegger who coincidentally would hire Ken Taylor, who at the time of the 1983 leadership convention was Canada's consul-general in New York. After the leadership campaign, and before Taylor went to work for Johnson, Pocklington and Taylor crossed paths in New York and become close friends.

6. By the time Pocklington ran for the Progressive Conservative leadership, he had abandoned the sport. In April 1982, when he was in the process of selling Westown Ford, he explained how he got involved in jet-boat racing in the first place. "A girl came over to sell me an ad on the Smoky Lake race in the Peace River area. Instead I bought a boat and finished third. I've since given it up. It's too dangerous."

7. Mulroney's advice to Pocklington is recorded in L. Ian MacDonald's *Mulroney: The Making of the Prime Minister*.

CHAPTER 8

1. The impetus to change the penalty rule was provided by a Jean Beliveau hat trick during one power play against the Boston Bruins in 1955/56.

2. An undrafted free agent signing in September 1979 from the Oshawa Generals, Huddy was a strong defensive anchor who could also contribute offensively. With fifty-seven points in 1982/83, he led the NHL with a plus-minus of +62.

3. The trophy had never been physically lost. When the Soviets won in 1981, tournament organizer Alan Eagleson wouldn't let them leave the country with it.

4. The 11-2 score tied the record for most goals by a team in one playoff game, set by Montreal with an 11-0 defeat of Toronto in 1943/44. The Oilers set a new record in 1986/87 with a 13-3 defeat of Los Angeles. Edmonton also set a record in 1984/85 for most home victories by a team in the playoffs, with ten. They had tied the old record, with nine in 1983/84. They broke it again with eleven in 1987/88.

CHAPTER 9

1. Mulroney also allowed the Canadian Wheat Board to raise domestic prices from seven dollars a bushel to as high as eleven dollars.

CHAPTER 10

1. The deal specifics, which were confidential, are presented here as reported by Al Strachan in *The Globe and Mail* in 1988.

2. In 1993, after Eagleson had resigned as head of the NHLPA, Gretzky provided testimony to the U.S. grand jury investigation into Eagleson's actions.

CHAPTER 11

1. The game also tied the record Edmonton had helped set for most power-play goals by both teams in a single game (seven). In the 1983/84 playoffs Edmonton scored three and Minnesota four in an 8-5 Edmonton victory. In the 1984/85 playoffs, Chicago had five and Edmonton two as the Oilers won 10-5. In the 13-3 Edmonton win in 1986/87, Los Angeles had two, Edmonton five.

2. The twenty-six games Philadelphia played during the 1986/87 postseason was itself a record.

3. Gretzky was runner-up for the Lady Byng in four consecutive seasons, from 1987 to 1990, before winning in 1991 and 1992. He had already won in 1980, and been runner-up in 1981.

4. In January 1990, Gainers Inc., which was by then owned by the province, sued Pocklington Financial Corporation to recover advances it said had been improperly made by Gainers when Pocklington still owned it. In December 1995 a judgement was rendered in favour of Gainers, and $770,000 was recovered. The funds were placed in trust, as the government was appealing the decision, believing the judgement amount should have been higher. In 1998, Peter Pocklington told *Alberta Report*, "The province sued me for $15 million, saying I'd taken money illegitimately out of Gainers. It was entirely untrue. All they got was about $700,000, the same sum that I'd offered them seven years earlier. The judge not only threw out their case but made them pay my legal costs. What else can I say?"

5. In March 1994, Eagleson was indicted by a Boston grand jury while in Canada criminal investigations by the RCMP were still under way. In January 1998, a deal was struck between Eagleson and the authorities in both countries. He was fined $1 million and received an eighteen-month sentence in Canada for his fraud conviction, of which he served five months.

6. In addition to those already noted, the players Edmonton missed in the 1985 entry draft included Nelson Emerson, Steve Chiasson, Jeff Finley, Daniel Berthiaume, Brent Gilchrist, Fredik Olausson, Bill Houlder, Robert Kron, Chris Luongo, Ken Preistlay, Shane Churla, Randy McKay, Donald Dufresne, Joe Reekie, Tim Sweeney, Danton Cole, Paul Stanton, Randy Burridge, Jim Paek, Jamie Huscroft, Dave Williams, Tommy Sjodin, Rudy Poeschek and Ken Baumgartner.

7. In addition to Tugnutt, Tim Chevaldae, Rob Brown, Ron Stern, Hannu Jarvenpaa, Mark Janssens, Glen Featherstone and Frantisek Kucera were selected in the third round.

8. The only deep-draft coups were St. Louis's choice of Guy Hebert at 159th and Calgary's choice of Thereon Fleury at 166th.

9. The surrendered 1991 draft pick would haunt the Oilers. After the Oilers missed completely with their preceding four picks, Philadelphia used the pick acquired in the Brown deal to get Dimitri Yushkevich. In 1995, Philadelphia was able to deal Yushkevich to Toronto for upcoming first-, second- and fourth-round draft picks.

CHAPTER 12

1. Cross-ownership of cable and broadcast stations in the same market, banned under the 1984 U.S. Cable Act, was repealed in the 1996 Telecom Act, which also permitted restricted cross-ownership between television and telecommunications.

2. The television revenue picture was further complicated by the rise in the 1990s of cable-based regional sports networks, or RSNs. These functioned as both local cable services for individual teams and carriers of national television coverage when RSNs picked up specialty-channel feed from ESPN or Fox Sports. With the blurring of distinctions between cable (formerly solely local in nature) and network service, national television rights came to be split into two packages: traditional broadcast network and national cable.

3. In the summer of 1997, COMSAT spun off Ascent Entertainment by granting existing shareholders ownership of the subsidiary through a tax-free dividend. After the spinoff, Ascent struck the arena development deal for the Pepsi Center with the city of Denver, but then elected to focus on its core communications activities (Ascent Network Services and On Command). While subsidiary Beacon Communications had produced a summer film hit, *Air Force One*, in the summer of 1997, it followed up with a box office bomb, *Dear God*, starring Greg Kinnear. And while the Avalanche were a consistent sellout at home, the Nuggets were performing poorly. Ninety percent of Ascent's ownership of Beacon was offloaded in January 1999; on April 26, 1999, Ascent announced that it had sold the Avalanche, the Nuggets and the Pepsi Center to a partnership controlled by William and Nancy Laurie of Columbia, Missouri, for $260 million cash, with the Lauries also assuming $140 million in notes that Ascent had issued to finance the arena. A group of Ascent shareholders immediately sued the company to force an auction in hope of getting more money for these assets, and the company settled the action by holding one on July 27. A group led by Donald L. Sturm acquired the sports properties for $321 million, in addition to assuming the financing obligations for the arena.

4. On April 5, 1999, Fox's parent, The News Corporation, announced that it

would acquire "substantially all of" Liberty Media's 50 percent interest in Fox/Liberty Networks. It would pay with equities worth $1.425 billion. The deal was complete on July 15.

5. In August 1997, Fox/Liberty's wholly owned Fox Sports Rocky Mountain signed a seven-year local television rights deal with Ascent Entertainment for the Colorado Avalanche of the NHL and the Denver Nuggets of the NBA. Ascent predicted that, with licence fees, the contract could net more than $100 million. Fox/Liberty also acquired a $15 million interest in the Pepsi Center, the new arena under development for the Nuggets and Avalanche. This interest was bought out when the Sturm Group acquired Ascent's sports properties in July 1999.

6. It was still small change, compared with the dollars commanded by the NHL's fellow arena league, the NBA. In 1998/99, the NBA inked four-year national television contracts with NBC and Turner Sports worth a total of $2.6 billion in aggregate fixed revenues to league teams, with further opportunities for revenue sharing. The aggregate revenues for the NHL and NBA television contracts cited in this chapter are contained in financial documents of Ascent Entertainment, owners of the Colorado Avalanche of the NHL and the Denver Nuggets of the NBA.

7. ESPN had used a controlling shareholder veto to scuttle a purchase offer by CanWest that had been made to (and accepted by) other NetStar shareholders, who included members of NetStar's management. ESPN then invited a bid from CTV. The CTV Network, the only private English-language television network in Canada, had just been taken over by Baton Broadcasting Inc., which until August 31, 1998, had owned 28.6 percent of CTV. Baton completed a total acquisition of the network on December 21, 1998, and reincorporated as CTV Inc., a public company, before making the NetStar purchase.

8. In the summer of 1999, it appeared that the Toronto Maple Leafs might counter the retreat made from broadcasting holdings by Molson and the Montreal Canadiens. Maple Leaf Sports, which owns the Maple Leafs, the Raptors of the NBA, and their new arena, the Air Canada Centre, was rumoured to be considering buying CTV's share of SportsNet, should the CRTC force CTV to sell it in order to gain approval for the investment in TSN's parent, NetStar. If such a deal came to pass, the Maple Leafs would join the ranks of NHL teams like the Philadelphia Flyers and the New York Rangers in fully integrating ownership of the team, its arena and local cable broadcasting.

9. Left out of this windfall were Edmonton, Winnipeg and Quebec, who were not allowed to share in national television revenues in Canada as a condition of their admission to the NHL in 1979.

10. As William Houston reported in *The Globe and Mail* (February 27, 1999), the Oilers and Flames were averaging about 75,000 cable viewers per game

in 1998/99, compared with Toronto's 260,000 and Montreal's 290,000. The Leafs had been able to command about $25 million a season for their local audience in a four-year deal with TSN. (Ottawa's middling audience of 147,000 seemed comparable to Vancouver's 155,000, but the fact that only about 37,000 of the Senators' cable audience was on the English-speaking SportsNet greatly reduced the value of the viewer package.)

CHAPTER 13

1. In 1983, former Oilers owner Billy Hunter tried to finesse the relocation of the St. Louis Blues to Saskatoon.

2. The Central Professional Hockey League dropped "Professional" from its name in 1969.

3. The Phoenix Roadrunners lasted twenty-seven games in the CHL in 1977/78, and after the Oilers and three other WHA teams joined the NHL in 1979, the Birmingham Bulls and Cincinnati Stingers entered the CHL, while Houston, which had been home to the WHA Aeros, got the Apollos, reborn from the CHL's original slate of teams. But Cincinnati lasted only thirty-three games in 1979/80, and Houston had an equally brief tour in 1980/81.

4. Conoco rid itself of the Dome Petroleum takeover bid by surrendering HBOG to Dome in exchange for $245 million U.S. in cash and the 22 million Conoco shares Dome had been able to acquire on the open market. Conoco was promptly set upon by two other hostile bidders: Canada's Joseph E. Seagram & Co., and Mobil. A takeover was avoided by arranging a merger with DuPont.

5. The Edmonton Eskimos of the CFL had drawn a number of star players from the University of Oklahoma's Sooners. Roger Nelson was an All-American tackle who was drafted by the Washington Redskins, but signed with Edmonton, where he was coached by former Sooner All-American end and assistant coach Frank "Pop" Ivy. Nelson played with Edmonton from 1954 to 1967, making four All Star team appearances and winning the Schenley Award as the CFL's Most Outstanding Lineman in 1959. In 1964, Nelson was the first recipient of Edmonton's Jackie Parker Award for leadership and ability. Nelson became a Canadian citizen in 1962, and worked in the oil business in Alberta for thirty years before returning to the United States. He was inducted in the CFL Hall of Fame in 1986. Nelson's teammate Frank Anderson was also a former Sooner who played in Edmonton for five years in the 1950s and settled there.

6. Opryland USA was built upon the Grand Ole Opry, a live country music radio show created in 1925, which had blossomed into an entertainment and convention/resort complex in Nashville. It includes the Opry House, the Opryland Hotel, which Gaylord Entertainment asserts is "one of the nation's largest convention/resort hotels," and the Opryland theme park.

CHAPTER 14

1. In 1995, Klein's government passed legislation preventing the province from making any investments in private enterprise, thereby precluding a direct bailout of the Oilers by the Alberta taxpayer.

2. The Minnesota-San Jose swap and the subsequent move of the North Stars to Dallas are related in greater detail by Gil Stein in *Power Plays*.

3. Having been unable to relocate the Edmonton Oilers to Hamilton's Copps Coliseum in 1993, Pocklington moved his AHL Oilers there from Nova Scotia for 1996/97 and renamed them the Bulldogs.

4. This arm of the holding company grew to contain six Florida properties: the Boca Raton Resort and Club; the Registry Hotel and the Edgewater Resort in Naples; the Hyatt Regency Pier 66 Hotel and Marina, and the Radisson Bahia Mar Resort and Yachting Center in Fort Lauderdale; and the Rolling Hills Golf Club (where the movie *Caddyshack* was filmed) in Davie. It also acquired the Arizona Biltmore Hotel in Phoenix.

5. British Gas and Nova Chemicals each held 24 percent of Dynegy; Chevron held 29 percent. Nova Chemicals invested about $225 million U.S. in Dynegy in 1994 and 1995, and sold its share in June 1999.

6. After Kent Cooke's death, McNair voiced interest in buying the Redskins, but vowed he would leave them in Washington. This put him in direct competition with Howard Milstein, one of the new owners of the New York Islanders in 1998. McNair also considered acquiring the Denver Broncos and moving them to Houston.

7. John Wolfe was one of Columbus's leading citizens. He had considerably enhanced his personal wealth—and perhaps even made possible the Columbus NHL bid—by playing a major role in the limited partnership Columbus-America Discovery Group Inc., which was formed locally in 1984 to finance a high-tech search for the passenger ship S.S. Central America, which sank off the Carolinas in 1857 with 21 tons of California gold aboard. The search located the wreck in 1988 and began recovery of the treasure, valued in the hundreds of millions of dollars. Lawsuits by insurance companies seeking a claim to the find, however, tied up the treasure, and were not resolved until August 1996. The court ruling awarded Columbus-America virtually all of the gold. Two months later, Wolfe participated in the creation of the Columbus NHL franchise bid. (The search for the wreck is recounted in *Ship of Gold in the Deep Blue Sea*, by Gary Kinder.)

CHAPTER 15

1. Leslie Alexander would not discuss his ownership bid with the author. His assistant, Angela Blakeney, who attended the meeting with the mayor, said that "The meeting was to see what the city could do with regard to keeping the team in Edmonton," and was not intended to discuss the specifics of

Alexander's offer to Pocklington.

2. The intentions of characters like Largue are difficult to read. Was he an innocuous, delusional wannabe, who just liked being in the limelight and never signed on the dotted line? (His 1994 bid for the Whalers was conveniently received too late to be part of the formal bid process.) His fraud conviction suggested he was at least capable of criminal deceit with other people's money, but he never came close to executing the massive fraud achieved by John Spanos when he bought the New York Islanders franchise in 1997. Spanos forged letters of reference and credit to secure an $80 million U.S. bank loan to buy the team from John Pickett. Once in control of the team, he made off with $400,000. When he didn't meet scheduled payments on the purchase, Pickett took back the team and the inside job was discovered. Spanos had pleaded guilty to fraud on January 12, 1998, about one month before Largue showed up in Edmonton.

3. Bruce Saville founded Saville Systems in 1982 (with just one employee) and had a breakthrough creating the long-distance customer billing system for Ed Tel, Edmonton's municipal telephone service, in 1984. For tax reasons he incorporated the company in the Republic of Ireland as Saville Systems Ireland Limited in June 1993, a private limited company. In 1995 the company was reincorporated in Ireland as Saville Systems PLC as Saville took the company public with a share issue on NASDAQ that November. The company has its headquarters in Galway, Ireland; the North American headquarters is in Burlington, Massachusetts. Its consolidated subsidiary, Saville Systems Canada Ltd., is located in Edmonton. At the time of the Oilers purchase, Bruce Saville controlled 6.2 percent of the common stock (about 1.1 million shares of Saville Systems PLC) through Invoice Systems (Canada) Inc., of which he owned 94 percent. Saville Systems PLC revenues doubled in 1997, from US$53.9 million to $107 million, and shares reached a high of $41.50 in the fourth quarter. This placed Bruce Saville's net worth at about US$45.6 million, based on the Invoice Systems holdings alone. The fifty-three-year-old Saville was withdrawing from day-to-day business, resigning as chief executive officer effective April 1, 1998. Sales increased to US$167.7 million in 1998, but the company posted a surprise loss in the first quarter of 1999. In June 1999, Saville Systems was purchased by ADC Telecommunications Inc. of Minneapolis for US$700 million. The stock's value on NASDAQ was down to $15 3/8; ADC paid $17.94 per share.

4. The final investment group consisted of Ed Bean, Gordon Buchanan, the *Edmonton Journal*, Ernie Elko, Gary Gregg, Ron Hodgson, Jim Hole, Larry Makelki, Lloydminster Consortium of Five, Melcor/Springwood, Art Mihalcheon, Cal Nichols, Al Owen, Cathy Roozen, Bruce Saville, Barry Weaver, Todd McFarlane and Jim Woods/Dick Paine.

ACKNOWLEDGEMENTS AND SOURCES

I F YOU HAVE, by now, finished reading this book, you will know that I have a bent for context. In six books on hockey, I have pursued to varying degrees the world off the ice as well as on it. From the perspectives of both culture and economics, understanding the game cannot, in my mind, be limited to the view afforded solely by a seat in an arena. In the course of writing my second book on the sport, *A Breed Apart*, I was confronted with what seemed to me to be the patent absurdity of trying to explain hockey during the Second World War without making more than a passing nod to the very existence of the Second World War. The result was another book, *War Games*, which was as much about politics and combat as it was about sports. I consider *The Glory Barons* something of a companion volume to that work: a book that deals with political and economic issues, as I felt that it absolutely must, in the name of better understanding the rise and fall of a championship National Hockey League franchise. This conviction has led me to drag readers hither and yon not only through the Stanley Cup playoffs, but also through political leadership campaigns, labour unrest, and deregulation of American cable and telecommunications industries. I have been able to resist writing he-shoots-he-scores hockey books and instead employ such wide-screen enthusiasm in works like *War Games* and *The Glory Barons* solely because of the support and confidence of my publisher,

Penguin Books Canada. In particular, I am indebted to president and publisher Cynthia Good, who continues to green-light my endeavours. Editor Scott Sellers did his best to harness and clarify my meandering storyline, and copy editor Nick Gamble strove to keep consistent the names, dates, dollar figures and narrative logic. Chris Cuthbert graciously gave the results a careful read, offering corrections and suggestions. Responsibility for the final product is utterly mine. I thank Ralph Lean, Rich Winter, Bill Smith, Bob Turner, Rick LeLacheur, Ken Taylor, Peter Regenstreif and Harry Sinden for their insights and observations. Bob Turner in particular was extraordinarily patient in walking me through the complexities of the Edmonton Oilers' 1994 Location Agreement at Northlands Coliseum and its consequences in the ensuing sale of the team.

Every book you write within a particular genre makes you (hopefully) a little bit smarter, and you end up drawing on the cumulative experience they represent when the next project is tackled. I am grateful to the many people, who now number in the hundreds, who have given of their time over the course of writing my hockey titles. I have also enjoyed, yet again, the courteous cooperation of the staff of the Hockey Hall of Fame Archives in Toronto, in particular Craig Campbell, Phil Pritchard and Jane Rodney.

A wide variety of newspapers and periodicals were drawn upon in assembling this work, and direct sources are duly cited within the text. I should single out several sources for particular merit: *The Hockey News,* the *Edmonton Journal* and *The Oklahoman* of Oklahoma City. For player and team records and for general information on NHL and WHA history, two sources were indispensable—*Total Hockey: The Official Encyclopedia of the National Hockey League* (to which I am proud to have contributed two essays), and Ralph Slates's outstanding *Internet Hockey Database* (www.hockeydb.com).

The Internet was an indispensable research tool. Living a goodly distance from a large urban centre, I was pleased not to have to make a single trip to a reference library in the course of writing this book.

Official government sites too numerous to mention were accessed in search of reliable information. In compiling financial information, I relied especially on the EDGAR database of the U.S. Securities and Exchange Commission (www.sec.gov/edgarhp.htm) and the SEDAR database of Canada's SEC equivalent, CDS Ltd. (www.sedar.com). On-line financial information posted by Forbes Inc. was also helpful. Books used as references (some of which have already been cited in the text or in footnotes), in addition to *Total Hockey*, follow in alphabetical order.

The Acquisitors: The Canadian Establishment, Volume II,
    by Peter C. Newman
*The Complete Historical and Statistical Reference to the World Hockey
    Association*, by Scott Adam Surgent
Game Misconduct: Alan Eagleson and the Corruption of Hockey,
    by Russ Conway
The Game of Our Lives, by Peter Gzowski
Mulroney: The Making of the Prime Minister, by L. Ian MacDonald
Mulroney: The Politics of Ambition, by John Sawatsky
Net Worth, by David Cruise and Alison Griffiths
*Power Plays: An Inside Look at the Big Business of the National Hockey
    League*, by Gil Stein

353

357